POLITICS, &
POLICY, &
MANAGEMENT
in the AMERICAN
STATES

D1565244

POLITICS, POLICY,& MANAGEMENT
in the AMERICAN STATES

DENNIS L. DRESANG
University of Wisconsin–Madison

JAMES J. GOSLING
University of Wisconsin–Madison

Longman

New York & London

Politics, Policy, and Management in the American States

Longman Inc., 95 Church Street, White Plains, N.Y. 10601

Associated companies:
Longman Group Ltd., London
Longman Cheshire Pty., Melbourne
Longman Paul Pty., Auckland
Copp. Clark Pitman, Toronto
Pitman Publishing Inc., New York

Senior editor: David J. Estrin
Production editor: Elsa van Bergen
Cover design: Susan J. Moore
Production supervisor: Eduardo Castillo

Library of Congress Cataloging in Publication Data

Dresang, Dennis L.
  Politics, policy, and management in the American states / Dennis
L. Dresang, James J. Gosling.
    p.   cm.
  Includes index.
  ISBN 0-8013-0002-9 (pbk.)
  1. State governments—United States.   I. Gosling, James J.
II. Title.
JK2408.D69   1989
353.9—dc19   88-10096
                                                  CIP

ISBN 0-8013-0002-9 (pbk.)

88 89 90 91 92 9 8 7 6 5 4 3 2 1

Contents

ISSUES OF CONTEMPORARY STATE POLICY MAKING

Preface

The idea for this book was born out of our experiences teaching courses on state politics and working at top levels in state government. We wanted to write a textbook that marries theory and practice and is attentive to the many real-life issues and choices that regularly confront state officials on the job, that highlights the substance and politics of state policy making and management, and that is contemporary and comparative in its treatment of the subject matter. We also wanted to write a book replete with examples and illustrations drawn from among the fifty states, to give students a feel for the diversity of experience that exists among the states, while still conveying, and accounting for, the broad-based rejuvenation of the states as focal points of domestic policy in the federal system.

Beyond the traditional and important elements common to all state government textbooks, such as introductions to the intergovernmental context of state politics, state political parties and elections, and the institutions of state government, this book includes a number of features that set it apart from the rest. It has a consistent focus on "the state as policy maker," whether that be in covering the institutions of state government, the policy-making process, relationships with the federal government and local units of government, or the major contemporary public policy issues facing state policy makers. In addition, this book includes separate chapters on direct citizen democracy, state regulation, budgeting and financial management (including a section on financial and program auditing), and personnel management. It also incorporates a substantial section on the state attorney general along with its discussion of state courts.

For students to appreciate the increasingly vital role that states play in domestic public policy making and management, and the politics accompanying each, this book follows a developmental approach, providing successive building blocks of information and analysis. The first section deals with the intergovernmental context within which state policy makers operate. The second covers political parties and elections, for if political parties hope to control the institutions of state government they must do so through victories at the polls. Once the election outcomes are known and the winners assume office, they are positioned to use the institutions of state government to realize their policy objectives, recognizing that the voters who elected them can also vote them out of office in the next election if the incumbents prove unresponsive to the electorate's concerns. The third section therefore deals with the major policy-making institutions of state government: the governor, the bureaucracy, the legislature, and the courts (along with the attorney general). These institutional participants, often in competition with each other, shape state public policy. But in several states, laws can be made and voided outside of the traditional legislative process, using the initiative and the popular referendum, whereby citizens can get propositions on state ballots and pass them into law directly. It is these distinct processes of direct democracy that are also covered in the fourth section of the book. Section 5, moving away from a focus on process, looks at the major contemporary issues of state policy making in the areas of education, health and welfare, transportation, taxation, and economic development. In addition to making laws, state governments also regulate certain aspects of individual and organizational behavior; but in doing so, state regulation can involve implementing policy as well as making it. Once individuals get control of the institutions of government, they inherit the responsibility to manage the funds made available to support state programs and the people employed to carry them out, as discussed in the sixth section. The book concludes by speculating on the future of the states.

Throughout the text, and in suggested classroom exercises, we emphasize understanding the issues facing state policy makers today. Those issues can take the form of substantive policy problems, the adequacy of financial resources, procedural challenges and opportunities, or political relationships. Although the contemporary debate, with its underlying focus on values, is important for students to understand, they also need to appreciate the historical context from which the contemporary issues arose.

State governments represent a comparative laboratory of sorts. And the objective of any comparative endeavor is to be able to identify consistent similarities and differences amid diversity and to explain them when possible. The ability to make supportable generalizations, with significant and appropriate exceptions identified and accounted for, lies at the heart of comparative politics. This is the approach that we have taken.

A number of persons contributed to this book. Several colleagues reviewed earlier drafts of chapters. Special thanks goes to William Gormley, who read and commented on the entire manuscript.

Families can provide the love and support to enable each member to achieve self-fulfillment. We are fortunate to be members of such families, and we appreciate the ways in which our families shared and participated in this project. Accordingly, we dedicate this book to our wives and our children.

Dennis L. Dresang and James J. Gosling
Madison, Wisconsin

To
Eliza, Lee, Steve, and Anna Ruth
and
Connie, Amy, David, and Michael

CHAPTER 1

Introduction
The American States: The Diverse Focal Points of Policy Making

The 1980s represent a renaissance of state activism in domestic policy making. Not only have states undertaken major reforms in education, welfare, taxation, and public employee compensation policy, as well as seriously questioned the present federal-state relationship in transportation policy, they have also become actively involved in efforts to expand their industrial base and create new jobs within their borders. Although some of these state initiatives were prompted by changes in federal policy, others had their origins largely within the states. The Reagan administration's policy of federal retrenchment in intergovernmental relations clearly set a tone that encouraged a reemergence of state domestic policy leadership. Economic pressures and growing interstate competition reinforced that inclination toward activism.

Examples of increased activism can be found in all regions of the United States—regions that show significant differences in their patterns of in-migration and settlement, their natural resources and economic bases, and their political cultures. Yet selective differences can be found within the same region and even the same state, as the following discussion illustrates.

COMPARISON OF REGIONS OF THE UNITED STATES

The U.S. Bureau of the Census identifies four regions nationally: the Northeast, the South, the Midwest, and the West. Each, in turn, has its own identifiable regional subdivisions.

The Northeast

The Northeast comprises New England and the Middle Atlantic states. New England shares many common characteristics that give it regional distinctiveness, including its early colonial settlement, the strength of its local governments, its ethnic-based politics, and its strong regional identity. The concept of "I'm a New Englander" is embedded in all the region's residents, perhaps with the exception of those living in the southwestern third of Connecticut, who identify more with New York City. In comparison, not many Californians would take pride in identifying themselves as "westerners." They consider themselves Californians, or perhaps even northern or southern Californians, symbolizing the split identity of that state.

Politics in New England is a serious business. It is a preoccupation not characteristic of any other region. It has deep historical roots dating back to the local town meeting in colonial times. New Englanders expect to participate in political decision making, and do so both locally and at the state level. New England has regional voter turnout second only to the Plains states.[1]

Despite New England's common characteristics, the states have their differences. Maine, New Hampshire, and Vermont retain much of their historical tradition, remaining largely rural, Protestant, and Republican. Connecticut, Massachusetts, and Rhode Island, with their much larger Catholic immigrant populations from Ireland, French Canada, and southern and eastern Europe, who were drawn by the economic promises of early industrialization, have more strongly developed and heavily supported Democratic parties.[2]

Beyond political differences, the states differ economically. Maine and Vermont can be found well into the bottom half of the states nationally on per capita personal income. In contrast, the other four states rank high in the top half, with Connecticut, Massachusetts, and New Hampshire all in the top ten.[3]

Although residents of New England have relatively high incomes, they are also taxed fairly heavily. Property taxes in New England are among the highest in the nation, and all but Maine and New Hampshire rank in the top half of the states in per capita state and local revenue, as Table 1.1 illustrates. New Hamp-

TABLE 1.1. STATE RANKINGS FOR PER CAPITA STATE-LOCAL REVENUE AND EXPENDITURE 1985

State-Local General Revenue			State-Local General Expenditure		
Rank	*State*	*Per Capita*	*Rank*	*State*	*Per Capita*
1	Alaska	$12,910	1	Alaska	$9,513
2	Wyoming	5,274	2	Wyoming	4,166
3	New York	3,631	3	New York	3,355
4	Minnesota	3,106	4	Minnesota	2,842
5	Delaware	3,067	5	North Dakota	2,696
6	North Dakota	2,846	6	Delaware	2,688
7	New Mexico	2,843	7	California	2,647

continued

TABLE 1.1., *continued*

State-Local General Revenue			State-Local General Expenditure		
Rank	State	Per Capita	Rank	State	Per Capital
8	California	2,789	8	Montana	2,616
9	Montana	2,763	9	Wisconsin	2,561
10	New Jersey	2,737	10	Rhode Island	2,550
11	Connecticut	2,709	11	New Mexico	2,536
12	Michigan	2,695	12	Washington	2,521
13	Hawaii	2,673	13	Nevada	2,519
14	Oregon	2,667	14	Michigan	2,505
15	Massachusetts	2,663	15	New Jersey	2,486
16	Rhode Island	2,654	16	Hawaii	2,472
17	Wisconsin	2,610	17	Oregon	2,471
18	Nevada	2,602	18	Massachusetts	2,445
19	Utah	2,578	19	Colorado	2,420
20	Maryland	2,575	20	Vermont	2,410
21	Washington	2,545	21	Connecticut	2,368
22	Colorado	2,538	22	Maryland	2,352
23	Vermont	2,525	23	Utah	2,327
24	Louisiana	2,428	24	Iowa	2,316
25	Kansas	2,397	25	Louisiana	2,308
26	Illinois	2,375	26	Arizona	2,305
27	Nebraska	2,317	27	Nebraska	2,256
28	Arizona	2,298	28	Kansas	2,220
29	Pennsylvania	2,292	29	South Dakota	2,214
30	Iowa	2,290	30	Illinois	2,173
31	Maine	2,275	31	Ohio	2,120
32	Ohio	2,255	32	Maine	2,111
33	Georgia	2,251	33	Oklahoma	2,034
34	Oklahoma	2,244	34	Pennsylvania	2,032
35	Texas	2,173	35	Texas	2,004
36	South Dakota	2,168	36	Virginia	1,993
37	Virginia	2,121	37	West Virginia	1,983
38	Florida	2,109	38	Alabama	1,972
39	West Virginia	2,069	39	Georgia	1,970
40	Indiana	2,047	40	Florida	1,956
41	Alabama	2,029	41	Idaho	1,869
42	Kentucky	1,958	42	Indiana	1,853
43	North Carolina	1,951	43	New Hampshire	1,816
44	New Hampshire	1,925	44	Kentucky	1,798
45	South Carolina	1,920	45	North Carolina	1,785
46	Missouri	1,908	46	Mississippi	1,784
47	Idaho	1,906	47	South Carolina	1,782
48	Mississippi	1,886	48	Missouri	1,775
49	Tennessee	1,848	49	Tennessee	1,743
50	Arkansas	1,789	50	Arkansas	1,695
	United States	$2,504		United States	$2,321

Source: Significant Features of Fiscal Federalism, 1987 Edition *(Washington, DC: U.S. Advisory Commission on Intergovernmental Relations, 1987), pp. 130 and 137.*

shire, indeed, is the maverick when it comes to taxation. It has neither a state personal income tax nor a state sales tax. Instead, it relies on taxes from state lotteries and dog-racing tracks and earnings from its state liquor stores. And since its taxes are low, so is the level of government services it provides. Among the fifty states, New Hampshire is lowest in total state and local expenditures per $1,000 of personal income. It is also lowest nationally in per pupil state school aid.[4] Massachusetts Governor Michael Dukakis, reflecting on New Hampshire's recent economic growth, stated that although New Hampshire might be "a nice place for talented young workers to live, its services were so shabby that it wasn't a nice place in which to be old or sick or handicapped or uneducated or down and out."[5] Vermont, although sharing many of the same topographical and social features as New Hampshire, provides a marked contrast. Vermont taxes and spends at much higher per capita levels than does its eastern neighbor. In fact, in terms of relative tax effort (per $1,000 of personal income), Vermont consistently ranks among the top ten states nationally.[6]

The Middle Atlantic states—New York, New Jersey, and Pennsylvania—are part of the nation's "Foundry," as author Joel Garreau describes them in his *The Nine Nations of North America*.[7] They are heavily populated and urban; heavily industrial; energy dependent; and in their large, older metropolitan areas, share many of the problems of congestion, pollution, and infrastructural decay. They are also wealthier than most other parts of the United States, especially New York and New Jersey, which rank sixth and third, respectively, on per capita personal income. Pennsylvania, feeling the effects of the 1981–1983 recession, dropped from nineteenth in 1980 to twenty-second in 1985. New York and New Jersey take advantage of that higher ability to pay, as both states rank in the top ten nationally in state and local revenues. New York ranks second nationally in its use of the personal income tax.

Politically, all three Middle Atlantic states have strong, competitive parties. The Democratic party in New York and Pennsylvania clearly reflects the strength and influence of organized labor. And well it should, since both rank in the top ten nationally in the percentage of workers who are union members. In fact, New York tops the list.[8] Yet although interest groups play a major part in Middle Atlantic politics, voter turnout falls below the national median.

The South

There are different ways of identifying which states comprise the South. The South can be limited to the eleven states forming the Confederacy: Alabama, Arkansas, Florida, Georgia, Louisiana, Mississippi, North Carolina, South Carolina, Tennessee, Texas, and Virginia. The U.S. Bureau of the Census adds Delaware, Kentucky, Maryland, Oklahoma, and West Virginia to the list. Others might also include the border state of Missouri. In fact, although Kentucky and Missouri never seceded from the Union, their stars are included in the Confederacy's flag, representing their attempt at secession.

Although the South, as a whole, shared the homogenizing influences of slavery and the Civil War, significant differences obviously exist between such southern states as Alabama, Arkansas, Georgia, Mississippi, North Carolina, South Carolina, and Tennessee, on the one hand, and Delaware, Florida, Maryland, and Virginia, on the other. The former epitomize the "Deep South." They consistently rank toward the bottom on per capita income, state and local revenues, and state and local spending, as well as on levels of education[9] and unionization. They rank near the top, however, on the percentage of the population living in poverty[10] and on infant mortality rate.[11] Politically, with a predominant Democratic electorate, they tend to have minimal party competition in state elective races and low voter turnout. Their politics tend to be conservative, hierarchical, and paternalistic—largely dominated by traditional elites. The general populace is not expected to be politically active, but it is expected to defer to those with political influence attained through family ties, social position, and wealth. Government functions are more centralized at the state level than in any other region nationally. Consequently, local governments tend to be weak, particularly in comparison to those of New England.

In contrast, the states of Delaware, Florida, Maryland, and Virginia are more closely akin to their northern neighbors economically and socially. Politically, they have somewhat more competitive parties, particularly in Delaware; but they do not differ that much on voter participation.

Of the four Southwest Central states (Arkansas, Louisiana, Oklahoma, and Texas), Arkansas is the most similar economically and socially to the states of the Deep South. Arkansas ranks last among the states in state and local revenues and expenditures, sharing the bottom ten with six southern neighbors in each category. On per capita personal income it ranks forty-eighth, at home among the Deep South states. Like its southern brethren, it has a low percentage of unionized workers. And politically it is solidly one-party Democratic, having relatively low voter turnout. Louisiana, Arkansas' immediate neighbor to the south, is also solidly one-party Democratic but more divided by factions. In fact, the Democratic party factions in Louisiana take on many of the appearances of competing political parties. Historically, the Huey Long and anti-Long factions battled to control the state's political apparatus, being replaced today by the Edwin Edwards and anti-Edwards factions. In Louisiana, personalities have been as important as, and some say more important than, the issues. The politics of faction and personality have brought Louisiana voters to the polls at rates far in excess of the rest of the South.

Oklahoma and Texas, despite their significant economic and population growth over the past fifteen years, politically and socially fit in with the other southern states. They both have low levels of voter turnout; Texas' is the lowest among the fifty states. In both states the Democratic party is dominant, although Oklahoma's parties are somewhat more competitive than those of Texas. Oklahoma and Texas tax and spend at levels more in line with the rest of the South than with states farther north. They also rank low on unionization, like the rest of the South.

Several states classified as ''southern'' have split personalities and allegiances. Virginia, West Virginia, Kentucky, and Florida are good examples. Northern Virginia has very little in common with most of the rest of the state. It is really an extended suburb of the District of Columbia, with per capita income well in excess of the state median. Its ways are northern, and its transitory population comes from throughout the United States. Its residents generally take relatively little interest in Virginia politics, preferring to look more to national political events. Northern West Virginia is also a much different place from the rest of the state. With its industrial smokestacks and predominantly blue-collar work force, it economically and socially resembles Pittsburgh or Youngstown more than it does Dixie. Given northern West Virginia's heavy industrial base, together with the coal mines of the Southeast, it is not surprising that West Virginia, as a state, ranks far above its southern neighbors in unionization. Kentucky likewise has its northern industrial belt, which resembles that of Cincinnati or Dayton more than the Bluegrass horse country of its central and southern part. Finally, south Florida, with its transplanted population and its heavy Cuban influence, is hardly reminiscent of the Old South. Party competition is stronger in south Florida than in the rest of the state, and its ethnic-based politics more resembles Chicago's than Tallahassee's.

The Midwest
The Midwest is the least homogeneous of the four regions. The Census Bureau divides the Midwest into two parts, the East North Central states (Ohio, Indiana, Illinois, Michigan, and Wisconsin) and the West North Central states (Minnesota, Iowa, Missouri, North Dakota, South Dakota, Nebraska, and Kansas). Another way of looking at the Midwest is to divide the states into the midwestern Great Lakes states and the Plains states, which entails adding Minnesota to the East North Central division. This latter categorization makes sense given Minnesota's shared political culture with Wisconsin, deeply embedded in the farmer and labor Progressive tradition. Minnesota's politics today, with its competitive two-party system and Democratic advantage, more closely resembles Wisconsin's than that of its western or southern neighbors. Politics in Wisconsin and Minnesota are highly issue-oriented, reflecting the political heritage of their German and Scandinavian settlers. Voter turnout has been high in both states historically. Both states also have highly professional, well-paid bureaucracies that are free of corruption. A highly publicized scandal in Wisconsin government involved the use of state telephones by government officials for personal business, hardly deemed worthy of media attention in most other states.

Of the other Great Lakes states, Michigan is closer to Wisconsin and Minnesota in its politics. Michigan's politics also tend to be largely issue-oriented, reflecting similar patterns of ethnic in-migration, but its politics reflect a stronger management-labor cleavage than is found in the other two states. Its powerful labor unions, dominated by the United Auto Workers, significantly influence the policy positions taken by Michigan Democrats. After all, Michigan has the second largest percentage of its workers belonging to labor unions nationally. Yet its rural and suburban areas have traditionally been the strongholds of the Republican party, giving it a competitive party system statewide. It also enjoys high voter turnout.

Minnesota, Wisconsin, and Michigan are higher taxing and spending states than their Great Lakes neighbors, again a likely product of a political culture that views government as playing a positive role in society by promoting the "common good." Using per capita general expenditures as a measure, Minnesota and Wisconsin both rank in the top ten nationally, and Michigan stands a close fourteenth. In contrast, Illinois, Indiana, and Ohio rank in the bottom half of the states nationally.

Illinois, Indiana, and Ohio share a different political culture from that of Minnesota, Wisconsin, and Michigan, one that is less concerned about how government can be used to improve the general welfare and that views politics as just another means by which individuals can improve their economic and social position. Such an environment fosters greater political patronage and corruption than is found in the more public-regarding cultures of Minnesota, Wisconsin, and Michigan. Political parties are competitive in Illinois, Indiana, and Ohio but tend to be more interested in winning control of government to dispense its perquisites to the faithful than to enact a substantive policy agenda. Voter turnout is considerably lower than in the western Great Lakes states.

The Plains states comprise this country's "breadbasket." Its flat and fertile terrain yields a bounty of wheat, to the north, and corn and soybeans, to the south. And although only a small percentage of its residents are engaged in farming, the region is highly dependent economically on agriculture, with many of its major industries involved in the production of agricultural supplies and machinery and in food processing. Commercial enterprises, such as banking and insurance, also have a significant agricultural and agribusiness base. Main-street businesses in small town, rural areas rise and fall with the economic welfare of agriculture. Per capita income for the region, as an average, falls pretty much toward the middle nationally, with Kansas ranking the highest, at eighteenth, and South Dakota the lowest, at fortieth.

The Plains states lack the major population centers of the midwestern Great Lakes states. Kansas City and Des Moines dominate the region as centers of commerce and culture. Socially, the Plains states tend to be conservative and pragmatic. Missouri's state motto, "The Show Me State," could be applied to the region as a whole. Residents of the homogeneous Plains states prize the traditional values of hard work, family, and religion. The crime rate is the lowest of any region, the divorce rate is well below the national average, and the abortion rate is less than half the national average.[12]

Politically, the Plains states were significantly affected by the Populist movement of the late nineteenth century. The Populist creed was built on active political participation by the populace as a whole, not just by the influential elites in society or those who happen to be organized into interest groups. That heritage is evident today, as the Plains states continue to have the highest voter turnout of any region in the country. Another legacy of the Populist era is institutionalized "direct democracy," in the form of the initiative and popular referendum, in which residents can petition to get propositions on the statewide ballot and enact them into law directly, without approval of the governor or legislature. Among the Plains states, Missouri, Nebraska, North Dakota, and South Dakota possess both the initiative and popular referendum.[13] In terms of party politics, the Plains states tend to be more Republican than the rest of the country.

The West

The western states make up two geographical divisions, the Rocky Mountain states (Montana, Idaho, Wyoming, Colorado, New Mexico, Arizona, Utah, and Nevada) and the Pacific states (Washington, Oregon, and California). For convenience, the U.S. Bureau of the Census adds Alaska and Hawaii, but they probably should be treated as distinct and unique cases.

The Rocky Mountain states are part of what Garreau refers to as the "Empty Quarter" of North America.[14] This region can be differentiated from others on the basis of its sparse and diffused population, huge empty spaces, mineral resources, and uneven distribution of water. In addition, much of its land is owned and managed by the federal government. The federal government owns 86 percent of the land in Nevada, and in no Rocky Mountain state does its ownership drop below 43 percent.[15] Federally held lands include national parks, national forests, national wildlife refuges, public lands (some of which is leased for grazing rights), and Indian reservations. This sizable federal presence has generated controversy in several of the states, as a growing number of residents view this land as a potentially valuable tax resource and strive to obtain more local control over the region's future. Even beyond issues of land ownership and management, Rocky Mountain residents just do not like outsiders telling them what they can and cannot do. The recent push for reinstitution of a national 65 mph speed limit on interstate highways had its impetus in the "Big Sky Country."

Environmental issues also divide residents of the Rocky Mountain states. The lines have been drawn between developers and preservationists on issues involving mining, environmental damage, and water diversion, but a clear majority sympathizes with development and the economic benefits that accompany it. However, national conservation groups and a majority in Congress see themselves as protectors of a national treasury belonging to all the people, not just those in the Rocky Mountain states.

Given the controversy surrounding issues related to rapid development, politics in the region tend to be issue-oriented but with a thick symbolic wrapping. Strong feelings on the public debate in the northern tier states bring voters to the polls in high percentages. A strong civic-minded Mormon culture in Utah adds to a regional average turnout that is in third place nationally, behind the Plains states and New England.

Although political scientists have traditionally classified all the Rocky Mountain states as two-party competitive—except for Nevada and New Mexico, which are given a decided Democratic advantage—the Republicans have made major gains in several Rocky Mountain states, capitalizing on the region's aversion to government intervention in society and the economy to become today the most Republican region in the country. In the 1986 election, the Republican party won control of both legislative chambers in Montana, Idaho, Wyoming, Utah, Colorado, and Arizona, accounting for six of the eleven states so held nationally. In Montana, the Republicans hold a majority in the lower chamber and are tied with the Democrats in the Senate.

Despite the region's distrust of big government, its sparse population and expansive territory mean that the costs of government have to be spread over a relatively small tax-paying public. Therefore, its per capita cost of government tends to be higher than in most other regions. All the Rocky Mountain states, except for Idaho and the more heavily populated Arizona, are found in the top half of the states on per capita state and local general expenditures (and Arizona ranks twenty-sixth).

Like several of its neighbors to the east and west, a number of Rocky Mountain states possess the initiative and popular referendum, including Arizona, Colorado, Idaho, Montana, and Wyoming. However, as in the Plains states, the mechanisms of direct democracy are not used as much as they are in the Pacific states.

Political party organizations are weak in the Pacific states, but the parties themselves are competitive, with the Democrats traditionally holding a decided advantage in California and Oregon. The Democrats in 1986 won control of both legislative chambers in California; held a majority in the Senate and tied in the House in Oregon; and relinquished control of both chambers in Washington, losing by one seat in the Senate—a marked contrast to the Republican party's success in the Rocky Mountain region.

Beyond the arena of party politics, major political battles take place in the Pacific states over direct initiative propositions, which had their birth in the West Coast's Progressive era early in this century. The political contests begin with petition drives aimed at getting the requisite number of signatures to qualify propositions on the statewide ballot and continue up to the general election, as supporters and opponents of initiatives work to see their positions prevail. Voters in the Pacific states make extensive use of the initiative. Between 1982 and 1986, for example, Oregonians alone voted on more initiatives than the voters of all the Rocky Mountain and Plains states combined.[16] California was a close second nationally. Moreover, the issues dealt with were far from insignificant, involving questions of tax limitation, abortion, legalization of marijuana, and the quarantine of AIDS patients. Such popular use of the initiative has gone a long way in accounting for the weakness of political parties in the Pacific states.

California stands out as the behemoth of West Coast politics. But California's politics are far from homogeneous. If an imaginary line were drawn south of Santa Barbara, California could be divided into two discrete states politically: the one south of the line being politically conservative, strongly Republican, and growth-oriented (despite an already considerable concentration); the one north being much more liberal, Democratic, and preservation-oriented. Among the several factors dividing northern and southern California, a significant one is water. Northern California is water rich, and southern California is water poor. Obviously the south would like to divert more of the north's water, but the political intransigence of the north has forced southern California to look east for its water—water that is diverted from Utah and Arizona.

Washington and Oregon clearly resemble northern California in their politics more than they do southern California. Garreau places Washington, Oregon, and northern California together socially and politically into what he calls "Ecotopia," with San Francisco as its capital. Southern California is included within "Mexamerica," with Los Angeles as its capital, dramatizing the social and political chasm between the two substate regions.

California, of the three states, is strongest economically, benefiting from a well-developed, highly diversified economy. That diversity, spanning high-technology industry, agriculture and agribusiness, service industries, and government employment, cushions California against national economic shocks. Washington and Oregon are less diversified: Washington is highly dependent on the fortunes of the aerospace industry, although it has lately been attracting high-technology growth; and Oregon is dependent on the lumber industry. Of the three, Oregon is the poorest, having a per capita personal income in the bottom half of the states nationally. California and Washington respectively rank fifth and sixteenth nationally. All three states rank in the top half nationally on per capita state and local general expenditures, consistent with their long-standing state commitment in support of public services.

As mentioned earlier, Alaska and Hawaii each represent a unique case among the states. Alaska, with its low and far-flung population, has by far the greatest per capita costs of government of any state in the union, at over five times the national average. To compensate for the higher costs of government, Alaska has the highest per capita income nationally; yet even at that, its relative tax bite, per $1,000 of personal income, is also the highest in the country. Faced with major economic problems tied to the recently depressed price of oil, Alaska's government has been engaged in serious cutback management.

Alaska, largely a land of first-generation immigrants, has a competitive two-party system, with surprisingly high voter turnout given its diffuse population. Alaskans also possess the initiative and the popular referendum but have not used them to a significant extent.

Hawaii's economy is more diversified than Alaska's, although it relies primarily on agriculture and tourism. But tourism is its biggest business. Its per capita income is very close to the national average, and it spends slightly above the national average on a per capita basis. Hawaii also provides the lowest property tax support for education in the nation but has the second highest per pupil state school aid, consistent with Hawaii's tradition of highly centralized government services.

Hawaii's politics have a decided racial element; Japanese-Americans hold most of the major political offices in Hawaii, and the Japanese-Americans, about one-quarter of the state's population, make up 42 percent of the registered voters.[17] For the state as a whole, voter turnout falls below the national average.

Politically, the Democratic party holds a distinct advantage in Hawaii, and in 1986 the Democrats maintained a majority in both chambers of the state legislature.

CHANGING PATTERNS OF GROWTH AND DECLINE

Increased state competition among regions and even states within the same region has been a reality of the 1980s. The states have not been competing "on a level playing field" during this time, and the field's tilt has changed in the span of just a few years. The 1981–1983 recession affected the states differently. Hardest hit were the heavy industrial states, as demands for pig iron, steel, rubber, glass, industrial machinery, automobiles, and other vehicles fell off precipitously. The Midwest lost almost 1.2 million jobs between 1980 and 1983 alone, with the five East North Central states accounting for 988,000 lost jobs: Illinois (319,000), Ohio (274,000), Michigan (220,000), Indiana (100,000), and Wisconsin (73,000). On its western border, Iowa lost 70,000 jobs, and Minnesota lost 52,000. Other states suffering sizable employment reductions included Pennsylvania (229,000), West Virginia (64,000), and Kentucky (62,000).[18] The last two states, although not geographically part of the Midwest or Northeast, are an important part of this nation's heavy industrial belt. Down the river from Pittsburgh, the West Virginia panhandle, as an example, includes such major steel, glass, and chemical centers as Morgantown, Parkersburg, and Wheeling. Moreover, both West Virginia and Kentucky, as major bituminous coal-producing states, suffered from a marked downturn in the national demand for coal.

At the same time that unemployment reached post-Great Depression heights in the industrial states of the Snowbelt, business was booming in the noncoal, energy-producing states. As steel and auto workers were laid off in Pennsylvania and Michigan, prospective employees flocked to oil-field jobs, many paying $3,000 a month. Opportunities in the oil and natural gas industries appeared almost unbounded in the early 1980s, as rapidly rising prices encouraged expanded exploration and production. The energy boom meant good things for states such as Alaska, Texas, Louisiana, Oklahoma, New Mexico, North Dakota, Wyoming, and Montana. But the highest riders were clearly Alaska, Texas, and Louisiana. Rapidly expanding severance tax revenues swelled their state treasuries. For them, it was a period of boom, compared to the bust conditions of the heavy industrial belt.

In contrast, the treasuries of many northeastern and midwestern states took a beating. Not only did revenues come in far below projections, and in some cases below the level necessary to finance even last year's spending level, but also greatly increased public assistance costs pushed up expenditures. State budgets had to be recast. Spending had to be cut, taxes increased, or a combination of the two.

However, by the mid-1980s the tables had turned. An upturn in the nation's economy—associated with reduced inflation, lower interest rates, and federal tax cuts—reawakened demand for industrial products. Many of the states hardest hit by the 1981–1983 recession had turned things around by 1986. For example, Pennsylvania's unemployment rate dropped from a high of 11.8 percent in 1983 to 6.8 percent in 1986. Michigan's rate fell from its 1982 high of 15.5 percent to 8.8 percent in 1986. During the same period, Indiana's dropped from 12.5 to 6.7 percent, Ohio's fell from 12.5 to 8.1 percent, and Wisconsin's dropped from 10.7 to 7.0 percent. West Virginia's employment picture also brightened somewhat from its 1983 high of 18 percent, but a continued depressed price of coal kept it from dropping any lower than 11.8 percent in 1986.[19]

Just as fortunes improved for the industrial states, they worsened for both the energy-producing and agricultural states. The downturn in agriculture—associated with reduced international demand, depressed commodity prices, and high levels of farm debt from overextended credit in the face of unusually high interest rates—proved to be shorter-lived than that facing the energy-related industries. But it hit the farm belt hard during the middle part of the 1980s, depressing the fortunes not only of farmers but also of agribusinesses. It effects could be felt in greatly reduced agricultural land values as well as in increased, related industrial unemployment. However, the U.S. dollar's weakness toward the end of the decade made American agricultural commodities and farm implements more financially attractive in international markets, showing signs of reversing the earlier period of decline. For the energy-producing states, the breakdown of cartelized price controls on petroleum, together with the increased oil production of Middle Eastern and Latin American nations, resulted in a rapidly dropping international price of oil beginning in early 1985 and continuing throughout the decade. The per barrel price of oil fell from a high of $27 in January 1985 to under $15 in late 1987. The depressed energy economy had it effects on employment in the key energy-producing states. By 1986, their unemployment rates (Alaska, 10.8 percent; Texas, 8.9 percent; and Louisiana, 13.1 percent) no longer compared favorably to the industrial states of the Northeast and Midwest.

This localized energy-induced recession could well be viewed as a temporary aberration in a longer-term trend of economic ascendancy for the West and South, at the expense of the Northeast and Midwest. Disregarding the dampening economic effects of energy price declines on a number of western and southern states, the past fifteen or so years have witnessed a dramatic shift of population and jobs from the so-called Snowbelt (or more pejoratively, the Rustbelt) to the Sunbelt states. (See Figure 1.1.) The 1981–1983 recession accelerated an already established pattern.

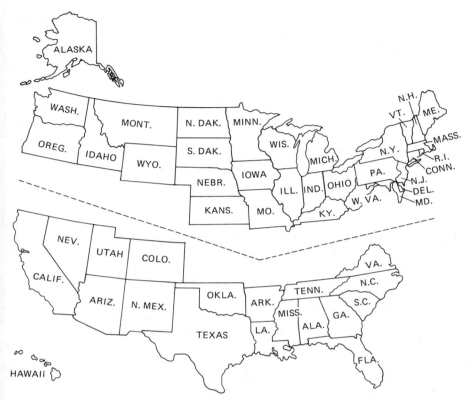

Figure 1.1. Sunbelt and Snowbelt (Source: Thomas R. Dye, *Politics in States and Communities*, 5/e, © 1985, p. 14. Reprinted by permission of Prentice-Hall, Inc., Englewood Cliffs, New Jersey)

Table 1.2 shows changes in metropolitan area populations, by state, between 1970 and 1985. Whereas metropolitan areas of the West and South grew by an average annual rate of 2 percent during the 1970s, the Midwest had only a 0.3 percent average annual increase over the same period. The Northeast actually saw its population decline. During the first half of the 1980s the Midwest's population remained just about constant, at the same time the Northeast had only marginal population growth. In comparison, the West and South continued to enjoy substantial population growth, again at about 2 percent a year.

Turning to individual metropolitan areas, the ten fastest growing areas during the 1970s and the first half of the 1980s were in the West or South, whereas the ten areas of greatest population decline could be found in the Northeast and Midwest.

The contrast becomes more obvious as we compare growing and declining cities. As Table 1.3 illustrates, St. Louis lost more than a quarter of its population during the decade of the 1970s; Buffalo, Cleveland, Detroit, and Youngstown lost over one-fifth of their populations during the same period. And that decline continued in the 1980s. In comparison, cities in Arizona, California, and Texas led the nation in population growth. The population of Mesa, Arizona, nearly tripled between 1970 and 1986. The population of Arlington, Texas, grew by 176 percent over the same period, and Colorado Springs' population doubled. But dramatic growth was not restricted to the smaller cities of the Sunbelt. Since 1970, Austin, Texas, almost doubled its population, picking up over 212,000 new residents. San Diego added over 300,000 new residents, San Jose and San Antonio over 250,000, and Houston nearly 500,000.

Industrial and commercial growth provided ample employment opportunities to attract new residents. Between 1970 and 1985, nonagricultural employment

TABLE 1.2. CHANGING METROPOLITAN AREA POPULATIONS,* BY STATE, 1970 TO 1985

Region, Division, and State	Total (000s)			Average Annual Percentage Change	
	1970	1980	1985	1970–1980	1980–1985
Northeast	43,742	43,291	43,906	(.1)	.3
New England	9,822	10,020	10,230	.2	.4
Maine	365	404	420	1.0	.7
New Hampshire	404	511	560	2.3	1.8
Vermont	99	115	122	1.5	1.1
Massachusetts	5,266	5,231	5,291	(.1)	.2
Rhode Island	868	878	896	.1	.4
Connecticut	2,819	2,879	2,940	.2	.4
Middle Atlantic	33,921	33,272	33,676	(.2)	.2
New York	16,647	15,869	16,091	(.5)	.3
New Jersey	7,171	7,365	7,562	.3	.5
Pennsylvania	10,102	10,038	10,023	(.1)	—
Midwest	40,460	41,549	41,837	.3	.1
E. No. Central	31,621	32,204	32,156	.2	—
Ohio	8,565	8,521	8,467	(.1)	(.1)
Indiana	3,551	3,719	3,737	.5	.1
Illinois	9,125	9,339	9,488	.2	.3
Michigan	7,361	7,481	7,291	.2	(.5)
Wisconsin	3,019	3,145	3,174	.4	.2
W. No. Central	8,840	9,345	9,681	.6	.7
Minnesota	2,434	2,621	2,741	.7	.9
Iowa	1,154	1,223	1,218	.6	(.1)
Missouri	3,170	3,226	3,301	.2	.4
North Dakota	196	234	250	1.8	1.2
South Dakota	155	180	198	1.5	1.8
Nebraska	650	708	747	.9	1.0
Kansas	1,082	1,153	1,227	.6	1.2

continued

TABLE 1.2., *continued*

Region, Division, and State	Total (000s)			Average Annual Percentage Change	
	1970	*1980*	*1985*	*1970–1980*	*1980–1985*
South	42,282	51,489	56,813	2.0	1.9
So. Atlantic	22,051	26,777	29,496	1.9	1.8
Delaware	386	398	413	.3	.7
Maryland	3,668	3,920	4,082	.7	.8
Dist. of Col.	757	638	626	(1.7)	(.4)
Virginia	3,279	3,745	4,069	1.3	1.6
West Virginia	683	718	710	.5	(.2)
North Carolina	2,755	3,204	3,433	1.5	1.3
South Carolina	1,504	1,865	2,010	2.2	1.4
Georgia	2,807	3,403	3,816	1.9	2.2
Florida	6,213	8,885	10,337	3.6	2.9
E. So. Central	6,913	7,903	8,195	1.3	.7
Kentucky	1,550	1,677	1,694	.8	.2
Tennessee	2,630	3,048	3,173	1.5	.8
Alabama	2,169	2,462	2,558	1.3	.7
Mississippi	564	716	769	2.4	1.4
W. So. Central	13,318	16,809	19,123	2.3	2.5
Arkansas	730	885	922	1.9	.8
Louisiana	2,439	2,892	3,095	1.7	1.3
Oklahoma	1,432	1,724	1,925	1.9	2.1
Texas	8,716	11,307	13,180	2.6	2.9
West	29,320	35,975	39,968	2.0	2.0
Mountain	5,155	7,263	8,316	3.4	2.6
Montana	169	189	201	1.1	1.2
Idaho	112	173	192	4.3	1.9
Wyoming	108	141	146	2.7	.7
Colorado	1,772	2,326	2,623	2.7	2.3
New Mexico	456	609	686	2.9	2.3
Arizona	1,323	2,040	2,433	4.3	3.3
Utah	822	1,128	1,262	3.2	2.1
Nevada	394	657	774	5.1	3.1
Pacific	24,165	28,712	31,652	1.7	1.9
Washington	2,752	3,322	3,566	1.9	1.3
Oregon	1,415	1,763	1,805	2.2	.4
California	19,241	22,689	25,231	1.6	2.0
Alaska	126	174	236	3.2	5.8
Hawaii	631	763	815	1.9	1.3
United States	155,805	172,304	182,525	1.0	1.1

*Includes metropolitan areas of 250,000 or greater. *(Source: Bureau of the Census,* Statistical Abstract of the United States, 1987 *[Washington, DC: U.S. Department of Commerce, 1987], p. 25.)*

TABLE 1.3. POPULATION OF SELECTED CITIES' GROWTH AND DECLINE 1970–1980 AND 1980–1986

Growth

	1970–1980			1980–1986		
City	1970	1980	Percent Growth	City	1986	Percent Growth
Mesa, AZ	63,000	152,000	58.6	Mesa, AZ	251,430	65.4
Arlington, TX	90,000	160,000	43.8	Arlington, TX	249,770	35.9
Modesto, CA	62,000	107,000	42.1	Austin, TX	466,550	26.1
Garland, TX	81,000	139,000	41.7	Fresno, CA	284,660	23.4
Colorado Springs, CO	136,000	215,000	36.7	Garland, TX	176,510	21.3
				Colorado Springs, CO	272,660	21.1
San Jose, CA	460,000	629,000	26.9	Modesto, CA	132,940	19.5
Austin, TX	254,000	345,000	26.4	San Antonio, TX	914,350	14.0
El Paso, TX	322,000	425,000	24.2	San Diego, CA	1,015,190	13.7
Fresno, CA	166,000	218,000	23.9	El Paso, TX	491,800	13.6
Charlotte, NC	241,000	314,000	23.2	San Jose, CA	712,080	11.7
Houston, TX	1,234,000	1,595,000	22.6	Charlotte, NC	352,070	10.8
Tucson, AZ	263,000	331,000	20.5	Dallas, TX	1,003,520	9.9
San Diego, CA	697,000	876,000	20.4	Oklahoma City, OK	446,120	9.7
San Antonio, TX	654,000	786,000	16.8	Tucson, AZ	358,850	7.8
Oklahoma City, OK	368,000	403,000	8.7	Houston, TX	1,728,910	7.7
Dallas, TX	844,000	904,000	6.6	New York, NY	7,262,700	2.6
				Boston, MA	573,600	1.8
				Chicago, IL	3,009,530	.2

Decline

	1970–1980				1980–1986	
City	1970	1980	Percent Growth	City	1986	Percent Growth
St. Louis, MO	622,000	453,000	(27.2)	Detroit, MI	1,086,220	(9.7)
Cleveland, OH	751,000	574,000	(23.6)	Buffalo, NY	324,820	(9.3)
Buffalo, NY	463,000	358,000	(22.7)	Flint, MI	145,590	(9.0)
Youngstown, OH	141,000	111,500	(20.9)	Pittsburgh, PA	387,490	(8.6)
Detroit, MI	1,514,000	1,203,000	(20.5)	Cleveland, OH	535,830	(6.6)
Pittsburgh, PA	520,000	424,000	(18.5)	Youngstown, OH	104,690	(6.1)
Flint, MI	193,000	160,000	(17.1)	St. Louis, MO	426,300	(5.9)
Newark, NJ	382,000	329,000	(13.9)	Milwaukee, WI	605,000	(4.9)
Baltimore, MD	905,000	787,000	(13.0)	Baltimore, MD	752,800	(4.3)
Boston, MA	641,000	563,000	(12.2)	Newark, NJ	316,240	(3.9)
Milwaukee, WI	717,000	636,000	(11.3)			
Chicago, IL	3,369,000	3,005,000	(10.8)			
New York, NY	7,896,000	7,072,000	(10.4)			

Source: Bureau of the Census, Statistical Abstract of the United States, 1987 (Washington, DC: U.S. Department of Commerce, 1987), pp. 31–33.

grew by 65 percent in the West and 60 percent in the South, compared to only 13 percent in the Northeast and 15 percent in the Midwest. The regional disparities in employment growth come into sharper focus as we compare states at both ends of the spectrum. Heading the growth list are Alaska (148%), Arizona (137%), Nevada (120%), Florida (105%), Colorado (90%), Texas (84%), and New Mexico (77%). Although employment in California grew by 58 percent, slower than the fastest growing states, California still added over 4 million jobs between 1970 and 1985—nearly 3.3 million more than in Arizona during the same period.

The employment picture in several Snowbelt states stands in sharp contrast. More jobs were created in Arizona than in New York between 1970 and 1985, as New York's employment grew by only 6 percent during that time. Other states having only moderate job growth during that period included Pennsylvania (9%), Illinois (10%), Ohio (13%), West Virginia (15%), Michigan (17%), and Indiana (18%).[20]

The Snowbelt also offers a few economic success stories, most notably among them New Hampshire, which increased its jobs by 80 percent between 1970 and 1985 and is going strong in the late 1980s. Massachusetts, although feeling the bite of the 1981–1983 recession, still managed to increase its employment by 29 percent during those fifteen years. But Massachusetts has also recently undergone an economic revival based on high-technology growth, spurred by attractive state-sponsored industrial location incentive packages, including applied research and industrial incubation arrangements with the Massachusetts Institute of Technology and other universities.

The top story in comparing the fortunes of the Snowbelt and the Sunbelt is the dramatic growth of the latter. The growth surely has come at the expense of the Snowbelt, but not in the sense that large industries in the North have pulled up stakes and moved to the South and West. Instead, the Sunbelt has disproportionately benefitted from industrial and business *expansion* as well as from new industrial starts. Faced with increasing national and international competition, corporate officers have been looking for ways to maximize their company's operating efficiency, which has often entailed closing their least efficient industrial operations. In that competitive environment, the older, often technologically dated plants of the Northeast and Midwest have emerged as the prime candidates for closing. Conversely, the Sunbelt's generally favorable business climate has fostered expansion and new development as entrepreneurs compare the states in terms of their prospective costs of doing business, including taxes, government regulations, and state and local development incentives, as well as labor, energy, and transportation costs.

The West has recently had its share of economic success stories, largely tied to high-technology or energy-related growth. Several of the nation's fastest growing cities have based their expansion on the fortunes of high technology. Austin, Texas, is no longer considered as just a university town; it is today a major high-technology center of the Southwest, having attracted IBM, Texas Instruments,

Tracor, Motorola, and Data General. San Jose, California, in the heart of the Silicon Valley, has accumulated the highest concentration of high-technology industries in the world, including Apple, Atari, Intel, National Semiconductor, IBM, Hewlett-Packard, and Lockheed, to name a few. Colorado Springs, Colorado, has assumed the high-technology leadership of the northern Rocky Mountain states, having attracted such blue-chip companies as Hewlett-Packard, Texas Instruments, TRW, and Honeywell. This list could readily be expanded to include other high-technology growth centers such as Albuquerque, Phoenix, San Diego, and Tucson.[21]

A state's location on the growth spectrum can greatly influence its policy agenda and politics. State policy makers know where their states fit both regionally and nationally. Several prominent national rankings of the states not only provide conspicuous reminders but also tend to reinforce the stereotypes of states commonly held by business and industry leaders. Rankings such as the Grant & Co.'s Manufacturing Climate Score and *Inc.*'s Small Business Climate Rank become simplified, easily understood approximations for states' efforts to foster economic development. They readily take on symbolic meaning as popular and well-publicized representations of the good and bad of economic development. And because they are reduced to a single rank, they become naturals for widespread media coverage.

State officials know that economic growth brings with it expanded job opportunities, general prosperity, and increased state revenues. At the same time, both they and local officials recognize that growth increases the demands for government services. Generally, however, that is a tradeoff they are willing to accept because they recognize that decline, or even stagnation, places its own demands on government, in the form of increased welfare and other human services costs.

CONTEMPORARY STATE POLICY AGENDAS

In reference to the faster growth of the West and South in relation to the rest of the country, a certain "leveling" appears to have taken place. Although the Sunbelt states have clearly *grown* faster than the Snowbelt states, the latter maintain an advantage on a number of measures, including per capita income, educational attainment, and lower levels of poverty. The relative gap is closing, but the Snowbelt states still have higher absolute levels of income and education and fewer poor people. The states are also becoming more alike in their spending.[22] Growth has required that Sunbelt states increase their spending for services such as transportation and education. But it would be foolhardy to suggest that regional differences are no longer important politically, for they clearly are.

Despite the great diversity that still exists among the states, competition for economic development has topped state policy agendas across all regions during most of the 1980s. Governors and legislators in those states that have become less attractive to business and industry have sponsored legislation aimed at improving their state's allure. Toward that end, reform packages have included proposed reductions in state personal and corporate income taxes, elimination of taxes on manufacturing machinery and equipment, and reduced regulatory requirements. States have also made land available for industrial developments, helped finance plant expansions, developed state-owned industrial parks (often in concert with university research parks), and retrained workers.

Educational reform has also assumed a prominent position on state policy agendas of the 1980s. Reform initiatives have not come largely from school administrators or teachers' organizations; rather they have come from governors and state legislatures. The call for reform from the state capitals even foreshadowed that of several national commissions charged with assessing the status of American education. The national bodies found what many state policy makers had already sensed, that educational performance fell during the 1970s even though states had greatly increased school aid during that decade. Governors and legislators reasoned that if their states were to continue to increase state financial support for education, they were going to make education more accountable. Toward that end, state policy makers focused their attention on getting back to the academic basics. Legislation variously strengthened core curricular requirements, established statewide progress assessment tests and graduation examinations, required that teachers be tested for competency in their teaching fields, and mandated merit pay for teachers. Governors and legislators were also quick to relate educational performance to economic development, viewing educational improvement as an important ingredient of enhanced competitiveness.

Transportation policy is another area in which the states have been proactive during the 1980s. Faced with declining motor fuel tax revenues at the beginning of the decade, state legislatures, usually at the governor's recommendation, raised motor fuel taxes and vehicle registration fees, along with cutting back on planned highway projects. In fact, states that had not increased their motor fuel tax since the 1960s raised their rate at least once during the 1979–1983 period, and several increased taxes as many as three times in those few years.[23] Transportation provides an example of where elected state officials have been willing to take the political heat for acting responsibly and enacting higher taxes in a situation of marked need. But these same state officials, later in the decade, questioned whether the Reagan administration had acted responsibly by placing limits on how much federal funding could be released to the states each year for highway construction and repair, even though the federal tax revenues provided for a growing unobligated surplus in the Federal Highway Trust Fund. With released funding levels falling well below those earlier approved by Congress, state governors increasingly questioned publicly whether their states were getting a fair shake from the federal partner.

Beyond transportation finance, the states have acted responsibly in their general fiscal management. In contrast to the federal government, the states have had to make the tough political decisions necessary to balance state budgets during the difficult and unpredictable years of the 1980s. During the economic bad times, governors and legislatures have had to cut budgets and increase taxes, despite their unpopularity. During the 1981–1983 recession, twenty-eight states increased their personal income tax, and thirty states raised their sales tax.[24] In these times of economic stagnation, it was common practice for governors to call their state legislatures back into session to enact emergency legislation. In the mid-1980s, a new wave of tax increases became necessary for a largely different collection of states—those most affected by declining energy prices and agricultural recession. During the 1984 and 1985 fiscal years, five states were forced to raise the personal income tax, and fourteen raised the sales tax.[25]

The states have also taken the lead in restructuring civil service systems to establish pay equity. Several states during the 1980s have altered their compensation plans to correct for the effects of past practices of paying jobs disproportionately held by women at lower rates than comparable jobs disproportionately held by men. As of 1987, all but fourteen states had begun so-called "comparable worth" studies, and legislatures in twelve states approved appropriations to bring undervalued jobs into line with their counterparts.[26]

Although the states have been proactive in several policy areas, federal budget reductions have forced them into more reactive postures in other areas. In contrast to annual real-dollar increases averaging over 17 percent between 1960 and 1980, federal financial aid to state and local governments dropped by nearly 18 percent, in real-dollar terms, between 1980 and 1986.[27] The states, in turn, were put in the position of having to decide whether or not, and for which programs, to fill the gap. The states were also given somewhat greater discretion by the federal partner in deciding how those fewer funds could be spent, as Congress, at President Reagan's behest, consolidated several categorical grants into block grants. In addition, the Reagan administration's brand of "New Federalism" greatly reduced the number of federal programs that had provided aid directly to local units of government, and thereby effectively bypassed the states.

In one particular area, welfare, federal legislation provided incentives for the states to enact reforms, especially those that would require able-bodied recipients to work for their benefits and would make welfare recipients more employable. Within federal guidelines, the states have had considerable, but not complete, discretion in designing their reforms. In a similar vein, Congress also gave the states greater freedom to pursue a number of cost-cutting alternatives in the Medicaid program—a federal-state health-care program for needy individuals. As with welfare, the states generally seized the opportunity by moving to "managed health care" for welfare recipients, frequently adopting prepaid plans that give physicians incentives to stress preventive care and limit unnecessary or marginal treatment, thus reducing overall costs. Similarly, states have also adopted prospective payment plans, which reimburse hospitals on a fixed scale for services associated with treating a particular ailment, regardless of the actual services required. Again the emphasis has been on cost control and its resulting savings.

STRONGER STATES

It is not surprising that the states have exercised policy leadership in the 1980s. States are better equipped today to assume leadership than at any time before. Executive branch reforms have strengthened the ability of governors to set policy agendas and to see them through to implementation. Gubernatorial staffs have increased, as have executive budget and program evaluation support staffs. In addition, federal reforms have given state agencies increased responsibility for planning, auditing, and program review of federal grants, significantly displacing prior federal responsibility in these areas. Legislatures have also become more professional and better staffed in their own right. And vastly improved computerized information systems have given both branches the information and simulation capability they need to make better-informed policy choices.

The states have also joined forces in national organizations to advance their common interests. Such interstate associations as the National Governors' Association, the National Association of State Budget Officers, the Council of State Governments, and the National Conference of State Legislatures have been used to share information and recent state innovations. State agency officials also have their own functionally based interstate associations. For example, there are national organizations of state highway and transportation officials, state welfare officials, state natural resource officials, state school superintendents, and state university administrators, to list the most prominent associations. These organizations provide important channels for collecting and sharing information. They also constitute institutionalized avenues for transfer of innovation, as the staffs of these specialized associations share new state initiatives with all the other member states. Finally, interstate associations serve as a lobby arm of the states in Washington, representing the states' interests with Congress and the federal bureaucracy. Yet even beyond the lobbying role played by the interstate associations, many states have their own lobbying offices in the nation's capital, watching out for their own particular interests.

The key question facing interstate cooperation today, however, is whether heightened state competition for economic development will undercut the established forms of cooperation and sharing. Will states tend to abandon investments in interstate cooperation in favor of increased expenditures for promotion of their own state? The most likely course is that they will attempt to do both, continuing to marshal their common interests in Washington while expanding their own promotional efforts toward getting a bigger slice of the economic pie.

One thing is clear: The states have taken a proactive role in public policy making; they are identifying what is important to them substantively, and they are marshaling their resources toward accomplishing those ends, whether that entails initiating program or tax reforms, raising taxes when necessary, or selectively assuming administrative functions previously performed by the federal government. In addition, local units of government are asking the states for increased financial assistance, as municipalities and cities are feeling the effects of cuts in their federal financial aid. In responding, state policy makers will have to determine whether they can help their localities and still meet their own state objectives within available revenues.

SUMMARY AND CONCLUSIONS

The states, faced with rapidly shifting economic circumstances and reductions in federal aid, have met the many challenges of the 1980s. During adverse economic times, state policy makers have cut their budgets and increased taxes to make fiscal ends meet. During periods of recovery they have reduced taxes to avoid building undue surpluses. And where fiscal resources have permitted, states have advanced new policy initiatives in areas ranging from education to welfare and tax reform.

The resurgence of state activism can be found in all regions of the nation, regions that have significantly different historical, cultural, economic, and political roots and patterns of development. Yet despite these differences, state responses to the challenges of the 1980s have shown remarkable similarity. Their responses, at the same time, also have reflected increased competition among the states—primarily over economic development. Even state-initiated educational reforms at the secondary and postsecondary levels have been enacted with an eye toward improving the quality of a state's labor force and developing the technological know-how to attract and keep businesses. State officials know that business expansion brings with it increased jobs and the new tax revenues that accompany them.

The South and the West have been winning the interstate competition over growth, but several Snowbelt states have recently shown signs of making a comeback, as they have reformed their tax systems and increasingly provided incentives for businesses to locate and expand within their borders. Their state officials, in search of growth, point to the infrastructure that is already in place—sewers, roads, and schools—in contrast to the Sunbelt's need to finance new development.

Besides pursuing their own policy initiatives, the states are being asked by local units of government—which also are facing major cutbacks in federal aid—to expand state local assistance programs. Yet although states have made it clear that they are not in a position to make local governments whole for lost federal revenues, states are assessing ways in which they can help local governments while advancing their own policy initiatives within available revenues.

REFERENCES

1. John F. Bibby et al., "Parties in State Politics," in Virginia Gray et al., eds., *Politics in the American States: A Comparative Analysis,* 4th ed. (Boston: Little, Brown, 1983), p. 63; Bureau of the Census, *Statistical Abstract of the United States, 1987* (Washington, DC: U.S. Department of Commerce, 1987), p. xxii. This source is also used for subsequent references to voter turnout, by state.

2. Bibby et al., "Parties in State Politics," p. 66. This source is also used for subsequent references to the relative competitiveness of political parties among the states.
3. Bureau of the Census, *Statistical Abstract, 1987*, p. xxiv. This source is also used for subsequent references to the ranking of states on per capita personal income.
4. Brizius and Foster, Inc., *State Policy Data Book, 1987* (Alexandria, VA: State Policy Research, 1987), Table G–15. This source is also used for subsequent references to the ranking of states on per pupil state school aid.
5. Joel Garreau, *The Nine Nations of North America* (Boston: Houghton Mifflin, 1981), p. 28.
6. Brizius and Foster, *Data Book, 1987*, Table D–1.
7. Garreau, *Nine Nations*, pp. 49–97.
8. Bureau of the Census, *Statistical Abstract, 1987*, p. xxiii. This source is also used for subsequent references to the percentage of workers who are unionized, by state.
9. Brizius and Foster, *Data Book, 1987*, Table G–49.
10. Ibid., Table A–19.
11. Bureau of the Census, *Statistical Abstract, 1987*, p. xviii. This source is also used for subsequent references to the ranking of states on the infant mortality rate.
12. David C. Saffell, *State Politics* (Reading, MA: Addison-Wesley, 1984), p. 12.
13. David B. Magleby, *Direct Legislation* (Baltimore: Johns Hopkins University Press, 1984), pp. 38–39.
14. Garreau, *Nine Nations*, pp. 287–327.
15. Saffell, *State Politics*, p. 12.
16. *Initiative Quarterly*, Vol. 3, Issue 3 (1984), 9; *Monthly Initiative Bulletin*, Vol. 1, No. 1 (Sept. 1986), 11.
17. Garreau, *Nine Nations*, p. 120.
18. Bureau of the Census, *Statistical Abstract, 1987*, p. 395.
19. Ibid., p. 393; Bureau of Labor Statistics, U.S. Department of Labor, telephone inquiry for 1986 data, Dec. 1987.
20. Bureau of the Census, *Statistical Abstract, 1987*, p. xxiii; Bureau of the Census, *Statistical Abstract of the United States, 1980* (Washington DC: U.S. Department of Commerce, 1980), p. 412; Bureau of Research and Statistics, Michigan Employment Security Commission, telephone inquiry for Michigan's 1970 nonagricultural employment figure, Dec. 1987.
21. John Naisbitt, *Megatrends* (New York: Warner Books, 1984), pp. 245–58.
22. Harvey J. Tucker, "The Nationalization of State Policy Revisited," *Western Political Quarterly*, Vol. 37, No. 3 (Sept. 1984), 435–42.
23. *State Highway Funding Methods, 1983* (Washington, DC: The Road Information Program, 1983); telephone update, July 1986.
24. *Fiscal Survey of the States, 1985* (Washington, DC: National Association of State Budget Officers, 1985), p. 7.
25. Ibid.
26. *Options for Conducting a Pay Equity Study of Federal Pay and Classification Systems* (Washington, DC: Comptroller General of the United States, 1985), p. 3; telephone update, March 1987.
27. *Significant Features of Fiscal Federalism, 1985–86* (Washington, DC: U.S. Advisory Commission on Intergovernmental Relations, 1986), p. 19.

THE INTERGOVERNMENTAL CONTEXT

CHAPTER 2

Federalism and Intergovernmental Relations

State governments operate within a federal system. The U.S. Constitution, and its subsequent interpretation by the federal courts, establishes the legal structure for the relationship between the national government and the states. The Constitution does not, however, tell us how federal and state policy makers choose to use the legal framework in dealing with each other. It does not tell us how far policy makers are willing to stretch the boundaries of that constitutional authority. For that dimension, we have to move beyond a discussion of formal and legal federalism and examine patterns of intergovernmental relations that have evolved along with the federal courts' interpretations of the structural relationship. But to understand intergovernmental relations, we have to understand the contextual structure of federalism.

The Constitution created a strong national government, establishing clearly its supremacy over the states. Article I, Section 8 of the U.S. Constitution lists seventeen powers expressly given to Congress, including such powers as levying taxes, regulating interstate commerce, printing and coining money, maintaining a national military force, and so on. Article I also notably gives Congress the authority to "make all laws which shall be necessary and proper for carrying into execution the foregoing powers." This *"implied powers"* clause has served as the basis for Congress' expansion of the enumerated powers. In addition, Article VI establishes the U.S. Constitution as the "supreme law of the land," having legal ascendancy over state constitutions and state law.

The Tenth Amendment to the Constitution, in contrast, appears to limit the powers of the federal government, providing that any powers not explicitly given to the national government are "reserved" to the states. Thus a strict interpretation of the *"reserved powers"* clause would suggest that the states can constitutionally exercise great discretion in their governance. This apparent tension between the rightful powers of the federal government and the states has been the subject of several landmark U.S. Supreme Court decisions.

That role for the Supreme Court was firmly established in *Marbury v. Madison.*[1] Under Chief Justice John Marshall, the Court asserted its authority as the final judicial arbiter of disputes between the national government and the states. In so doing, the Court relied heavily on Article III, which declares that "the judicial power of the United States shall be vested in one Supreme Court." Marshall argued that "judicial power" entails the authority to interpret the law, including the highest law of the land, the U.S. Constitution. In balance, the Supreme Court's rulings over nearly the past two centuries have expanded the powers of the federal government vis-à-vis the states. Such major decisions have come in the areas of interstate commerce[2] and civil rights.[3]

A more recent landmark case, *Garcia v. San Antonio Metropolitan Transit Authority* (1985),[4] cemented the national supremacy of the federal government. In a 5 to 4 decision, the majority ruled that if the states, "as states," want protection from the national government within the constitutional system, they must look to Congress, not to the courts. The Supreme Court, in *Garcia,* appears to have abdicated its historic role as arbiter of disputes between the federal government and the states. As Justice Blackmun, author of the majority opinion, wrote, "State sovereign interests . . . are more properly protected by procedural safeguards inherent in the structure of the federal system than by judicially created limitations on federal power."[5] The Court, in effect, has suggested that state officials contact their elected federal representatives and work out differences through the federal legislative process.

But even before the *Garcia* decision, Congress probably shaped the evolving nature of American federalism more than did the courts. And Congress, since the Great Depression, has taken its policy lead from the president. Presidential policy initiatives—from Franklin Roosevelt's "New Deal" and Lyndon Johnson's "Great Society" through Ronald Reagan's policies of extrication and devolution of federal financial responsibilities to the states and local units of government—have greatly shaped the contours of intergovernmental relations. This is *not* to suggest that the courts' role has been modest, particularly as federal courts have acted to protect individual liberties in the face of state assaults. The civil rights area provides several notable illustrations of such protection. What it does suggest is that the federal government, through Congressional lawmaking, has involved itself in nearly every aspect of American life; and federal funds have served as the vehicle for expansion.

THE PHASES OF FEDERALISM

Federal-state relations have taken a number of different turns since the Constitution's ratification in 1787, but the general direction has been toward broader intervention of the federal partner in affairs traditionally the domain of the states. Four phases in the evolving relationship are discernible.[6]

Dual Federalism (1787-1913). During this early period in American political history, a clearer separation divided the functional responsibilities of the national government and the states than in later years. The national government largely pursued its enumerated powers, including matters of national defense, foreign affairs, tariffs, interstate commerce, mail delivery, and limited road construction. The states, on the other hand, assumed responsibility for education, social welfare, health, and criminal justice.

Cooperative Federalism (1913-1964). The great population growth accompanying two major waves of European immigration, the Industrial Revolution, two world wars, and the destabilizing effects of the Great Depression created a significantly different environment for the federal-state relationship than during earlier years. Popular demands on government increased greatly during this period, putting tremendous pressure on the states' ability to go it alone. The massiveness of the Great Depression forced the states to seek federal assistance in confronting its effects. In response, federal assistance programs were created to *help the states* meet the heightened demands. In addition, industrial development and population growth rendered inadequate the existing state highway network, and federal financial assistance was increased to support new construction. The federal government had become a cooperative partner. The states still largely provided program direction and administration while accepting growing federal financial support.

Centralized Federalism (1964-1980). This period marked a departure from the national government's supportive role in domestic policy making. Instead of assisting the states to develop programs to meet emerging domestic needs, the federal government articulated "national" policy goals and held out a greatly increased fiscal carrot to entice state participation, which often involved state administration. During the early years of this period, federal programs were created to provide financial aid and medical care to the poor, construct low-cost housing, provide compensatory education for the underprivileged, and revitalize inner cities. A number of new federal programs even bypassed the states, providing direct assistance to municipalities. This was also a period of rapidly growing federal mandates and regulations that accompanied the receipt of federal funds.

New Federalism: Federal Extrication and Selective Penetration (1981-   ). This period represents a reexamination of the federal government's relationship with the states (and local governments). Many federal programs were eliminated, and others were consolidated. Overall, federal financial support was reduced, in constant dollar terms, for grants-in-aid. The federal partner, in several areas, was drawing back on the program and funding commitments made during the previous decades of federal expansionism. At the same time, state officials were given greater discretion in program administration, as federal regulations were increasingly reduced and simplified. Yet despite this general movement toward a reduced federal presence, several notable examples of increased federal penetration can be cited—instances where greater national involvement in areas of traditional state prerogative appeared paradoxical in the context of a general pattern of federal extrication.

FEDERAL INVOLVEMENT AND THE ROLE OF GOVERNMENT

The degree of the national government's involvement over time in the affairs of the states has been clearly influenced by environmental factors such as two world wars and the Great Depression, but it has also been a product of presidents' and Congress' willingness to enact legislation enlarging or, more recently, contracting the federal government's role. And that relative willingness to legislate expanded involvement has been related to changing views about the role of government in society, in general, and about the balance between nationalization of policy and local responsiveness, in particular.

What is the appropriate role for government in society? Is the best government a greatly limited government? Is it the basic operating presumption that government should keep its hands off the affairs of society unless an overwhelming case can be made for its intervention? Is the private marketplace of supply and demand really the best and most effective allocator of value in society? Or conversely, is the best government one that proactively intervenes in societal affairs to protect what is viewed as the public interest or to correct for "market failure" and ensure that all citizens have at least a minimally adequate quality of life, including subsistence, health care, housing, and educational opportunity? If the answer to this last question is affirmative, is that improved relative position likely to be enduring or only transitory, ending with the termination of government assistance? How our elected representatives at all levels of government answer these questions greatly shapes the nature of what they try to do or choose not to do. The answers have also significantly shaped the nature of intergovernmental relations over time.

Political philosophers and policy makers have debated these questions across continents and centuries. Even ordinary citizens have acquired a "gut-level" response to them. As Americans, steeped in the tradition of democratic liberalism, we tend to emphasize the individual, and his or her rights and needs, over those of society. In doing so, we are wary of government intervention that goes much beyond protecting the rights of individuals guaranteed by the Constitution. We believe in the wisdom of mutual adjustment and of the marketplace. But that faith in "rugged individualism" is tempered by a deep-seated concern over fairness, over ensuring that people have a chance to succeed—free from the constraints of social position at birth, religion, sex, or race. Yet they are the "cutting points" over which policy debates take place in America. How broad are individual rights, and how far should government go to protect them? Conversely, how far should government go in protecting the public interest if it means constraining the rights of individuals? Where does fairness begin and end in providing public assistance to those who fail to succeed in the private marketplace, and what is the popularly perceived reason for that failure? Do some fail because of circumstances that are viewed as beyond their control, such as being old or disabled; or are other reasons imputed, such as laziness or taking self-interested advantage of overly generous public benefit levels, which depress the incentive to "make it on one's own"? The ways in which these lines have been drawn have shaped the nature of intergovernmental relations in this country, even more so than philosophical or legalistic concerns about the inherent authority of the federal government or about the reserved powers of the states.

The Great Society and Its Aftermath

These different ways of viewing government and its appropriate role in society can be illustrated by comparing the decade of the 1960s with that of the 1980s. Domestic public policy in the 1960s can best be characterized by President Lyndon Johnson's call for a "Great Society," in which government, through the federal partner's lead, established public programs that improved the overall quality of life. But the key to that effort involved programs aimed at improving the lot of the underprivileged; for a truly great society was defined as one that assured an adequate quality of life for the less fortunate. At President Johnson's call, Congress enacted most of the programs designed by the administration's Great Society architects, including programs providing cash transfer payments to poor families with dependent children, the aged, the blind, or the disabled not qualifying for Social Security; for medical care for the poor and other eligibles not qualifying for Medicare; for housing subsidy; for community development; for greatly increased need-based educational assistance; for job training; and for law enforcement assistance. During the Johnson administration alone, 209 new grant programs were created toward these ends.[7]

These grant programs took one of two forms: formula-based or project-based. *Formula grants* are made available to all recipients who meet the legally constituted eligibility requirements. Those who are eligible have a right to the cash transfer or service. Accordingly, the federal treasury is required by law to make available whatever amounts are necessary to finance the "entitlement" spending. *Project grants,* on the other hand, require specific approval and are often awarded on a competitive basis by the federal bureaucracy. Although the vast majority of all federal grants fall into the project category, the cost of formula grants far exceeds that of project grants.

Most grants-in-aid require *matching* funds from state and/or local governments as a demonstration of state and/or local interest in, and commitment to, the aided programs. But the balance of sharing has characteristically tipped over to the federal side of the scale, with the "feds" characteristically picking up between 50 and 90 percent of the costs, with the remainder falling to state and/or local governments. For some programs, the state picks up the full nonfederal share, but for other joint state-local-administered programs, it passes a percentage of the costs on to local units of government.

Although federal grant programs were created by the federal government's design, they were structured to incorporate state and/or local governmental administration and, selectively, financial participation. A partnership was offered, with federal funds serving as the financial carrot for state and local participation.

Federal grants-in-aid grew from $8.6 billion during the last year of the Kennedy administration to nearly $19 billion at the end of the Johnson administration.[8] That major increase was consistent with the view that the federal government needed to lead the way in improving the condition of America's poor and disadvantaged. Government was viewed as having an obligation to make such a financial investment in society, even if that meant transferring resources from the private sector to the public sector, a perspective popularized by economist and presidential advisor John Kenneth Galbraith.

As Table 2.1 shows, although federal aid to the states and local governments almost doubled between the 1964 and 1969 fiscal years, the most dramatic in-

TABLE 2.1. FEDERAL GRANTS-IN-AID TO STATE AND LOCAL GOVERNMENTS, SELECTED YEARS, 1949–1987

Calendar Year	Amount ($ Billions)
1949	2.2
1954	2.9
1959	6.5
1964	10.1
1969	20.3
1972	34.4
1974	43.4
1976	59.1
1978	77.9
1980	91.5
1982	88.2
1984	97.6
1986	102.6e
1987	100.4e

e = estimate *(Source:* Significant Features of Fiscal Federalism, 1985–86 *[Washington, DC: U.S. Advisory Commission on Intergovernmental Relations, 1986], pp. 10, 19.)*

creases can be found during the 1970s. A good share of that growth can be attributed to inflation, as Figure 2.1 illustrates. If one looks at changes in federal aid on a biennial basis, using constant dollars, the Great Society years did represent, on the average, the period of greatest real growth. Nevertheless, the 1970s still represented a period of sustained growth in federal aid. Throughout both the 1960s and 1970s federal grants-in-aid rose as a percentage of state and local own-source revenue. (See Figure 2.2.) States and local units of government became increasingly dependent on federal financial support, and the very availability of the growing federal "kitty" enticed state and local policy makers to align their priorities with the availability of financial aid.

During this period of sustained growth, the *categorical* grant-in-aid served as the primary vehicle for enticing state and local governments to follow federal priorities. Categorical grants have to be used for the narrowly specific purposes prescribed in the enabling legislation and in the federal administrative code. Grants are made for specific purposes such as building bridges, providing medical care for the needy, and subsidizing housing. In accepting the assistance, state and local governments become obliged to comply with the various grant requirements. And the requirements often not only designate the purpose(s) to which the funds may be put but also stipulate the services that are to be provided and any conditions attached to their provision.

By the 1968 fiscal year, there were nearly 400 separate grants available to state or local jurisdictions.[9] As a step toward simplifying federal aid programs and reducing federal direction over state and local governments, President Richard M. Nixon initiated *block grant* programs.

Block grants can be applied much more broadly than can categorical grants, and with fewer restrictions or regulations. State and/or local governments may

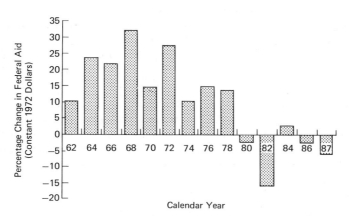

Figure 2.1. Change in Federal Aid to State and Local Governments (Source: *Significant Features of Fiscal Federalism, 1985–86* [Washington, DC: U.S. Advisory Commission on Intergovernmental Relations, 1986], p. 19.)

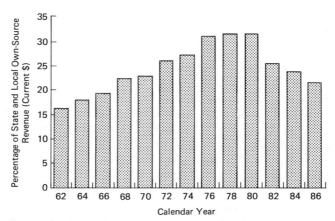

Figure 2.2. Federal Grants-in-Aid to State and Local Governments (Source: *Significant Features of Fiscal Federalism, 1985–86* [Washington, DC: U.S. Advisory Commission on Intergovernmental Relations, 1986], p. 19.)

choose among a variety of related purposes consistent with the block's design. One such example is the Social Services Block Grant, also known as the Title XX amendments to the Social Security Act, which consolidated several discrete categorical social services into a single block grant. Thus, rather than applying for federal assistance to provide activity therapy or personal-care services for the elderly, and then making a separate application for children's day-care services and still another for foster-care assistance, funds from a single grant can be used to finance whatever social service activities that fall within the grant's umbrella. Higher relative percentages of a block's funding can be used for certain activities deemed to be of higher local priority. Lower-priority activities can be lightly funded or not funded at all. States can set their own priorities and allocate block grant funding accordingly, all within the general functional limits of the block.

During the Nixon administration, three block grant programs were enacted into law: the Comprehensive Employment and Training Program (CETA), providing training and employment in public service jobs; the Community Development Block Grant, tying together a number of preexisting urban development and renewal programs; and Title XX of the Social Security Act, discussed above.

Moving even further away from the philosophy underlying the categorical grant, the Nixon administration introduced the concept of *general revenue sharing,* a proposal Republican candidate Richard Nixon had made during the 1968 presidential campaign, and which was based on earlier suggestions made by economist and Democratic presidential advisor Walter Heller. In that election campaign Nixon argued that the Great Society had concentrated too much decision-making authority in the hands of the federal government. The plethora of categorical grants was held up as symptomatic of a pervasive "Washington knows best" mentality. With revenue sharing, the federal government would simply provide funds, without strings, to state and local governments based on an allocation formula. In turn, state and local officials would use the monies as their own priorities dictated. Having the strong, broadly based support of governors and mayors, general revenue sharing overwhelmingly passed Congress in 1972.

Revenue sharing was popular because it met a number of needs. For conservatives, it represented a retrenchment from federal program direction and provided greater state and local choice, where public decisions are closer to the people affected by them. For liberals, it meant additional funds for urban areas. And politically, for Republicans it meant lessened hostility from big-city mayors, who traditionally allied their interests with those of the Democratic party.

Based on a formula that takes into account population, relative income, urbanization, and tax effort, over 39,000 jurisdictions—states and local units of government—received funding. Revenue-sharing money came with relatively few restrictions. The initial authorizing legislation provided approximately $30 billion over a five-year period. Congress subsequently reauthorized the program for an additional four years, through 1980, providing $25.6 billion for that period. Roughly one-third of the funds characteristically went to the states, two-fifths to municipalities, and about one-fourth to counties.[10]

With the introduction of revenue sharing and block grants in the 1970s, the normative (or some might say, "rhetorical") pendulum had swung back from centralization of choice toward greater local decision making. However, even in 1980 categoricals still comprised nearly four-fifths of all federal grants-in-aid. Although movement had been made toward centralization, significant change did not occur until President Ronald Reagan took office in 1981.

The Reagan Administration's New Federalism

David Stockman, in a postelection, November 1980 memorandum to newly elected President Ronald Reagan, offered advice on how to avoid an "Economic Dunkirk." His advice focused on three initiatives: cutting the federal budget, cutting taxes, and reducing federal regulation. These three objectives, particularly the first two, proved to have major implications for the Reagan administration's policy of "New Federalism." As we shall see, the actual pursuit of New Federalism became in large part subjugated to the attainment of these highest-priority objectives. And the effects of that quest greatly modified President Reagan's policies toward state and local governments during the course of the administration's two terms.

The Blueprint for Change. The first plank of Stockman's campaign called for a substantial personal income tax reduction, particularly benefitting taxpayers in the upper-income tax brackets, combined with more favorable depreciation rates. Stockman characterized both as necessary incentives to increase investment. That the tax changes would tend disproportionately to benefit the more well-to-do was viewed as totally appropriate because such individuals were seen as those most inclined to put their newly found after-tax savings to work, thus spurring economic development and pulling the country out of recession. But the new federal budget director-to-be cautioned that tax reductions had to be accompanied by major budget reductions, as a second plank, arguing that "the pre-eminent danger is that an initial economic policy package that includes the tax cuts but does not contain decisive, credible elements concerning outlay control, future budget authority reduction, and a believable plan for curtailing the federal government's massive direct and indirect credit absorption (as a result of excessive debt) will generate pervasive expectations of a continuing 'Reagan inflation.' ''[11] Stockman went on to warn Reagan that "the federal budget has now become an automatic coast-to-coast soup line that dispenses remedial aid with almost reckless abandon, converting the traditional notion of automatic stabilizers into multitudinous outlay spasms throughout the budget.''[12] The third plank called for pulling back on federal regulations. These "calls-to-arms" provided the policy structure on which the Reagan administration's initiatives were based.

Shortly after his inauguration, President Reagan on February 18, 1981 presented his tax-relief package to Congress. After some give-and-take with Congress, resulting in several tax-break concessions to business, Congress approved a package that closely followed the lines proposed by Reagan—one that included income tax cuts and investment incentives, albeit with a few compromise-oriented "sweeteners" included. But since there is no such thing as a free lunch, the tax-cut package reduced would-be federal revenues drastically, amounting to $37 billion in fiscal year (FY) 1982, $93 billion in 1983, and a whopping $150 billion in 1984.[13] At the same time that revenues were reduced, federal expenditures grew significantly. Actual expenditures (outlays) increased by 46 percent over the five-year period between FY 1981 and 1986, rising from 22.7 to 23.8 percent of the gross national product (GNP). In other words, federal spending exceeded the growth in the economy, just the opposite of what had been expected.

The combined effect of reduced revenues and increased expenditures has meant one thing: that the federal budget deficit would increase—and increase it did. The deficit rose from $78.9 billion in FY 1981 to a record $220.7 billion in 1986. Again, as a percentage of GNP, the deficit took a greatly increased share, rising from 2.6 percent in FY 1981 to 5.3 percent in 1986—a staggering 104 percent increase in just five years.[14] This experience can be contrasted to the Reagan administration's initial projection (in March 1981) of a marginal budget surplus by the end of the 1984 fiscal year.

The 1986 fiscal year marked a highpoint in federal spending and in the federal deficit. The following year, however, represents a point of departure, as Congress began to assert itself more aggressively in the federal budgetary process. Whereas defense appropriations had grown by an average of 8 percent per year—after inflation—between FY 1981 and 1986, Congress approved a 1987 budget calling for only a 1 percent increase above the 1986 spending level, an amount well within inflation.[15]

This major reduction in the growth of defense spending, approved despite strong presidential opposition, in large part contributed to a FY 1987 aggregate budget increase of only 2 percent. Such spending restraint, together with revenue growth triggered by an improved economy, resulted in a $46 billion drop in the federal deficit projected for the end of the 1987 fiscal year.

The overall increase in spending during the first five years of the Reagan administration masked major shifts across program areas, reflecting the administration's agenda of restoring real-dollar defense spending to the level of the late 1950s while reducing the post-Great Society growth in domestic spending. The Reagan administration, to a great extent, achieved these objectives. As Figure 2.3 shows, while defense spending rose from 23 percent of total federal expenditures in FY 1981 to a projected 28 percent in 1987, nondefense discretionary spending dropped from 25 to 17 percent during the same period. Entitlement spending[16] increased only marginally, reflecting some administration success in modifying authorizing law. And as we shall see later, federal aid to state and local governments bore a significant share of the retrenchment in domestic spending.

The Initial Outlines. The "reach" of the federal government, for President Reagan, had become far too extensive. The Great Society years had launched an explosion of federally directed grant-in-aid programs that provided federal financial assistance for a plethora of discrete programs viewed by Washington to be in the national interest. Not only had the overall number of separate federal grant programs mushroomed to 534 by Reagan's first year in office, at a cost of over $90 billion, but also the proportion of direct federal to local aid increased from 14 percent of all federal aid in 1968 to 30 percent in 1980.[17] For President Reagan, these trends had to be reversed. The unprecedented growth in narrow federal prescription had to be turned around because the states were viewed as better able

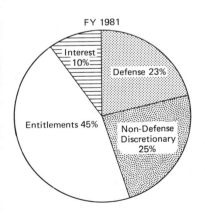
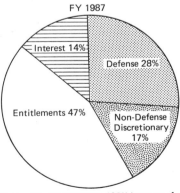

Note: Figures add up to 106% because of offsetting receipts

Figure 2.3. Federal Spending Priorities (Source: *Congressional Quarterly Weekly Report,* Vol. 44, No. 46 [Nov. 15, 1986], 88.)

to decide what programs are most in their interest and best meet their needs. In President Reagan's words,

> Our citizens feel they have lost control of even the most basic decisions made about the essential services of government, such as schools, welfare, roads, and even garbage collection. They are right. A maze of interlocking jurisdictions and levels of government confronts the average citizen in trying to solve even the simplest of problems. They do not know where to turn for answers, who to hold accountable, who to praise, who to blame, who to vote for or against. The main reason for this is the overpowering growth of federal grants-in-aid programs during the past few decades.[18]

For the Reagan administration, the federal government's direct dealing with local units of government also had to be reversed since President Reagan viewed the states as best positioned to set priorities within their boundaries. In that vein, the administration looked toward the governor's office as being most appropriate to initiate the sorting out of relative policy priorities. The governor was viewed by the administration as being in the best position to consider what is in the state's best interest, not merely what is in the best interest of the state's major city or cities.

Consolidation of Grants-in-Aid. In pursuing the consolidation of categorical grants-in-aid into block grants, the Reagan administration positioned itself to kill the proverbial "two birds with one stone" by reducing federal directedness and, at the same time, cutting back on financial assistance. President Reagan offered a trade: more state flexibility in exchange for a drop in the level of financial support. Congress, riding the high waves of presidential popularity during Reagan's first year in office, went along with the deal, amid only mild protestation coming primarily from municipalities. The cities feared that the movement to block grants, under the allocative discretion of the states, would further the interests of suburban and rural areas at the expense of the urban. The concern was that the rurally dominated state legislatures, in reviewing gubernatorial recommendations, would slant allocations in ways disadvantageous to the major cities. The cities' voice had been muted not only by the fiscal exigencies facing Congress but also by support for categorical consolidation from such groups as the U.S. Advisory Commission on Intergovernmental Relations, the National Governors' Association, and the National Conference of State Legislatures. The lure of greater state-level flexibility, along with the prospects for lessened federal regulation, prompted support from these influential organizations.[19]

The Reagan administration made the most of the opportunity. As part of the FY 1982 block grant reforms, the president proposed the consolidation of eighty-five existing categorical grant programs into seven new block grants. Congress concurred in the general outline of the conversion but made a few marginal adjustments. The somewhat reconfigured result found seventy-seven categoricals consolidated into nine block grants, including two existing blocks that underwent some modification. (See Table 2.2.) In addition, forty-three other categorical pro-

TABLE 2.2. CATEGORICAL GRANTS CONSOLIDATED BY BLOCK GRANTS: PROPOSED BY REAGAN ADMINISTRATION, ENACTED BY CONGRESS

Proposed

Block	Number of Categoricals
1. Local Education	10
2. State Education	33
3. Health Services and Mental Health	17
4. Preventive Health	10
5. Social Services	12
6. Emergency Hardship Assistance	2
7. Community Development	1
	85

Enacted

Block	Number of Categoricals
1. State Education	37
2. Preventive Health and Health Services	6
3. Alcohol, Drug Abuse, and Mental Health	10
4. Maternal and Child Health	9
5. Social Services	1
6. Community Services	7
7. Primary Care	2
8. Low-Income Home Energy Assistance	2
9. State Community Development	3
	77

Source: David B. Walker, Albert J. Richler, and Cynthia Cates Colella, "The First Ten Months: Grant-in-Aid, Regulatory, and Other Changes, Intergovernmental Perspective, *Vol. 8, No. 1 (Winter 1982), 12.*

grams were eliminated, at the administration's recommendation. They included programs in the following areas: seven in energy conservation and regulation; eight in pollution control and abatement; five in migrant and refugee care; six in area and regional development; three in health maintenance; and fourteen in the general area of state and local government "capacity building," including programs aimed at upgrading management, personnel training, and planning assistance.[20]

Consolidation, and the inherent increased flexibility accorded the states, did not come without a price. The seventy-seven superseded categorical programs totaled approximately $8.2 billion for FY 1981, whereas the nine block grants were funded at $6.1 billion for 1982—a decline of slightly over 25 percent.[21] Thus the Reagan administration learned concretely that reforms directed at federalism could make good economic sense, contributing to the goal of restraining federal domestic spending.

In implementing the newly created block grants, the Reagan administration made good on its promise of enhanced state flexibility of choice within the terms of each block grant program. During a series of briefing sessions with state and local government officials in 1982, the Office of Management and Budget (within the Office of the President) emphasized three themes that were to guide the federal role in implementing the programs:

- simplicity and flexibility through minimal, ''bare bones'' regulations and paperwork requirements;
- absolute neutrality by the federal executive branch concerning priorities among program purposes, with no interference and no interpretation of the statutes;
- accountability at the state level, so that state officials will be held accountable for their choices by state residents instead of federal administrators.[22]

Since the initial success of the 1981 block grant initiatives, the Reagan administration made twenty-three additional proposals to expand existing block grants or to consolidate other categorical grant programs into new block grants, but with only one success—replacing the increasingly disreputed Comprehensive Employment Training Assistance (CETA) program with the business-endorsed Job Training Partnership Act program in April 1982. But these later proposals carried with them major reductions in the dollar value of the consolidated programs. For state and local officials, grant program consolidation took on the growing appearance of a subterfuge for the administration's fiscal policy of budget restraint.

The Big Swap. Bolstered by his earlier successes, President Reagan called for further reform. In his January 1982 State of the Union address, he proposed a substantive sorting out of state and federal responsibilities. Having quickly acquired the tag of the ''big swap,'' Reagan's proposal called for the federal government to turn over to the states sole responsibility for the nation's basic income maintenance programs, involving Aid for Families With Dependent Children (AFDC) and food stamps, whereas the ''feds'' would assume full responsibility for Medicaid. In addition, the president's package included fully turning back to the states sixty-one other grant-in-aid programs, involving those in the areas of transportation, education, community development, social services, and general government assistance. The states would assume total responsibility for administering and financing the turnbacks. In some cases, state officials might even decide that, without federal support, the programs are not of sufficient priority to be continued. Under Reagan's proposal, a comparable amount of tax revenue would be returned to the states. Toward that end, a "New Federalism Trust Fund" would be created, providing a vehicle, during a transitional ten-year period, to help the states pay the costs of their newfound program responsibilities. After the transition, the states would assume full financial responsibility. Presumably they would use the transitional period as a time to enact the necessary state revenue increases.

However, the president's proposal, other than the general sketch just discussed, contained little concrete elaboration—a fact that greatly bothered state policy makers. Precise amounts were not mentioned; nor was any schedule provided for federal support over the ten-year period. The concept of program turnbacks met with general sympathy among state governors and legislators, but both shared great concern over how the transitional funding arrangement would work and how the states would ultimately pay the full bill. Top program administrators and affected interest groups promptly turned from a discussion of the relative conceptual and theoretical merits of the proposals to very narrow assessments on a function-by-function basis. In the public welfare area, for example, interest groups (as well as program-supportive administrators) became concerned that devolution would result in lower benefit rates and stricter eligibility standards.[23]

Another significant issue in the debate over program and revenue devolution dealt with whether the federal government should play the role of "fiscal equalizer" within the federal system. In other words, is it appropriate for the federal government to step in and ease the disparities in fiscal capacity among the states? Fiscal capacity is a hypothetical measure of how much revenue a state could raise if it levied national average tax rates in relation to its tax base. Employing that measure, fiscal capacity among the states ranges from 70 percent of the national average in Mississippi to 250 percent in Alaska. As might be expected, southeastern states, on the average, possess the lowest fiscal capacity, at 84 percent of the national average, compared to those of the Far West, at 138 percent.[24] The issue of relative fiscal capacity is important because, with program turnbacks, the states would be in quite different positions in their ability to assume the added fiscal responsibility. Since many of the federal grants-in-aid programs were designed with some measure of fiscal capacity affecting allocations among the states, state officials (particularly through the National Governors' Association) demanded that any transitional revenue transfer be allocated, in part, on an equalized basis. But the dilemma still remained about how the less well-off states would be able to pick up the full program costs after the transitional period ended. These nagging, practical concerns took some of the luster off the theoretical attractiveness of devolution.

The big swap and its associated package of program turnbacks never really got much beyond the preliminary discussion stage. Although in general agreement over the desirability of realignment, both the states and the Reagan administration got scared off by its fiscal implications. State policy makers were worried about the added fiscal burden that might be imposed, particularly in an environment in which the strength of well-entrenched interest groups would make it very difficult for the states to shed any of the inherited responsibilities. The Reagan administration, in light of the growing national deficit associated with the national recession of 1982, appeared to develop serious second thoughts, not only about the fiscal viability of transitional revenue assistance, but also about the extent to which the administration would make major budget cuts in the affected programs as another means of restraining domestic spending and balancing the federal budget. On the administration's side, faced with a worsening budget picture, Reagan became unwilling to make the fiscal concessions that appeared necessary to win gubernatorial backing for his initiative. When it came right down to it, the integrity of the president's fiscal policy proved to be too high a priority when put on line with his New Federalism initiative.[25]

THE NEW UNWRITTEN POLICY OF FEDERAL EXTRICATION

Cutting the Grants-in-Aid Budget

Although Reagan's New Federalism package never became a reality, that is not to say that the Reagan administration has had little effect on intergovernmental relations, for its effect has been considerable. The administration was successful in significantly reducing the number of categorical grant programs, but its impact has probably been more strongly felt in the area of budget reductions. Confronting an inability to reduce federal expenditures for state and local assistance *while* reforming federalism, the Reagan administration went for budget cuts alone. Yet as just discussed, the fiscal "bottom line" increasingly appeared to be the primary motivation even behind the New Federalism initiatives. Or, put differently, when the competing priorities of structural reform of federalism and budget cutting came into prospective conflict, the former was quickly set aside in favor of the latter.

Figure 2.1 shows the Reagan administration's success in drastically turning around the pattern of federal assistance inherited from previous administrations. In contrast to *annual* real-dollar increases averaging over 17 percent between 1960 and 1980, federal aid dropped by nearly 18 percent, in real-dollar terms, between the 1980 and 1986 fiscal years. Direct grants to the states and local units of government, as contrasted to programs directly aiding individuals, such as income support and Medicaid, bore the greatest share of the reductions by far.

Ending General Revenue Sharing

In another area, the Reagan administration dealt the final death blow to general revenue sharing (GRS). It was not President Reagan who first called for the program's termination. That call came from President Carter, during his last year in office, as part of a move to balance the federal budget. However, the Carter administration agreed largely with the Democratic-led Congress to provide continuing funding after it became clear that the budget would be in deficit even with the termination of GRS. As a compromise, Congress extended the revenue-sharing program for three years but eliminated states from participation. The act was again continued in 1983 for three more years, but with only the local government portion intact. Finally, with the strong urging of the Reagan administration, Congress failed, in 1986, to reauthorize the program further, reducing aid to local governments by about $4.4 billion a year.[26]

Beyond expenditure reductions, the Reagan administration also went after tax expenditures that benefit state and local governments. (Tax expenditures are monies lost because of tax breaks written into the Internal Revenue Code; they are considered ''expenditures'' because, like spending, they draw down the would-be fiscal bottom line.) The Reagan administration pushed its efforts on two fronts: eliminating the federal income tax deduction for all state and local nonbusiness taxes, and reducing the costs to the federal treasury of tax-exempt interest on state and local bonds.

THE SQUEEZE ON LOCAL GOVERNMENTS

Local governments particularly found themselves negatively affected by the Reagan administration's policies. They lost local general revenue sharing, faced restrictions on borrowing, and felt the pinch of considerably reduced federal grants-in-aid. And with the creation of new block grants, local government officials felt more beholden to state legislatures, whose sympathy toward the major urban areas has not always been apparent. But local governments also knew that they had to turn to the states for help. Faced with federal aid cuts and growing taxpayer disenchantment with rising property taxes, municipalities and counties increasingly lobbied governors and state legislatures to increase state aid to local units of government. Local officials argued that they had been forced to ''tighten their fiscal belts'' and that their present plight warranted additional assistance from the states. After an explosive period of local government spending increases during the 1960s and most of the 1970s, peaking in 1978, real-dollar local government expenditures actually declined over the next four years, leveling off in the early 1980s. (See Table 2.3.)

In addition to cutting expenditures, local government policy makers turned their attention to the revenue side of fiscal management. There they faced a real problem. Along with declining federal grants-in-aid, the traditional major source of local government revenues, the property tax, increasingly came under pressure. Whereas property taxes made up 60 percent of municipal own-source tax revenues in 1977, that percentage dropped to about 49 percent only eight years later.[27] Property values leveled off, and even dropped in some places, at the end of the 1970s and through the mid-1980s, following the steep record growth of much of the 1970s. In addition, the property tax revolt, begun in California with Proposition 13 in 1978, which reduced property revenues there by about half, spread to other states. Sixteen states imposed fiscal limitations on their local governments between January 1978 and June 1981. Today thirty-eight states impose some form of limitation on local governments' ability to raise property taxes. Twenty-nine

TABLE 2.3. LOCAL GOVERNMENT EXPENDITURE,
SELECTED YEARS, 1949-1986 (PER CAPITA
1982 DOLLARS)

Calendar Year	Amount ($ Billions)
1949	357
1954	452
1959	560
1964	710
1969	946
1974	1,119
1979	1,142
1981	1,098
1982	1,079
1983	1,093
1984	1,112
1985	1,150e
1986	1,201e

e = estimate *(Source:* Significant Features of Fiscal Federalism,
1987 Edition *[Washington, DC: U.S. Advisory Commission on
Intergovernmental Relations, 1987], p. 4.)*

limit rate increases, and nineteen restrict increases in the actual levy itself.[28] Obviously, some states have imposed both.

Although local governments attempted to diversify their revenue sources in response to property tax controls, their flexibility to do so has been greatly limited by state law. Since local governments are statutorily creatures of the states, they do not have the absolute freedom to institute alternative taxes, such as local income or sales taxes. Unless such authority already exists in state statutes, or unless the state legislature enacts the authority in those states where such taxes are not proscribed constitutionally, local governments are limited to existing authority. That explains why local government officials, particularly those of municipalities, have increasingly turned to increases in existing user fees or to the establishment of new fees (which are not usually affected by state law). In a 1982 survey of municipal finance officers, user fee increases stood out as the most frequent nonproperty tax action taken to bolster sagging municipal revenues, as 78 percent of the 438 respondents reported increased or new user fees instituted by their jurisdictions.[29] Prominent examples of such user fees include new or higher charges for garbage collection; increased fees for municipal or county-issued permits; new or increased charges for municipally provided ambulance service; higher parking fees; and increased fees for municipal or county-owned recreational facilities, such as golf courses, swimming pools, and boat-launching areas. This practice appears to be continuing throughout the 1980s, as pressures continue against the property tax.

LOCAL GOVERNMENTS TURN TO THE STATES

Local government officials, particularly those of municipalities and counties, saw their jurisdictions in the unenviable position of sitting between the proverbial rock and a hard place. In facing cuts in federal assistance, they reduced real-dollar expenditures and increased user charges, but they still faced a precarious fiscal situation. The states, with which local governments have had a checkered love-hate relationship, appeared to be one remaining viable source of help.

But based on recent experience, local governments' hopes may be misplaced. Since FY 1980, state aid has declined as a percentage of local governments' own source revenue—dropping from an historic high of 62.5 percent in that year to 53.8 percent in FY 1985.[30] Clearly, the states' recession-induced fiscal "belt tightening" of the early 1980s occurred, in part, at the expense of local governments. The contemporary query focuses on whether state policy makers, having broken the pattern of steadily increasing local assistance, will turn their attention to the current fiscal plight of their municipalities and counties.

State aid grew during the 1970s, as state policy makers applied the resources of the state to pursue policies of statewide significance. State legislatures, often at the governors' prodding, used rapidly growing revenues to equalize the distribution of such major local aids as state shared revenues, general school aids, and local transportation aids. (Equalization involves allocating state-collected revenues in terms of some measure of need or ability to pay, not strictly on a population or return-to-source basis.) In addition, states raised their levels of support for social welfare programs, matching increasingly higher amounts of available federal aid. In several instances, states also assumed the heretofore local match requirements for such programs as AFDC and Medicaid. In contrast, states in the 1980s have been called on not to pursue new state policy initiatives but to act as bankers, providing additional funds to offset reduced federal aids and help local governments finance local services and pursue local priorities. However, as will be illustrated in subsequent chapters, the states have had their own policy initiatives to pursue.

SUMMARY AND CONCLUSIONS

The U.S. Supreme Court's rulings over the past two centuries, on the whole, have expanded greatly the powers of the national government in relation to the states, particularly in the areas of interstate commerce and civil rights. But the national government's penetration into areas of traditional state prerogative has been largely the product of federal legislation, characteristically in response to presidential initiatives. Growing federal programs to meet national policy goals won state support in large part because of the federal government's willingness to share high percentages of program costs with the states.

Contrary to the expansionist domestic policy orientation of presidents since

Franklin Roosevelt, President Ronald Reagan has generally pursued a policy of federal retrenchment, reducing federal regulations and cutting constant-dollar financial aid to the states. Moreover, the Reagan administration has altered the structure of federal assistance, consolidating many categorical grants into block grants and eliminating others.

Local governments also have felt the pinch of recent federal retrenchments. Although direct federal aid to local governments grew during the Great Society and into the 1970s, the 1980s have seen a reversal. Local governments lost general revenue sharing and a number of direct aid programs, had reductions of pass-through grants-in-aid to the states, and faced growing federal restrictions on borrowing. In turn, local governments have turned to the states for help. But the pattern of state response has been mixed. Although some states have been able to increase local assistance, others—facing their own fiscal problems—have been unable to meet the call. Overall, the trend toward steadily increasing state aid appears to have been sidetracked.

Faced with checkered recession and prosperity along with reductions in federal aid, state policy makers have confronted the many challenges, raising and cutting taxes where necessary or feasible and pruning budgets. Overall, more is being asked of the states in the federal system, but there are solid grounds, based on the experience of the 1980s, to expect that the states will respond responsibly.

REFERENCES

1. 1 Cranch 137 (1803).
2. *McCulloch v. Maryland*, 17 U.S. 316 (1819); *National Labor Relations Board v. Jones and Laughlin Steel Corporation*, 301 U.S. 1 (1937); and *E.E.O.C. v. Wyoming*, 460 U.S. 226 (1983).
3. *Brown v. Board of Education of Topeka, Kansas*, 347 U.S. 483 (1954); *Harper v. Virginia State Board of Elections*, 383 U.S. 663 (1966); and *South Carolina V. Katzenbach*, 383 U.S. 301 (1966).
4. *Garcia v. San Antonio Metropolitan Transit Authority*, 105 S. Ct. 1005 (1985).
5. *Garcia*, 1018 (1985).
6. The first three phases are identified in Thomas R. Dye, *Politics in States and Communities*, 5th ed. (Englewood Cliffs, NJ: Prentice-Hall, 1985), pp. 60–61.
7. Jeffrey R. Henig, *Public Policy and Federalism* (New York: St. Martin's Press, 1985), p. 16.
8. *Significant Features of Fiscal Federalism, 1985–86 Edition* (Washington, DC: U.S. Advisory Commission on Intergovernmental Relations, 1986), p. 19.
9. Henig, *Public Policy*, p. 16.
10. David C. Saffell, *State Politics* (Reading, MA: Addison-Wesley, 1984), p. 51.
11. David A. Stockman, "How to Avoid an Economic Dunkirk," *Challenge*, March-April 1981, 17.
12. Ibid., 18.
13. *Congressional Quarterly Weekly Report*, Vol. 39, No. 32 (Aug. 8, 1981), 1435.

14. House Committee on the Budget, *President Reagan's Fiscal Year 1988 Budget* (Washington, DC: U.S. Government Printing Office, 1987), p. 19.
15. Elizabeth Wehr, "Signs of Thrift Seen in Largest-Ever Money Bill," *Congressional Quarterly Weekly Report,* Vol. 44, No. 44 (Nov. 1, 1986), 2730.
16. As a general rule, entitlement programs are those for which eligible recipients are entitled, as a property right, to receive the benefits authorized by law. The federal treasury must pay the required "bill," whatever the actual amount turns out to be.
17. Charles A. Bowsher, "Federal Cutbacks Strengthen State Role," *State Government News,* Feb. 1986, p. 18; Saffell, *State Politics,* p. 36.
18. President Ronald Reagan, *State of the Union Address,* Jan. 1982.
19. "Intergovernmental Focus," *Intergovernmental Perspective,* Vol. 8, No. 3 (Summer 1982), 4–6.
20. Susan Golonka, "Whatever Happened to Federalism?" *Intergovernmental Perspective,* Vol. 11, No. 1 (Winter 1985), 13.
21. David B. Walker et al., "The First Ten Months: Grant-in-Aid, Regulatory, and Other Changes," *Intergovernmental Perspective,* Vol. 8, No. 1 (Winter 1982), 5.
22. Ibid., 13.
23. George E. Peterson, "Federalism and the States: An Experiment in Decentralization," in John L. Palmer and Isabel V. Sawhill, eds., *The Reagan Record* (Cambridge, MA: Ballinger, 1984), pp. 224–26.
24. Carol E. Cohen, "1984 State Tax Wealth: Preview of the RTS Estimates," *Intergovernmental Perspective,* Vol. 12, No. 3 (Summer 1986), 25.
25. See Timothy J. Conlan, "Federalism and Competing Values in the Reagan Administration," *Publicus,* Vol. 16, No. 1 (Winter 1986), 29–47.
26. Ibid., 36.
27. *Significant Features of Fiscal Federalism, 1987 Edition* (Washington, DC: U.S. Advisory Commission on Intergovernmental Relations, 1987), p. 45.
28. Richard D. Bingham, *State and Local Government in an Urban Society* (New York: Random House, 1986), p. 308.
29. Robert J. Cline and John Shannon, "Municipal Revenue Behavior After Proposition 13," *Intergovernmental Perspective,* Vol. 8, No. 3 (Summer 1982), 25–26.
30. *Fiscal Federalism, 1987 Edition,* p. 45.

COMPETITION TO CONTROL STATE GOVERNMENT

—————————— CHAPTER 3 ——————————

Political Parties and Elections in States

To say that in the United States the people govern is a gross oversimplification. Elected officials who claim they have a mandate from the people make a rhetorical point; they do not describe reality. In presidential elections, slightly less than two-thirds of the eligible voters actually vote. In state elections, more eligible voters do not participate than do. Only a relative handful go beyond voting to campaign actively for candidates.

Despite the sobering record of low participation in elections and in political party activity, it is through the electoral process that we fill legislative positions and several positions in the executive and judicial branches of state government. Similarly, although relatively few take advantage of the opportunity, the electoral process allows citizens to shape their state's public policy agenda. This chapter examines the nature of participation and nonparticipation in politics and explains the important roles of political parties and elections in the formation and implementation of public policy in the states.

THE ROLES OF POLITICAL PARTIES

Responsible Parties
One role of political parties, at all levels of government, is to advocate for certain public policies and to bring together groups and individuals interested in those policies. This perspective of political parties is often referred to as ''responsible

party government'' or the "party democracy" school. This role presupposes a basic common and distinct identity within each party and a set of mechanisms that the parties can use to screen new members and to reward and sanction existing members so that everyone conforms to the same strategies and objectives.[1]

The Democratic party, for example, is characterized as one that regards government as responsible for ensuring a minimum quality of life for everyone. Democrats also believe that government ought and can improve the quality of life for everyone in society. That general philosophy is matched by a traditional coalition of workers, ethnic minorities, and service professionals who stand to gain from this orientation of government.

The Republican party, in contrast, has been labeled the party of the business community and is identified with a philosophy that the role of government is primarily to ensure a vibrant and healthy economy, in large part by staying out of the way and letting the market operate. The Republican philosophy is to rely on general economic activity and individual generosity to provide for the welfare of the less fortunate. Although the images of the parties are based in part on their respective records and their formal positions, the distinctions are not always clear and predictable.

The basic unit of political parties in the United States is the state party. In most states, the basic building block is the county. The national Democratic party and the national Republican party are loose confederations of state organizations. Although the national parties have a structure and establish platforms that include the positions the parties have taken on various policy issues, no major party has required its members to support the platform. State parties have not been expelled or disciplined for deviating from the national platform. State parties have, in fact, developed their own identities and at times worked in direct opposition to the positions of the national party. The most dramatic and long-standing example of this was the conflict between the national Democratic party and Democratic party organizations in southern states over racial issues.[2]

State parties are not themselves highly cohesive, homogeneous organizations. Democrats in Illinois were embarrassed in 1986 when members of a nationwide extremist group successfully ran in the primary and became the party's candidates for lieutenant governor and secretary of state. The Democratic candidate for governor, Adlai Stevenson, Jr., whose father had been the national party's candidate for president and who had himself long been associated with the party, took the unusual and somewhat ironic step of resigning from the state party ticket and running as an independent in order to avoid being on the same ticket with the extremists.

The role of political parties as coalitions pursuing a common political philosophy or a common set of public policies is, in short, imperfect at best. Parties do not exert discipline to maintain adherence to party positions. Parties at times contain widely diverse groups and individuals. What distinguishes parties from one another, if anything, is tradition and a general image.[3] The labor orientation of the Democratic party and the business orientation of the Republican party are general and imprecise portraits that tend to attract people and groups that favor labor causes, on the one hand, and respond to business concerns, on the other. Yet some Democratic governors have been particularly kind to business, and some Republican governors have established especially close ties with labor. Party labels allow us to make some guesses about public policy positions, but we cannot make confident predictions.

Electoral Parties

When Lee Sherman Dreyfus was elected governor of Wisconsin in 1978, he quipped that he thought it would be a good idea to join the Republican party before he took it over.[4] Governor Dreyfus viewed the role of parties as vehicles candidates could use to get elected to office. Indeed, parties often provide an organizational shell that gets filled temporarily each electoral period by those eager to get their candidates elected. Party campaign workers include some who are active each election on behalf of the party and others who are participating because of their interest in specific candidates.

The classic use of parties primarily as vehicles for elections was in the period from the Civil War until the middle of the twentieth century, when political machines were at their peak.[5] Machines emerged primarily in urban areas, and they had their base of support in ethnic neighborhoods. Immigrants from various parts of Europe formed neighborhoods, with their own restaurants, churches, grocery stores, social clubs, and the like. These neighborhoods coincided with wards and precincts used by urban governments for conducting elections and providing services. Political parties responded to this situation by developing organizations that were based on a quid pro quo; that is, a neighborhood or ward that turned out a sizable vote for a party candidate received services and jobs if the party got into power. Once a party machine established control over a city or state government, it set in motion a cycle of patronage and services for votes that retained control of government for the party in power. Several state parties were built on these machines and contributed to machine politics the spoils available through control of state governments.

The Progressive movement led by Theodore Roosevelt, Woodrow Wilson, Robert M. La Follette, Sr., Hiram Walker, and others attacked and dealt fatal blows to machine politics during the first quarter of the twentieth century. Although some machines lingered through the middle of the century, the effects of primary elections, civil service reform, and the direct election of many executive officials were to deprive machines of the closed control and rewards and punishments that were so critical to their operations.[6] The end of strong machines did not, however, end the role of parties in elections.

State laws and traditions make parties essential to the electoral process. State laws define how candidates can get on the ballot, who will be declared a winner, how election results can be challenged, and what rules must be followed by parties and by candidates. States, for example, sponsor the primary elections that parties use to determine their nominees. Primary election winners gain added publicity and a sense of legitimacy that advance party candidates over independents. States write ballots with party nominees listed first, an advantageous position. Most states register voters with their party preferences indicated, thus providing party candidates with lists of those eligible to vote in their primary and those who might be willing to assist in campaigning.

Political parties must be registered with the secretary of state in each respective state. State laws provide constraints on the organization, financing, and ethical conduct of parties. In some states public funds are available to help candidates meet campaign expenses. Invariably, as we shall see later in this chapter, the ways in which public funds are channeled to candidates assume the existence of parties and work to maintain their importance.

Traditions are important for compliance with election laws and for the voting patterns of the electorate. Corrupt practices can make a mockery out of the best laws. During Mayor Richard Daley's reign over Chicago, a powerful party machine played a major role in local, state, and even national government while a model civil service law prohibiting patronage languished on the books. Similarly, an understanding of California politics requires attention to the grass-roots political organizations associated with parties, more than awareness of legal requirements on the parties themselves. Clubs, some based on issues, some on philosophies, and some on regions, are the major vehicle through which many individuals participate in politics. The parties are, in a sense, loose coalitions of these clubs.

About 60 percent of the voters have a tradition of identifying with and voting for a particular party.[7] Candidates thus regard parties as an important element in their electoral strategies. Because of the effects of party loyalties, candidates can generally count on a certain core of support and a certain core of opposition even before they begin their campaigns. In districts that traditionally vote for the party of a candidate, the strategy is to emphasize party identification. Those candidates running in districts that have a history of supporting the party of their opponents will downplay party and stress issues and personal traits. The strategy for campaigning in districts without strong party traditions is obviously more complex.

In short, political parties are integral to the electoral process and to some extent can be regarded as important to campaigns, even if ideological differences are not always clear or predictable. State laws on elections assume and to some extent perpetuate the existence of parties. Traditions of party identification are critical to campaign strategies and in some cases are the most important determinant of probable success.

PARTY ORGANIZATION

Because political parties exist primarily to get candidates elected, party organization parallels the geographical boundaries of constituencies. Typically, in urban areas, parties have ward units that are identical to the wards represented on a city council. Rural areas tend to use counties as their basic unit of organization, in large part reflecting the election of county boards. The leaders and staff of state parties loosely coordinate and serve the local units and represent the state in national parties.

Links between political parties and interest groups are usually informal. Business organizations do not have seats on the executive committees of Republican parties, nor do labor unions with Democrats. Although some parties have traditions that their executive committees include individuals from certain interest groups, ethnic backgrounds, parts of the state, and the like, this is not to be confused with, for example, the formal and explicit ties in England between the labor unions and the Labour party. Some interest groups in the United States, in fact, provide support to both major parties and to opposing candidates, thereby being in a position to work with whoever wins.

Candidates, as already mentioned, have their own ad hoc organizations, usually formally established as "Committee for. . . ." Some states, in fact, require all candidates to register the name or names of their organizations, along with the names and addresses of people serving as treasurer. Campaign organizations have links to party organizations. Candidate-centered organizations are fundamentally separate, however, and they utilize staff and volunteers who serve the candidate first and the party second.

Political parties, in short, are not neat, hierarchical organizations. Interacting with the ward, county, and state party structures are informal ties to interest groups and, even more important, the ad hoc organizations that emerge to support specific candidates. Political parties are open and do not emphasize paid, formal membership. Political parties are also open arenas for organizations supporting various causes and candidates to spar with one another, to coalesce, and to claim a banner that has its own core of supporters.

PARTY NOMINATIONS

In part, the openness of American political parties is a result of the use of primary elections to determine who will be the candidate for a given party. Primary elections are a legacy of the Progressive movement, as mentioned previously. Those opposing the closed processes of political machines, where machine bosses determined who would be candidates and thus, in effect, who would be governor, mayor, state senator, and so on, saw primary elections as a way of wresting this role from the machine elite and placing it in the hands of the voters. Candidates for a party's nomination would have to secure the support of a majority of those voting in the primary, rather than merely the favor of a machine boss.

Between 1886 and 1915, all forty-eight states adopted some form of a primary election for determining who got a party's nomination for the general election. Connecticut and New York adopted a "challenge primary," in which party conventions select a nominee, but anyone who gets 20 percent (Connecticut) or 25 percent (New York) of the delegates' votes can challenge the convention's choice in a primary. Iowa and South Dakota use a somewhat reverse process. In these two states, if no candidate receives more than 35 percent of the votes cast in a primary, the party must call a convention to select a nominee. Minor parties—those who garnered less than 5 percent of the votes cast for secretary of state (Kansas) or 15 percent of the votes cast for governor (New Mexico)—must select their nominees in conventions, not primaries. In Alabama, Colorado, Georgia, South Carolina, and Virginia, the executive committees can choose to call conventions rather than use primaries. In all other states, primaries by themselves determine party nominees.

Thirty-nine states adopted a *closed primary* system, in which voters identify their party membership or preference and then are allowed to vote only in the primary elections of that party. In 1986, the Democratic party in Alabama overturned the results of its primary election for governor when the party's executive committee found evidence that the apparent winner had garnered votes from Republicans, who were not supposed to vote in the Democratic primary. The Democrats declared the runner-up in the primary to be their nominee. This action was challenged in court. The U.S. Supreme Court upheld the decision of the Alabama Democratic party since it was consistent with Alabama state law restricting participation in a party primary to voters registered with that party. States with closed primaries vary their requirements on when and how one must register with a party. Thus some closed primaries are more closed than others.

The laws in eleven states would not have disallowed Republicans voting in a Democratic party primary. In eight states (Idaho, Michigan, Minnesota, Montana, North Dakota, Utah, Vermont, and Wisconsin), an *open primary* law exists. Voters in these states do not register with a party or as independents, and they may choose which party primary they want to participate in when they appear at the voting booth. They may not vote in more than one party's primary, however.

Alaska and Washington have a *blanket primary,* in which voters can choose, office by office, the party in which they will cast their vote. The only restriction is that they cast only one ballot per office. A voter might, for example, vote for one of the Republican candidates for governor and one of the Democrats for secretary of state. A voter could not vote for one of the Republican and one of the Democratic candidates for governor.

In Louisiana, all candidates, regardless of party identity, run in the same primary—a *single primary* system. Based on the assumption that Louisiana would always be a single-party (Democratic) state, the legislature passed a law that provided for all candidates to run in the same primary election, and if any candidate wins more than 50 percent of the votes, he or she is declared the winner and no general election is held for that office. If no candidate receives a majority of the votes cast, the top two run against one another in the general election. This law almost backfired in 1986, when W. Henson Moore, a Republican candidate for the U.S. Senate, came within a whisker of getting a majority of votes in a field otherwise crowded with Democrats. Moore went on to launch a formidable campaign in the general election and lost to John Breaux, the Democratic candidate, by a 6 percent margin, relatively narrow for Louisiana.

CAMPAIGNS

Campaigns are most focused and visible in the period between the selection of party nominees and the general election. Nonetheless, campaigns by individuals seeking office and by parties seeking majority control begin in the immediate aftermath of an election.

Victors claim clear mandates from the people, and both victors and losers plot strategies for success in subsequent elections. Reelection, especially for those in two-year posts, seems all too soon. Legislative leaders eye gubernatorial positions. Public statements and private musings are influenced as heavily by concerns about the next elections as by the results of the current balloting.

Campaign Techniques

Public appearances and commentaries are integral to campaigns. Aspirants to public office, whether for election or reelection, need to build bases of support and to provide an attractive public image. Constant concern for electoral success is in part a fundamental dynamic on which a representative democracy is built. If public officials did not care about their support among the electorate, they might rule arrogantly, pursuing policies opposed by the governed.

Formal campaigning begins with an announcement of intent to run for a particular office as a candidate of a specific party—or in rare cases, as an independent. Typically, campaigning consists of the following activities:

1. Speaking before small groups and major organizations to seek their support and their formal endorsement
2. Soliciting funds from supporters, individually and through organizations
3. Getting media attention through press conferences, interviews, press releases, rallies and other media events, paid advertisements, and debates with other candidates
4. Securing grass-roots visibility through bumper stickers, pins, brochures, and yard signs
5. Mailing to specific groups letters or brochures that address their particular concerns
6. Encouraging supporters and potential supporters to vote. This effort includes identifying potential supporters through surveys, helping them register to vote if they are not already registered, and then reminding them to vote and in some cases giving them rides to and from the polls

In part because there are no studies that indicate conclusively which campaign activities are more or less effective, and in part because of uncertainty and anxiety, campaign managers use all of the preceding strategies. They emphasize some activities more than others simply because of the abundance of volunteer campaign workers, on the one hand, and the availability of funds for media ads and brochures on the other.[8]

For many elections for state legislative seats, the constituencies are small enough so that the candidates are personally involved in almost all campaign activities. Especially in assembly or house races, candidates can and do go door to door, trying to meet everyone in their district. This is not always possible in the larger senate districts. For statewide offices, heavy reliance on television and radio is common.

Media

Media campaigning is a growing business. In 1984, $300 million was spent on the over 6,600 state legislative races waged that year. In 1986, almost $500 million was spent on about the same number of races.[9] The twenty-two gubernatorial contests in 1984 cost $55 million, and the thirty-six in 1986 cost $91 million. The bulk of these funds went to media consultants, the production of radio and television advertisements, and the purchase of air time. Media costs vary widely from state to state. A thirty-second spot on "The Bill Cosby Show," which frequently has been television's top-rated program, costs $800 for covering all of South Dakota, in contrast to $30,000 for just New York City.

Although the creation and dissemination of media ads is obviously an art, research on public opinion has led to some standard practices. An individual generally must see an ad five times before it makes a meaningful impression. Ads must not only be aired repetitively but also at times when persuadable voters are likely to be viewing or listening. In the 1986 elections, each gubernatorial candidate produced between twenty and thirty different radio and television ads.[10] Campaign commercials selling a candidate usually follow a common sequence:

1. Early ads introduce a candidate by describing his or her life and accomplishments.
2. Testimonials by both prominent and "common" people present the candidate's empathy and problem-solving abilities.
3. Short, often ten-second, spots highlight a policy position.
4. As the campaign comes to a close, the candidate is identified with good feelings—patriotism, progress, hope, and general satisfaction.

Consultants and pollsters tend to acquire clients from either one party or the other, despite the similarities in what consultants and pollsters must do. The Communications Co.; Frank Greer; Doak, Shrum and Associates; Peter D. Hart Research Associates; and Cambridge Survey Research, Inc., are prominent firms with Democrats as clientele. Republican candidates, on the other hand, use The Robert Goodman Agency, Inc.; Bailey, Deardourff, Sipple and Associates; Decision/Making/Information, Inc.; Tarrance, Hill, Newport and Ryan; and Market Opinion Research.

Negative Campaigning

Hamburgers had a profound impact on the 1986 elections. This impact is likely to continue in the near future. Advertisers found that an effective way to sell one kind of fast-food hamburger was to say negative things about the hamburgers sold by the competition. Accordingly, in Pennsylvania, the Democratic gubernatorial candidate, Robert P. Casey, ran an ad caustically citing his Republican opponent, William Scranton III, for missing meetings; he concluded, "You can't fight for Pennsylvania's future if you don't go to work." In Texas, former Governor William P. Clements, Jr. (Republican), who was beaten by Governor Mark White (Democrat) in 1982, got revenge in part by using an ad that decried White for breaking promises and raising taxes. In a salvo of negative ads from both sides, White shot back with an ad that made fun of Clements' secret plan to solve the financial crisis in Texas brought about by the decline in oil prices. In Wisconsin, Republican Tommy Thompson labeled Democrat Tony Earl a high taxer and a runaway spender, even though Governor Earl had just engineered a major cut in the state's income tax and reduced spending growth.

Negative campaign ads were not the norm in 1986, but they were highly visible. While candidates continued to run negative and at times misleading ads against their opponents, at the same time they outdid one another in bemoaning the use of such approaches. Common forms of attack were to question an opponent's sincerity and competence by citing inconsistent positions on issues, to poke fun at something a candidate did or said, and to charge that a candidate was self-centered and negligent. Negative ads may reflect badly on the fast-food industry generally, but they do sell hamburgers. Likewise, negative campaigning may reinforce images of government and politics as dirty and insincere. Nonetheless, negative campaigning is regarded as effective. Karl Struble, a media consultant who helped engineer a number of successful campaigns, expressed the consensus of his profession: "People have become very cynical about positive advertising. People hate negative ads, but they remember them."[11]

Thirty-second and ten-second spots almost inevitably lead to simplifications and misstatements. The electronic media, nonetheless, provide the technology to reach almost all voters, and most candidates are obliged to use this technology effectively. This means not only accepting the challenge to compete in presenting an effective message and image through the media but also raising the money necessary to pay for the air time.

CAMPAIGN FINANCES

Elections for federal offices are most expensive. In 1984, the average cost of campaigning for a seat in the House of Representatives was $250,000, and $2.9 million for the Senate. These costs increased by about 10 percent in 1986, more than the rate of inflation.

In 1986, about $325 million was spent on state legislative races. Almost $50 million was spent in California alone. Candidates in key races in the Michigan State Senate spent $300,000 each. Gubernatorial contests waged in 1986 cost each candidate, on the average, over $2 million.[12] Not surprisingly, the most expensive races are hotly contested in states with relatively high populations. In 1986, those states were California, Florida, New York, Texas, Pennsylvania, Ohio, and Illinois.

The need for campaign funding has prompted two major developments: state regulations and the emergence of political action committees (PACs). In the 1970s, state governments responded to a growing concern about the influence that financial contributions to campaigns might have on elected officials by passing laws regulating campaign financing. All fifty states have laws requiring public disclosure of who makes campaign contributions to a candidate and of the amount contributed. In every state except Ohio, Utah, Alabama, Illinois, and Indiana, candidates are directly responsible for filing complete and accurate information. In the five states mentioned, plus most of the others as well, campaign committees must disclose contributions and expenditures.[13] The reasoning behind public disclosure is that this information will enable anyone interested to expose an elected official who provides special treatment and favors to those who have made generous contributions.

Another approach to the regulation of campaign financing is to set limits on the contributions that can be made. Twenty-three states have set such limits. South Dakota, for example, has set $250 as the maximum contribution that anyone may make to a candidate. In contrast, the limit in New Hampshire is $5,000.

Montana has focused its attempts to control campaign spending by targeting PACs. Political action committees have been formed by business associations, labor unions, and organizations to promote special causes or policies. Most prominent among the latter are the National Abortion Rights Action League and the National Right-to-Life PAC. Montana stipulates that candidates for its House of Representatives may accept no more than $800 from all PACs combined. Candidates for the Senate may accept no more than $1,300. (See Table 3.1.)

Little systematic data have been collected on the activities and records of PACs operating at the state level. Inferences might, however, be made from the success ratios of PACs supporting candidates for the U.S. Senate and House of Representatives in the 1986 elections.

Generally, business PACs support Republicans and labor PACs support Democrats. Those formed to promote a special issue quite naturally contribute to individual candidates that support the positions of the respective PACs. Political action committees that are especially active in state government elections are professional groups, like teachers, chiropractors, physicians, and lawyers, who recognize that states regulate and license professionals. Moreover, through school financing, insurance regulation, and requirements for processing wills and divorces, state governments have profound effects on these professions.

Twenty states use yet another approach to the regulation of campaign financing. They provide public funds to major candidates for state government offices. The reasoning behind this is that public funding, accompanied by limits on expenditures, provides candidates with equivalent levels of resources to get their messages to potential voters. This can work against challengers, who may need more resources to offset the name recognition that incumbents usually have. Nonetheless, candidates who use public funds for their campaigns avoid any obligations to special interests that can accompany funding from private sources.

TABLE 3.1. PAC SCORECARD: THE BIG WINNERS

	Winners Backed	Losers Backed	Percentage Winning
Associated Milk Producers	205	10	95.3
American Bankers Association	232	16	93.5
Philip Morris (tobacco)	186	14	93.0
American Medical Association	310	27	92.0
National Education Association	248	24	91.8
National Association of Life Underwriters	260	24	91.5
National PAC (pro-Israel)	42	4	91.3
National Association of Realtors	297	29	91.1
Lockheed (defense)	163	18	90.1
National Rifle Association	114	13	89.8
Handgun Control Inc.	81	10	89.0
United Auto Workers	198	39	83.5
National Abortion Rights Action League	44	10	81.5
Tenneco Inc. (energy)	105	24	81.4
National Committee for Effective Congress	20	5	80.0
Fund for a Conservative Majority	60	26	69.8
National Right-to-Life PAC	28	18	60.9

Source: Federal Election Commission; USA Today research 11/6/86. Copyright 1986, USA Today. Reprinted with permission.

Political action committees obviously hope the candidates they support will be elected so that the public policies supported by the PACs will be enacted and enforced. Incumbent officials hope that the campaign finance laws they pass will work to their benefit, rather than provide advantages to challengers. Campaign consultants and political pollsters want to be identified with winning candidates in order to generate more business.

INTERPRETING THE 1986 ELECTIONS

To illustrate and apply what has been discussed in this chapter, we can examine the results of the elections held in November 1986. Like other elections, there are both unique and general patterns that can be observed.

Voter Turnout

Only 37.3 percent of eligible voters cast ballots on November 4, 1986. This was the lowest voter turnout in U.S. history, breaking the previous low of 37.5 percent in 1978. As noted previously, the turnout in years when we do not elect a president is generally low. The visibility and perceived importance of presidential contests are higher than contests for state government offices and attract more people to the polls than do state races alone.[14] This fact, however, does not explain the record low vote in the 1986 state elections.

No studies have been completed, but two hypotheses have been offered: (1) an effect of negative campaigning is to disgust voters with politics generally, and they stay away from the polls as a result; and (2) the absence of any crisis or burning issue in 1986 made it more difficult than usual for candidates to generate interest. Most citizens either do not participate in politics or participate only minimally. It is to be expected that these people could easily get cynical and/or disgusted enough to stay home when nothing earth-shattering seems at stake and when candidates are simply slinging mud at one another.

Another possible explanation of the record-breaking low turnout is weak political parties. Political scientists Paul R. Abramson and John H. Aldrich found a high correlation between a decline in party organization and activity and a decline in voter turnout.[15] Parties and campaign organizations, as noted, do include get-out-the-vote efforts as part of their activities. It follows, then, that weaker parties may contribute to lower voter participation.

As illustrated in Figure 3.1, the 1986 low point is part of a trend that is noticeable from 1960.[16] Weak parties, negative campaigning, lack of either crisis or vision, and a feeling of alienation all seem to be contributing factors. An obvious concern is how to reverse this trend.

Party Nominations

The 1986 elections were affected by three events associated with the processes of party nomination. The first two illustrate the importance of formal rules estab-

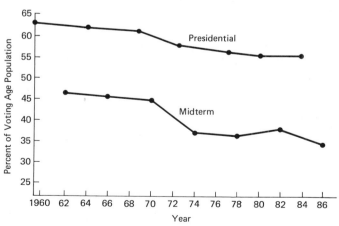

Figure 3.1. Voter Turnout, 1960–1982 (Source: *Elections '84: Strategies, Issues and Outlook* [Washington, DC: Congressional Quarterly, 1983], p. 14 and updated with news files.)

lished by state laws in determining party nominees. The third instance is an example of the force of traditional ties and informal rules.

1. The Louisiana no-party primary, as mentioned, was based on an assumption that the Democratic party was the only viable party in the state. That is no longer true, and the Republican candidate for the U.S. Senate almost won more than half the votes cast in the primary, which could have resulted in outright election. He then ran a campaign that almost garnered a victory in the general election. Louisiana may change its laws for party nominations.

2. The Alabama primary results were, with Supreme Court approval, set aside by the Democratic party because of indirect evidence that Republicans voted in the Democratic primary and influenced the outcome. The process itself seemed to draw the ire of the electorate, and Alabama elected its first Republican governor (Guy Hunt) in 112 years.

3. The Republican party was successful in getting prominent Democrats to switch parties, but with only two exceptions (including Bob Martinez, who was elected governor of Florida) voters were not sufficiently impressed to elect these nominees to office. In most instances, the switch in party label was used against these candidates in the primary campaign by opponents who could cite their own toil in party vineyards. Party labels are not the best indicators of what a candidate stands for. Switching party labels, however, seems to be interpreted as opportunism and disloyalty, traits not favored by the electorate.

Party Realignment

Ever since the election and continued popularity of Ronald Reagan as president, political pundits have speculated that a realignment of party loyalties was occurring that would make the Republican party the party of the majority.[17] During the 1986 elections, President Reagan campaigned extensively for Republican candidates. He consciously attempted to transfer his personal popularity, telling voters that they could vote for him by voting for Republican candidates.

Despite gains made by Republicans in gubernatorial races, Democrats showed no signs of becoming a minority party. Democrats posted gains in state legislatures, the U.S. House of Representatives, and the U.S. Senate. Gains in the Senate were particularly important since the Democrats took control back from the Republicans even though Reagan campaigned so hard to keep this from happening.

According to national polls by NBC News of voters as they left voting booths, Republican support has fallen, not risen, from 1980 levels. Even when breaking down the population by age, occupation, race, gender, education, and income, there are no noticeable Republican gains. These poll results are for the country as a whole. (See Table 3.2.)

Austin Ranney has developed a widely used and cited scale based on only

TABLE 3.2. HOW THE PUBLIC VOTED ON ELECTION DAY
(The table, based on polling by NBC News of voters as they left their polling places, shows the Republican share of total votes cast for major-party House candidates.)

	1980	1982	1984	1986
Nationwide	49%	45%	47%	43%
Party identification				
Republicans	89	89	87	85
Independents	56	51	51	44
Democrats	16	7	9	8
Ideology				
Liberals	29	24	29	27
Moderates	46	40	44	38
Conservatives	64	66	68	62
Sex				
Women	47	42	45	41
Men	51	48	50	45
Race				
Whites	52	49	53	47
Blacks	7	6	8	8
Education				
Not high school graduate	40	34	37	33
High school graduate	47	41	46	40
Some college	50	47	51	46
College graduate	53	52	53	48
More than college	47	45	45	45
Religion				
Protestants	54	53	54	50
Catholics	44	37	45	38
Jews	27	22	26	24
Occupation				
Professional/managerial	50	49	51	47
White collar	50	44	51	44
Blue collar	43	38	41	35
Retired	50	44	48	44
Union households	39	33	37	32
Income*				
Less than $10,000	NA	27	31	28
$10,000 to $20,000	NA	38	42	38
$20,000 to $30,000	NA	43	45	43
$30,000 to $40,000	NA	45	50	45
More than $40,000	NA	55	58	50
Age				
18–24	NA	40	45	41
25–34	NA	41	44	39
35–49	NA	47	48	44
50–64	NA	46	50	44
65 and older	NA	45	52	46

*Income categories slightly different in 1982, reflecting adjustments for inflation. *(Source:* National Journal, *Nov. 8, 1986, 2709.)*

state government elections to measure party dominance. Table 3.3 presents the fifty states as classified by Ranney for electoral activity during 1956 to 1970, accompanied by party control of the governorship and party distribution in state legislative chambers in the aftermath of the 1986 elections. Republicans have fielded winning gubernatorial candidates in states otherwise dominated by the Democratic party strongholds. The Democratic party has cracked Republican dominance in North Dakota and Vermont by electing the governor and capturing control of one of the legislative houses. Nonetheless, when we focus on the party identity of state legislators, the striking feature of this table is the continuity and stability of the patterns over the past three decades.

As a result of the 1986 elections, Democrats controlled sixty-six chambers (senate and house or assembly) and Republicans twenty-eight. Democrats controlled both houses in twenty-six states and Republicans in eight states. In the remainder, control was split, there was a tie, or for Nebraska, there is a single chamber with nonpartisan elections.

The issue of realignment, when applied to state government in particular, needs to be put into perspective. Democratic party dominance in state legislatures is itself a relatively recent phenomenon. When Richard Nixon was elected to the presidency in 1968, Republicans controlled a majority of the houses in state legislatures and only two fewer senates than the Democrats. The major shift to the pattern evident in the 1986 elections took place in 1974, during the Watergate scandal. In that year, Republicans lost 498 state legislative seats and control of nine state houses, and they lost 135 seats and control of eleven state senates. They have been in the minority, nationally, ever since.

Although party realignment has not been happening, one might ask whether "dealignment" might be. Here the evidence is mixed. As noted, the trend since 1960 has been for lower voter turnout. That shows general disaffection with politics, however, rather than disappointment with one party and attraction to another. In an analysis of election survey data from 1952 through 1984, the Advisory Commission on Intergovernmental Relations found a growth in the percentage of those voters identifying themselves as independents, from 5 percent in 1952 to 14 to 15 percent in the period from 1974 through 1978, with a corresponding decline in the proportion of voters identifying themselves as either strong Democrats or strong Republicans. As Table 3.4 illustrates, the trend since 1978 has been a decline in voters identifying themselves as independents and a return to previous patterns of party identification. A noticeable difference in previous patterns is the increase in those leaning Republican in 1980 and 1984, probably a reflection of Reagan's appeal in those presidential election years. A very consistent feature of party identification patterns from 1952 through 1984 is that around 24 percent continually are weak Democrats and 14 percent are weak Republicans. Fundamental to the bases of parties in the United States are these small, steady cores with links to the parties that are not intense. These data, in other words, provide more evidence of the rather weak and loose party structures in this country.

TABLE 3.3. INTERPARTY COMPETITION AND PARTY CONTROL AFTER THE 1986 ELECTIONS

State	Ranney Classification*	Governor	Party Control After 1986 Elections			
			Senate		House	
			Dem	GOP	Dem	GOP
Louisiana	One-party Democratic	Dem	38	1	83	22
Alabama	"	GOP	30	5	88	17
Mississippi	"	Dem	49	3	115	7
South Carolina	"	GOP	36	10	92	29
Texas	"	GOP	25	6	94	56
Georgia	"	Dem	45	11	153	27
Arkansas	"	Dem	31	4	91	9
North Carolina	Modified one-party Democratic	GOP	40	10	85	35
Virginia	"	Dem	31	9	65	33
Florida	"	GOP	25	15	75	45
Tennessee	"	Dem	23	10	61	38
Maryland	"	Dem	40	7	25	16
Oklahoma	"	GOP	31	17	69	32
Missouri	"	Dem	21	13	111	52
Kentucky	"	Dem	28	10	73	27
West Virginia	"	GOP	27	7	78	22
New Mexico	"	GOP	21	21	48	22
North Dakota	Modified one-party Republican	Dem	27	26	45	61
Kansas	"	GOP	16	24	51	74
New Hampshire	"	GOP	8	16	133	267
South Dakota	"	GOP	11	24	21	49
Vermont	"	Dem	19	11	75	75
Hawaii	Two party	Dem	20	5	40	11
Rhode Island	"	GOP	38	12	80	20
Massachusetts	"	Dem	32	8	129	30
Alaska	"	Dem	9	11	24	16
California	"	GOP	24	15	44	36
Nebraska	"	GOP	Unicameral, nonpartisan			
Washington	"	Dem	24	25	62	36
Minnesota	"	Dem	47	20	83	51
Nevada	"	Dem	9	12	29	13
Connecticut	"	Dem	26	10	93	58
Delaware	"	GOP	13	8	19	22
Arizona	"	GOP	13	19	24	36
Montana	"	Dem	25	25	48	52
Oregon	"	Dem	17	13	30	30
New Jersey	"	GOP	23	17	30	50
Pennsylvania	"	Dem	24	26	104	99
Colorado	"	Dem	10	25	25	40
Michigan	"	Dem	18	20	63	47

continued

TABLE 3.3., *continued*

State	Ranney Classification*	Governor	Party Control After 1986 Elections			
			Senate		House	
			Dem	GOP	Dem	GOP
Utah	"	GOP	8	21	27	46
Indiana	"	GOP	20	30	49	51
Illinois	"	GOP	31	28	67	51
Wisconsin	"	GOP	20	13	54	45
Idaho	"	Dem	16	26	20	64
Iowa	"	GOP	30	20	58	42
Ohio	"	Dem	15	18	60	39
New York	"	Dem	26	35	94	56
Maine	"	GOP	20	15	86	65
Wyoming	"	Dem	11	19	20	44

*States are listed within each category according to the ranking by Ranney of how well the state fits the category. *(Source: "Parties in State Politics," by Austin Ranney from Politics in the American States, 2nd ed. by Herbert Jacob and Kenneth Vines, (Boston: Little, Brown, 1971, 87) and USA Today, Nov. 6, 1986.*

SUMMARY AND CONCLUSIONS

Given the nature of political parties and election campaigns, the relationship between voting and setting a public policy agenda are imperfect. We do not follow the "responsible party" model, where Republicans and Democrats face off with clear and sharp differences and the internal discipline to ensure that everyone in the party will pursue common policy objectives. Party ties are weak, for voters and for elected officials. Parties are important as a vehicle for getting elected but not as a source for direction once in office. Local issues, campaign strategies, and personalities are the most important determinants. In Texas, the financial crisis because of the drop in oil prices was important. In Alabama it was a reaction to the confusion surrounding the Democratic primary. In New York, California, and Massachusetts, voters seemed to be registering their satisfaction with recent economic development activity. In Wisconsin, the key was campaign strategies and the siting of a prison.

As will be seen in subsequent chapters, the policy-making process begins with setting an agenda. That agenda is set by public officials, but often with vague and sometimes contradictory messages from the voters. Even a message as loud as the "taxpayer revolt" of the late 1970s is not always clear about precisely what to do about cutting taxes or limiting spending. Economic development, welfare reform, and educational reform were recurring themes in state campaigns in the mid- and late 1980s. Here, too, however, the messages and the mandates were not clear and precise.

Parties and elections, in short, are used primarily for getting people into

TABLE 3.4. TRENDS IN PARTY IDENTIFICATION

	1952	1954	1956	1958	1960	1962	1964	1966	1968	1970	1972	1974	1976	1978	1980	1982	1984
Strong Democrat	22%	22%	21%	23%	21%	23%	26%	18%	20%	20%	15%	17%	15%	15%	16%	20%	18%
Weak Democrat	25	25	23	24	25	23	25	27	25	23	25	21	25	24	23	24	22
Independent, leaning Democrat	10	9	7	7	8	8	9	9	10	10	11	13	12	14	11	11	10
Independent, middle of the road	5	7	9	8	8	8	8	12	11	13	13	15	14	14	12	11	6
Independent, leaning Republican	7	6	8	4	7	6	6	7	9	8	11	9	10	9	12	8	13
Weak Republican	14	14	14	16	13	16	13	15	14	15	13	14	14	13	14	14	15
Strong Republican	13	13	15	13	14	12	11	10	10	10	10	8	9	8	10	10	14

Source: The Transformation in American Politics: Implications for Federalism (Washington, DC: Advisory Commission on Intergovernmental Relations, 1986), pp. 50, 51.

office. Images, personalities, campaign organization, and strategies, as well as general issues, are important determinants of electoral contests. Issues and policies are not resolved at the ballot box. Their resolution involves the full array of processes and institutions of state government.

ELECTIONS EXERCISE: DEVELOPING A CAMPAIGN STRATEGY

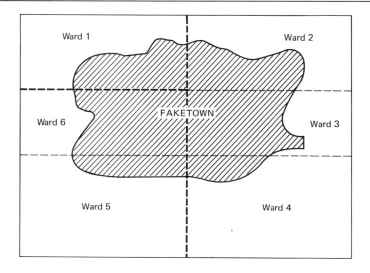

POLITICAL DATA FOR ASSEMBLY DISTRICT 999

	Ward 1	Ward 2	Ward 3	Ward 4	Ward 5	Ward 6
Population	5,000	5,000	5,000	5,000	5,000	5,000
Eligible Voters	2,000	2,000	2,000	2,000	2,000	2,000
Registered Voters	1,400	1,400	1,200	1,200	1,100	800
Average Family Income, 1985	$34,000	$36,000	$25,000	$15,000	$16,000	$10,000
Average Education— Adult	15 years	16 years	13 years	11 years	11 years	10 years
Voter Turnout:						
Presidential Primary, 1984	40%	42%	34%	27%	26%	20%
Fall 1984	65%	69%	60%	56%	54%	45%
Vote (expressed as % GOP) President, 1984	77	73	67	58	51	47
U.S. Senate, 1986	67	64	59	49	40	33
U.S. Congress, 1986	62	58	52	44	40	25
Governor, 1986	63	61	55	51	47	38
State Senate, 1984	64	60	53	45	44	36
State Assembly, 1986	60	54	48	43	41	26
County Sheriff, 1986	72	69	63	52	49	37

District includes Faketown, population 20,000, and surrounding agricultural community, population 10,000. The major economic activities in Faketown are the sale and servicing of farm equipment, two food-processing plants, a printing company with contracts for several national magazines and a major national book publisher, a manufacturer of bicycle parts and mechanical toys, as well as the retail, service, and commercial businesses common to a town of this size.

According to a survey conducted for a local newspaper, eligible voters in this district have the following attitudes on issues:

	Yes	No	No Opinion
State should have lottery	69%	17%	14%
State should help farmers	43	44	13
Raise gasoline tax for better roads	21	62	17
Require those on welfare to work or learn	58	22	20
Eliminate inheritance tax	34	37	29

The survey identified the following issues as the ones of major concern to the electorate:

- Property taxes
- Quality of education
- Farm crisis
- Environmental protection
- Unemployment due to technological changes and foreign competition

Directions
The incumbent Assembly representative, a Democrat, has announced he will not seek re-election. A popular member of the school board, a liberal Democrat, has announced that she will run for the seat. It is safe to assume she will win the primary.

You are the campaign staff for a conservative Republican who is about to announce his candidacy. He is thirty-three years old and has been practicing law for the past three years in Faketown. The major opponent in the primary is sure to be a farmer who, like others in the district, has been alarmed at the bleak prospects for family farms.

Use the information provided and develop a general design for a campaign strategy. As you develop a strategy, answer the following questions:

1. What is the major message your candidate wants to convey about himself and the issues?
2. To whom, if any particular group, will this message be aimed?
3. Is there any need for increasing voter registration and/or voter turnout?
4. In what ways will the candidate reach voters with his message?
5. Will the strategy change from the primary to the general election?
6. What further data or information would you like? How will you proceed if this information is not available?

REFERENCES

1. Austin Ranney, *The Doctrine of Responsible Party Government* (Urbana: University of Illinois Press, 1962), pp. 8–22.

2. V. O. Key, Jr., *Southern Politics in State and Nation* (New York: Knopf, 1949).
3. Sarah McCally Morehouse, *State Politics, Parties and Policy* (New York: Holt, Rinehart and Winston, 1980), pp. 45–94.
4. William M. Kraus, *Let the People Decide* (Aurora, IL: Caroline House, 1982), p. 27.
5. Bruce M. Stave, ed., *Urban Bosses, Machines, and Progressive Reformers* (Lexington, MA: D. C. Heath, 1972); Milton L. Rakove, *Don't Make No Waves—Don't Back No Losers: An Insider's Analysis of the Daley Machine* (Bloomington: Indiana University Press, 1975); and V. O. Key, Jr., *Politics, Parties and Pressure Groups*, 5th ed. (New York: Crowell, 1964).
6. Stave, *Urban Bosses*, pp. 115–47.
7. Lester Milbrath, *Political Participation* (Chicago: Rand McNally, 1965); and Paul R. Abramson and John H. Aldrich, "The Decline of Electoral Participation in America," *American Political Science Review*, Vol. 76 (Sept. 1982).
8. Marjorie Randon Hershey, *The Making of Campaign Strategy* (Lexington, MA: Lexington Books, 1974).
9. Karen Hansen, "PACs and Politics," *State Legislatures*, Vol. 12, No. 9 (Oct. 1986), 18–20; and Thad L. Beyle, "The Cost of Becoming Governor," *State Government*, Vol. 59, No. 3 (Sept./Oct. 1986), 95–101.
10. *The Transformation in American Politics: Implications for Federalism* (Washington, DC: Advisory Commission on Intergovernmental Relations, 1986), pp. 163–206; and "Comparisons of Campaign Commercials," *National Journal* (Nov. 1, 1986), 2610–2614.
11. "Comparisons of Campaign Commercials," 2621.
12. *National Journal*, November 8, 1986.
13. Council of State Governments, *The Book of the States, 1986-87* (Lexington, MA: Council of State Governments, 1986), pp. 185–88.
14. Paul R. Abramson and John H. Aldrich, "The Decline of Electoral Participation in America," *American Political Science Review*, Vol. 76 (Sept. 1982); see also Stephen D. Shaffer, "A Multivariate Explanation of Decreasing Turnout in Presidential Elections, 1960–1976," *American Journal of Political Science*, Vol. 25 (Feb. 1981), 77–89.
15. See, for example, Everett Carl Ladd, "As the Realignment Turns: A Drama in Many Acts," *Public Opinion*, Vol. 7 (Dec./Jan. 1985), 6; and Martin P. Wattenberg, *The Decline of American Parties, 1952-1980* (Cambridge, MA: Harvard University Press, 1984).
16. Advisory Commission on Intergovernmental Relations, *The Transformation in American Politics*, 42–47.
17. Ladd, "As the Realignment Turns."

STATE POLITICAL INSTITUTIONS

_____ CHAPTER 4 _____

Governors

Consider the following job vacancy announcement:

> WANTED: Chief Executive Officer. Complex organization of 50,000 employees: annual operating budget exceeding $8 billion. Wide diversity of responsibilities, including policy leadership; public relations and negotiations; and managerial direction over programs in education, criminal justice, social welfare, health, corrections, highway construction, occupational licensing, environmental protection and regulation, agriculture, and economic development. Responsible to two boards of directors, usually in conflict with one another. Travel and long hours. Job security for four-year term only. Annual salary: $70,000—not negotiable.

No sane person would apply. The complexity and demands of the job are not at all commensurate with either the job security or the salary. Someone with aspirations to be a chief executive officer would be advised instead to pursue such a position in, for example, a medium-sized insurance company, where typically the number of employees is half of that listed above, where the scope of functions is singular (insurance), and where the salary is two to three times that in the announcement. (In 1987, the salaries of most governors ranged between $60,000 and $75,000 per year. The lowest was $35,000—Arkansas and Maine—and the highest was $100,000—New York.)[1]

Despite the high job demands and low pay, individuals and groups spend millions of dollars and hundreds of hours fighting to fill one of the fifty jobs in the country described in the preceding ad. Clearly these efforts do not reflect widespread insanity. Despite the unattractive features of the position of governor, people of character and ability have sought the office. Their motivations vary from a sincere commitment to public service to a lust for power and prestige. Whatever the array of intentions, states have, with few exceptions, been fortunate that able men and women have usually been available to occupy gubernatorial offices.[2]

In an examination of personal, institutional, and circumstantial factors associated with the accomplishments of governors, Lee Sigelman and Roland Smith concluded that it is difficult to identify what leads to productive governors. They tested the competing hypotheses that (1) great people made great governors, (2) strong gubernatorial offices made great governors, and (3) great governors are products of crises and opportunities. No single explanation had much empirical support. The strongest predictor of accomplishments Sigelman and Smith found was age (mid-forties), which they interpret as a general indicator of personal dynamism and ambition.[3] These traits certainly seem like important requirements. The job is unusually demanding and challenging and needs someone with energy and commitment.

Being the governor of a state is, at least for some, not just an end in itself but a step toward other offices. Past and current governors include some of our country's most colorful and famous people, many of whom have served—or will serve—as members of Congress, ambassadors, and even presidents. This chapter will first discuss the institutional aspects of the governorship and then return to the individuals who are and have been governors.

HISTORICAL DEVELOPMENTS

A legacy of the colonial period was a guarded mistrust of governors and severe limitations on the authority of the office. The British Empire was structured so that governors not only represented the Crown but also ruled their respective territories with substantial autonomy. The discontent that led colonists to seek independence from England was focused primarily on governors, and the governors figured prominently in the struggles that led to independence. Thus, in the aftermath of revolt, few were inclined to endow the office of governor with much power.

The constitutions of the first states made legislatures the dominant institution. Only four of the thirteen original states directly elected their governors. The legislatures in the other nine states selected the governor. Budgets and personnel appointments originated in and were considered by the legislatures. Initially, only South Carolina, New York, and Massachusetts gave their governors the right to veto legislation—and South Carolina revoked that power after a few years. Governors, in short, did little other than represent their states in ceremonial roles.

With Jacksonian democracy and the enfranchisement of all white men, regardless of their income or whether they owned property, states—old and new—provided for the direct popular election of their governors. This provided governors with their own base of power, independent from state legislators. It did not, however, lead inexorably to a gradual strengthening of the office. Other events and concerns placed important constraints on state chief executives.

In an attempt to keep southern political leaders weak after the Civil War, governors in the states of the former Confederacy were not allowed to succeed themselves in office, and gubernatorial terms were set at two years in these states. As part of the effort to destroy political machines, the Progressive movement at the turn of the century established the direct election of state agency heads and the appointment of citizen boards and commissions to direct state executive and regulatory bodies. Governors in progressive states were elected to head the executive branch, but they did not have the authority to name the heads of all the various executive agencies.

Simultaneous to the efforts of the Progressive movement to locate more power in the people rather than in machines, the country confronted the challenges of rapid urbanization, industrialization, international strife, and westward expansion. These challenges required responses that presupposed effective managerial leadership. The country looked to Washington, not to state capitals, for that leadership.

After the Depression, the New Deal, and major wars, state governments were increasingly regarded as irrelevant or even as impediments to effective problem solving. It appeared that governors would simply head federal administrative units, rather than direct a government with meaningful discretion and authority.[4] It was not until the 1970s, when political sentiment against the size and scope of the federal government emerged, that state governments generally, and governors specifically, became strengthened, in status and in power. The legacy of distrust of powerful executives is still apparent, but it is tempered by the requirements for effective leadership and management.

FORMAL POWERS

Term of Office

A one- or two-year term is almost a guarantee for a weak chief executive. By the time an individual gets acquainted with the formal and informal rules for getting something done, the term is almost over and/or it is time once again to run for reelection. One-year terms and prohibitions against running for reelection were common provisions in the constitutions of the first thirteen states. Two-year terms and bars against immediately succeeding oneself were, likewise, common for the former states of the Confederacy. These provisions were conscious attempts to prevent a strong, monarchical-like executive.

As a way of providing for managerial continuity and allowing a governor to provide meaningful direction, states have been moving toward four-year terms and removing some of the limitations on reelections. Table 4.1 shows the changes that have taken place since 1960. In 1984, for example, Arkansas passed an initiative that lengthened its gubernatorial term from two to four years and provided for a maximum of two terms for any individual. New Hampshire, Rhode Island, and Vermont are the only states that still have two-year terms.

TABLE 4.1. GUBERNATORIAL TERMS OF OFFICE

Four Years	1960	1987
No limits on reelections	12	20
One reelection allowed	7	21
No reelections allowed	15	6
Two Years		
No limits on reelections	14	3
One reelection allowed	2	0

Sources: The Book of the States, 1959–60, pp. 21–22, and 1986–87, pp. 51–52 (Lexington, KY: Council of State Government).

Appointment Powers

A corollary to the four-year term is the opportunity for the governor to appoint his or her own people to head major state agencies. It makes little sense to acknowledge the need for a chief executive who can exert meaningful managerial leadership and then to keep that executive from assembling his or her own team of managers and policy makers. On the other hand, most would agree that if governors have only two-year terms, they should not have full discretion to hire and fire all agency heads. To allow for wholesale changes in top executive leadership would foster too much instability throughout state government. In part, in other words, the combination of a four-year term and the authority to appoint and terminate the heads of major agencies is a significant step toward strengthening governors and the executive branch generally. This reform is often called the ''establishment of cabinet government.''

The term *cabinet government* is used to refer to situations in which agency heads serve at the pleasure of the governor. This usage differs from its original meaning in Europe, where agency heads are legislators from the majority party or the ruling coalition in parliament and where there is a tradition of collective decision making and collective responsibility for running government. Cabinets in state governments rarely make decisions together and, in fact, rarely meet. And when they do, it is usually done as a media event. Nonetheless, the opportunity for a governor to determine who heads state agencies is important for his or her establishment of policy priorities and managerial style.

Executive branch reorganizations since the 1960s invariably have included providing governors with more positions than they can fill, often with the advice and consent of the state senate. These reorganizations have typically also involved consolidating many small agencies into larger departments, thus allowing for more central and coherent executive direction.[5] Still, small independent agencies continue to be a part of the organizational landscape, and less than a majority of state agency heads in 1981 were gubernatorial appointments. Of the 1,982 top agency positions, 46.8 percent were appointed by governors; 38.2 percent were appointed by boards, commissions, or legislatures; and 15 percent were elected.[6] As shown in Table 4.2, the positions of attorney general, secretary of state, treasurer, and auditor were most commonly elected.

An agency head elected to office independently from a governor can present even more limits on gubernatorial power than an agency head with indefinite job security. At times, an attorney general or a superintendent of public education who is elected to office is posturing for a try in the next election to become governor. Such a situation obviously triggers conflict and competition that are a far cry from what would exist if these individuals served at the pleasure of the governor. An attorney general who is a rival to the governor may consciously try to embarrass the governor, whereas a secretary of natural resources beholden to the governor for his or her position is not likely to give the governor problems. In short, although the trend has been to strengthen the appointment power of governors, that is still a limited power of the office.

Budget and Fiscal Management

Until the 1920s, the common pattern in state governments was for the legislature to have the responsibility for initiating a budget proposal, passing it, and submitting it to the governor for approval. Governors, in other words, played at best only an informal role in establishing the policies and priorities reflected in the budget. They instead were in the position of reacting to legislative deliberations.

As pointed out in Chapter 8, all but four states have statutorily defined a central role for the governor in the budget process. Most governors have the upper hand in that they formulate and propose a budget to the legislature and then, after legislative approval, can approve or veto what the legislature has done. For those who want funds from the state treasury, the key is getting gubernatorial support.[7] To rely on the legislature is to risk inaction and, if both houses do agree and do act, to risk gubernatorial veto. The budgetary process is described in detail in Chapter 8. Here, however, it is important to note the central position of the governor in this essential policy-making process.

Once a budget is passed, it must be administered. Governors have responsibility for assuring that funds are spent within established limits and for the purposes outlined in the budget. Inevitably, this means that despite directives and limits in budget laws, governors enjoy important discretion regarding exactly how, where, and when money will be spent. A budget may, for example, include funds for modernizing and expanding state prison facilities. The budget is unlikely to say exactly what modernization involves, however, and may also leave it up to the governor to determine which of the state's prisons will be scheduled first. In this situation, a governor might emphasize the construction of training facilities as opposed to solitary confinement cells. Some governors will even have the flexibility to use the funds to experiment with contracting with private firms for the care or rehabilitation of prisoners.

Not only do governors have responsibility for administering state funds, but they are also responsible for federal funds. Here, too, there are certain rules and

TABLE 4.2. ELECTED STATE AGENCY OFFICIALS

State	Secretary of State	Attorney General	Treasurer	Auditor	Comptroller	Education	Agriculture	Labor	Insurance	Other (number)
Alabama	x	x	x	x			x			2
Alaska										
Arizona	x	x	x			x				2
Arkansas	x	x	x	x						1
California	x	x	x		x	x				1
Colorado	x	x	x							2
Connecticut	x	x	x		x					
Delaware		x	x	x					x	
Florida	x	x	x		x	x	x			
Georgia	x	x			x	x	x	x		1
Hawaii										
Idaho	x	x	x	x		x				
Illinois	x	x	x		x					1
Indiana	x	x	x	x		x				
Iowa	x	x	x	x			x			
Kansas	x	x	x						x	1
Kentucky	x	x	x	x		x	x			1
Louisiana	x	x	x				x		x	2
Maine										
Maryland		x			x					
Massachusetts	x	x	x	x						1
Michigan	x	x								2
Minnesota	x	x	x	x						
Mississippi	x	x	x	x			x		x	2
Missouri	x	x	x	x						
Montana	x	x		x		x				1
Nebraska	x	x	x	x						3
Nevada	x	x	x		x					2
New Hampshire										1
New Jersey										
New Mexico	x	x	x	x						3
New York		x			x					
North Carolina	x	x	x	x		x	x	x	x	
North Dakota	x	x	x	x		x	x	x	x	2
Ohio	x	x	x	x						1
Oklahoma		x	x	x		x			x	1
Oregon	x	x	x			x		x		
Pennsylvania		x	x	x						
Rhode Island	x	x	x							
South Carolina	x	x	x	x						1
South Dakota	x	x	x	x						2
Tennessee										1
Texas		x	x		x		x			2

continued

TABLE 4.2., *continued*

State	Secretary of State	Attorney General	Treasurer	Auditor	Comptroller	Education	Agriculture	Labor	Insurance	Other (number)
Utah		x	x	x						1
Vermont	x	x	x	x						
Virginia		x								
Washington	x	x	x	x		x			x	1
West Virginia	x	x	x	x			x			
Wisconsin	x	x	x			x				
Wyoming	x		x	x		x				

Source: The Book of the States, 1986–87 *(Lexington, KY: Council of State Governments, 1987),* pp. 51 and 52.

regulations that must be followed, but also opportunities for creativity and leadership. In any case, the billions of federal and state dollars, annually, that governors manage enhance the power and prestige, as well as the challenges, of the office.

Veto

A tool to help governors manage state finances, avoid certain expenses, and balance budgets is the line-item veto. This power, discussed as part of the policy process described in Chapter 8, allows a governor to delete parts of a bill passed by the legislature while signing the bill as a whole into law. With a package or general veto, in contrast, the governor must either approve or reject the bill in its entirety. Presidents do not have line-item veto authority, but they may exercise a package veto. Governors in all but seven states may use the line-item veto on bills that have financial provisions. North Carolina's governor has no veto authority— line-item or package—at all. That had been a common pattern among the first states in the Union.

Veto authority is a substantial power. Only 6 percent of all vetoes by governors were overridden between 1945 and 1975.[8] Creative use of the line-item veto can be awesome. Governors in some states have, for example, deleted the decimal point from a figure or, at the other extreme, deleted one or more zeroes at the end of a number. Legislative language can be turned on its head by using a veto to strike such words as *not* and *whenever* and *with the approval of* . . . from sentences.

When something like a veto can be used to thwart legislative action, the threat of its use can be as effective as its actual use. It is impossible to cite the number of times governors have successfully influenced legislative action through threats. We can, however, examine its actual usage. One study shows that the frequency with which the line-item veto and the package veto are used varies considerably from state to state. In 1980, for example, one-fourth of the bills passed by the New York legislature were vetoed, but none of those passed in Vermont or Wyoming was vetoed. Not surprisingly, there were noticeably more vetoes in states where the legislature was controlled by a different party than the party to which the governor belonged.[9] Indeed, in a detailed study of the use of the line-item veto over a twelve-year period in Wisconsin, it was found that governors were acting primarily out of concern for partisan conflict and policy choices rather than fiscal constraint.[10]

Staff

An important resource for public officials, including governors, is staff. Time, energy, and ideas are precious commodities. They are also inextricably linked to human resources. Governors have never been without staff. Even governors of the early states had assistants to help with scheduling and with correspondence. Since the 1960s, governors have hired individuals to assist with policy analyses, legal work, and intergovernmental relations. The increase in responsibilities and the increases in staff for gubernatorial offices have gone hand in hand. In 1987, most governors had a staff of thirty to forty people. New York and Texas were far from the norm, with 216 in the former and 215 in the latter. Wyoming, on the other hand, had only seven.[11]

Today a typical staff in a governor's office will include:

1. Press secretary—maintains contact with the media. This includes issuing press releases, scheduling press conferences, notifying the media of the governor's schedule, answering media questions on behalf of the governor, and assisting with speech writing.

2. Legal counsel—provides legal advice. This usually includes explaining legal options to the governor in various situations, advising the governor on how to respond to requests for pardons and clemency; and assisting with negotiations with contractors, the federal government, unions, and the like.

3. Policy advisor—identifies and analyzes policies the governor might want to pursue. Some of these policies are initiatives of the governor and others are responses to the actions or proposals of others. An increasingly common pattern is to have several policy advisors, each with a specialty like education, human services, and transportation, and to have a director in charge of this policy staff.

4. Appointments secretary—schedules the public appearances of the governor. This position or the chief of staff, described below, may perform a "gatekeeper" function, determining who may have access to the governor. The implications of having access to the governor are, of course, very significant.

5. Legislative liaison officer(s)—work with legislators to ensure favorable

treatment of gubernatorial initiatives and to ensure informed responses by the governor to legislative action.

6. Intergovernmental relations officer(s)—maintain communications with local governments and represent their concerns to the governor and/or operate an office in Washington to keep the governor informed about federal government activities relevant to the state and to represent the governor to federal officials.

7. Constituent relations staff—drafts responses to correspondence the governor receives, sends replies, and files correspondence. This task is often done by volunteers and student interns, under the direction of a full-time staff person. Replies that require detailed, technical information are usually drafted by personnel in the relevant administrative agency and then reviewed by the governor's constituent relations staff.

8. Chief of staff—manages the employees and volunteers in the governor's office.

Beyond this core of staff, governors may also have analysts focusing on specific policy areas. Some governors hire their own analysts to cover all issues of concern to state government. Others assemble a staff to emphasize those areas of greatest interest to the governor and then rely on agency employees for analyses on the remaining issues.[12]

Considerable symbolic significance is attached to staff positions in the governor's office. If someone is publicly identified as, for example, responsible for the development of small businesses or assistance to the elderly or efforts to achieve affirmative action goals, the policies and the people affected are accorded high priority on the governor's agenda. The symbolic messages conveyed by these appointments are usually loud and clear, regardless of what substantively is accomplished.

Transition

One indication that states are taking their governors seriously is the conscious provision of personnel, funds, and legal authority for transitions from one gubernatorial administration to another. Prior to the mid-1970s, the issues of transition were left to be worked out between the incoming and the outgoing administration. It was assumed that if those involved could work out arrangements, they would, and that if they could not work together, it really didn't matter.

Now thirty-four states have legislation related to gubernatorial transitions. A change in administration is not regarded as inconsequential. State budgets have become very complex. States recognize that gubernatorial teams should work together at least minimally to avoid unnecessary delays and disruptions in programs and state fiscal management. A newly elected governor, for example, might delay payments of state aids to local school districts in order to consider using some or all of that money for some other purpose. The implications of the delays and uncertainties that this would cause are, of course, enormous. It would be far better, for the orderly establishment of new policies and priorities, if that governor-elect could be involved in whatever budget and financial decisions were being made in the months between election and inauguration.

Although structures and resources are provided, transitions still depend heavily on personalities and politics.[13] Probably the best circumstance is when a governor decides not to run for reelection, and the worst is when a governor has been defeated in a bid for another term. Nonetheless, those leaving office voluntarily may not make the effort to ensure a smooth and orderly transition. Gracious losers, on the other hand, can counteract the inherent tensions when they leave involuntarily. Fundamental to smooth transition is communication. An outgoing staff can comply with transition laws and still not communicate fully. Likewise, an incoming administration that is arrogant and haughty can block communication.

National Governors' Association

A supplement to staff resources within a governor's own state is the National Governors' Association (NGA). The NGA is an organization to which all states belong and which provides the fifty governors with a forum to take positions on issues and to press the federal government for policies and procedures that the states find advantageous. The NGA also sponsors a series of meetings and symposia in which suggestions are offered for everything from how to manage a smooth transition when assuming office to what can be done to deal with certain policy and political issues. The staff of the NGA is located in Washington, DC. It is valuable as a source of information regarding the activities of the federal government related to states. The NGA played a major role in negotiating with the White House after President Reagan proposed his ''big swap'' New Federalism plan, discussed in Chapter 2. The NGA has also been effective in shaping state responses to concerns in the 1980s for the quality of elementary and secondary education. Establishing tougher standards for teacher certification and administering standard tests for those graduating from high school are measures that got enhanced visibility through the NGA.

The formal powers and resources of the governor are used for a variety of purposes. They are used by individual incumbents for pursuing their own aspirations, whether that be to get reelected, to win some other race, or to establish a legacy of certain policy accomplishments. Within state governments, these powers and resources are used in the performance of certain institutionalized roles.

ROLES

Agenda Setting

The most important policy-making role that governors play is to establish the agenda for state governments. Agenda setting is a critical first stage in the deliberative process. Obviously, if an issue is never raised, it will never be addressed.

How a governor raises an issue is important to how it will be addressed. A proposal to require all able recipients of welfare benefits to get job training or work for their benefits can, for example, be presented as a way of helping those on welfare become self-sufficient and independent. This proposal might, on the other hand, be presented as an effort to discourage recipients from remaining on welfare, and thereby cutting welfare costs. The former approach conveys the image of an empathetic governor and focuses attention on job-training programs, placement services, support systems, and the like. The latter way of defining the issue pictures the governor as tough on deadbeats and cheaters and emphasizes compliance with welfare eligibility rules.

The role of the governor in determining which issues will be addressed offsets many of the formal limitations of the office. The agenda-setting role is a leadership role. Governors can let the legislature legislate and then decide whether or not to approve or veto its work. With such a passive approach, a governor will not be able to take responsibility for policy direction or policy initiatives. In contrast, a governor can work with his or her staff in identifying an issue and developing a proposal and then campaign publicly for that proposal much like the governor campaigned for office. Such a governor, particularly if persuasive, will leave a legacy and will be remembered for vision, even by those who might oppose the governor's initiatives.

It should be added that state policy making depends heavily on how a governor plays the agenda-setting role. Legislatures are typically too fragmented to be a major source of policy initiative. If a governor wants simply to be a passive caretaker of state government, little cohesive change is likely to occur, even in response to external political and economic events. It is very rare that legislative leaders can fill the void and provide a central source of direction. They have more limited constituencies than the governor, and they lack his or her overall authority and resources.

Ceremonial

The oldest and most enduring role of governors is as the chief representative of the state. Even when the office had few formal powers, the governor was regarded as the most visible, central figure in state government. The governor was called on to represent the state at key functions and to preside at solemn occasions. The challenge to contemporary appointment secretaries is to assign priorities to the myriad of requests for the governor to be present at opening ceremonies, hand out awards, greet guests, and so on. Governors cannot afford to reject all such requests, yet it would be easy to let ceremonial opportunities "nickel and dime" all the governor's time. One strategy is to define this role personally and politically rather than in terms of representing the state. Thus invitations to appear before large gatherings or important groups of supporters are preferred. Also, an emphasis is placed on making sure that appearances become media events, for broader exposure and publicity.

Party Leader

The governor is not only the most visible, central official in state government but also usually the most visible, central figure in his or her political party. Most state political parties defer to their respective governors in naming chairs of the party. At national political conventions the governor is typically the leader of his or her party's state delegation.

However, except for some of the machines that once prevailed in several states, parties are not strong, monolithic, disciplined organizations in the United States. Governors rarely can eliminate factions within their parties. They must cope with them. Governors, moreover, do not regard their party as a source of policy guidance, nor do they think of party leadership as their most important role. Lynn Muchmore and Thad L. Beyle interviewed fifteen governors who left office between 1976 and 1979 and found a consistent attitude that party platforms were meaningless, parties were not ideological, and patronage appointments to maintain party strength were inappropriate.[14] Governors, in short, appear to agree with the description of parties offered in Chapter 3. They are somewhat useful in electoral strategies but not as sources for policy guidance.

Manager

An elementary civics lesson is that chief executives—presidents, governors, and mayors—are the chief administrators of their respective jurisdictions. Studies of state administrators have found, however, that although governors set in place certain managerial styles and processes, legislators tend to have more influence over policy direction of agencies.[15] Primarily through their appointments of agency heads and through fiscal management devices, governors influence whether state governments will emphasize centralized control or local discretion and whether specific efficiency goals or a more casual approach will prevail. Most administrators in most states, however, reported that governors do not use their appointment, budget, or other powers to establish policies that emphasize mass transit over roads or pollution controls over industrial activity. Those priorities are attributed mostly to legislators.

Governors are increasingly concerned about their role as managers. The National Governors' Association has devoted more attention to this subject since the mid-1980s, and governors individually are focusing on how they might provide more effective direction to state agencies.[16] The frustrations arise not so much because governors face hostile agencies but rather because time periods are so different. Administrators have perspectives that are influenced by their careers, whereas governors must operate within four-year or two-year terms.

The general pattern of limited influence by governors over administrative agencies should not be interpreted as an indictment of those who have held this office. Given the broad scope of responsibilities and the relatively short time spent in office, even the most effective governors will have only a limited impact on what state governments do. In her study of Governor Francis Sargent of Massachusetts, for example, Martha Weinberg found that Governor Sargent began to exert effective policy leadership only when he defined a very short list of goals and then concentrated his personal time and the resources of his office on accomplishing those goals. That, for Governor Sargent, meant providing special leadership over the Department of Public Works and the Department of Public Welfare. Meanwhile, other policies and other agencies continued on their existing courses, receiving virtually no gubernatorial attention unless a crisis emerged.[17]

Governors with fairly specific agendas and with the willingness to concentrate their personal energy and their political capital can accomplish policy change. Gubernatorial leadership does not occur automatically as a function of having been elected. The kind of governor that someone will be is determined only in part by the formal duties and powers of the office. To understand fully the nature of governors in state governments requires an understanding of the personalities of those who become governors. Because the governorship centers attention and whatever authority and powers that formally exist on one individual, this office is more heavily influenced by those who occupy it than is true for other institutions of state government.

GOVERNORS AS INDIVIDUALS

We need not resolve the age-old debate about whether great leaders are products of their times or whether leaders are responsible for great times. As governor, few individuals will have the opportunity to change the course of history—the scope of a governor's influence and authority is simply too limited. The exceptions to this rule—Nelson Rockefeller of New York and some of the progressive governors in the early decades of this century—are people who had unusual leadership skills and a long enough tenure to accomplish major change.

Within the context of a state, it seems clear that the interaction among formal authority, political and social circumstances, and gubernatorial accomplishments must include the personal aspirations and strengths of individual governors. Given similar circumstances and times, governors with vision, governors inclined toward corruption, and governors not willing or able to lead will perceive opportunities differently and will react differently. The variation in state responses to the emergence of high technology and the decay of traditional industries is explained in part by differences in gubernatorial leadership. Similarly, governors have provided different direction in response to the partial withdrawal of federal support for social welfare and for urban and agricultural conditions.

As a whole, governors look alike. They tend to be male, white, married, Protestant, college-educated, lawyers or business leaders, and in their mid-forties.[18] However, women and minority group members made new gains in securing governorships in the 1980s. Between 1950 and 1980 only three women, all Democrats, were elected governors: Lurleen Wallace (who succeeded her husband) in Alabama in 1966; Ella Grasso, Connecticut, 1974 and 1978; and Dixie Lee Ray, Washington, 1976. In 1983, Martha Collins was elected governor of Kentucky, and in 1984 Madeline Kunin was elected governor of Vermont. In 1986, Governor

Kunin was reelected, and Kay Orr (who had a woman opponent) won the governorship in Nebraska. Since 1974, four Hispanics and one Japanese-American have become governors. No black has been elected, but Thomas Bradley was the Democratic nominee in California in 1982 and 1986.

To understand their differences requires rather detailed information about governors as individuals rather than just data about age, race, sex, and educational background. Some governors have been prominent and colorful enough to capture the attention of biographers and historians. Huey Long, Orvil Faubus, George Wallace, Nelson Rockefeller, Earl Warren, Pat Brown, Robert La Follette, and James Folsom are some who have etched prominent places in U.S. history. Governors who have become president, ambassador, justice of the Supreme Court, or member of Congress have also generated biographical accounts.

What emerges from these studies are qualitative descriptions of individuals with ambition, vision, agendas, fervent supporters and detractors, and a bit of luck. Notable governors usually were not caretakers, as many governors have been. They were—or tried to be—change agents. They used the formal authority of their office and the informal but real influence of their prestige and their respective power bases to pursue specific objectives. In most cases they evoked both intense devotion and intense hatred. The progressives, like La Follette, were loved by farmers and workers and hated by the old machine bosses and some business leaders. Segregationists, like Faubus and Wallace (in his first years as governor), were heroes to white conservatives and villains to blacks and liberals.

As are chief executive officers in a private company, governors are vulnerable, whether or not they exert leadership. Policy initiatives risk failure or the perception that the consequences are not desirable. Circumstances outside the realm of a governor's authority or influence can redound to the governor's benefit or detriment. Generally, the expectations of a governor's ability to lead and to react are not matched by the institutional or personal abilities to do so. Whether governors come near, or appear to come near, to those expectations affects not only the directions pursued by state governments but also the personal careers pursued by individual governors.

GOVERNORS AND MOBILITY

Slightly more than one-third of the governors who have run for reelection since the mid-1970s have been defeated, either in the primary or in the general election—a rather high percentage. Only about 10 percent of the incumbents of other offices fail to win their bids for reelection.[19] The name recognition and the ability to control events that are enjoyed by incumbents are generally formidable obstacles for challengers to overcome. In his study of governors, Larry Sabato found that the single issue most associated with the defeat of governors running for reelection was taxes. This was particularly true between 1960 and 1975, when tax increases were especially common to support the expanding responsibilities of state government.[20] Most gubernatorial elections are not on the same cycle as presidential contests, so local issues and personalities are more important than presidential coattails.

Governors leave office, voluntarily or involuntarily, to go on to a wide variety of positions. Many resume their professions or their businesses. Some become chief executive officers in private, educational, or not-for-profit organizations. Some assume other public service responsibilities. Former governors are judges, cabinet officers, ambassadors, and regulatory commissioners. One-fourth of the U.S. senators used to be governors. Of the first thirty-eight presidents, thirteen were governors.

A few governors retire in disgrace or obscurity. After he was out of office, Governor Dan Walker of Illinois was found guilty of bribery and conspiracy charges and sentenced to a prison term. Louisiana had an incumbent governor indicted but not convicted. Alaska and Arizona went through impeachment proceedings in the 1980s. Arizona, in 1988, actually impeached its governor. These instances are, it should be emphasized, rare exceptions. For the most part, as stated at the outset of this chapter, governorships have attracted high-quality men and women.

SUMMARY AND CONCLUSIONS

Primarily out of recognition of the need to manage the dramatically increased scope and size of state governments, steps have been taken since the 1960s to provide governors with more resources and power. The terms have increased, staff resources have grown, and more agency heads are now appointees of the governor. Governors themselves regard their positions as primarily managerial, as a chief executive officer.

Governors can make a difference if they have personal vision and energy and if they use their authority strategically. Most important, governors can have a major role in shaping the agendas of state governments. They can define the issues that need to be addressed and they can begin the deliberations by offering their own proposals. Governors who want to have any impact at all on policy must limit their agenda and concentrate their own energies and political capital on a few agencies and a few issues. Governors are central figures in state government, and they can, if they wish, play a major role in shaping public policy.

REFERENCES

1. Council of State Governments, *The Book of the States, 1986–87* (Lexington, KY: Council of State Governments, 1987), p. 30.
2. For a study of the traits of governors, see Larry Sabato, *Goodbye to Good-Time Charlie,* 2nd ed. (Washington, DC: Congressional Quarterly Press, 1983).
3. Lee Sigelman and Roland Smith, "Personal, Office and State Characteristics as Predictors of Gubernatorial Performance," *Journal of Politics,* Vol. 43 (Feb. 1981), 169–80.

4. Sabato, *Good-Time Charlie,* p. 9; and Ira Sharkansky, *The Maligned States* (New York: McGraw-Hill, 1972).

5. James L. Garnett, *Reorganizing State Government: The Executive Branch* (Boulder, CO: Westview, 1980), pp. 8, 9; also, Diane Kincaid Blair, "The Gubernatorial Appointment Power: Too Much of a Good Thing?" *State Government,* Vol. 55, No. 3 (Summer 1982), 88–91.

6. Thad L. Beyle and Robert Dalton, "Appointment Power: Does It Belong to the Governor?" *State Government,* Vol. 54, No. 1 (1981), 6.

7. Ira Sharkansky, "Agency Requests, Gubernatorial Support, and Budget Success in State Legislatures," *American Political Science Review,* Vol. 62 (Dec. 1968), 1220–31.

8. Coleman Ransone, Jr., *The American Governorship* (Westport, CT: Greenwood Press, 1982), p. 140.

9. Charles Wiggins, "Executive Vetoes and Legislative Overrides in the American States," *Journal of Politics,* Vol. 42 (Nov. 1980), 42. Also, Glenn Abney and Thomas Lauth, "The Line-Item Veto in the States," *Public Administration Review,* (Jan./Feb. 1985), 66–79.

10. James J. Gosling, "Wisconsin Item Veto Lessons," *Public Administration Review,* (July/Aug. 1986), 292–300.

11. *Book of the States, 1986-87,* p. 35.

12. Donald R. Sprengel, *Gubernatorial Staffs: Functional and Political Profiles* (Iowa City: Institute of Public Affairs, 1962); and Alan J. Wyner, "Staffing the Governor's Office," *Public Administration Review,* Vol. 30, No. 1 (Jan./Feb. 1970), 17–24.

13. Thad Beyle and J. Oliver Williams, eds., *The American Governor in Behavioral Perspective* (New York: Harper & Row, 1972), pp. 76–104.

14. Lynn Muchmore and Thad L. Beyle, "The Governor as Party Leader," *State Government,* Vol. 53, No. 1 (1980), 13–22.

15. F. Ted Hebert, Jeffrey L. Brudney, and Deil S. Wright, "Gubernatorial Influence and State Bureaucracy," *American Politics Quarterly,* Vol. 11, No. 2 (Apr. 1983), 243–64; and Glenn Abney and Thomas P. Lauth, "The Governor as Chief Administrator," *Public Administration Review,* (Jan./Feb. 1983), pp. 40–49.

16. See the July/August 1986 issue of *State Government.*

17. Martha Wagner Weinberg, *Managing the State* (Cambridge, MA: MIT Press, 1977).

18. Sabato, *Good-Time Charlie,* pp. 20–32.

19. J. Stephen Turett, "The Vulnerability of American Governors: 1900–1969," *Midwest Journal of Political Science,* Vol. 15, No. 1 (Feb. 1971).

20. Sabato, *Good-Time Charlie,* pp. 33–42.

CHAPTER 5

Bureaucracy

State bureaucracies are the most stable of state government institutions. They have employees that, for the most part, work full time and continue in their jobs regardless of changes in the personalities, partisanship, and policy orientation of the governorship or the legislature. The work of administrative agencies, often referred to as "the bureaucracy," remains very much the same over the years, notwithstanding the speeches of elected officials claiming responsibility for dramatic reorientations of state government. State agencies are responsible for ensuring compliance with state laws, providing state services, and operating state institutions. These agencies include the highway patrol and tax departments, state parks and social welfare departments, and prisons and public universities, among others.

State bureaucracies almost tripled in size in the years 1950 to 1970. At the beginning of this period, almost 1.2 million employees worked for state governments. In 1970, the number was slightly over 3 million. While the number of state employees tripled, the population in the United States grew by 11.6 percent. Since 1970, the growth of state bureaucracies has been at a slower pace. In 1985, 3.2 million individuals were state government employees.

Most of the growth represents the expanding scope of the role of state governments. Some of the expanded scope is caused by programs, like those in health care and environmental protection, funded by the federal government but administered by state governments. Table 5.1 shows the growth in total state government employment between 1952 and 1984. Note that a major area of growth has been education. For state governments that means public universities and technical colleges. (Remember that elementary and secondary education is the responsibility of local school boards.) In 1952, state employees in education represented 25 percent of the total, and in 1984 the percentage had grown to 31 percent.

As in other areas, states differ in the size of their bureaucracies. In 1978, for

TABLE 5.1. SUMMARY OF STATE GOVERNMENT
EMPLOYMENT: 1952–1984

Full-Time Equivalent

Year	All	Education	Other
1984	3,177	1,091	2,086
1983	3,116	1,072	2,044
1982	3,083	1,051	2,032
1981	3,087	1,063	2,024
1980	3,106	1,063	2,044
1979	3,072	1,046	2,026
1978	2,966	1,016	1,950
1977	2,903	1,005	1,898
1976	2,799	973	1,827
1975	2,744	952	1,792
1974	2,653	929	1,725
1973	2,547	887	1,660
1972	2,487	867	1,619
1971	2,384	841	1,544
1970	2,302	803	1,499
1969	2,179	746	1,433
1968	2,085	694	1,591
1967	1,946	620	1,326
1966	1,864	575	1,289
1965	1,751	508	1,243
1964	1,639	460	1,179
1963	1,558	422	1,136
1962	1,478	389	1,088
1961	1,435	367	1,068
1960	1,353	332	1,021
1959	1,302	318	984
1958	1,259	284	975
1957	1,153	257	896
1956	1,136	250	886
1955	1,081	244	837
1954	1,024	222	802
1953	966	211	755
1952	958	213	745

Source: The Book of the States, 1986–87 (Lexington, KY: Council
of State Governments, 1987), p. 295, from U.S. Bureau of Census,
1987

example, 36 percent of all state employees and 39 percent of all state payroll costs
were located in seven of the wealthiest and most populous states: California, New
York, Illinois, Michigan, Ohio, Pennsylvania, and Texas.[1] Table 5.2 presents for
each state the number of state employees and the ratio of state employees per
10,000 population.

The newest states, Alaska and Hawaii, appear to have, in relation to their
population, the largest state bureaucracies. It should be noted, however, that be-

**TABLE 5.2. STATE GOVERNMENT EMPLOYMENT,
BY STATE: OCTOBER 1984
(FULL-TIME EQUIVALENT EMPLOYEES)**

State	Number	Number per 10,000 Population
United States (total)	3,177,199	135
Alabama	64,007	160
Alaska	20,866	417
Arizona	36,091	118
Arkansas	36,288	154
California	260,536	102
Colorado	42,122	133
Connecticut	48,461	154
Delaware	16,173	264
Florida	112,285	102
Georgia	82,220	141
Hawaii	37,763	363
Idaho	14,636	146
Illinois	116,890	102
Indiana	65,661	119
Iowa	45,544	157
Kansas	38,848	159
Kentucky	59,247	159
Louisiana	86,193	193
Maine	18,718	162
Maryland	79,358	182
Massachusetts	75,340	130
Michigan	113,426	125
Minnesota	54,406	131
Mississippi	42,632	164
Missouri	61,497	123
Montana	15,182	184
Nebraska	29,255	182
Nevada	12,559	138
New Hampshire	15,323	157
New Jersey	88,066	117
New Mexico	32,254	227
New York	259,648	146
North Carolina	88,276	143
North Dakota	13,484	197
Ohio	113,314	105
Oklahoma	60,714	184
Oregon	41,292	154
Pennsylvania	121,881	102
Rhode Island	20,484	213
South Carolina	61,500	186
South Dakota	11,874	168
Tennessee	64,991	138
Texas	185,486	116
Utah	29,092	176

continued

TABLE 5.2., *continued*

State	Number	Number per 10,000 Population
Vermont	10,496	198
Virginia	94,849	168
Washington	71,702	165
West Virginia	34,798	178
Wisconsin	61,540	129
Wyoming	9,921	194

Source: The Book of the States, 1986–87 *(Lexington, KY: Council of State Governments, 1987), p. 298,* from U.S. Bureau of Census, 1987.

cause of their unique histories and geography, these states have responsibilities not common to the others. Alaska's state government, for example, operates its maritime industry—a private sector activity in other states. Hawaii and Alaska administer welfare programs directly rather than through city and county governments as is done in some states. Both Hawaii and Alaska need more state workers to serve their scattered populations. California, Pennsylvania, and Ohio, in contrast, can serve their more dense population centers more efficiently. Their ratio of state employees to population is among the lowest of all the states. In short, Alaska and Hawaii do not have a penchant for bloated government but rather define the responsibilities of government in a way that requires more state employees than other jurisdictions.

This chapter discusses the characteristics of state government bureaucracies. As will become apparent, administrative agencies play key roles in policy making. It is simplistic and misleading to regard bureaucracies merely as passive implementors of whatever is decided by governors and legislatures.

TYPES OF STATE AGENCIES

State agencies reflect what state governments do. Although each state has its own variations, it is common to find the following agencies or their equivalents in a state government:

1. Department of public instruction—provides financial and programmatic assistance to public elementary and high schools and monitors compliance with regulations regarding compulsory school attendance, basic curriculum, and programs for children with special needs.
2. Department of transportation—constructs and maintains state highways throughout the state and implements federal interstate highway programs; also, in some states, is responsible for highway safety and licens-

ing drivers; may also have mass transit programs or responsibility for water and air transportation facilities.

3. Department of justice—defends the government in legal actions brought against the state, investigates and prosecutes certain crimes, and assists local law enforcement and prosecution agencies.
4. Department of revenue—collects state taxes and provides economic analyses to project the income the government can expect to receive through taxes and fees.
5. Department of corrections—operates the state's prison system and directs the parole programs.
6. Department of health and social services—administers the variety of institutions and programs for the poor, the elderly, the mentally ill, the handicapped, and other groups with special needs. Monitors compliance of private and nonprofit providers of these services with state regulations.
7. Departments of agriculture, commerce, and economic development—promotes economic activities in the state through technical assistance, ensuring compliance with minimum quality standards, and sometimes, advertising.
8. State university and vocational-technical education—operates public colleges and universities and, in some states, administers programs for vocational and technical education.
9. Department of natural resources—ensures compliance with state and federal environmental protection regulations, enforces hunting and fishing laws, and manages state parks and forests.
10. Public utility commissions—regulates pricing, production, and investment policies of telephone, gas, electric, and other utility companies.
11. Licensing and regulatory boards and commissions—enforces compliance with state laws licensing occupations; regulating insurance companies; mandating equal employment opportunities; specifying health and safety standards for buildings and industries; providing for labor relations agreements; and regulating the sale of food, liquor, and drugs.
12. Budget, purchasing, and personnel departments—provide administrative services to other state agencies and ensure compliance with purchasing, personnel, and other policies and procedures state government has set for itself.

Table 5.3 shows how many state employees are hired for the various agencies or responsibilities of state government. This is descriptive information only. The number of employees hired is not an indication of how important a function is but rather how labor-intensive the work is. It takes, obviously, many more employees to operate a public university, a prison, and a mental health institution than it does to collect taxes or to regulate insurance companies or health-care professionals.

TABLE 5.3. EMPLOYEES IN STATE GOVERNMENTS, BY FUNCTION (OCTOBER 1984)

Higher education	2,084,000
Highways	248,000
Public welfare	179,000
Hospitals	556,000
Health	120,000
Police	131,000
Natural resources	158,000
Corrections	215,000
Social insurance administration	105,000
Financial administration	126,000
General control	134,000
Local utilities	25,000

Source: The Book of the States, 1986–87 (Lexington, KY: Council of State Governments, 1987), p. 296, from U.S. Bureau of Census, 1987.

Organizational Patterns

The size and organization of these agencies vary, of course, from state to state and from one agency to another. Several rather distinct patterns can, however, be described. The variations are due primarily to the functional responsibilities or the technical tasks of the agency. Scholars of public administration generally agree that there is no single organizational structure that is best for all activities. The variations in administrative responsibilities require a variation in organizations.

Hierarchical Organization. A relatively large organization that has a single purpose and a well-defined chain of command, like a prison or an institution for the mentally ill, fits this category. Employees can be placed in a pyramid structure with three or four layers. The lowest layer has the narrowest and least skilled set of responsibilities; each higher layer has a more general range of responsibilities.

Decentralized Organization. Agencies with responsibilities for state field operations and/or for dealing with the general public often have a decentralized structure. A department of natural resources and a department of transportation, for example, are likely to have units dispersed throughout the state to manage parks, monitor pollution control, maintain highways, and administer drivers' licensing examinations. The central headquarters provides supervision and ensures consistency in behavior through training, directives, and periodic reviews, but it must allow for a certain level of autonomy for the field offices.

Boards. Licensing and regulatory boards typically consist of a handful of individuals who review and rule on specific cases. If the workload is heavy, as is usually the case with public utility commissions and insurance regulatory bodies, the board members work full time. Many other state boards meet only once or twice a month and the members have other full-time jobs.

Teams. Some agencies and some units within agencies are organized like a team, with a "captain" as leader, but everyone is treated essentially as an equal. The emphasis is on contributing in a fairly open way to a common effort. One example is a budget office where analysts use their own work to shape a budget that reflects the goals of elected officials, the needs of agencies, and the constraints of state revenues. Another example that is common in state governments is an interagency committee or task force established to solve a problem or coordinate a special project.

Despite the variation within and among state administrative agencies, the usual image from outside is that government has an imposing, complex, and intimidating bureaucracy.[2]

THE NATURE OF BUREAUCRACY

For many people, the term *bureaucracy* has acquired a derogatory connotation. The negative image of bureaucracies comes primarily from the rules and routines—commonly referred to as "red tape"—established by these organizations. Ironically, the creation of bureaucracies was intended to ensure fairness, effectiveness, and efficiency.[3] The idea was to arrange a flow of work and to hire workers in ways that emphasized specialized skills and that minimized wasted effort.

Bureaucracies, as traditionally defined, share four basic characteristics. These characteristics, discussed below, best fit the hierarchical organizations that have been discussed, but all administrative agencies share these fundamental traits. Bureaucracies, it should be noted, are distinct from legislatures, governors, and courts, in large part because of organizational traits that emphasize rules, expertise, and hierarchy rather than representation, compromise, negotiation, and consensus. Efficiency, not democracy, is the primary, traditional goal of administration.

1. Job Specialization. An organizational innovation that was key to the Industrial Revolution was the establishment of assembly lines. Rather than relying on a single crafts worker to master all the skills needed to build a car or a radio, the producer of goods used many individuals, each of whom specialized in a particular task. The work of these specialists was orchestrated so that they made the contribution in the proper sequence and so that they would be kept constantly busy. The concept of assembly line specialization and organization is fundamental to most medium- and large-scale firms and to all state governments.

2. Hierarchy of Authority. The specialized skills that go into providing a service or making a product must be coordinated. That is typically done through control and direction from a central source exercised through a chain of command from the top to the bottom of an organization. Information may be encouraged from various levels within the organization, but direction comes from a single source.

3. System of Rules. Coordination depends not only on supervision but also on an understanding by everyone about what must be done and how it should be done. Rules and routines are best viewed as decisions that apply to problems or circumstances that are common and repetitive. Rather than considering anew what response should be made every time a common situation occurs, a rule provides a quick and consistent response. Rules—whether formal or informal, mutually agreed on or ordered from the top—are crucial to the smooth functioning of a large, complex organization.

4. Impersonality of Operation. If the administrative operations of any large organization are to proceed efficiently, employees must not let their personal feelings affect their decisions. Fairness and efficiency demand that rules be applied without regard for subjective concerns or personal stereotypes. State agencies that collect taxes or make welfare payments, for example, devise a set of rules so that all individuals who fit a certain category are treated the same. The alternatives would be to negotiate with each taxpayer or to distribute welfare to those who, subjectively, one liked or for whom one felt sorry. The standardized forms that must be completed are to determine, objectively, tax liability and welfare eligibility.

One of the concerns of critics of bureaucracy is that each or all of these four traits will take on a life and value of their own.[4] Rules might be pursued without regard for the purposes behind them. Impersonalization might be so prized that agencies neglect a service-orientation. A university might, for example, set a minimum grade-point average as a requirement for continuing to enroll in courses. Presumably, that rule is to maintain educational standards for the institution and to prompt students to be serious about their studies. In applying the rule, the university needs to be consistent and fair, regardless of the race of a student or whether the student's parents are alumni who contribute generously. On the other hand, some provision needs to be made for students who do poorly not because of limited abilities but because of illness, a trauma in the family, or poor advising. Giving these students another chance to continue—assuming the problem has been rectified—does not do harm to either the goals of the university or to the development of the student.

Some of the behavior of administrative agencies as they wrestle with themselves as institutions and with what they were established to accomplish can be understood by recognizing that agencies pursue two general types of goals: transitive and reflexive.[5] Transitive goals are those that are intended to have an impact on individuals or on society. Examples are the desire to improve the quality of water in a river or to aid farmers squeezed by low commodity prices and high production costs or to provide job training for workers affected by changes in technology. Reflexive goals concern the health and character of the agency itself. Agencies need an adequate budget, qualified personnel, and support from governors and legislatures.

Administrators must pursue reflexive goals to accomplish their main mission. A correctional system without adequate resources risks prison riots, and a tax department with few auditors cannot identify most of the mistakes made on returns. Agencies can be so successful in achieving reflexive goals that they acquire more employees or money than they need to do their job. This is the "fat" that budget cutters and efficiency experts attempt to identify.

The ideal balance between reflexive and transitive goals is often difficult to define. The activities of many state government agencies defy any precise or widely accepted articulation of what the proper level should be. The extent of highway maintenance and construction that government should complete is a subject of continuing debate. In a very real sense, that debate is resolved temporarily every time a department of transportation receives an allocation of funds. Likewise, a state tax-collection agency can set its goals for catching cheaters in accordance with the number of employees the agency is allowed to hire. The more employees the agency has, the more extensive it can be in discovering errors.

The imprecision of goals makes state agencies vulnerable to charges of waste and inefficiency. Since it is difficult to define exactly what an agency should be accomplishing, it is also difficult to know exactly what the agency needs in money, staff, equipment, and supplies. Moreover, government agencies do not always have competitors, and so it is hard to make comparisons in order to know whether an agency could get its job done (however defined) quicker or with fewer resources.

Moreover, it is not always clear what prompts an attack on the bureaucracy. An accusation that an agency is too big can be a comment on how many employees and how much money it takes to get something done. It can also be a comment on how many people are on welfare; on the harassment of taxpayers over small, inadvertent errors; or on the quality of students allowed to enroll in public universities. Given the favorite refrain of politicians to cut government spending, this vulnerability makes public agencies perennial targets. Thus there is an ongoing cycle of suspicion and tension in which politicians assume waste and inefficiency and try to cut, whereas administrators assume they do not have all that they need or could use and try to expand. The ideal is elusive, and probably no one would recognize it if it were reached.

PROFESSIONAL AUTONOMY

A common, and understandable, reaction of administrators is to resent being every politician's favorite scapegoat and target.[6] Agency employees typically regard themselves as competent and committed professionals. They often spend their working years as transportation engineers, tax collectors, prison guards, safety inspectors, clericals, and the like. From their standpoint, the best prescription for the ills of government is to let government employees alone so that they can use their full energy and expertise to do their jobs.

State agency professionals get support from one another. Virtually every professional in state government has an association that brings together members from various states and, sometimes, from the private sector to share concerns and expertise. Lawyers, social workers, engineers, budget officers, and personnel managers all have their own associations. Important norms for appropriate approaches and ethics are conveyed through these associations. Individuals get suggestions from one another and secure a standard by which to measure their own performance. These interactions are important, ongoing supplements to the formal education acquired at a university and contribute to the competence of state administrators and to the professional autonomy of state agencies.

As a general rule, agencies' powers and expertise are enhanced through relationships with interest groups.[7] Professionals in state agencies and their counterparts in various societal organizations share concerns and information that are mutually beneficial. In addition, each has an interest in the competence of the other. A state bar association, for example, wants a competent and efficient department of justice so that cases can be tried in timely and professional ways and so that investigations of crime are done legally and well. Advocates for mental health programs are important allies of those in charge of mental health efforts of state government. Even when state administrators are defending themselves from attacks from these advocates, the issue is usually over whether state government is doing enough rather than whether state government should be active at all.

The effects of interaction with relevant interest groups is similar to the effects of interaction with professional associations. In both instances, agency personnel and agency missions are supported. On the one hand, increased agency support and expertise are to be celebrated. On the other hand, there is a concern about accountability when standards for guiding, judging, and supporting the behavior of state employees come from outside organizations rather than from elected state officials.

POLITICAL ACCOUNTABILITY

State government is the property of the people of a state, not the members of the National Association of State Budget Officers or the American Bar Association or the American Society for Public Administration. Although governors and legislators appreciate the need for expertise and professionalism in the bureaucracy, they understandably insist that administrative agencies pursue the agenda and the policies set through the electoral process or through judicial policy making. Just as the engineers in General Motors are instructed by their bosses to design a medium-sized sedan that carries six passengers comfortably and costs less than $10,000 to retail, so also might correctional officials be told to design a system of early release and parole that relieves overcrowding in a state's prison system.

Accountability to the Governor

The traditional view is that the governor is the head of the executive branch and therefore directs administrative agencies. In fact, however, state administrators identify the legislature as the major body from which they receive direction. In a survey of senior administrators in the fifty states, Abney and Lauth found that governors generally seemed primarily concerned with how efficiently something was being done.[8] Legislators even more than governors played a major role in providing policy direction. Accountability includes both how something is done as well as what is done.

Perhaps the most visible evidence of gubernatorial concern with managerial control, rather than policy control, is the flurry of reorganization common to the beginning of a governor's term.[9] The major purpose of reorganizations sometimes is not to reflect new policies but rather to run state government better, that is, more efficiently.[10] Agencies are combined to eliminate redundancy and to provide better coordination. Agencies are created to reduce complexity and to provide better managerial control. Governors launch reorganizations with promises of cutting costs and improving services. These are all laudable goals, of course, but they do not represent attempts at making agencies accountable for policy direction.

Although most reorganizations promise a better-run state government, some agencies are created, abolished, or merged to signal new policy. The signal can be symbolic. This was the case in the federal government when President Jimmy Carter created the Department of Energy. The new department brought together several offices concerned with energy that had been located in a number of different departments. Little new was put in place, at least initially, but establishing the agency sent an important message in the midst of a growing national concern about energy availability. State governments in the 1980s have launched new agencies to promote economic development, a top item on the agenda in almost all the state capitals. One way of demonstrating its importance is to create or reorganize a department of economic development.

Governors can also use budgets to exercise policy control. Given the complexities of budgets and state governments, major new directions are likely to be limited to a few areas. Budgets can reallocate resources to emphasize those items most important on a governor's agenda. Budgets, moreover, implicitly and explicitly, have policy content in the way they authorize spending. A budget, for example, that provides funds for road construction but not for mass transit, or one that spends on rehabilitation and probation programs rather than new prisons, are budgets that embody fairly clear policy statements.

Abney and Lauth's survey of senior state administrators indicated that budgets are recognized as policy instruments of governors. Respondents cited the budget as even more important than appointments of agency heads in setting policy direction. Nonetheless, the general sense was that the major arena was the legislature and that the primary need agencies had for gubernatorial support was in getting help for the passage of favorable legislation.[11]

Accountability to the Legislature

In its most obvious form, state agencies are held accountable through the laws establishing the agencies and giving them authority to provide certain services, regulate certain activities, or pursue certain goals. A private company is relatively free to change its product line or to expand its operations as opportunities appear in the marketplace. A public agency may only do what the statutes allow it to do. A state university concerned about the preparation of entering freshmen, for example, cannot start running high schools. At most, it can provide advice and limited assistance to high school faculty and counselors. Likewise, a correctional system cannot use its acquired experience and expertise to branch out into nursing homes or day-care facilities.

A key concept in determining agency accountability is "legislative intent." The scope of an agency's activities and the way it uses its resources must conform to legislative intent. Laws are passed because a majority in both houses voted in favor of a bill. It is not always the case that all or even most of the affirmative votes reflected the same motive or intent. Legislative compromises, in fact, sometimes consciously produce ambiguous and even contradictory language. In these instances, administrative agencies may have an opportunity to exercise some freedom in interpreting the law and what it mandates and/or authorizes. Disputes over legislative intent can be resolved through subsequent clarifying legislation or through litigation in court.

Agencies are rarely passive while legislatures deliberate over their missions and their resources. In fact, the origin of legislative intent sometimes is the agency itself. Agencies work with concerned legislators and with relevant interest groups in initiating new laws and revising old ones. Agencies lobby to affect legislative behavior. They, like other lobbyists, have information important to legislative deliberations, and they mobilize support from the governor, from interest groups, from the media, and from local government officials. The stakes are simply too high for agencies to stand on the sidelines.

With statutory authority in hand, agencies can elaborate on the law through the promulgation of administrative rules. These rules, which in most states can only be implemented if they are written in a process that allows for public comment and objection, have the effect of law. A statute, for example, authorizing the Department of Transportation to license drivers, might be followed by rules specifying what the tests must include, who may administer them, where and when they may be administered, and what appeals may be made by those who fail them. State legislatures typically establish a committee or committees to review administrative rules that are promulgated to be sure they conform to legislative intent. These committees, in several states, can even suspend the rules for a limited period of time to allow the legislature to pass a clarifying law. If the legislature fails to act, the rules take effect.

Once laws are passed and rules promulgated, the ongoing work of administrative agencies gets very limited legislative scrutiny, except when they come back before the legislature at budget time. Further legislative involvement is usually either through casework for constituents or in response to a problem. Legislators are asked by some of their constituents to get information or pursue a complaint that leads them to administrative agencies. A common response from agency personnel is to be annoyed with these inquiries, but recognizing a serious response is important in maintain,ng good relations with legislators.[12] Rarely does constituent casework lead to anything significant, for the agency or the constituent . . . or the legislator.

Problems and crises, however, can lead to new legislative directives. A prison riot almost inevitably leads to an investigatory commission to review the correctional system. Sharp increases in welfare costs lead to assessments of welfare policies and their administration. A resignation of a prominent administrator in public protest will prompt an inquiry into the complaints. Sometimes these problems are pursued by ad hoc commissions or task forces; sometimes standing legislative committees take jurisdiction. Legislatures also rely on their audit bureaus to identify and examine problems with administrative agencies. Note that invariably a negative event or the hint of a scandal is what attracts the attention of elected officials. Achievements tend to go unnoticed.

Governors and legislators, understandably, get upset when they feel that laws they helped enact are implemented by agencies in ways that disregard or are contrary to their major intent. Public officials are also concerned that administrators act as efficiently as possible, reaching objectives while using the least amount of time, money, and human resources. The challenge to administrators in state government agencies is simultaneously to act in accordance with professional norms, to be responsive to the intent of policies, to communicate effectively with the public and public officials, and to develop routines that are fair and simple. Fortunately, in most instances these principles converge to prescribe the same course of action.

STATE ADMINISTRATION AND FEDERAL PROGRAMS

Many state administrative agencies have yet another boss, namely, the federal government. Especially since the late 1960s, a major role of state bureaucracies has been to implement federal programs. Federal grants-in-aid to state governments prior to the 1960s were for general purposes like highway construction and vocational education and had virtually no restrictions, mandates, or reporting requirements. Municipalities participated in some complicated federal programs for community development, but state governments were not involved.

Federal programs that emerged out of the "War on Poverty" and in response to the civil rights movement of the 1950s and 1960s, however, depended on state governments for implementation, and federal dollars were attached with a myriad of directives, mandates, prohibitions, and reporting requirements. The federal government—with some justification in some states—had little confidence in the administrative competence of state governments. Moreover, federal officials did not trust state officials in all states to be cooperative in serving the poor and the disadvantaged. Yet the federal government was committed to working through state governments. To compensate for the limited competence and sometimes downright hostility of its partners, the federal government gave specific directives for how programs should be administered and devoted enormous energy to monitoring state government activities. In a real sense, state agencies became administrative units of the federal government.

In response to federal mandates and the strings attached to federal monies, state governments reorganized, hired almost twice as many employees as they previously had, and altered their own policies and priorities. A federal rent subsidy program, for example, prompted state governments to hire new employees to conduct studies and complete reports showing state eligibility for funds. Still other employees were hired to determine which families qualified for the federal assistance. State inspectors were required, moreover, to certify that participating housing units met minimum standards of safety and sanitation and that rents fell within the "fair market" criteria established by the federal Department of Housing and Urban Development. State agencies hosted teams of federal inspectors and filed long and complicated reports to ensure that federal requirements were met.[13]

Frustrations and frenzied activity were common. Sometimes federal funds had to be spent before federal guidelines were established. One study by Peterson, Rabe, and Wong noted,

> . . . decisions on federal guidelines were constantly delayed, the guidelines were often published several months after they were officially announced, and they could be very unclear. The first set of rules and regulations was established almost a year after Congress passed the legislation. Federal officials took six months to clarify the exact formula on rent payments for large, low-income families and did not publish fair market rental rates for months after they went into effect.[14]

Confusion and misunderstandings reigned until the late 1970s. By that time, most states had a corps of trained and experienced personnel, and federal officials felt more comfortable with the programs they were designing. The federal government backed off on both the number of directives issued and the intensity with which it proceeded with inspection and enforcement. The mutual accommodation and comfort that had been accomplished, in fact, caused unexpected resistance to the move by President Reagan to deregulate these state-federal relationships. In part, this resistance reflected satisfaction with current arrangements, and in part it reflected anxiety that deregulation might lead later to the same kind of suspicion, directives, and auditing that everyone had just been through.[15]

The pattern was not, however, uniform. In the environmental area, for example, the federal government, both through intent and through neglect, gave states considerable discretion in determining the extent to which antipollution measures had to be taken.[16] As states experimented with different ways of including programs for recipients to work and study as a part of the welfare program, the federal government was besieged with requests to allow states to make exceptions to general rules.

By the end of the 1980s, state administrative agencies continued to implement many federal as well as state policies and programs. For some of these agencies, half or more of their funds came from the federal government rather than the state treasury. The perennial anxiety in these agencies has been over the possibility that efforts to reduce the federal deficit will lead to severe cuts or even the elimination of these federal funds. Indeed, some state agencies have already suffered major reductions in federal funding. It seems that state governments have for the most part accommodated to the role of administering federal programs. What might be more difficult to adjust to is the loss of financial support for these programs.

ADMINISTRATIVE ALTERNATIVES

In the never-ending quest to construct a better mousetrap, state governments are searching for approaches to administer programs and enforce laws that are cheaper, fairer, and more effective. Whereas in the 1960s and 1970s that quest focused primarily on government itself, in the 1980s attention shifted to alternatives outside government. Instead of trying to improve administrative agencies, state governments gave serious consideration to relying on private businesses and nonprofit organizations.

Contracts with private vendors are not new to governments generally or state governments specifically. Everything from the construction of roads and buildings to the typing of reports has been contracted out.[17] Likewise, state governments have provided funds or vouchers to individuals and organizations needing services and then told them to find those services in the private sector or among not-for-profit organizations. The federal food stamp program is an example of providing vouchers for meeting a need (food) instead of directly distributing cheese, flour, sugar, and the like. Vouchers are common for health care and for services to the disabled. What is new in the 1980s is the level of emphasis, which could be a matter of kind as well as degree.

Another alternative to state administrative agencies for some policies and functions is the greater use of county and municipal agencies. State governments, like the federal government, have relied on local government agencies to implement its programs. States, too, have issued a plethora of directives, mandates, and prohibitions accompanying its funding. Local governments often harbor the same fears of the loss of continued state funding that states have regarding federal support.

SUMMARY AND CONCLUSIONS

The development and enhancement of alternative administrative arrangements that might involve local governments, nonprofit organizations, and private businesses have a common intuitive appeal. The field of public management has certainly learned that there is no single approach that is appropriate for the many tasks and responsibilities of government agencies.

A central concern for all arrangements, in and out of government, will continue to be the need for accountability to the ballot box. Inherently and inevitably a democracy requires the sometimes conflicting mandates of professionalism, efficiency, and the public will. The ambiguities of each mandate allow for some latitude and creativity, but in the final analysis the bureaucracy, which is not a democratic institution, cannot be aloof and arrogant but instead must be a full and active participant in public policy making.

REFERENCES

1. Leon M. Blevins, *Texas Government in National Perspective* (Englewood Cliffs, NJ: Prentice-Hall, 1987), pp. 175 and 176.
2. Robert I. Kahn et al., "Americans Love Their Bureaucrats." *Psychology Today* (Feb. 1975, 22–29).
3. Peter M. Blau and Marshall W. Meyer. *Bureaucracy in Modern Society,* 2nd ed. (New York: Random House, 1971), p. 58.
4. Michael M. Harmon and Richard T. Mayer, *Organization Theory for Public Administration* (Boston: Little, Brown, 1986).
5. Lawrence Mohr, "The Concept of Organizational Goals," *American Political Science Review,* Vol. 67, No. 2 (June 1973), 470–81.
6. See Hugh Heclo, *A Government of Strangers* (Washington, DC: Brookings Institution, 1977), for a lucid description of the tension between administrators and politicians in the federal government.
7. Glenn Abney and Thomas P. Lauth, *The Politics of State and City Administration* (Albany: State University of New York Press, 1986), pp. 84–105.
8. Ibid., p. 45.
9. James L. Garnett, "Strategies for Governors Who Want to Reorganize," *State Government,* (Spring 1979), 135–43.
10. Kenneth J. Meier, "Executive Reorganization of Government: Impact on Employment and Expenditures," *American Journal of Political Science,* Vol. 24, No. 3 (Aug. 1980), 396–412.
11. Abney and Lauth, *State and City Administration,* pp. 47–60.
12. Ibid., p. 79.
13. Paul E. Peterson, Barry G. Rabe, and Kenneth K. Wong, *When Federalism Works* (Washington, DC: Brookings Institution, 1986), p. 119.
14. Ibid., p. 123.
15. Ibid., pp. 145 and 146.
16. R. Tobin, "New Federalism and State Implementation of the Clean Water Act," *Environmental Management,* Vol. 10 (1986), 785–96.
17. E. S. Savas, *Privatization. The Key to Better Government* (Chatham, NJ: Chatham House, 1987).

CHAPTER 6

State Legislatures

Whereas the governor is elected on a statewide vote to represent all the people of the state, legislators are elected from subdivisions of the state, called districts, to represent the interests of their constituents. In every state except Nebraska, legislative representatives are organized into two chambers, and the population basis of representation differs between them. Representatives to the lower chamber, commonly referred to as the house or assembly, usually represent fewer state residents than do their upper-chamber colleagues, who are organized into senates. Usually house or assembly districts are subdivisions of the larger senate districts, with three lower-chamber districts, on the average nationally, comprising a senate district. Both the population basis of the respective districts and the number of house or assembly districts encompassed within each senate district vary considerably among the states.

Legislators in highly populous states represent more people than do their counterparts in the less populous states. Each state senator in California, for example, represents an average of about 600,000 constituents. In New York the comparable figure slightly exceeds 300,000. On the other end of the spectrum, state senators in Wyoming and North Dakota represent approximately 11,000 and 12,000 constituents, respectively. Lower-chamber districts also vary greatly in represented population among the states. California assembly districts average nearly 300,000 residents, and New York house districts average about 122,000. In contrast, Vermont's house districts average only 1,800 residents.[1] However, regardless of this variation among the states, legislative districts of the same chamber must be nearly equal in population *within* each state.

Although the principle of representative government had been enunciated centuries earlier in England and continental Europe, its operationalization was significantly reinterpreted only two decades ago. The 1962 U.S. Supreme Court decision in *Baker v. Carr*[2] affirmed the principle of equal representation, arguing that unequal representation on the basis of population violates the Fourteenth Amendment of the U.S. Constitution, which guarantees equal protection under the law. A subsequent Supreme Court decision, *Reynolds v. Sims*,[3] rendered in 1964, enunciated the "one-man, one-vote" principle—that each person's vote should secure an equal amount of representation in state legislatures. In some states a legislator from a rural area represented only one-quarter of the population represented by an urban colleague. With the Supreme Court's action, such practices became unconstitutional. As Chief Justice Earl Warren noted, "Legislatures represent people, not trees or acres. Legislators are elected by voters, not farms or cities or economic interests. . . . The right to elect legislators in a free unimpaired fashion is a bedrock of our political system."[4]

Westbury v. Sanders,[5] in 1964, applied the one-man, one-vote principle to both state legislative chambers, making it illegal to apportion representation in state senates on any basis other than equal population. Representation in the U.S. Senate was not recognized as an analogous case for state senate representation, for U.S. senators are elected statewide and represent all residents of the state. State senators, on the other hand, are elected from substate electoral districts and represent only their local constituents. Moreover, states enjoy a special sovereignty that is recognized in the U.S. Constitution in that each state has two senators, regardless of population. Legislative districts, whether state house or state senate, do not have "sovereign" status.

Federal courts, in overseeing implementation of the Supreme Court's ruling, have allowed state legislatures only marginal deviation from the one-man, one-vote rule, permitting limited retention of some district lines that coincide with existing municipal boundaries.

State legislators face the problem of representing the preferences of their constituents and, at the same time, making policy for the entire state. In reconciling these interests, legislators also have to weigh their own policy preferences with what they perceive to be their constituents' preferences. And to complicate matters, constituents' interests often tend to be unclear or in competition with each other. Ultimately, legislators themselves have to decide how to exercise the responsibility of representation, including deciding about the appropriateness of the compromises and accommodations that are made in the process of putting together legislative majorities. In doing so, they cannot stray too far from their constituents' interests for fear of future rejection at the polls.

Legislative districts can be equally apportioned on population, and therefore not violate the law, but be drawn to provide a distinct advantage for one party over another. Two methods can be employed to maximize one party's representative strength over another. The first involves dividing, or "splintering," the opposition party's areas of electoral strength; the second involves "packing" areas of partisan strength in ways that quarantee high majority votes for winners but that limit the number of victors. The first method distributes votes to create several marginally competitive districts with a clear advantage to one's party. The second "sacrifices" one or two big defeats to retain a majority in numerous other districts.

Figure 6.1 provides an illustration of "gerrymandering"—drawing district lines to gain a partisan advantage in legislative representation or to minimize or maximize the electoral representation of minority populations. As an example of partisan gerrymandering, the dark solid lines divide three legislative districts. Districts 1 and 2 are basically competitive districts, with the Republicans holding a slight advantage in District 1. District 3, however, is solidly in Republican hands. With redistricting, represented by the heavy, dotted line, District 3 becomes even more dominated by Republicans. District 1 swings to a decided Democratic advantage, and District 2 picks up enough Democratic support to provide the Democrats with a moderate advantage.

The redrawing of District 3's lines serves as an example of packing. An already large Republican majority is made even larger. But such an expansion of electoral support comes at the expense of the Republicans' relative strength in District 1. Whereas District 1 had a marginal Republican advantage prior to redistricting, it subsequently picked up enough Democratic support from a slice of the old District 3 that it has assumed a decided Democratic advantage. Similarly, the new District 2 picked up sufficient Democratic support from the redrawing of District 1, so that it has gone from a "nip and tuck" competitive district to a moderately Democratic advantage. The slicing of Democratic strength from District 3 to District 1, and from District 1 to District 2, serve as examples of splintering. The net result, then, is to go from a Republican advantage in two districts and close competition in a third to a Democratic advantage in two districts and a solid Republican majority in a third. Obviously, in this example, such gerrymandering would be promoted by a Democratic legislative majority.

Despite its partisan implications, legislatures do not redistrict themselves every time majorities change, but they usually do so after a new census is completed at the beginning of each decade since the official U.S. Bureau of the Census

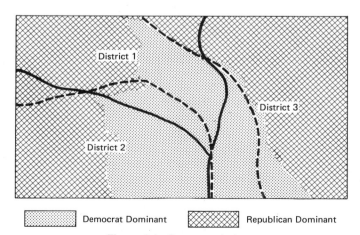

Figure 6.1. Gerrymandering

figures from the last decennial census must be used as the basis for reapportionment.

This practice of gerrymandering has not been proscribed across the board by the Court's landmark decisions. However, gerrymandering for the purpose of minimizing the electoral representation of racial minorities has been expressly forbidden. In a 1977 U.S. Supreme Court ruling, *United Jewish Organization of Williamsburg, Inc. v. Hugh L. Carey,*[6] such racially motivated districting was deemed in violation of the equal protection clause of the Fourteenth Amendment. However, that same decision also provided the leeway for state legislatures to draw boundaries that preserve the viability of minority representation.

In response to the Supreme Court's rulings, state legislatures across the country have reapportioned their legislative districts and thereby corrected some glaring inequities. Three very different states provide vivid illustrations of the problems to be addressed. Before court-induced reapportionment, 18 percent of the voters in Florida could elect a majority of legislators in both the Florida house and senate. Voters in Connecticut's five largest cities, containing over one-quarter of the state's population, could elect only ten of 294 representatives in the lower house. Finally, California's Los Angeles County, with about 40 percent of the state's population, was accorded only one seat in the forty-seat California senate.[7] These examples, although among the most extreme, highlight the monumental task of reapportionment.

What differences did state reapportionments make? One study of thirty-eight state legislatures found that the effects on partisan representation were not all that staggering. Democrats increased their legislative strength by less than 3 percent of the seats contested. And given the Democrats' disproportionate control of state legislative chambers, that percentage appears to be marginal at best.[8] Reapportionments did result, however, in an increase in the number of state representatives and senators from urban and suburban areas, at the expense of rural representation. But such was expected, given the dramatic post–World War II population growth that occurred in urban and suburban areas.[9]

LEGISLATIVE ORGANIZATION

With the exception of Nebraska, which is unicameral, legislative representatives are organized into lower and upper chambers. The size of each chamber bears no relationship to a state's population or geographical size. The lower house among the states varies from a high of 400 representatives in New Hampshire to a low of forty in Alaska. Senates range from sixty-seven members in Minnesota to twenty in Alaska. Nebraska's unicameral legislature has forty-nine members, called senators. (See Table 6.1 for a listing of legislative membership in each of the states.)

State senates can be distinguished from the lower houses on several dimensions. First, as was noted earlier, senate districts encompass several house or assembly districts and are therefore larger in size than the individual districts that comprise them. Thus, within the same state, senates are smaller in size than their

TABLE 6.1. NUMBER OF LEGISLATORS BY CHAMBER

State	Senate	Lower House	Total
Alabama	35	105	140
Alaska	20	40	60
Arizona	30	60	90
Arkansas	35	100	135
California	40	80	120
Colorado	35	65	100
Connecticut	36	151	187
Delaware	21	41	62
Florida	40	120	160
Georgia	56	180	236
Hawaii	25	51	76
Idaho	42	84	126
Illinois	59	118	177
Indiana	50	100	150
Iowa	50	100	150
Kansas	40	125	165
Kentucky	38	100	138
Louisiana	39	105	144
Maine	35	151	186
Maryland	47	141	188
Massachusetts	40	160	200
Michigan	38	110	148
Minnesota	67	134	201
Mississippi	52	122	174
Missouri	34	163	197
Montana	50	100	150
Nebraska	Unicameral		49
Nevada	21	42	63
New Hampshire	24	400	424
New Jersey	40	80	120
New Mexico	42	70	112
New York	61	150	211
North Carolina	50	120	170
North Dakota	53	106	159
Ohio	33	99	132
Oklahoma	48	101	149
Oregon	30	60	90
Pennsylvania	50	203	253
Rhode Island	50	100	150
South Carolina	46	124	170
South Dakota	35	70	105
Tennessee	33	99	132
Texas	31	150	181
Utah	29	75	104
Vermont	30	150	180
Virginia	40	100	140
Washington	49	98	147
West Virginia	34	100	134
Wisconsin	33	99	132
Wyoming	30	64	94
Mean	40	112	152

Source: The Book of the States, 1986–87 *(Lexington, KY: Council of State Governments, 1986), p. 87.*

lower-house counterparts—most commonly by a 1:3 ratio. Fourteen states have an exact 1:2 ratio, whereas the ratio approaches 1:5 in Texas and Vermont and reaches a high of 1:16 in New Hampshire.

Second, the terms of state senators are usually longer than those of state representatives. Such is the case in thirty-four states, where senators serve four years compared to representatives' two. In four other states both senators and representatives serve four-year terms. The remaining eleven states, except for Nebraska, have two-year terms for both upper-house and lower-house legislators.[10]

Both a chamber's size and the length of its members' term can affect its character. Larger bodies tend to be more unwieldy and bound by greater organizational rules and procedures. They also tend to have more pronounced and rigid leadership hierarchies. Because of their larger size and the corresponding greater volume of legislative business before them, houses and assemblies appear to be less collegial and "clubbish" than do senates. Lower-house representatives will be the first to suggest that the senate debating club is not where the bulk of the legislature's work gets done. Representatives are usually quick to point to the "roll up the sleeves and get the job done" mentality of the house, in contrast to the senate's decorum of sartorial splendor.

The general difference in length of terms between the two chambers can also influence the nature of politics in each. Shorter terms may prompt incumbents to pay closer attention to the electoral implications of their legislative choices. They may weigh their actions more in terms of their immediate political ramifications than their longer-term policy implications. Yet such a pragmatic orientation can also carry with it greater responsiveness to one's constituency. Knowing that you are going to be judged by the voters within a time frame that allows them to remember prominent instances of disregard may prompt more responsive representation.

LEGISLATIVE LEADERSHIP

Political parties compete in elections in order to win and take control of the government. Not only does a party hope to win the governorship and thus be in a position, through gubernatorial appointments, to oversee the operations of the executive branch; it also strives to win majorities in both chambers in order to control the legislative process. We know, however, that political parties are not monoliths. Members of the same party do not always act in concert. They are frequently pulled simultaneously in several directions, as they individually respond to competing influences and problems. Yet despite the forces that work to divide would-be solidarity, party affiliation plays an important role in the legislature's organization.

As Figure 6.2 illustrates, the Democrats in 1986 controlled the legislature in twenty-nine states, the Republicans had control in ten states, and control was split between the chambers in another ten states. (Nebraska's legislature is elected on a nonpartisan basis.) Geographically, Democratic control is concentrated in the

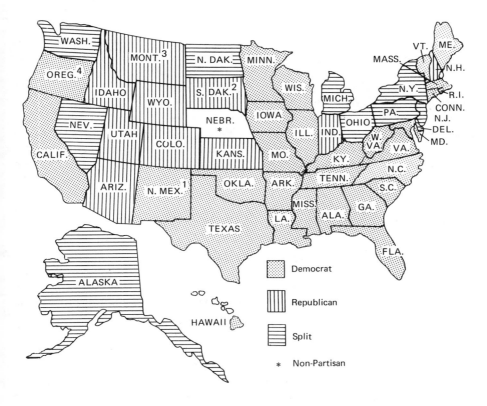

1. The Dems. and Reps. are tied in the Senate with 21 seats apiece.
2. The Dems. and Reps. are tied in the House with 75 seats apiece.
3. The Dems. and Reps. are tied in the Senate with 25 seats apiece.
4. The Dems. and Reps. are tied in the House with 30 seats apiece.

Figure 6.2. Partisan Control of State Legislatures 1986

Deep South, whereas Republican control of both chambers can be disproportionately found in the Rocky Mountain region.

The majority party in each legislative chamber is in an excellent position to hold all the key legislative leadership positions, although in some states minority party members hold committee chairs. All the majority party needs to do is to hold together its members' votes when the state legislature elects its leadership at the beginning of the legislative session. Would-be party leaders vie for leadership positions within their respective partisan caucus. Candidates "run" for specific leadership positions, but as in general elections, incumbents have a decided advantage. During their tenure incumbents have incurred debts from their legislative colleagues and have established a proven track record. Often, however, leadership positions become vacant as a result of retirement, election to higher political office, appointment to administrative positions, or as happens rarely, defeat within the incumbent's own district election. Where vacancies occur, competition for leadership positions much more resembles a free-for-all, although apparent "heirs to the throne" stand prominently in the queue.

The leadership structure is similar in both chambers, even though office titles differ selectively. In the lower house the presiding officer is called the "speaker." In the senate the presiding officer is usually called the "president." The lieutenant governor is the Senate's presiding officer in thirty states, but the legislative authority vested in the lieutenant governor varies considerably among the states.[11] Where the lieutenant governor presides, but with a limited legislative role, the majority leader exercises the real power.

The power of the speaker and the president has essentially three bases: great influence over the process of legislative agenda setting and the flow of legislation within the chamber; the authority to make appointments to key legislative leadership, committee, and staff positions; and the many debts owed by legislative colleagues that have accumulated over the speaker's or president's tenure. Of the two legislative leaders, it is the speaker who tends to possess the greater power within their respective chambers, reflecting the higher degree of centralization generally found in the lower house—centralization necessary to bring order to the larger, more unwieldy chamber.

One of the more powerful speakers in the nation is California's Willie Brown. A self-made man from a poor Texas family, Brown worked his way through law school to become the second most powerful figure, next to the governor, in California politics. As Brown himself once said, being speaker in California is the "closest thing you will ever know in the world to the Ayatollah."[12] Brown has used his power as speaker adeptly, whether that be by guiding his legislative agenda through the assembly, making key committee appointments, employing assembly staff, assigning office space, or even deciding whose offices get carpeting. A black representative from liberal San Francisco, Brown has known how to mix accommodation with hardball partisan politics, as needed.

Speaker Brown has allowed the Republicans to author and, with endorsed Democratic help, pass some major legislation that traditionally would have been allowed to pass only under the majority party's authorship.[13] But Brown, with a sizable majority in the assembly, knows that he can pass almost any legislation that he wants just by retaining the support of his own party, an ability he has often demonstrated. Toward that end, not only has he skillfully employed the traditional prerogatives of the speaker's office, but he has also used his powerful legislative position to raise sizable amounts of money—approaching $2 million in an election year—in support of assembly candidates. As one Democratic assemblyman put it, "When you get that kind of money, you get grateful."[14]

The next most powerful leadership position in both chambers is that of the majority leader. The majority leader can be viewed as the party's chief lieutenant—the "right-hand man" of the speaker or president. Although the positions of deputy speaker and president pro tempore exist, the majority leader really functions as "second in command," usually assuming the role of chief legislative floor leader. In contentious floor debate it is the majority leader who gains the recognition of the presiding officer to enunciate the official party position on a bill. When the majority leader speaks in his or her official role, the membership is expected to heed the message. The majority leader also plays a key role in caucus deliberations, working continually, both inside the formal caucus (in which members of the same party meet to discuss partisan strategy and assess the strength of members' proposals) and outside in the halls, to shape a clear-cut majority position on legislation—one that will marshal a sizable majority of votes on the floor. Although a caucus chairperson presides at caucus sessions, it is the majority leader who generally plays the dominant role in amassing support. The speaker or president may selectively insert himself or herself into the caucus debate on particularly difficult or divisive issues, but such involvement is usually reserved for the "biggies."

In a few states, such as New York and Wisconsin, the majority leader exercises the real leadership in the senate. The president presides over the chamber, but the majority leader sets the legislative agenda and shepherds it through the legislative process. In New York, for example, the majority leader makes committee appointments, including naming the chairpersons; controls the legislative staff payroll and dispenses individual staff allowances; establishes the majority party's legislative agenda; and refers bills to committees. But an effective majority leader has to use these substantive and procedural resources judiciously. Instead, senators are frequently wooed and cajoled into compliance. As a perceptive observer of the New York State senate, John Pitney, Jr., has noted,

> In a tough floor vote, the majority leader uses his knowledge of the senators' needs and beliefs to choose who will be let off the hook. If their objections are rooted in principle, he and his staff can muster facts to change their minds. Persuasion conserves his resources: the more he can convince them that they are doing the right thing, the less they think of their vote as a favor to be repaid. And even if he fails to win their hearts, he can at least provide them with a defense against those who attack their vote.[15]

Under the majority leader come the deputy majority leader and floor "whip" positions, held by senior party members who are responsible for garnering the support of the rank and file. These agents of the top leadership buttonhole members and try to persuade them to follow the party line. Yet there may not be a party line on every bill passing through the chamber. Often, when a bill is not of importance to the legislative party leadership, members are free to vote their own choice. But it should be understood that when official party positions are taken on legislation, it is the speaker or president and majority leader who exercise the greatest leadership in setting legislative priorities. Such is particularly the case in the waning days of the session, when huge backlogs of unfinished legislative business accumulate. In those cases the support of the chamber's top leadership is an essential requirement even for that legislation to receive consideration on the floor. Without such singling out from among the mass of legislation awaiting action, a bill will probably die from lack of attention.

The minority party in the legislature is similarly organized, with the major exception that minority party members generally hold none of the top leadership positions in the chamber. Rare situations do occur in which a minority party leader may be elected speaker or president by a combined majority of both parties' members, but such an anomaly normally occurs only in closely divided chambers when a heated battle for majority party leadership positions has badly divided the majority party.

The minority party elects its own leaders as well as its floor whips. They play very similar roles to their majority party counterparts in floor debate and caucus deliberations. And their importance is very much a function of the relative competitiveness of their party in the state. Where legislative membership is more evenly divided, minority party strategy becomes important; for with a few defectors from the other side, the minority might be able to forge a majority position on any given piece of legislation. In such instances minority solidarity becomes essential as a core building block of a winning coalition.

The committee chairperson represents another key leadership position in the legislature. Just as the majority party generally controls the speaker's and president's office, committee chairpersons are usually drawn from among majority party members. Among lower houses, the speaker appoints committee chairs in four-fifths of the states.[16] In the others, the caucus as a whole may elect committee chairs, or appointments are made by a committee on committees made up of the majority party's top legislative leadership. The senate often presents a different picture. In several states a committee on committees (or a rules committee) makes the appointments. This is the case in Arkansas, Georgia, Illinois, Kentucky, Michigan, Montana, Nebraska, New Mexico, North Dakota, Ohio, Oklahoma, and Vermont. The full senate elects committee chairpersons in Virginia.[17] This difference in appointments between the lower house and the senate is another reason why the speaker tends to be more influential than the senate president.

Beyond the selection of committee chairpersons, the majority party is in a position to determine both the number of committees and their jurisdictions. The majority party can also establish the relative ratio of majority-to-minority members that each committee will have. That partisan ratio need not be the same for every committee. However, the majority party may give itself a higher percentage of seats on the most important committees, such as appropriations or budget. For the less significant committees, the margin of majority may be much narrower. But the majority party runs some major risks if it goes too far in skewing party representation. Not only may the majority party selectively need cooperation from the minority party on key legislation when some defection occurs, but also majorities can become minorities in the coming election. One's party might well be treated as it treated its competitor. There often is a line that, if crossed, undermines the prospects for interparty cooperation and creates a climate of partisan antagonism.

LEGISLATIVE COMMITTEES

Committees represent the "front line" of a legislature in its role as lawmaker. Committees develop subject matter expertise and get the first substantive crack at introduced legislation. They can hold bills indefinitely (short of the full legislature's action to discharge them), in effect impounding them, or they can report legislation—with or without amendment. The committee phase of the legislative process also gives members of the public an opportunity to be heard on legislative proposals since all bills assigned to committee must be scheduled for public hearing before they can be acted on by the full legislature.

Although committees exist in every state legislative body and perform similar functions in the legislative process, marked differences do exist among states. Most states have separate standing committees in each chamber of the legislature. For example, both the house and senate may have an education committee made up of members appointed from their own respective chamber and chaired by one of their own. In contrast, four states—Connecticut, Maine, Maryland, and Massachusetts—make exclusive use of joint committees, that is, committees made up of representatives from both chambers and co-chaired. Other states, like Wisconsin, rely on standing committees for the most part but employ joint committees selectively, generally for the most demanding, and often technical, substantive areas such as finance and audit. Joint committees tend to give the leadership somewhat more control over the legislative process, more readily accommodating earlier in the process the sometimes divisive rivalries that exist between the chambers. The recommendations that go to the first house for consideration have already been the subject of interchamber negotiation in the joint committee. And to facilitate such negotiations, joint committee members are frequently appointed to create a committee closely representative of the legislature as a whole. The legislative leadership makes a clear effort to ensure that not only are constituent and geographic differences reflected in the committee's membership but also the appointees have demonstrated a willingness to represent the "corporate partisan good."

The typical state senate has fifteen standing committees, and the typical lower house has twenty. The New York State senate has the most standing committees, with thirty-one, followed by the senates in North Carolina and Mississippi, with twenty-nine and twenty-eight, respectively. On the other end of the spectrum lie Massachusetts, Maryland, and Rhode Island, with six *joint* committees each, and New Mexico and Nevada, with eight and nine single-chamber committees, respectively. Among state houses or assemblies, North Carolina has the greatest number of standing committees, with fifty-eight, followed by Missouri with fifty-four. The fewest single-chamber committees can be found in South Carolina and Colorado, with eleven and twelve each. (See Table 6.2.)

Beyond standing committees, state legislatures frequently also create special

TABLE 6.2. NUMBER OF STANDING COMMITTEES

State	Senate	Lower House	Total
Alabama	22	23	45
Alaska	9	9	18
Arizona	11	16	27
Arkansas	10	10	20
California	22	30	52
Colorado	11	12	23
Connecticut			NA
Delaware	18	14	32
Florida	16	23	39
Georgia	24	28	52
Hawaii	16	19	35
Idaho	10	14	24
Illinois	18	25	43
Indiana	18	25	43
Iowa	15	15	30
Kansas	18	21	39
Kentucky	15	15	30
Louisiana	15	15	30
Maine			NA
Maryland	6	7	13
Massachusetts	6	7	13
Michigan	15	30	45
Minnesota	16	18	34
Mississippi	28	30	58
Missouri	22	54	76
Montana	17	14	31
Nebraska	Unicameral		14
Nevada	9	13	22
New Hampshire	17	23	40
New Jersey	14	19	33
New Mexico	8	16	24
New York	31	35	66
North Carolina	29	58	87
North Dakota	20	19	39
Ohio	12	26	38
Oklahoma	18	30	48
Oregon	11	13	24
Pennsylvania	21	24	45
Rhode Island	6	7	13
South Carolina	15	11	26
South Dakota	11	11	22
Tennessee	12	12	24
Texas	11	34	45
Utah	10	10	20
Vermont	12	15	27
Virginia	11	20	31
Washington	12	16	28
West Virginia	15	13	28
Wisconsin	11	26	37
Wyoming	11	12	23
Mean	15	20	35

Source: The Book of the States, 1986–87 (Lexington, KY: Council of State Governments, 1986), p. 123.

legislative committees, which are formed to examine a particular issue or problem and after the issuance of their report are dissolved. Special committees may look at such things as how to improve a state's business climate or whether and how to revamp the state budgetary process.

A pecking order exists among committees. Some are clearly more prized than others—both in the members' eyes and among close observers of a state's policy-making process. The "money" committees generally hold the greatest prestige. In most states it is within the appropriation, budget, or finance committees that the major recommendations most broadly affecting state residents are made. "Money talks," representing programmed resource commitments that cut through political rhetoric. It is also within these money committees that levels of aid for local units of government are first set by the legislature. And in those states in which the executive budget serves as the major policy-making vehicle, a seat on the appropriations or budget committee gains added importance—not just for setting appropriations but for shaping programmatic initiatives as well.

In seeking particular committee assignments, legislators are motivated by several factors. Beyond being in a position to influence the most important state policy decisions, other key factors relate to how the assignment situates the legislator to be of greatest service to his or her constituents (and thus improve one's prospects for reelection) and to pursue personal or political ambitions.

MEMBERS

The typical state legislator today is a white male whose occupation is listed as attorney or owner of his own business, as was the case a decade ago. But this fact should not lead one to believe that significant changes have not occurred in state legislative membership. First, between 1975 and 1986, the percentage of women serving in state legislatures has risen from 8 to 17 percent[18] Second, the percentage of black state legislators has also increased significantly, rising from 3.6 percent to 5.4 percent over the same period.[19]

In addition to the increased numbers of women and blacks serving in state legislatures, the occupational mix has changed. Two changes have been most notable between 1976 and 1986: a decline in attorneys, followed by business owners and farmers, and an increase in full-time legislators. Over the decade, the most dramatic change has been the decline in attorneys, from 22 percent of all legislators in 1976 to 16 percent ten years later. Looking at different regions of the country, the greatest declines in the number of attorneys occurred in the Middle Atlantic states (from 32 percent to 21 percent) and the South Central states (from 33 percent to 24 percent).

Almost matching the drop in attorneys has been the rise in full-time legislators. A 1976 study of legislators' occupations relegated the full-time legislator to a category labeled "insufficient information," which included retired members, vacant seats, and those cases where no information was available at all—collectively comprising only 9 percent of the total. By 1986 a separate category of "full-time legislator" had been added to the occupational survey, alone comprising 11 percent of all legislators. A new category of "homemaker" was also added in 1986, comprising another 2 percent of the total. With the other three headings— "retired," "seat vacant," and "insufficient information"—totaling 10 percent in 1986, the equivalent category to "insufficient information" in 1976 had increased to 23 percent of all legislators, amounting to a 144 percent increase over the ten-year period. Thus the only conclusion that can be drawn from this comparison is that the ranks of the full-time legislator have grown significantly over the past decade.

In reality, however, there are probably even more full-time legislators among the states than the recent National Conference of State Legislatures' study suggests. Many legislators list an occupation even though they spend the vast majority of their time on legislative business and have essentially ceased to practice their professions or pursue their former occupations.[20]

The rise of the full-time legislator is a phenomenon deserving of attention, having both its supporters and detractors. Supporters argue that full-time legislators are in a better position than part-timers to spend the rapidly growing time necessary to discharge their legislative duties professionally. They contend that the legislative business has significantly changed over the past decade or two. The demands now placed on legislators greatly exceed those of earlier years. State legislatures today, so the argument goes, face more numerous and complex policy issues; have become more involved in state budgeting; and have become much more active, on many fronts, in exercising oversight of the executive branch. Such demands, supporters argue, require full-time legislative attention.

Detractors take a different perspective. For them, full-time legislators can too easily become detached from the "real world." They can too easily get caught up in the "artificial capital-city mentality" of the politicians and bureaucrats who make and administer state laws. In contrast, legislators who actively pursue their "real" professions and occupations, detractors allege, better understand the problems and needs of working people; and they have a more realistic knowledge of how government affects people's lives. Detractors also often take issue with the "career paths" of full-time legislators, who increasingly, upon graduation from college, have worked as legislative aides before running for office on their own.

Despite the different perspectives on the full-time legislator, it is clear that the legislative environment has changed in most states. The exclusiveness of the "good ol' boy" legislative club has broken down. The growth in the number of women, blacks, and full-time legislators, together with the reduction in the number of attorneys, business owners, and farmers, has changed the makeup of many state legislatures. But the political culture of state legislatures has also changed. The closer social camaraderie of earlier years has given way to a more autonomous, and perhaps more competitive, professionalization of independent legislative pursuits. However, there are a few states, such as New Hampshire, Vermont, and Wyoming, where amateur legislators have remained amateurs, by choice, and where the legislative culture has remained largely unaltered. On the whole, though, the position of legislator is increasingly taking on the characteristics of a profession in its own right, and is not just a membership in an exclusive club.

LEGISLATIVE REFORM

State legislatures have undergone considerable change over the past couple of decades. Not only have the personal characteristics of the individual members changed, but the legislative institution has changed as well. One phrase might sum up the change that has occurred: professionalization of the legislative institution.

The need for reform was well documented by an exhaustive study of state legislatures conducted by the Citizens' Conference on State Legislatures in the late 1960s. Although the conference study found considerable variation in the institutional strength and professionalism of state legislatures, many were identified as being in need of major reform. Too many state legislators were popularly characterized as part-time dabblers in the business of legislating, constituency service, and administrative oversight. Legislatures were criticized for being too large and unwieldy, for meeting too infrequently, for possessing inadequate authority to initiate special sessions, for being inadequately staffed to meet the rising demands placed on the legislative institution, for providing inadequate office facilities for members, for providing insufficient compensation to attract better-quality legislators, and for not reducing the inordinate influence of interest groups through more effective regulation of lobbying.

In the course of its work, the conference established a number of factors by which each state might be rated on its relative capability. The principles underlying them were identified as follows:

1. Each chamber should be manageable in size to encourage full participation by its members.
2. Committees should be manageable in number and reasonable in member assignments.
3. Legislatures should not be limited by restrictions on frequency, length, or flexibility of sessions.
4. The legislative process should insure the fair and effective consideration of bills by all legislators and should be comprehensible to the public.
5. Competent professional and clerical staff should be available to legislative leaders and members as well as to legislative service agencies.
6. Legislative salaries should reflect the demands and importance of the job. Reimbursement should be provided for necessary expenses.
7. The powers, methods of election, and length of terms for legislative leaders should be fair, and effectively distribute power and authority.
8. Adequate office space and other facilities should be provided.
9. Provision should be made for regulating lobbyists and conflicts of interest.[21]

These nine principles were then incorporated into the following five criteria, which, in turn, were used to rate the fifty state legislatures: functional, accountable, informed, independent, and representative. A brief description of each follows:

1. *Functional*—getting the job of legislating and administrative oversight done (a legislature's workability). The functional legislature has the ability to devote adequate time and to organize itself in such a way that it can handle the growing volume of legislative business in a competent, professional manner.
2. *Accountable*—being responsive to the public it represents. The accountable legislature provides for public understanding of, and involvement in, its deliberative decision making. Members of the public have access to key documents used in the process of legislative deliberation, and the legislative process is open to public observation and input so that constituents can make judgments on how well their elected representatives are doing.
3. *Informed*—having the information necessary to make knowledgeable public choices. The informed legislature is not dependent on the executive branch or organized interests for the information it has to assess issues and analyze problems.
4. *Independent*—exercising legislative decision making apart from undue executive influence. The independent legislature is not merely a "handmaiden" to the governor or administrative agencies. It is capable of criticizing executive initiatives and of initiating viable policy alternatives, as well as overseeing the activities of executive branch agencies. Not only is the independent legislature free from executive dominance, but also it is not beholden to organized interest groups.
5. *Representative*—reflecting the diversity of the electorate who gave legislators the privilege of representing constituents' interests. The representative legislature is based on the one-man, one-vote principle. It also is responsive to its constituency's interests, whether that be in legislating, overseeing executive branch activities, or providing services for constituents.

Table 6.3 provides a comparison of the conference's ratings for each of the criteria discussed. Clearly certain states ranked high across all the measures of legislative capability. California and New York, the most populous and perhaps complex of the fifty states, led the list overall. But midwestern states accounted for six of the top ten places. Of the bottom ten, six were southern states.

Given the significant increase in the workload of state legislatures, pressures on the capacities of legislative bodies to meet the challenge have prompted state legislatures to expand their time in working sessions. In 1965 only eight states had unlimited sessions, but by 1980 that number increased to seventeen. In addition, although only four states held annual legislative sessions in 1960, that number grew to thirty-six in just two decades.[22]

With legislating becoming more of a full-time business, state legislatures turned their attention to their levels of pay and the facilities provided them. In 1970 the median salary for legislators from states holding annual sessions was $7,248, and $8,093 for those from states with biennial sessions.[23] By 1984 average annual compensation increased to $17,305, and ten states paid their legislators at least $25,000 a year. In addition, most states provided per diem payments exceeding $50 for each day the legislature was in session.[24] This higher compensation, in turn, has made it economically possible for legislators to make their elected position a full-time job.

Office facilities for legislators were also greatly improved. Instead of having to work out of one's desk on the chamber floor, legislators were given private offices. In many states this meant the construction of new legislative office buildings; in others it resulted in other nonlegislative occupants of state capitols being booted out of their capitol offices. In Wisconsin, for example, the state treasurer and secretary of state were relocated to state executive office facilities.

As legislative workloads have grown, and as more legislators have become full time, the need for additional staff and better information storage and processing capabilities became apparent. Expanded staff not only were needed to help process the increased volume of legislation but were also increasingly called on to assist legislators in their rapidly expanding supervision of state administrative agencies. And as an important tool, most legislatures established or greatly expanded their information systems, including the acquisition and upgrading of computer hardware and applications software.

With greater professionalization came an increased desire on the part of legislators to challenge the traditional prerogatives of the governor and the executive branch. But for that to become feasible, many additional staff members were needed; for one of the traditional resources available to governors, but not to legislators in many states, was the breadth of staff assistance available from within their own executive offices and from the vast resources of cabinet agencies. Most legislators were simply "outmanned." That picture, though, has been changing over the past fifteen years or so, and today most state legislatures are very much up to the task of competition.

LEGISLATIVE STAFF

Staffing state legislatures has been a real growth industry over the past two decades, and the greatest increase has come in the area of professional employment. During the six years from 1968 to 1974 alone, the number of professional legislative staff members increased by nearly 130 percent across the states.[25] The actual numbers of professional staff vary considerably among the states, even though all

TABLE 6.3. STATE LEGISLATURES: OVERALL RANKING AND FAIR CRITERIA RANKINGS

Overall	State	Functional	Accountable	Informed	Independent	Representative
1	California	1	3	2	3	2
2	New York	4	13	1	8	1
3	Illinois	17	4	6	2	13
4	Florida	5	8	4	1	30
5	Wisconsin	7	21	3	4	10
6	Iowa	6	6	5	11	25
7	Hawaii	2	11	20	7	16
8	Michigan	15	22	9	12	3
9	Nebraska	35	1	16	30	18
10	Minnesota	27	7	13	23	12
11	New Mexico	3	16	28	39	4
12	Alaska	8	29	12	6	40
13	Nevada	13	10	19	14	32
14	Oklahoma	9	27	24	22	8
15	Utah	38	5	8	29	24
16	Ohio	18	24	7	40	9
17	South Dakota	23	12	15	16	37
18	Idaho	20	9	29	27	21
19	Washington	12	17	25	19	39
20	Maryland	16	31	10	15	45
21	Pennsylvania	37	23	23	5	36
22	North Dakota	22	18	17	37	31
23	Kansas	31	15	14	32	34
24	Connecticut	39	26	26	25	6

25	West Virginia	10	32	37	24	15
26	Tennessee	30	44	11	9	26
27	Oregon	28	14	35	35	19
28	Colorado	21	25	21	28	27
29	Massachusetts	32	35	22	21	23
30	Maine	29	34	32	18	22
31	Kentucky	49	2	48	44	7
32	New Jersey	14	42	18	31	35
33	Louisiana	47	39	33	13	14
34	Virginia	25	19	27	26	48
35	Missouri	36	30	40	49	5
36	Rhode Island	33	46	30	41	11
37	Vermont	19	20	34	42	47
38	Texas	45	36	43	45	17
39	New Hampshire	34	33	42	36	43
40	Indiana	44	38	41	43	20
41	Montana	26	28	31	46	49
42	Mississippi	46	43	45	20	28
43	Arizona	11	47	38	17	50
44	South Carolina	50	45	39	10	46
45	Georgia	40	49	36	33	38
46	Arkansas	41	40	46	34	33
47	North Carolina	24	37	44	47	44
48	Delaware	43	48	47	38	29
49	Wyoming	42	41	50	48	42
50	Alabama	48	50	49	50	41

Source: Citizens' Conference on State Legislatures, The Sometime Governments (New York: Bantam Books, 1971), pp. 52–53.

states have had considerable growth. The legislatures of California, New York, Florida, and Michigan employ the greatest numbers of professional workers, and those of Delaware, North Dakota, Vermont, and Wyoming employ the fewest.[26]

Staffs have grown in all areas of legislative support—bill drafting; committee assistance; leadership and individual member assistance; partisan caucus support; and other specialized areas such as information systems, reference services, and auditing and evaluation activities. One area of particularly notable growth has been legislative fiscal staff support. Whereas the average state legislature employed 8.7 professional fiscal staff members in 1975, that number increased to 15.3 by 1981.[27] In contrast, to put that increase in perspective, professional staffs in state budget offices grew less than half as much, by about 35 percent, from an average of twenty, to twenty-seven.[28]

Who constitutes the ranks of recently hired professional staff members? Although a systematic study of legislative staffs has not been undertaken, observation of state legislatures at work, and of staff participation at national meetings, suggests that newer staff members tend to be young, having come to their new positions either directly out of college or after only a few years of work experience. Their prior employment most characteristically appears to be with other agencies of state government. Those who have established favorable reputations in state agencies, frequently while working in support areas such as budget, planning, program evaluation, and audit, are often lured away by the appeal of greater personal exposure and first-hand participation in the excitement of legislative politics and policy making.

THE CHANGING EXECUTIVE-LEGISLATIVE BALANCE

Critical observers of state politics have pointed to the governor as being best able to set the state's policy agenda.[29] After all, scholars traditionally viewed the governor as possessing most of the resources necessary for successful political competition. Beyond drawing on executive office staff, the governor can tap the vast staff resources available in the many cabinet agencies of the state bureaucracy. In addition, the governor is in a position to create task forces and commissions to consider issues and offer recommendations for gubernatorial and legislative action.

In contrast, academic observers in the 1960s and early 1970s characterized state legislatures as institutionally weak and reactive to the chief executive's initiatives.[30] Legislatures were understaffed, and the severe constraints on legislative activity, associated with limited sessions and part-time legislators, yielded a marked advantage to the governor and the executive branch. But not only have state legislatures become far better staffed today, they have also challenged the governor in areas of traditional executive prerogative. The following discussion covers several areas of legislative penetration.

Legislative Budgeting

Legislative fiscal bureaus and budget offices have been created and well staffed in order to add coherence to legislative budgeting—to bring some central order to an otherwise fragmented and disjointed legislative appropriations process. In addition to summarizing executive budget recommendations, legislative budget staffs develop and present alternatives to gubernatorial recommendations and, in some states, even present recommendations to legislative fiscal committees and their respective chambers. A prominent example of the latter can be found in California, where the Legislative Analyst's Office, with a professional staff of about sixty, presents a comprehensive package of alternatives to the governor's executive budget recommendations, complete with an analysis of their collective fiscal effect.[31] In other states, like Wisconsin, fiscal staffs may offer alternatives but not make recommendations as such. Yet the way in which the alternatives are presented often clearly suggests the staffs' preferences. Staffs also play an important role in "keeping score" of how legislative budget decisions modify the executive budget and affect the fiscal "bottom line."

State legislatures have also gotten more involved in the *review of federal funds*, an area of long-standing executive prerogative. Under the "separation of powers" doctrine and closely tied to the governor's role of chief state administrator, the receipt and use of federal funds has traditionally been viewed as a matter of executive discretion. As recently as 1979, most state legislatures failed to appropriate federal funds. Instead, estimates of federal expenditures usually appeared in the appropriations schedule in place of sum-certain appropriations (in which the appropriation numbers are binding and serve as the basis of financial control). Conversely, where estimates were used, actual expenditures often varied from them considerably.

This picture had changed dramatically by the early 1980s. In the 1981 legislative session alone, almost half the state legislatures enacted statutes increasing their oversight of federal funds and placing controls on the administration and expenditure of federal block grants.[32] By 1983, thirty-seven state legislatures had acquired the authority to make sum-certain appropriations of federal funds.[33] State statutes in twenty-five states require the executive branch to seek the advice and/or approval of the legislature before spending interim federal funds (i.e., funds received by the state after the state budget has been passed by the legislature).[34] In addition, nineteen states established computerized information systems to track the receipt and expenditure of federal funds.[35]

The courts have been drawn into the issue of executive-legislative competition. Pennsylvania provided the setting for a landmark case. In 1980 the Pennsylvania legislature gave itself the authority to appropriate federal grant dollars on a line-item basis. Upon petition by the governor, a lower state court and, subsequently, the state supreme court ruled that the law was not in violation of the state's constitution. The U.S. Supreme Court, upon appeal, refused to consider the case, thus in effect sustaining the state court's decision in *Shapp v. Sloan*. Other subsequent state litigation shows a mixed pattern. Whereas decisions in the state courts of Kansas, Montana, and New York supported the position of the legislature, state courts ruled against the legislature in Arizona, Colorado, Massachusetts, and New Mexico.

The issue of *interim* legislative control over federal funds has been the subject of other litigation. But the pattern is more consistent. Courts in Alaska, Missouri, Montana, North Carolina, and Oklahoma all ruled against legislative committees acting on behalf of the full legislature.[36] It is one thing for legislatures to assume control of federal funds, and quite another for them to delegate that responsibility to a single committee. The former practice has been adjudged tenuous among the states, but the courts have consistently found delegation to be unlawful.

Legislative Review of Administrative Rules

As mentioned in Chapter 5, state agencies promulgate administrative rules that have the force of law. Such rules cover everything from the criteria to be used by a state highway department in ranking highway construction projects to safety requirements for commercial buildings in providing public access. Although administrative agencies have the authority to make rules following a statutorily prescribed process that involves public notice and hearing requirements, the rule-making process in most states provides a role for legislative supervision. In structuring that supervision, state legislatures have assumed various degrees of authority. Whereas legislatures in forty-one states have adopted some form of legislative oversight, whether that be review of proposed or existing rules, twenty-one have assumed the authority to veto, suspend, or modify agency rules.[37] Thirteen state legislatures give a legislative standing committee the authority to suspend rules, but in nine of those states the entire legislature must sustain the committee's action.[38]

That power has not been exercised without controversy. The point of contention concerns whether legislatures are empowered to veto executive acts without passing legislation, which the governor, in turn, has the opportunity to veto. What is in question is the authority of a legislative committee to suspend or repeal administrative rules outside of the normal legislative process.

Numerous state courts have ruled that the delegated legislative veto is in violation of their state constitutions, among them Alaska, Connecticut, Montana, New Hampshire, New Jersey, and West Virginia.[39] At the federal level, the U.S. Supreme Court has held that the legislative veto by Congress represents a violation of the "separation of powers" doctrine.[40] But since the decision was directed at the U.S. Congress, the implications of this decision for the states are presently unclear.

Sunset Laws

Another form of legislative oversight of the executive branch is the "sunset" law. Sunset laws mandate the termination of designated agencies after prescribed periods unless the legislature acts to continue them. Sunset laws are based on the premise that state agencies should periodically be forced to justify their existence, to demonstrate that they are accomplishing what they are statutorily charged to do and that they are doing it efficiently. Agencies that are determined to have outlived their usefulness, the theory goes, can be allowed to go out of existence. In addition, discrete laws can have sunset provisions attached, which wipe a law off the books unless the legislature acts to extend it.

In practice, sunset laws have accomplished very little of substance. Instead, they have served primarily a largely symbolic function, creating a perception that legislators are cracking down on unbridled government growth or pruning ineffective government activities. Rather than resulting in termination of major state agencies, sunset laws have largely been used as the basis for "beating up on the barbershop inspectors." A few of the smaller regulatory agencies, most often those involving the licensing of some occupations, have been eliminated in a few states. As Alan Rosenthal, a close observer of state government, has observed, "Often what is removed is merely a nominal organizational structure, and not much else."[41] Pennsylvania, however, appears to be an exception. There, sunset review led to reform of the state's public utility commission, and it may soon lead to the abolition of state liquor stores, which have a monopoly on liquor sales within the state.

What sunset laws have accomplished in several states, apart from their sparse record of bureaucratic reduction, is reinforcement of the legislature's role in oversight or administration. Through the review process associated with planned termination, legislative committees have come to learn much more about agency programs and operations. Even though it is not very realistic to expect that a highway or welfare department will be allowed to go out of business, the process of legislative review might turn up a number of issues or problems that could receive further attention in budget reviews or legislative audits.

The Legislative Audit

Whereas the legislature appoints auditors in most states, the people directly elect them in twenty states. Where popularly elected, state auditors tend to work more independently of the legislatures. In addition, ten states have both an elected state auditor and a legislative auditor, who is usually appointed by the legislative leadership or by the chairperson of the legislature's fiscal committee. In five other states the state auditor is an executive branch official, appointed by the governor or the head of the state's chief administrative agency.[42]

Legislative audit agencies across the states have recently been turning away from financial audits to program or performance audits. Instead of exclusively examining whether the state's "books" balance, auditors have turned their attention toward assessing the degree to which programs are achieving their intended objectives. Such a review might assess, for example, the extent to which "halfway house," work-release programs have contributed to reduced recidivism, that is, lowered repeat criminal offenses. Another example might be a legislative assessment of the degree to which state universities have complied with statutory requirements governing the award of state-funded student financial aid. These new priorities have meant that legislative audit agencies in several states have refused to perform customary end-of-year agency or grant financial audits, arguing that they simply do not have sufficient staff members to continue business as usual with the added program auditing responsibilities. The resulting void in several states has had to be filled through the increased use of private audit firms under contract to state agencies.

Legislative auditors do not function autonomously; legislative committees approve the auditors' agenda, oversee the audit process, accept or reject audit reports, and propose legislation that takes corrective action. But although the committees may vote on which audits should be undertaken and in what order, the legislative auditor (referred to as the "state auditor" in some states) can greatly influence audit agenda setting—not only in terms of which audits are undertaken but also concerning what is actually examined. The auditor is also in a position to suggest how aggressively an audit committee should air its findings in public hearings and how doggedly it should hold agencies accountable for complying with audit recommendations.

Program or performance audits generally result in recommended administrative or managerial changes that state agencies are charged with implementing. In the course of the audit process, agencies are characteristically given the opportunity to comment on audit findings and proposed recommendations in draft form. After reviewing the agencies' responses, the audit bureau may make changes in what will become the final report. However, once a determination is made about the content of the final report, the agencies may be given a last opportunity to submit written comments, which most often are transmitted to the audit committee along with the report. Upon receiving the audit report, the committee schedules a public hearing at which the affected agencies are invited to appear. The committee will then vote to accept or reject the report's recommendations and may endorse legislative proposals offered to the full legislature for consideration.

An eight-year study of legislative program audits, involving nearly 500 reports from thirty-one states, reviewed the nature of their recommendations. Almost 90 percent recommended that agencies adopt administrative and managerial improvements on their own. About one-half proposed statutory changes, and about one-quarter recommended that the legislature pursue budgetary adjustments—providing a significant source of legislative initiatives.[43]

LEGISLATIVE DECISION MAKING

On what bases do legislators make their decisions? Studies of legislative decision making consistently point to seven factors that most systematically appear to influence legislative choice: (1) partisanship—party positions or stances taken by party leaders, (2) the individual legislator's ideology, (3) committee recommendations, (4) staff recommendations, (5) organized interest group positions, (6) the governor's recommendations and wishes, and (7) constituent interests. Of these factors, research most consistently supports political parties as exercising the most consistent and enduring influence on the policy choices made by state legislators. Yet this finding is in need of qualification because the relevance of party as a major factor in legislative decision making varies among the states, depending on the relative strength and competitiveness of parties in a given state and, to a lesser extent, on the nature of the issues being debated. Partisanship appears to be of stronger influence in urbanized and industrial states, which generally have greater electoral competitiveness, reflecting urban, suburban, and rural divisions. And in competitive industrial states, Democrats tend to represent the urban residents, whereas Republicans generally represent suburban and rural interests.

Ideology appears to exert an influence on legislative decision making that is independent of partisanship. Ideology can be defined as "a set of general attitudes about the proper role of government in the allocation of values in society, containing a general evaluation of the status quo of wealth and power, and a general orientation toward the extent and nature of any changes that government should pursue."[44] Partisan competition and ideology appear to be related; the greater the competition, the more likely that legislatures will adopt liberal policies.

Chapter 8 provides an in-depth discussion of how the legislature, as an institution, makes policy through its lawmaking function.

SUMMARY AND CONCLUSIONS

State legislatures have come a long way over the past couple of decades. They have generally come into their own as formidable competitors in state policy making. But this is not to suggest that governors or the executive branch have lost the resources that have made, and continue to make, them highly influential institutional participants in state policy making, for they certainly have not. What it does suggest is that the legislature, as an institution, has been greatly strengthened. Today, in most states one sees strong legislatures confronting strong governors on matters of policy, reflecting the overall strengthening of the state in domestic policy making. Divided partisan loyalties between the two branches may fuel that competition, but institutional rivalry and the issue of institutional prerogatives exert strong nonpartisan forces as well. Not only are legislatures exerting themselves in the legislative function, but they are also challenging the governor and executive branch in matters of traditional executive prerogative. They are dealing not from a position of structural weakness but from one of growing strength, and they are pressing their challenge on several fronts.

REFERENCES

1. *The Book of the States, 1980–81* (Lexington, KY: Council of State Governments, 1980), pp. 86–87.
2. 369 U.S. 186 (1962).
3. 84 S. Ct. 1362 (1964).
4. 84 S. Ct. 526 (1964).
5. Ibid.
6. 430 U.S. 144 (1977).
7. Sarah McCally Morehouse, *State Politics, Parties and Policy* (New York: Holt, Rinehart and Winston, 1981), p. 262.
8. Robert S. Erikson, "The Partisan Impact of State Legislative Reapportionment," *Midwest Journal of Political Science*, Vol. 15, No. 1 (Feb. 1971), 70.

9. Timothy O'Rourke, *The Impact of Reapportionment* (New Brunswick, NJ: Transaction Books, 1980).
10. *The Book of the States, 1986–87* (Lexington, KY: Council of State Governments, 1986), p. 87.
11. Alan Rosenthal, *Legislative Life* (New York: Harper & Row, 1981), p. 151.
12. Daniel J. Blackburn, "How Willie Brown Solidified His Speakership," in Thomas R. Hoeber and Charles M. Price, eds., *California Government Politics Annual 84–85* (Sacramento: California Journal Press, 1984), p.46.
13. Richard Zeiger, "The Odd Couple," in Thomas R. Hoeber and Charles M. Price, eds., *California Government and Politics Annual 86–87* (Sacramento: California Journal Press, 1986), p. 51.
14. Alan Rosenthal, "If the Party's Over, Where's All That Noise Coming From?" *State Government*, Vol. 57, No. 2 (1984), 53.
15. John J. Pitney, Jr., "Leaders and Rules in the New York State Senate," *Legislative Studies Quarterly*, Vol. 7, No. 4 (Nov. 1982), 502.
16. Rosenthal, *Legislative Life*, p. 163.
17. Ibid.
18. *National Directory of Women Elected Officials, 1985* (Washington, DC: National Women's Political Caucus, 1985), p. 10; *State Legislators' Occupations: A Decade of Change* (Denver, CO: National Conference of State Legislatures, 1986), p. 5.
19. Joint Center for Political Studies, Washington, DC, telephone inquiry, February 2, 1987.
20. *State Legislators' Occupations*, pp. 2–9.
21. *The Sometimes Governments: A Critical Study of the 50 American Legislatures*, 2nd ed. (Kansas City, MO: Citizens' Conference on State Legislatures, 1973), pp. 41–42.
22. Ann O'M. Bowman and Richard C. Kearney, *The Resurgence of the States* (Englewood Cliffs, NJ: Prentice-Hall, 1986), p. 82.
23. Ibid., p. 88.
24. *Book of the States, 1986–87*, pp. 95–96.
25. Gary J. Clarke and Charles R. Grezlak, "Legislative Staffs Show Improvement," *National Civic Review*, Vol. 65, No. 6 (June 1976), 292.
26. Lucinda S. Simon, *A Legislator's Guide to Staffing Patterns* (Denver, CO: National Conference of State Legislatures, 1979), p. 43.
27. The 1975 information was provided by the National Conference of State Legislatures, Denver, CO. The 1982 information is from *Legislative Budget Procedures in the 50 States* (Denver, CO: National Conference of State Legislatures, 1983), p. 75.
28. *Budgetary Processes in the States* (Washington, DC: National Association of State Budget Officers, 1976 and 1981), pp. 7 and 11, respectively.
29. Malcolm E. Jewell, "State Decision Making: The Governor Revisited," in Aaron Wildavsky and Nelson W. Polsby, eds., *American Governmental Institutions* (Chicago: Rand McNally, 1968); Alan J. Wyner, "Gubernatorial Relations with Legislators and Administrators," *State Government*, Vol. 41, No. 3 (Summer 1968), 199-203; Ira Sharkansky, "Agency Requests, Gubernatorial Support and Budget Success in State Legislatures," *American Political Science Review*, Vol. 62, No. 4 (Dec. 1968), 1220–1231; Sarah McCally Morehouse, "The Governor as Political Leader," in Herbert Jacob et. al., eds., *Politics in the American States*, 3rd ed. (Boston: Little, Brown, 1976), pp. 196–241; Coleman B. Ransome, Jr., *The American Governorship* (New York: Greenwood Press, 1982); Thad L. Beyle, "Governors," in Virginia Gray et. al., eds.,

Politics in the American States, 4th ed. (Boston: Little, Brown, 1983), pp. 180–221; Larry Sabato, *Goodbye to Goodtime Charlie*, 2nd ed. (Washington, DC: Congressional Quarterly Press, 1983).

30. J.D. Barber, *The Lawmakers* (New Haven, CT: Yale University Press, 1965); John Burns, *The Sometime Governments: A Critical Study of the Fifty American Legislatures* (New York: Bantam Books, 1971); Malcolm E. Jewell and Samuel C. Patterson, *The Legislative Process in the United States* (New York: Random House, 1966); William J. Keefe, "The Functions and Powers of State Legislatures," in Alexander Heard, ed., *State Legislatures in American Politics* (Englewood Cliffs, NJ: Prentice-Hall, 1966); D. B. Truman, *The Government Process*, 2nd ed. (New York: Knopf, 1971); Alan Rosenthal, *Legislative Performance in the States* (New York: Free Press, 1974).

31. *Report of the Legislative Analyst for Fiscal Year 1984-85* (Sacramento, CA: Legislative Analyst, 1986).

32. William Pound, "The State Legislatures," *The Book of the States, 1982-83* (Lexington, KY: Council of State Governments, 1982), p. 184.

33. *Legislative Budget Procedures in the 50 States*, p. 96.

34. Barbara Yondorf, *A Legislator's Guide to Budget Oversight* (Denver, CO: National Conference of State Legislatures, 1983), pp. 36–37.

35. *Book of the States, 1986-87*, pp. 138–39.

36. Yondorf, *Legislator's Guide*, pp. 79-80; Carol S. Weissert, "State Legislative Oversight of Federal Funds," *State Government*, Vol. 53, No. 2 (Spring 1980), 77–80.

37. *Book of the States, 1986-87*, p. 133.

38. Ibid.

39. Alan Rosenthal, "Legislative Oversight and the Balance of Power in State Government," *State Government*, Vol. 56, No. 3 (1983), 94.

40. *Immigration and Naturalization Service v. Chadha*, 1983.

41. Rosenthal, *Legislative Life*, p. 323.

42. Information provided by the State Auditor Training Program, Council of State Governments, Lexington, KY, Oct. 1986.

43. Rosenthal, *Legislative Life*, pp. 326–28.

44. Robert M. Entman, "The Impact of Ideology on Legislative Behavior and Public Policy in the States," *Journal of Politics*, Vol. 45, No. 1 (Feb. 1983), 165–66.

CHAPTER 7

State Courts and Attorneys General

Virtually everyone will have to be in court sometime. Obviously, those accused of crime and those doing the accusing will deal with lawyers and judges. Individuals also go to court when they have a dispute with someone else, over a contract or ownership of property or the like. Those serving on juries will also participate in the judiciary system.

Courts exist to resolve disputes. They play the role of a third, neutral party who knows the law and will apply it fairly. Courts also play administrative and legislative roles. The judicial branch of state governments certifies adoptions and name changes, processes wills, and licenses lawyers. These functions are not substantively different from those of administrative agencies that register births and deaths, process tax returns, and license workers in various professions.

Courts make public policy as they decide cases. It is not always possible for courts to resolve a dispute by ascertaining the facts of a case and then fitting those facts to the law. Even if the facts are clear, the law may be vague or even contradictory. Legislators and framers of constitutions cannot anticipate every unique instance. When the court clarifies the law while making a ruling on a case, in a very real sense new law is created, both for that case and for similar situations. Sometimes the clarifications are minor and not controversial. In other instances, like determining circumstances that meet the definition of obscenity or disturbing the peace, the court makes a major contribution to public policy making and can be at the center of debate and dispute.

Although the courts share the authority and the discretion of other policy-making institutions, they are distinct from the bureaucracy, the governor, and the legislature in one major way—the courts may not set their own agenda. Legislators, governors, and administrators can initiate new policies. Judges cannot initiate litigation. The policies made by judges are limited to the ambiguities and contra-

126

dictions that exist in the cases they adjudicate. The conflicts resolved by the courts are only those that are brought before the bench.

This chapter will discuss the roles and characteristics of state courts. A special part of this discussion will be the description of the attorney general's office in state government. The attorney general is the chief law enforcement officer in a state, and like the courts, engages in the formulation and clarification as well as the application of state laws.

STATE AND FEDERAL COURTS

Not only are we all bound to have some interaction in our life with courts, but also most of that interaction will be with state courts. State courts have jurisdiction over traffic violations, divorces, wills, most contracts, crimes against persons and property, and the decisions and processes of state institutions. Litigation in state courts includes, in other words, the areas that affect the daily lives of most people. The jurisdiction of federal courts is limited to disputes involving federal constitutional rights, federal laws, and the activities of federal agencies and institutions.

Contrary to common views, the courts in the United States are not all part of a single system, with the U.S. Supreme Court at the head. Instead, state and federal courts have their own systems, with their own types of cases and their own routes for appeals. These two systems only overlap when a case involves both state and federal laws or constitutions. If, for example, you were arrested for a traffic violation, you could contest the charge in a state court. You could not have the case tried in a federal court, and you could not appeal the verdict to a federal court unless you went beyond the traffic violation and involved some federal law or constitutional provision. To secure access to a federal court, you would have to allege, for example, that in making the arrest the local law enforcement official violated your right to due process. (The Fifth Amendment of the U.S. Constitution provides the right to know what crime one supposedly committed, the right to have a lawyer, and the right to avoid self-incrimination.) Figure 7.1 illustrates the state-federal court relationship.

When federal and state laws overlap, the general rule is that the federal law prevails. If a state, for example, said that employers may discriminate on the basis of race when they hire people, that policy would directly contradict the Fourteenth Amendment to the U.S. Constitution and Title VII of the federal 1964 Civil Rights Act. The federal law would be the one that applies. Not only would federal courts so rule, but state courts, through a process known as "inclusion," would on their own abandon the state law in favor of the federal. Federal courts and federal law are in this way regarded as supreme.[1]

Some issues are not "either-or" but instead raise questions of "more or less." For example, the Fifth Amendment to the U.S. Constitution provides basic due process rights, and the U.S. Supreme Court has through its rulings upheld and specified those rights. States can add to those rights, but they cannot subtract from them. The federal government, in other words, provides a floor and the

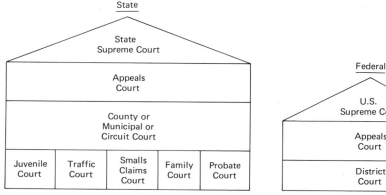
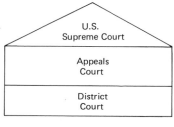

Figure 7.1. State and Federal Courts

states can determine ceilings. Where states supplement federally guaranteed rights, state courts are the arena for litigation regarding the added protections.[2]

Since the mid-1970s, state courts have taken the lead in elaborating individual rights under the constitution. Table 7.1 shows the dramatic increase in the number of times during the 1970s and 1980s that state courts have granted greater rights to individuals than those guaranteed under U.S. Supreme Court interpretations of the U.S. Constitution. Note that Table 7.1 includes only part of the decade of the 1980s.

This activity by state courts has been encouraged and monitored by the U.S. Supreme Court. Justice William J. Brennan wrote an essay in the *Harvard Law Review* in 1977 urging state courts to look to their own constitutions to enhance the rights of individuals.[3] Former Chief Justice Warren Burger celebrated the de-

TABLE 7.1. STATE SUPREME COURT DECISIONS EXTENDING CONSTITUTIONAL RIGHTS

Years	Number	Percent of Total
1950–1959	3	1.0
1960–1969	7	2.2
1970–1979	124	39.9
1980–1986	177	56.9
Total	311	100.0

Note: Figures are through August 1986. *(Source: Ronald K. L. Collins and Peter J. Galie, "State Constitutional Rights Decisions," National Law Journal, Aug. 11, 1986.)*

crease in rulings by the U.S. Supreme Court and the increase in state courts as the judicial version of "new federalism."[4]

It is easy to imagine widely different laws and court rulings on the same issues or crimes as one goes from state to state. The exercise of discretion by the fifty state court systems has not, however, entailed great diversity and inconsistencies in the courtrooms around the country. Several traditions and principles work to provide cohesiveness in our judicial system across state boundaries:

1. The "inclusion" of U.S. Supreme Court rulings into the framework within which state judges make decisions provides a common set of standards for state courts. Legal reasoning, by lawyers and by judges, applies to a dispute the precedents set by rulings in similar cases. This practice is reinforced by the desire of judges to avoid having their decisions overturned by courts hearing cases on appeal. Thus rulings by the U.S. Supreme Court not only set precedents but also provide clues to those judges wanting to have their decisions upheld.
2. Certain states have established reputations as leaders in developing and clarifying legal principles through the decisions of their courts. Judges and lawyers around the country look to these states and cite their rulings in presenting their own arguments, much like they watch and cite the actions of the U.S. Supreme Court.[5] The state supreme courts of New York and Massachusetts were cited by courts in other states most frequently in the first half of the twentieth century. California has been the most frequently cited court since World War II.[6]
3. The common law tradition, originating in the British jurisprudence system and becoming part of our colonial legacy, is central to state courts. Common law originated as an aggregation of the decisions made by judges in England in the thirteenth century. Although common law is not always in written form, it is nonetheless applied by courts as they decide issues regarding family disputes, charges of indecency and disorderly conduct, and allegations of criminal behavior. Even with its rich ethnic and regional diversity, the United States generally subscribes to the basic edicts of Anglo-American culture and common law. Louisiana used to be an exception. It followed the Napoleonic Code of French tradition. Today, however, even Louisiana subscribes to common law principles. The workload of state courts primarily involves family, criminal, and contractual matters, and common law traditions provide the standards for rulings in these areas.

Despite the inevitable diversity in different courtrooms and in different states, some basic common standards are useful so that individuals and organizations can predict the likely outcomes of their disputes. The knowledge of which party would probably prevail in litigation tends to reduce the workload of the courts. In addition, except for cases in which crimes are committed out of emotion or desperation, the predictability of what will happen in court may affect the behavior of those contemplating criminal acts.

The ability to predict process as well as outcome is also valuable. Like other government institutions, courts have established ways in which they consider issues and make decisions. Again, although there are some differences, there are also common patterns in the structures and procedures used in courts among the states.

STRUCTURES AND PROCEDURES

For a case to be brought to court, someone who has been injured or is in danger of being injured must bring a charge against someone else. The party bringing the charge is referred to as a *plaintiff*. The party being accused is the *defendant*. Our legal system is based on an adversarial process in which two (or more) sides argue facts and principles and rely on the court to act as referee.

Upon receiving a plea for action, the court first determines whether the plaintiff has standing and whether the complaint involves or potentially involves a violation of law. *Standing* is a legal determination that the plaintiff has indeed suffered some kind of damage or injury or is about to suffer damage or injury. Courts in the United States have avoided becoming the arena for a debate between people who simply have different opinions and want a judge or jury to decide who is right. People who think as a matter of principle that government should be stricter about false advertising by businesses do not have standing in court, but someone who has been lured into buying an appliance that cannot do all that was promised can proceed. Standing is not enough, however. The accusation must point to a law that was broken and someone (individual or organization) must explicitly be accused. A specific business must be named as having violated an existing law requiring truthful advertising. The purchaser of the overrated appliance cannot go to court complaining that the legislature should pass a better law protecting customers from overzealous salespeople.

Specialized and Lower Courts

With few exceptions, cases must begin at the most local level possible. The lowest traditional level of state courts is the justice of the peace. The justice of the peace, who has vanished in court reorganizations that many states adopted in the 1970s,[7] was a local official who handled everything from marriages to traffic violations. Justices of the peace have been a favorite subject of humor and ridicule in American theater and screen. Typical scenes depict an unscrupulous and sometimes pompous person of minimal intelligence enjoying the power he wields over a stranger passing through town. A justice of the peace decided cases without a jury. Often, the position was filled through patronage, and remuneration depended at least in part on the fines collected. All the ingredients for injustice existed, especially when the justice of the peace also doubled as local sheriff.

Figure 7.2 illustrates the common state court structure. State court systems

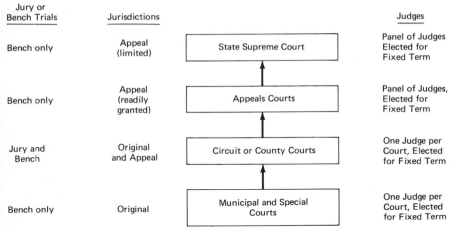

Jury or Bench Trials	Jurisdictions		Judges
Bench only	Appeal (limited)	State Supreme Court	Panel of Judges Elected for Fixed Term
Bench only	Appeal (readily granted)	Appeals Courts	Panel of Judges, Elected for Fixed Term
Jury and Bench	Original and Appeal	Circuit or County Courts	One Judge per Court, Elected for Fixed Term
Bench only	Original	Municipal and Special Courts	One Judge per Court, Elected for Fixed Term

Figure 7.2. General State Court Structure

typically begin with various courts that specialize in small claims (disputes involving less than $500), traffic violations, family issues, juvenile cases, and wills. In addition, courts that have general jurisdiction are at the lowest level. General jurisdictional courts can be found in both rural and urban areas. Specialized courts tend to exist only in urban areas. Most specialized courts have a single judge presiding with no jury.

The lowest level of general jurisdiction courts are most commonly called district, circuit, municipal, or county courts. Over 1,500 of these courts exist in the United States, and most of them have either a city or a county as their geographic area of jurisdiction. These courts also have one judge presiding, but litigants can petition for a jury trial. If specialized courts exist within a district or municipal court, the case can be appealed to the general jurisdiction court. If this happens, the case is presented and argued in its entirety as if it were the first time the case were being tried. An important role of judges and juries as they hear the evidence and the arguments is to make an assessment of the credibility of the litigants and witnesses. Especially when both sides have a reasonable case to present, the one who seems most sincere and honest (even if it is good acting) is likely to prevail.

Appeals Courts
Those unhappy with the decisions of district or municipal courts may appeal their cases. Depending on the state, appeals courts are either a panel of judges or a single judge. Appeals courts do not include juries, and they do not try the case over from the start. Appeals courts do not hear testimony from witnesses, and therefore they must defer to the conclusions of lower courts regarding the credibility of witnesses. The judges in state appellate courts review cases as they have already been presented and then consider the arguments of lawyers about whether

the original court used a flawed process and/or whether the judge or jury made an error in reasoning. Appeals in thirteen states are made directly to a state supreme court. The other thirty-seven states have an intermediate appeals court that hears cases, and the supreme court considers cases appealed beyond the intermediate level.[8]

Supreme Courts

As mentioned, the state supreme courts are the last step in litigation, unless the U.S. Constitution, a federal law, or a treaty is involved. State supreme courts must—in most states—rule on all cases presented to them. They may not, like the U.S. Supreme Court, refuse to hear some cases, thereby letting the judgments of lower courts stand. State supreme courts usually have seven members, although some states have as few as three and others as many as nine.

ROLE OF STATE'S ATTORNEY OR ATTORNEY GENERAL

In cases involving criminal law, where the victim or alleged victim has been killed, has been physically injured, or has suffered loss or damage to property, society acts as the plaintiff. The local district attorney will initiate and pursue the necessary legal action once he or she has evidence indicating who committed the crime. The state attorney general provides consultation, training, and investigatory assistance to district attorneys.

When government jurisdictions are involved in legal disputes other than criminal cases, the district attorneys at the local level and the attorneys general at the state level act as the lawyer. They can, in other words, be representing either the plaintiff or the defendant, depending on whether government is accusing or being accused. Agencies in state government sometimes have their own legal staff. The attorney general is available for advice and assistance, much like the assistance provided to district attorneys. The attorney general might also be acting as lawyer for one agency and in combat with the legal staff of another agency.

Most attorneys general and district attorneys, or state's attorneys, as they are called in some states, are elected to office. The governor appoints the attorney general in Alaska, Hawaii, Wyoming, Tennessee, New Jersey, and New Hampshire. In Maine, the attorney general is elected by both houses of the legislature every other year. Invariably, attorneys general are lawyers, although only twenty-seven states require this qualification. For those who must run for office, the keys to electoral success are, of course, the image, policy positions, party identity, and name recognition that are instrumental in getting any candidate into office. With election comes independence from the governor. The attorney general of the United States does not have independence, since he or she is appointed by and serves at the pleasure of the president.

The independence of the attorney general and the role of being the lawyer for state government can create conflict, especially when the attorney general and the governor are rivals. A governor cannot command an attorney general to defend a certain action or to sue a particular company, jurisdiction, or individual. When such a command is prompted more out of a governor's personal or political interest than concern for the state, the independence of the attorney general is celebrated. When conflict between the governor and the attorney general obstruct the operations of state government, on the other hand, this independence is bemoaned.

One of the roles of attorneys general that can have considerable policy and political impact is the issuance of legal opinions. As indicated in Table 7.2, all attorneys general provide formal legal opinions to other state officials. Unlike courts, a state's attorney general can conduct a legal analysis and then formally give an opinion on whether an action or a contemplated action is legal or constitutional. These opinions are not legally binding but can thwart or prompt legislative and administrative behavior in state governments. Participants in the policy-making process will seek an attorney general's opinion as a way of getting support for their own position or as a way of combatting a charge that a proposal is unconstitutional. The substance and the timing of an opinion can be critical to the success or failure of a policy initiative.

Some states have given their attorneys general responsibility beyond acting as lawyers for government. Table 7.2 presents these roles. The most common one is providing protection to consumers from reckless and unscrupulous businesses. In a sense, this is an extension of the role of monitoring businesses for unfair competitive practices in order to establish monopolies. The antitrust responsibilities assumed by attorneys general at the beginning of this century was supplemented with consumer protection authority in mid-century. Antitrust measures protect businesses from one another. The focus on individual consumer protection has led to action against mail-order fraud, schemes that entice sales or investments with false or misleading promises of prizes and trips, and tougher restrictions on how insurance policies can be sold.

PROCESS

One of the adages that applies to the judicial system is "Justice delayed is justice denied." A contested will can take so long that the principal beneficiaries may die before it is settled. That is certainly an example of injustice because of a slow judicial process. Likewise, someone who seeks damages because of an injury should have the matter resolved as soon as possible so that person can make financial and rehabilitation plans. Individuals accused of rape or murder should either begin a prison term or be declared not guilty rather than be held in jail or restricted by bail provisions for a long time awaiting trial.

To provide for a fair and expeditious court process, a number of practices are followed.

Grand Jury. The first practice, submission of a case to a grand jury before filing a case in court, is the least effective in providing for either fairness or expediency.

TABLE 7.2. ATTORNEY GENERAL'S ROLES

State	Serves as Counsel for State	Appears for State in Criminal Appeals	Litigates for State Agencies	Litigates Against State Agencies	Reviews Administrative Rules	Issues Advisory Opinions	Reviews Legislation Before Passage	Reviews Legislation Before Signing	Antitrust Duties	Administers Consumer Protection Agencies	Represents State Before Regulatory Agencies	May Intervene in Local Prosecutions	May Supersede Local Prosecutor
Alabama	×	×	×	×	×	×	×	×	×	×		×	×
Alaska	×	×	×	×	×	×	×		×	×	×	×	×
Arizona	×	×	×	×	×	×	×		×	×		×	×
Arkansas	×	×	×		×	×	×		×	×	×	×	
California	×	×	×	×		×	×		×	×	×	×	×
Colorado	×		×	×		×	×	×	×	×	×	×	×
Connecticut	×	×	×		×	×	×	×	×	×	×		
Delaware	×	×	×		×	×	×	×	×	×			
Florida	×	×	×	×	×	×	×	×	×		×	×	×
Georgia	×	×	×	×	×	×	×	×	×	×	×	×	×
Hawaii	×	×	×	×	×	×	×	×	×	×	×	×	×
Idaho	×	×	×	×		×	×	×	×	×	×	×	×
Illinois	×	×	×		×	×	×	×	×	×	×	×	×
Indiana	×	×	×	×	×	×		×	×	×	×		
Iowa	×	×	×	×	×	×	×	×	×	×	×		
Kansas	×	×	×	×	×	×	×		×		×	×	×
Kentucky	×	×	×		×	×	×	×	×	×	×	×	×
Louisiana	×	×	×	×	×	×	×	×	×	×	×	×	×
Maine	×	×	×		×	×	×	×	×	×		×	×
Maryland	×	×	×		×	×	×	×	×		×	×	×

State													
Massachusetts	x	x	x	x		x		x	x	x		x	x	x
Michigan	x	x	x	x		x		x	x	x	x	x	x	x
Minnesota	x	x	x	x		x		x	x	x	x	x	x	x
Mississippi	x	x	x	x		x		x		x	x	x	x	
Missouri	x	x	x	x		x		x	x		x	x		
Montana	x	x	x	x		x		x	x	x		x	x	x
Nebraska	x	x	x	x	x	x		x	x	x	x	x	x	x
Nevada	x	x	x	x		x		x	x			x	x	x
New Hampshire	x	x	x	x	x	x		x	x	x	x	x	x	x
New Jersey	x	x	x	x	x	x		x	x	x	x	x	x	x
New Mexico	x	x	x	x	x	x		x	x	x	x	x	x	x
New York	x	x		x	x	x		x	x	x	x	x	x	x
North Carolina	x		x	x		x	x	x	x		x	x	x	
North Dakota	x	x	x	x	x	x	x	x	x	x		x	x	x
Ohio	x			x	x	x		x	x	x			x	x
Oklahoma	x	x	x	x	x	x		x	x	x	x	x	x	x
Oregon	x	x	x	x	x	x		x	x	x	x	x	x	x
Pennsylvania	x	x	x	x		x	x	x	x	x	x	x	x	x
Rhode Island	x	x		x		x	x	x	x	x	x	x	x	x
South Carolina	x	x	x	x	x	x		x	x			x	x	x
South Dakota	x	x	x	x	x	x		x	x			x	x	x
Tennessee	x	x	x	x		x	x	x	x	x	x	x		x
Texas	x	x	x	x		x		x	x	x	x	x	x	x
Utah	x	x	x	x		x		x	x	x	x	x	x	x
Vermont	x	x	x	x	x	x	x	x	x	x	x	x	x	x
Virginia	x	x	x	x	x	x	x	x	x	x	x	x	x	x
Washington	x	x	x	x	x	x	x	x	x	x	x	x	x	x
West Virginia	x	x	x	x	x	x		x	x	x	x	x	x	x
Wisconsin	x	x		x		x		x	x	x		x	x	x
Wyoming	x	x	x	x		x		x	x			x	x	x

Source: The Book of the States, 1986–87 (Lexington, KY: Council of State Governments, 1987), pp. 71–73.

In accordance with British judicial traditions, some states require public prosecutors to seek an indictment (formal accusation of a crime) from a grand jury before going to court. A grand jury is made up of twelve to twenty-five citizens and is established to determine whether enough evidence exists to accuse someone of a crime. Grand juries operate in secret. They do not determine guilt or innocence but instead review the evidence and arguments of a district attorney and then decide whether the district attorney should proceed to trial.

The intent behind a grand jury process is to be certain that district attorneys are not accusing people without evidence and are not going to court with obviously weak cases. Individuals suffer in personal, financial, and professional terms just by being formally accused of a crime, even when they are innocent. Grand juries are, however, rarely effective in providing protection against frivolous or unwarranted cases. Grand juries tend to rubber-stamp the plans of public prosecutors and thus become a costly and needless step in the process. Grand juries typically spend five to ten minutes on each case and then vote unanimously to follow the recommendation of the district attorney. The only cases that seem to generate discussion and disharmony among members of grand juries are victimless sex crimes, like prostitution.[9] Because grand juries seem to be valuable in concept but unnecessary in practice, most states now allow district attorneys to file cases directly with the court, without first securing a grand jury indictment.[10]

Plea Bargaining and Out-of-Court Settlements. Many disputes that could be litigated are resolved outside courtrooms. Law schools, in fact, include courses that train students to negotiate as well as to litigate. Of those cases that are filed in courts, only about 10 percent actually go to trial.[11] Even after cases are filed, parties can and do reach accords through discussion and negotiation and then drop further legal action. In addition, of course, cases are dropped not through negotiation but because one of the parties realizes that his or her case is too weak to pursue.

In criminal cases, where the district attorney or state's attorney is prosecuting on behalf of society, individuals charged with a crime or a series of crimes can often reduce potential fines or sentences if they plead guilty and avoid the need for a court trial. This phenomenon is known as "plea bargaining" and may involve a plea of guilty or no contest to the charges as they have been lodged, to only some of the charges, or to crimes that are less serious than those in the initial complaint. For example, someone charged with assault, burglary, and trespass may agree after discussions with a district attorney to plead guilty to the burglary and trespass charges. In return, the district attorney will drop the assault charge and, perhaps in addition, suggest to the judge some leniency in sentencing. Someone charged with first-degree murder (intent to kill) may reach an agreement to plead guilty if the charge is reduced to homicide due to reckless behavior. In both cases, the individual charged receives a less severe penalty and the district attorney and courts have a reduced workload. Prosecutors sometimes are pleased to arrange a plea bargain when they are not certain they have all the evidence they would like to secure a conviction of the more serious crime. Plea bargains are negotiated between the district attorney and those accused of a crime, but the agreements are not enacted until approved by a judge.

Ideally, out-of-court settlements and plea bargaining achieves justice in an efficient and fair manner. The fear, of course, is that there may be instances in which criminals are not punished fully or in which innocent people without the necessary will or resources plead guilty under pressure from aggressive prosecutors. In civil cases, where one party is suing another for a breach of contract or malpractice or the like, out-of-court settlements may not always be ideal, either. Attorneys in these cases often are paid on a contingency basis and receive 25 to 40 percent of the award. One suspects at times that the lawyers have a strong incentive to settle, in order to get some kind of payment without having to go through the risk or the effort of going to trial, rather than a compelling commitment to timely justice.

Despite the potential for mischief and misfortune, plea bargains and out-of-court settlements continue to characterize much of what happens in litigation. Given the limited resources of courts and state attorneys, this action outside courtrooms is essential for the timeliness of justice achieved through trials.

Sharing Evidence. For purposes of efficiency and fairness, judicial procedures provide for the parties in a dispute to exchange information, evidence, and expert opinions before arguing their cases in court. Each side files motions of discovery with a court in order to secure from the other party information it needs that the other party has. A contractor, for example, who alleges that a state government violated the law in the way it received and considered bids for building a new prison will almost certainly need information in the files of the state agency responsible for the bidding process to proceed with a legal challenge. A motion of discovery will secure those files. Once a judge approves these (or other) motions, they become legally binding and a failure to comply fully and candidly can lead to contempt of court and/or perjury charges.

Similarly, the two parties may need to clarify issues and facts through interrogatories, that is, a series of questions that must be answered under oath and in writing. The contractor may need to know when certain decisions were made and who was at certain meetings. The agency may need to get more details about how the contractor feels he or she was disadvantaged. These can be done through interrogatories.

The two parties must also exchange the "exhibits," that is, documents, physical evidence, and visual aids they intend to use during the trial. If one of the parties objects to the use of an exhibit, he or she is supposed to make the objection before the trial, and the judge will rule on whether to allow the exhibit. Usually, neither new exhibits nor new objections are allowed during the trial.

The role of the judge receiving these motions and issuing orders underscores the importance of enabling both parties to have the information they need to argue their cases fairly and of doing so before the actual trial. Imagine the delays and frustrations if in the middle of a trial each side were demanding documents from one another.

Exchanging Lists of Witnesses and Taking Depositions. As with the sharing of documentary evidence, concerns over fairness and efficiency have prompted courts to provide for an exchange between litigants of the names and identities of witnesses they intend to call. Witnesses, including both those involved in the dispute and outside experts called to comment on specific aspects of the case, must be available to the opposing side before the trial to answer questions under oath. The answers are transcribed into written form and are called "depositions." Written statements, also made under oath, secured by a party in support of its own position are referred to as "affidavits." In some instances, the written deposition or affidavit is the only contribution made by a witness. In other instances, the written statements are supplemented by oral testimony at the trial itself.

Although exchanging lists of witnesses and securing testimony from them before the trial takes something away from the surprise and drama that television and movie scripts associate with trials, it does allow the two parties to come to the court better prepared. Lawyers can focus their presentations to make them more effective and they can anticipate the approach of their opponents. When the pretrial exchange of evidence, exhibits, and testimony reveals vulnerabilities, discussions leading to a settlement or to plea bargaining might well occur.

Courts, in sum, like other state government institutions, have rules and procedures to guide deliberations and to determine, at least formally, how decisions get made. These procedures provide a certain predictability about judicial behavior. But courts are more than institutions and rules. They are made up of people, with their own personalities and preferences. These people include plaintiffs, defendants, attorneys, witnesses, and interest groups. The central actors who make authoritative decisions are, of course, judges and, in district, county, or circuit courts, juries.

SELECTION OF JUDGES

In contrast to the appointment process for a judge in the federal government, most state governments rely on some method of election for selecting judges. Judges in the federal government are appointed by the president, confirmed by the Senate, and serve indefinitely. As shown in Table 7.3, thirty-seven states elect some or all of their judges. In fourteen states, governors appoint all the judges, and in six states some judges are gubernatorial appointments and some are elected.

Electing judges seems contrary to the role of the court. The judicial system is supposed to provide a neutral, wise, and objective arbiter of disputes. Electoral success, however, depends on relative popularity and not necessarily on evidence of competence and neutrality. In sixteen states, the elections are, in fact, partisan, and victories may reflect party strength more than judicial temperament.

TABLE 7.3. JUDICIAL SELECTION PATTERNS

Partisan Election	Nonpartisan Election	Election by Legislature
Alabama	Arizona	Connecticut
Arkansas	California	Rhode Island
Georgia	Florida	South Carolina
Indiana	Idaho	Vermont
Kansas	Kentucky	Virginia
Illinois	Michigan	
Louisiana	Minnesota	
Mississippi	Montana	
Missouri	Nevada	
New Mexico	North Dakota	
New York	Ohio	
North Carolina	Oregon	
Pennsylvania	Oklahoma	
Tennessee	South Dakota	
Texas	Washington	
West Virginia	Wisconsin	

Appointment		Merit Plan	
Delaware	Massachusetts	Alaska	Missouri
Hawaii	New Hampshire	California	Nebraska
Maine	New Jersey	Colorado	Oklahoma
Maryland	New York	Indiana	Tennessee
		Iowa	Utah
		Kansas	Wyoming

Source: The Book of the States, 1986–87 *(Lexington, KY: Council of State Governments), pp. 130–32.*

It is easy to exaggerate the significance of different methods of judicial selection. Governors, after all, can emphasize patronage in their appointments; thus partisanship can be important even when judges are not elected. Judicial elections are not always arenas for heavy partisan politics, however. Frankly, the election of a judge is often a bore, attracting few voters. Candidates traditionally do not discuss specific cases or run on issue-based platforms. At most, candidates seek images of being tough, reasonable, compassionate, or experienced. Campaigns focus on presenting differences (which are often subtle) in experience and qualifications and on achieving widespread name recognition.

Reforms of state court systems since the 1960s have been modeled after "the Missouri plan," an approach that combines appointive and elective processes. According to a system first adopted in Missouri, when a vacancy on a bench occurs, a select committee of judges, attorneys, and citizens nominates highly qualified individuals. The governor must then select someone from this list of nominees. After the person selected has served as a judge for a year, during a regularly scheduled election the following question is placed on the ballot: "Shall Judge (name of judge selected) of the (name of court) be retained in office?" Voters register a yes or no. If the majority of votes cast are yes, the judge serves a full term. If the majority of votes say no, the governor must select someone else from the original list of nominees, and they in turn must be "confirmed" by a yes vote in a general election.[12]

Although the Missouri plan is conceptually appealing, studies do not show that judges selected in this manner differ from judges selected through straight gubernatorial appointments, partisan elections, or nonpartisan elections. All selection methods appear to provide judges with similar educational, experiential, and social backgrounds.[13] Moreover, how an individual becomes a judge does not appear to influence whether he or she will tend to rule in favor of or against criminal defendants, corporations, government agencies, or poor people.[14] The way judges are selected, in other words, may be more significant for how comfortable the public is with the process than for how the courts will actually operate.

DISCIPLINE AND REMOVAL OF JUDGES

A crucial resource of courts is the image of judges as fair, impartial, honest, and intelligent arbiters. Courts rely primarily on this image for compliance with their decisions. They do not control armies or police forces that might enforce compliance, nor do they have financial resources to provide or withhold funds to affect behavior. Despite the importance of image to the court, it would be unreasonable to expect that all judges are going to maintain an aura of objectivity and integrity.

Judges have at times made statements or issued rulings on procedure that may have prejudiced the outcome of a trial. A check on these instances is the opportunity of litigants to appeal the case and to base the appeal on the prejudicial actions of a judge. Inappropriate behavior by judges have sometimes extended beyond what happens in the courtroom. Judges have been convicted of accepting bribes, fraudulently avoiding income taxes, engaging in sexual misbehavior, and driving while drunk.

Since most state judges are elected for specific terms, they can be removed from the bench by suffering defeat in a bid for reelection. Sometimes the mere publicity—quite apart from the facts—about an indiscreet or potentially criminal act is enough to thwart a bid for reelection or to dissuade a judge from running for reelection. Those states that allow for the recall of elected officials typically include judges among those subject to recall. Indeed, judges have been recalled from the bench in the midst of their terms.

Thirty-two states rely heavily on impeachment by the legislature to remove judges from office. This process, which also applies to governors, legislators, and other major officials, necessitates hearings and investigations by the legislature, a vote by the lower chamber to indict the accused judge, and a trial and vote in the upper chamber to convict. Because this process tends to be cumbersome and highly contentious, it is rarely used.[15]

Led by California, thirty states have established judicial review commissions to receive complaints of misbehavior by judges, to investigate those complaints, and when necessary, to prosecute the case—usually before a state supreme court.[16] Judicial review commissions typically include lawyers, judges, and citizens. The discipline meted out to convicted judges can range from reprimands to suspensions to dismissal. Contemporary court reformers prefer judicial review commissions to other ways of disciplining judges both because the wider range of punishments allows for sanctions appropriate to the indiscretion and because the process is more efficient and less expensive than impeachment or recall.[17]

JURIES

A hallowed principle of justice in the American and British jurisprudence systems is the opportunity to be tried by one's peers. The original implementation of this principle is quite different from contemporary practices. Initially, a "jury of one's peers" was interpreted to mean those in the community who knew the litigants and the circumstances of the dispute intimately. Today, however, the selection of a jury emphasizes the identification of individuals who will enter the courtroom without any previous knowledge of the people involved in the case and, ideally, the case itself. Judges will, for example, grant a motion for a "change of venue" and move a trial to another town when a case has been publicized or discussed so much in a community that it would be difficult to select jurors who lack information or an opinion on the dispute. While the case is being tried, jurors are instructed not to discuss it with anyone or read newspaper accounts of the trial. In sensational cases or ones that are being discussed extensively throughout the community, jurors may be "sequestered"—kept in a hotel and prevented from going home during the trial—to confine the influences on their decisions to the presentations made in the courtroom.

Juries, as mentioned, are used only in the lower-level courts, both in state and federal court systems. Once a case reaches the appellate levels, only judges will hear the case. The defendant usually has the option of choosing a jury trial or a "bench trial"—one before a judge only. States differ somewhat in the number of jurors that constitute a jury. In most states, the number is between eight and fifteen. Jurors are selected randomly from a list of registered voters and/or taxpayers. Individuals can be excused from jury duty if they satisfy the court that serving would cause a serious hardship. Lawyers on either side can ask that specific individuals be excused because they suspect that, based on answers to preliminary questions or on some other information, the individuals are likely to be prejudiced to the issues or the litigants in the case.

The role of the jury is like the role of the judge. Jurors must consider the evidence and the arguments presented at the trial, the credibility of the witnesses, and the law that applies and then render a verdict of guilt or innocence. The judge in a jury trial essentially makes certain that the litigants and their lawyers follow proper procedure in presenting their cases and that the jury receives instructions about the law that applies and the standards that must be applied to determine guilt or innocence. State laws specify whether the jurors must consider the defendant guilty only if the evidence meets the test of "beyond reasonable doubt," as for first-degree murder, or some other standard, like "preponderance of evidence." The latter requires a kind of balancing of the two sides to determine who is most convincing. Many states apply this standard, for example, to contract law.

A certain amount of subjectivity in jury decisions is almost inevitable. But this is true for decisions made by judges, too. Support for our system of jurisprudence depends in part on ignoring or downplaying this subjectivity. Appeals are always an option when the subjectivity is considered excessive or somehow in error.

SENTENCING

Guilty verdicts are accompanied by a sentence. The punishment to the guilty party can be a fine paid to government, an award paid to an injured individual or group, a period of imprisonment, a period of probation (out of jail but under supervision by an agent of the court), a requirement to participate in a program of rehabilitation or community service, or some combination of these. The sentence is determined by the judge or, in some cases, the jury. State legislatures give the options for punishment or sentencing to judges and juries in state courts. States, for example, determine if first-degree murder can be punished by execution or life imprisonment. Typically, when laws are passed, clauses are included that specify that violators will be subject to a fine of up to a certain amount, imprisonment of a certain range of years, or both. Judges and juries can exercise considerable discretion in meting out prison terms and fines and required participation in certain programs. One study presented forty-eight trial judges with a hypothetical case of breaking and entering, specifying the race, age, and sex of the person convicted. The judges responded to this same hypothetical case with sentences that ranged from thirty days of unsupervised probation to eleven months in jail.[18] Ranges in sentencing should not be surprising. Individuals, including judges, differ in how they treat offenders. Some have more faith in the effects of giving someone another chance and providing an opportunity for rehabilitation. Others are convinced that the best response, both for society and for the offender, is tough penalties that keep offenders off the streets.

A concern is whether different sentences are given for the same crimes by the same types of individuals. The time one spends in jail can be more a function of who the judge is rather than what one did. This concern has led state lawmakers to consider a reform known as "determinant sentencing," which gives to judges throughout the state guidelines that in a fairly specific way match sentences with crimes. Judges in this system must abide by the guidelines unless they can, in writing, justify an exception. Exceptions can be reviewed by appeals courts, at the request of the convicted individual.

Another sentencing reform considered by state governments in the 1980s concerns awards made by judges and juries in cases of medical malpractice and negligence by manufacturers and businesses. The focus of reform efforts, sponsored by the insurance industry and business organizations,[19] is tort law in state statutes. A tort is a wrongful act that is not criminal in nature and does not involve the violation of a contract. As a result of generous awards in the early 1980s to victims of medical malpractice and faulty products, physicians and businesses sought insurance policies to protect themselves financially. Physicians in some high-risk specialties had to pay between 3 and 7 percent of their income in insurance premiums. Although insurance companies collected $3.5 billion in 1986 in premiums, they paid $4.8 billion in damages.

In response, insurance companies developed a "model tort law" for state legislatures to adopt. The law includes a limit of $250,000 for "pain and suffering" damages, a stipulation that punitive damages (awards by judges and juries that are designed to punish the defendant rather than compensate the victim) be awarded only if intent to injure could be proven, and restrictions on collecting for the same medical expenses from more than one source. Another feature of the model law hits at how lawyers are paid. In many tort cases, lawyers are paid on a contingency basis, which usually gives lawyers one-third of the sum awarded to the plaintiff. This arrangement obviously encourages lawyers to seek high awards. The model law provides for a mandatory case-by-case review by the courts to be sure that the fees collected are "reasonable."

The model tort law was considered—but not always enacted—by thirty-two state legislatures by the beginning of 1988. The reform efforts and the issues raised illustrate the interdependency of the courts and the other institutions of state government. Court behavior has prompted efforts to seek legislative action. Courts will continue to receive cases charging medical malpractice and manufacturers' negligence, no matter how state legislatures and governors respond to the pleas for change. What is at stake are the standards that must be applied in making awards and the discretion available to the courts.

SUMMARY AND CONCLUSIONS

Courts have tried to maintain a position "above politics." The image of judges as fair and impartial is essential to the dispute settlement role that they must play. The selection process—even when electoral—and the provisions for discipline and removal have for the most part fostered the image of judges as being objective and professional. Attorneys general and district attorneys are more explicitly involved in partisan politics, but the aura of impartiality of the law and the courts generally tends to help these officers appear more like objective enforcers of the law than political hacks.

In addition to resolving disputes and enforcing the law, the judicial system is centrally involved in policy making. Attorneys general and district attorneys are politicians, by definition, and win in partisan and sometimes issue-oriented campaigns. Attorneys general increasingly provide services and pursue policies that are outside the strict boundaries of legal work. The application and interpretation of laws by judges and by prosecuting attorneys invariably involves the exercise of discretion.

Policies affecting more than the specific litigants in a lawsuit are made when judgments clarify ambiguities in statutes. Citizens and the legal community take note. Administrators, legislators, and governors are also attentive to court rulings as they exercise discretion and make and implement policy in their respective positions. These officials, obviously, feel compelled to operate within the boundaries of the law, as interpreted by the courts and the state's attorneys. In short, although courts and prosecutors maintain a certain distance from other government institutions and other actors in the political arena, they play a central and extensive role in the functions of state governments.

REFERENCES

1. Earl M. Maltz, "Federalism and State Court Activism," *Intergovernmental Perspective* (Spring 1987), 23–26.
2. Ronald K. L. Collins and Peter J. Galie, "Models of Post-Incorporation Judicial Review: 1985 Survey of State Constitutional Individual Rights Decisions," *Publius*, Vol. 16 (Summer 1986), 117 and 118.
3. William J. Brennan, Jr., "State Constitutions and the Protection of Individual Rights," *Harvard Law Review*, Vol. 90 (Jan. 1977), 489–504.
4. Douglas Ross, "Safeguarding Our Federalism: Lessons for the States from the Supreme Court," *Public Administration Review* (Nov. 1985), p. 723.
5. Gregory A. Caldeira, "The Transmission of Legal Precedent: A Study of State Supreme Courts," *The American Political Science Review*, Vol. 79 (1985), 178–93.
6. Ibid., 187; and P. Harris, "Some Predictors of the Insterstate Diffusion of State Common Law, 1870–1970," presented at the Annual Meeting of the Law and Society Association, San Francisco, 1979, p. 23.
7. Herbert Jacob, "State Courts and Public Policy," in Herbert Jacob and Kenneth N. Vines, eds., *Politics in the American States. A Comparative Analysis*, 3rd ed. (Boston: Little, Brown, 1976), p. 247.
8. *The Book of the States, 1986-87* (Lexington, KY: Council of State Governments, 1987), pp. 55–56.
9. Robert A. Carp, "The Behavior of Grand Juries: Acquiescence or Justice," *Social Science Quarterly*, Vol. 55 (Mar. 1975), 853–70.
10. David C. Saffell, *State and Local Government*, 3rd ed. (New York: Random House, 1987), p. 173.
11. Henry Robert Glick and Kenneth N. Vines, *State Court Systems* (Englewood Cliffs, NJ: Prentice-Hall, 1971), p. 179.
12. Richard A. Watson and Ronald G. Downing, *The Politics of the Bench and Bar: Judicial Selection Under the Missouri Nonpartisan Court Plan* (New York: Wiley, 1969).
13. Bradley Cannon, "The Impact of Formal Selection Processes on Characteristics of Judges—Reconsidered," *Law and Society Review*, Vol. 13 (May 1972), 570–93.

14. Stuart Nagel, "Unequal Party Representation in State Supreme Courts," *Journal of the American Judicature Society*, Vol. 44 (1961), 62–65.
15. *Book of the States, 1986-87*, p. 126.
16. *State Court Systems* (Lexington, KY: Council of State Governments, 1979), p. 57.
17. Herbert Jacob, *Justice in America*, 4th ed. (Boston: Little, Brown, 1984), Chap. 3.
18. Austin Sarat, "Judging Trial Courts," *Journal of Politics*, Vol. 39 (May 1977), 368–98.
19. "Tort-Reform Laws in Six States Get Mixed Results," *State Legislatures* (Feb. 1987), 8.

COMPETITION TO SHAPE THE STATE POLICY AGENDA

———————————— CHAPTER 8 ————————————

The Policy-Making Process

State governments affect the public in a number of ways. They tax state residents to obtain the revenues needed to finance the various operations of state government. They operate state prisons and mental health institutes, build new highways and maintain existing ones, manage the state's natural resources, operate public institutions of higher education, and administer and staff all the agencies and institutions of state government. State-collected taxes and fees also go to support municipalities, counties, school districts, and other local units of government. Major local assistance programs, in dollar terms, include general and categorical school aids, state revenue sharing, and property tax relief. A third category, also involving significant redistribution of resources, includes programs of direct aid to individuals. Prominent examples include Aid to Families with Dependent Children (AFDC), Medicaid, and state support for general welfare assistance.

States regulate individual behavior and commercial enterprise. The massiveness of most states' criminal and civil codes testify to the voluminous quantity of state law governing regulation in its broadest sense. Add to that the many volumes of state administrative code, and the vast extent of state regulation becomes apparent. Statutory law defines what are considered to be felonious crimes against others' persons and property and prescribes maximum jail or prison terms. The criminal code also covers those provisions governing probation and parole. Civil law governs noncriminal disputes between individuals and outlines the procedural and substantive basis on which multiparty grievances may be pursued in the courts and administrative agencies. Such disputes can involve contracts, personal injuries, divorce settlements, and the like.

States confer privileges on individuals, including the privilege of operating motor vehicles on public roads, fishing or boating in state waters, hunting game and wildlife, and providing professional and certain occupational services to others. Not only does each of these areas of privilege involve licensing, but also state regulation details the manner in which the state-conferred privilege can be legally exercised.

State governments also enforce standards in the areas of public building safety (including privately owned buildings providing access to the public), industrial discharge of air and water pollutants, sanitary conditions and health standards, trucking operations, and apprentice and equal rights employment practices. States also regulate financial institutions, insurance companies, and real estate practices. Significant regulatory concerns include disclosure of required consumer information, the financial viability of commercial enterprise, corporate investment practices, and maximum chargeable rates of interest.

Finally, states regulate intrastate public utilities, including telephone, gas, and electric services. State public service commissions oversee initiation and abandonment of service (including, in several states, the construction and location of power plants), evaluate energy load management and the adequacy of service, approve offers for the public sale of utility stocks and bonds, prescribe financial and accounting procedures, and approve the rates utility customers are charged.

Besides legally resolving disputes between parties, state courts also make public policy. For example, decisions regarding the banning of textbooks in the public schools may affect the quality of elementary and secondary education in a state; decisions regarding a highway department's compliance with state environmental protection laws may force a major highway project to be redesigned; decisions regarding legislative apportionment may result in the redrafting of legislative districts, thus shifting the partisan balance in a state legislature; and decisions regarding the governor's use of the item veto may affect the political balance between the executive and legislative branches of state government.

At the appeals level, judges not only decide whether the law has been properly applied by a trial court or a lower appeals court but also—most significantly at the state supreme court level—make collective judgments on whether state laws violate state constitutions. State appeals court judges produce written statements accompanying their decisions, which provide a context for other judges to use in deciding similar or analogous cases. This citing of decisions can even take place across state lines, thus broadening the precedential and policy-making effects of earlier decisions.

Public policies affecting these and other policy areas are made through the use of several policy-making processes. There are similarities among them; yet their procedural differences contribute toward significant political differences as well. They may be divided conceptually as follows: (1) the traditional single-bill legislative process; (2) the budgetary process, as a distinct variant of the former; (3) the formal administrative rule-making process; (4) the informal process of administrative determination, outside of formal rule making; (5) the process of regulatory commission review and decision; (6) the process of judicial decision making; and (7) the processes of direct citizen democracy, including the initiative, referendum, and recall.

The next chapter, Chapter 9, will cover the process of direct democracy. This subject should immediately follow a discussion of the executive-legislative policy-making process because plebiscitary democracy, like the substantive bill and budgetary processes, leads to the enactment of state statutory law or the amendment of state constitutions. These three political processes are appropriately covered together under the heading of Competition to Shape the State Agenda. Each leads to the making of law, rather than to the interpretation or clarification of law. This is not to suggest that interpretation or clarification of law does not involve policy making, for each does. But the state's policy agenda is most directly shaped through the processes of creating or amending state law, including the enactment of appropriations.

THE SUBSTANTIVE BILL LEGISLATIVE PROCESS

Putting aside for now a discussion of plebiscitary democracy, the process of law-making represents a shared executive-legislative function. Although only the legislature can pass legislation, that legislation is not enacted into law until the governor approves it or the legislature overrides the governor's veto. Then, upon its effective date, the legislation becomes law. The effective date may be specified in the legislation itself or governed by constitutional provision.

Legislatures may also approve joint legislative resolutions, which make a unilateral statement, without gubernatorial approval, but do not have the force of law. Examples might include the expression of the legislature on national affairs, such as its opposition to U.S. involvement in Nicaragua, or a proclamation rendering thanks to a retiring key legislative staff director. Joint resolutions can also be used as the means for the legislature to establish referenda, the results of which can be either advisory or binding, depending on the action of the legislature constrained by state constitutions or statutes. Such unilateral actions do not require the governor's approval.

Legislative Initiatives and Their Origin

Laws are enacted in all states through the medium of bills. A bill can propose a new law or change an existing one through amendment or outright repeal. Although bills may be introduced in the legislative process only by a legislator or legislative committee, they have many different points of origin. A bill can originate from within any one of the three branches of government: the executive, the legislative, or in very limited instances, the judicial.

Key policy staff in the governor's office, executive planning and budget officers, and top state agency administrators all get involved in policy initiation and its accompanying bill development. Governors and their executive office staffs often think in terms of their administration's broad policy agenda. A governor, for example, may commit his or her administration to property tax relief, welfare reform, new highway construction, and legalized gambling. Although these items provide the general policy outlines to be pursued, specific program proposals still have to be developed for submission to the legislature. And the governor and key executive office aides also have to decide which policy vehicles should be used to advance the proposals. Relevant considerations include whether initiatives should be floated as several separate bills; collapsed into a few broad-based, functionally related bills; or where permitted, included within the state budget bill. Such strategic decisions are geared toward increasing the prospects of successful attainment of the governor's policy objectives.

Not only do key gubernatorial aides help to set the administration's policy agenda; they also work with other administration officials to formulate the substantive proposals that embody the agenda. Agency heads and their top administrative officials, along with the state budget and planning directors, often assume the leadership for shaping specific proposals. But the real work of proposal design usually falls to program experts who occupy mid-level positions in the state bureaucracy. They have the in-depth program expertise to deal with the "nuts and bolts" issues of proposal development. They do so, however, under the close supervision of top administration officials.

The process differs somewhat for state agencies whose heads are not appointed by the governor nor serve at the governor's pleasure. For noncabinet agencies, the role of the governor's office becomes one of monitoring the status of bills and, when important enough, of trying to influence their outcome in the legislature. Here the customary proaction of the executive office gives way largely to review and reaction. This should not suggest that governors or their top aides do not occasionally attempt to convince noncabinet officials to withdraw or modify legislative proposals, for they surely do. But with noncabinet agencies, governors possess fewer tools with which to elicit compliance.

Gubernatorially appointed task forces and commissions provide still another vehicle for the initiation of legislation. Task forces and commissions are frequently formed to deal with controversial policy issues, serving as a sounding board for public opinion. As an illustration, the potentially divisive issues of tax or welfare reform could well become the subject of task force or commission review. Besides its potential substantive value, such action can also be of major symbolic value to an administration. Appointment of a task force or a commission allows a governor to separate himself or herself from the appointed body's recommendations while, at the same time, creating the popular image that the chief executive is taking steps to deal with a pressing public problem. If the recommendations engender broad political support, the administration can claim credit for the coup. Conversely, if they spell political trouble, the governor can ignore or deemphasize them, pursue only selective recommendations, or combine other gubernatorial initiatives with them.

Legislators and their staffs also initiate legislation. Individual legislators come into office with a sense of which policies they wish to advance, and they seek committee assignments that reinforce their policy preferences and help them best to serve their constituencies. For example, rural legislators in heavily agricultural states can somewhat predictably be expected to show an interest in farm matters, highway construction and repair (particularly farm-to-market roads), and property tax relief. They will also hire staff members who have expertise in these areas or will be expected to develop it. Both legislators and staffs tend to take proactive legislative postures; they usually perceive themselves as voted into office to *do* something, and that most often entails sponsoring or supporting legislation of benefit to their constituents.

Staffs, too, tend to be proactive. They are employed to help accomplish their bosses' objectives. Interacting with other legislative staff and agency officials, they readily get caught up in the heady activity of legislative business, while developing programmatic expertise of their own. Along with such subject matter expertise frequently comes insights into how programs can be "improved," or at least how they can be of greater political benefit to their legislators.

Unlike the executive and legislative branches, it is relatively unusual for the courts to initiate legislation directly. However, judges (particularly appeals court justices) occasionally suggest in their rulings that a particular contested issue would be most appropriately left to the state legislature for resolution. In addition, existing statutory law might be internally contradictory, requiring corrective amendment. Most states have a judicial council, which reviews cases in which statutory remedies appear necessary and endorses bills that accomplish the task.

Bills can also be initiated from sources outside of government. People contact their legislators or legislative staff about policies that they, as individuals, want to see enacted, changed, or eliminated. Legislation may be pursued that relates to one's views about how society could be improved, for example, through tougher penalties for drug trafficking, increased funding for schools, or laws against pornography. Or individuals may have a more personal concern, such as pursing a financial claim against the state through legislation, even though they may have unsuccessfully exhausted available administrative channels for remedy. Legislators, responding to this request for assistance, can introduce what is referred to as a "private" bill—one having very limited, particular interest. Such introduction largely amounts to a symbolic gesture, as the vast majority of such private bills fail to be enacted; most do not even make it out of committee.

Groups may also develop legislation that advances the collective interests of their members, whether they be economic or professional. Among the more active groups at the state level are the AFL-CIO, representing a large segment of both private and public sector organized labor; the American Federation of State, County and Municipal Employees (AFSCME), representing public sector employees; associations of manufacturers, representing the larger industries; chambers of commerce, representing local businesses; coalitions of road builders, representing engineering firms and highway contractors; associations of local governmental jurisdictions, including cities, counties, and school districts; and a wide range of professional associations, representing most of the major professions—from physicians and lawyers to schoolteachers and university professors.

These groups often supply friendly legislators or committees with drafts of proposed legislation, which can then be forwarded to the legislature's bill-drafting department for production in official bill form. Examples of such special-interest legislation might include proposals that eliminate a mandatory one-week waiting period before unemployment compensation benefits can be collected (benefitting organized labor), increase the state's share of financing local school costs (benefitting school districts and teachers' unions), include chiropractic services under the state's Medicaid program (benefitting chiropractors, while being adverse to the interests of physicians), and increase funding for new highway construction (benefitting civil engineering firms and highway contractors).

The Process of Legislative Consideration and Approval

Following a long-standing tradition begun in England, all bills must be "read" three times in each legislative chamber. Upon introduction, a bill is read for the first time by the clerk of the chamber of origin and referred to the standing committee determined to have jurisdiction over its subject matter, such as transportation, education, agriculture, or one of several others. The bill's number, the dates of its introduction and first reading, the committee to which it is assigned, and the date of referral are generally recorded on the bill's cover. Depending on state law, the bill may or may not contain an indication that it was introduced at the request of a specific constituent, public official, or state agency. Of course the introducer's identity is always noted on the bill.

The rules of legislative procedure, adopted by each chamber, require that committees hold public hearings on all bills assigned to them. Committee hearings may be held during the legislative session or during periods when the full legislature is formally in recess. However, most states—either by law or procedural rules of the legislature—prescribe a minimum period of time after a bill's introduction before the committee can act on it. This waiting period is required to give legislators and the public adequate time to consider a bill and determine what action, if any, to take.

A schedule of committee hearings is prepared at the behest of the committee, usually at its chairperson's direction. The schedule is then published and posted, satisfying public notice requirements where mandated by state law. Most states require a three- to five-day advance notice of hearing.

The full committee may conduct the hearing, or the bill may be assigned to a subcommittee for review and hearing. Both subcommittees and committees can recommend amendments to bills. The subcommittee makes its recommendations to the full committee, and the committee, in turn, makes its recommendations to the chamber as a whole. A bill can be reported out of committee in most states with either a positive or negative recommendation. In others, only bills receiving positive recommendations clear the committee. Failing to get a favorable vote, they simply "die" there.

Upon clearing the committee, the bill is usually read for a second time and scheduled by the chamber's legislative leadership for debate on the floor. Prior to floor debate, or during recesses, legislators of both parties may meet separately, in partisan caucus, to consider possible amendments and the relative support they are likely to receive on the floor. Both committee-endorsed amendments and those offered by individual legislators are considered on the floor. Amendments are approved usually by majority vote of the chamber; however, state constitutions or statutory law may require a "super majority" for certain amendments, such as those for appropriations or revenue bills.

After a bill has been passed by the house of origin, it is engrossed and sent to the second chamber, where all the above-described steps (see Figure 8.1) are repeated. (Engrossing involves the incorporation of all approved amendments into the bill and is considered the third and final reading.) That chamber can, in turn, pass, defeat, or amend the bill. If passed in identical form, the bill is returned to the house of origin and from there sent to the governor for signature or veto. If the bill is amended by the second house, it is sent back to the first for concurrence. If that chamber concurs, it goes to the governor. If concurrence cannot be attained, a conference committee, consisting of equal representation from each chamber, may be appointed to come up with a compromise version. State law may permit the full legislature to amend the conference report, or it may require an "up" or "down" vote without amendment. If the conference committee cannot reach agreement, other conferees may be named as replacements. If agreement fails, the bill dies. Conversely, if agreement is reached, rejection of the conference report by either house also results in the bill's death.

After a bill has been passed by both legislative chambers, it is enrolled with all approved amendments incorporated and sent to the governor. Usually the governor has only a limited number of days in which to sign or veto the bill. If not signed within that period, the bill automatically becomes law. If vetoed, the bill is returned to the house of origin, most often with a written statement of the governor's objections. The legislature then has a period of time in which to act on the veto. If no action is taken within the prescribed period, the veto is automatically sustained. If overridden by both houses of the legislature, usually requiring a two-thirds vote, the legislature-approved version stands. In other words, gubernatorial vetoes are usually upheld since the governor needs the support of only one-third, plus one, of the members of either house in order to sustain his or her veto.

Two Variants of the Legislative Process

Alan Rosenthal, a close observer of the state legislative process, draws a distinction between the legislative "assembly line" and the executive-legislative policy-making process.[1] The assembly line operates more like a "bill-passing machine" than a deliberative process, according to Rosenthal. Many bills are introduced with little or no expectation that they will ever come to the floor for a vote. Several are introduced at a constituent's request or as a symbolic gesture. They may be introduced, read, and referred to committee but fail to receive serious attention in the process, typically languishing there.

Other bills can be treated more seriously by their authors but simply fail to

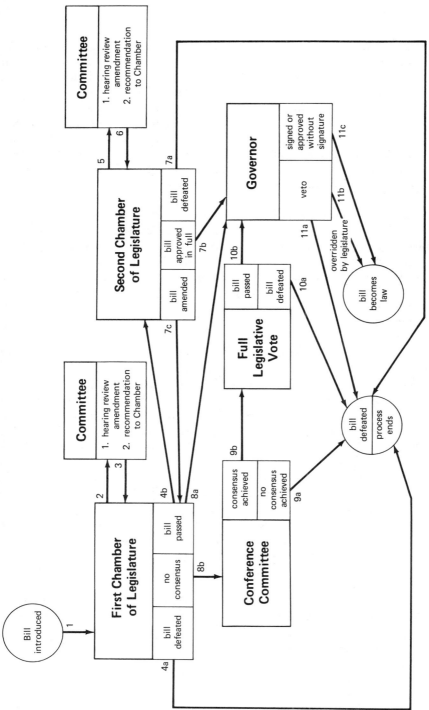

Figure 8.1. The Substantive Single-Bill Legislative Process

153

engender much interest on the part of legislative colleagues. In a crowded legislative docket, such bills may also fail to make it out of committee. Only so much legislative business can be conducted within the constraints of limited time and staff resources. Yet several bills fitting this description are enacted into law annually without the strong support of the legislative leadership, and often without even gaining much notice. That latter factor, though, could be a significant element in their success. Although these bills do not generate much support, they often attract little or no opposition. The leadership does not tag them for defeat; nor do others coalesce to stop their progress. The "press" of the docket becomes their greatest enemy. And as they compete for consideration, some will successfully make it through the legislative process uncontested. In such cases the executive branch may not even have become involved other than for the governor's ultimate signature. At that stage the governor may have no reason not to sign the approved legislation. The governor, like the legislators who earlier considered the bill, might not feel strongly enough to prevent it from becoming law.

Governors choose to use the veto sparingly, saving it for priority cases where it matters. Hence it is fair to say that a good portion of legislation makes it through the screening process because no party, legislative or gubernatorial, cares enough to sidetrack it. Saying no uses up some political capital and can make others less willing to go along with the naysayer's own initiatives.

The process for legislation that really matters is different. First, the executive branch is likely to be more closely involved throughout the legislative process. In fact, the executive branch may even have initiated a number of the major legislative proposals. A state agency may have drafted the bill and sought legislative introduction, often with the intercession of the governor's office. In some states, executive office staffs clear all legislation initiated by cabinet agencies. In others, appointed agency heads are relatively free to work directly with sympathetic legislators. Cabinet agencies may produce a draft bill, providing it to a legislator who requests that state's legislative reference bureau to prepare the official bill for introduction. Noncabinet agencies are free to work directly with supportive legislators. They face no obligation, other than the maintenance of good will, to seek the governor's support for introduction. In many cases the governor may even be an intense political rival of the attorney general or state superintendent of public instruction or another constitutionally elected public official. Or with boards or commissions, the current governor cannot have appointed, or control, a majority of their members.

For the most important bills, which generate executive and legislative interest, the participants in the lawmaking process are less willing to allow them to roll along unimpeded. Coalitions of support and opposition form around their deliberations—coalitions that often reflect political party lines, business or labor positions, or urban or rural divisions. Such legislation becomes more hotly contested in committee. Gubernatorial aides are more likely to take the trouble to appear in support or opposition at committee hearings. Legislative caucuses—separate meetings of the Democratic and Republican members of each house—flag the bill for discussion. Legislative leaders and other legislative supporters or opponents work to convince the governor and/or executive office staff to either support or, at a minimum, not oppose legislative initiatives. State officials may take the trouble to appear at committee hearings, either taking positions for or against legislation. The agency professional's testimony that a bill is technically or substantively flawed can "put the skids" on an otherwise fast-track initiative, often causing legislative reviewers to take note and possibly reconsider their support.

In most states, agencies or legislative staff offices are legally required by state statutes to review all introduced legislation in terms of its anticipated effect on state revenues and/or expenditures and to prepare fiscal notes. These notes, which must be appended upon referral of a bill to committee, provide an estimate of the extent to which the legislative proposal increases or decreases state revenues or expenditures. For example, a bill that stiffens parole eligibility laws, making it more difficult for prisoners to be released from prison before their mandatory release date, would increase the costs of prison operations because inmates would remain in prison longer. Thus the fiscal note would illustrate the cost implications of what, on face value, appears merely to be a statutory change.

Fiscal notes openly disclose the otherwise "hidden" costs of legislative initiatives. Like open meetings and public information laws, they are premised on making the public aware of the effects of government's activities. As the theory goes, full disclosure gives the public the information needed to make informed choices in support of, or opposition to, proposed legislation.

Organized interest groups may become involved in both the assembly-line and executive-legislative processes. Ideally, lobbyists would prefer to keep their initiatives within the assembly-line process, that is, if they could be assured that their proposals would not be waylaid within the crowded legislative hopper. Anonymity can serve as an asset once a bill gets out of committee and makes it to the floor of the first chamber for a vote. But it can be a detriment if the end result is that no one cares enough, not even the author, to report it out of committee with a favorable vote. The balance can be tenuous. If a bill can get just enough attention to keep moving, but not so much that it becomes closely scrutinized at any phase of the process, its chances for passage and signing are good. So when lobbyists champion legislative initiatives of limited scope that do not raise apparent overriding value issues, the assembly line fits their needs quite nicely. However, most issues of substance attracting interest group involvement have trouble getting treated within the assembly line. They regularly get sorted out into the executive-legislative process because of their broader policy significance or fiscal effect. Executive officials or other legislators care enough to single them out for closer scrutiny.

In this charged arena, advocates of legislation become proactive, seeking out executive and legislative participants with whom they can make their case. Once a bill has risen out of relative obscurity, and particularly when it has become a visible point of controversy, proaction becomes the strategy of choice. It no longer remains in one's interest to follow a strategy of acquiescence. Others are pushing strongly for support or opposition. The battle has begun. It has become time to influence choice overtly, to count votes and mold coalitions. The game has changed, and so have its rules.

One institutional effort to change the legislative process to make it more manageable has been for legislatures to institute "deadline" systems. Such systems provide deadlines for the introduction of bills, committee review, and floor consideration. They are aimed at reducing the end-of-session congestion that obligates legislatures to rush some bills through without the customary deliberation or to let other, late-introduced legislation die without adequate time to consider properly their relative merits. In that environment of late-session "logjam," the usually decentralized legislative process becomes much more centralized, with the top legislative leadership directing traffic. Earlier in the session a bill will pass unless the leadership singles it out for derailment; but at session's end, bills pass because they have the leadership's support. Most bills caught up in the final legislative rush die for lack of attention. But since there are several favored bills having the leadership's support, they must be rushed through during a session's waning days and hours—perhaps without the deliberation they deserve. The growing use of deadlines is directed at more evenly distributing the legislature's workload throughout the session. Under deadlines, a bill's failure to be introduced or moved to the next stage in the process can more readily be attributed to its lower priority (since a predetermined period of time has been reserved for consideration of those bills meeting the deadline) and not to its getting caught up in the figurative "last-minute" shuffle. The volume of legislative business is not necessarily eliminated, but it is spread over several deadline periods during a session.

So far we have been discussing the traditional single-bill legislative process, where bills embrace distinct subjects and where those bills are referred to standing committees having jurisdiction over a particular area of substantive policy. However, a major caveat needs to be interjected at this point. The state budget, often encapsulating several diverse subjects depending on the latitude granted by a state's constitution or statutes, necessitates a separate discussion. Not only does the budget differ from other bills in form and effect, but also the legislative process within which it is deliberated significantly differs. This distinctiveness of process, along with its associated distinctive politics, merits special attention. The significance of the budget bill, in both dollars and policy, assures that it takes center stage in the state policy-making process.

THE STATE BUDGETARY PROCESS:
AN IMPORTANT VARIANT

"Put your money where your mouth is" is an oft-heard refrain in everyday discourse. It captures the sense of folk wisdom that "money talks." Social scientists may instead choose to speak about the importance of "programmed resource commitments"; yet the gist is the same: that dollar commitments cut through rhetoric, clearly disclosing priorities. The state budget constitutes such a statement of a state's priorities—backed up by dollars—from one year or biennium to the next.

State legislative sessions are structured to accord the state budget a privileged position. The governor kicks off the budget-year legislative session with a "Budget Message" delivered to the legislature. This message, presented with considerable fanfare and media attention, and often preceded by selective attention-getting "leaks" of key elements, provides a substantive and highly symbolic statement of the administration's agenda for the coming budget period and often beyond. In most states, as well, no bill that makes an appropriation may be approved by the legislature or sent to the governor until the budget bill is enacted into law. From the governor's budget message—through committee hearings, caucus deliberations, and floor debate—the budget disproportionately focuses the attention of state policy makers and close observers alike. This is not to say that important state policies are not enacted outside of the state budget, for they surely are. Major matters of state policy, such as the death penalty, high school graduation requirements, abortion restrictions, and binding labor arbitration, are most commonly enacted as separate legislation apart from the budget. In fact, several state constitutions proscribe the inclusion of statutory authorizations or changes within the budget bill. In other states the budget bill may include appropriations as well as statutory authorizations and changes. It is in this environment that the budget bill can most readily serve as a policy vehicle; major policy initiatives can be included in the budget, whether or not they involve the appropriation of funds or have a fiscal effect. States having the greatest flexibility include California, Oregon, Pennsylvania, and Wisconsin, whereas Colorado, Mississippi, Montana, New Hampshire, New Mexico, and Wyoming are the most restrictive.[2]

Where permitted, the practice of including statutory provisions in the budget has many advantages from an executive perspective. First, it permits the governor to use the item veto, where that authority exists, on policy initiatives having no associated appropriation since once included in the budget bill they become subject to the item veto. Second, it is easier for the governor to work with the legislative leadership in managing the more contained budgetary process than to manage the more fragmented substantive bill legislative process. Third, the governor has greater opportunity to offer and entertain compromises when a number of major policy initiatives are considered in the same bill.

The legislature may wish to include policy in the budget for some of the same reasons. The budgetary process may afford the leadership an opportunity to bargain among the various policy items that are incorporated into the budget bill. The budgetary process restricts the number of legislative actors who are in a position to shape the outcome of policy initiatives. The appropriations or fiscal committees, variously named, exercise decision-making authority over the budget, referring their official version of the budget to their respective legislative chambers. The substantive standing committees play no official decision-making role in the budgetary process, although they may make nonbinding recommendations to the appropriations committees on matters of policy and budget levels affecting agencies and programs falling within their jurisdiction. In that vein they may hold committee hearings, but these generally have more of a palliative and symbolic, rather than substantive, value. Thus, where the budget is concerned, the real power at the committee stage rests with the appropriations or fiscal committees—a fact that is not lost sight of by other legislators, the executive branch, or lobbyists.

Herein lies a major difference between the state budgetary process and that of the federal government. At the federal level, the authorizing committees review requests and recommendations for changes in statutory authority. The money (appropriations and finance) committees approve the funds to be spent in a given budgetary period. Although this overly simple distinction between statutory authorization and appropriation generally applies at the federal level, the increasing practice in Congress of "loading up" appropriations bills with riders, restrictions, and expressions of congressional intent has weakened the distinction in practice.

States have either an annual or biennial budgeting period. As Table 8.1 shows, thirty are on an annual basis, and twenty have a biennial period. Yet whether a state has an annual or biennial budget does not materially affect the process leading up to budget enactment. It does, however, influence the char-

TABLE 8.1. BUDGETING PERIODS

State	Annual	Biennial	Beginning Month of Fiscal Year
Alabama	x		October
Alaska	x		July
Arizona	x		July
Arkansas		x	July
California	x		July
Colorado	x		July
Connecticut	x		July
Delaware	x		July
Florida		x	July
Georgia	x		July
Hawaii		x	July
Idaho	x		July
Illinois	x		July
Indiana		x	July
Iowa		x	July
Kansas	x		July
Kentucky	x		July
Louisiana	x		July
Maine		x	July
Maryland	x		July
Massachusetts	x		July
Michigan	x		October
Minnesota		x	July
Mississippi	x		July
Missouri	x		July
Montana		x	July

continued

TABLE 8.1., *continued*

State	Annual	Biennial	Beginning Month of Fiscal Year
Nebraska	x		July
Nevada		x	July
New Hampshire		x	July
New Jersey	x		July
New Mexico	x		July
New York	x		April
North Carolina		x	July
North Dakota		x	July
Ohio		x	July
Oklahoma	x		July
Oregon		x	July
Pennsylvania	x		July
Rhode Island	x		July
South Carolina	x		July
South Dakota	x		July
Tennessee	x		July
Texas		x	September
Utah	x		July
Vermont		x	July
Virginia		x	July
Washington		x	July
West Virginia	x		July
Wisconsin		x	July
Wyoming		x	July
Total	30	20	

Source: Legislative Budget Procedures in the 50 States *(Denver, CO: National Conference of State Legislatures, 1983), p. 6.*

acter of the legislative sessions, as budgeting tends to crowd out other executive and legislative activities. With annual budgeting, no off-year exists to give the governor and the legislature a ''breather'' from budgeting, which would allow them to concentrate on other legislative initiatives. Similarly, state agencies tend to devote more of their top-level managers' time to developing budget requests for additional resources as well as preparing defenses against attempts to cut or reduce existing programs and their funding.

Executive Budget Development

The budgetary process begins with the governor's state budget office issuing budget instructions in the summer of the year preceding the upcoming budget period. Materials generally include a timetable for budget submission, instructions for formatting and packaging requests, and most important, a statement of major policy guidelines that agencies should follow in structuring their requests. This last communication is usually reviewed by the governor's key executive office staff and often personally by the governor. The policy themes often include reference to a fiscal climate of austerity within which agencies are urged to limit their re-

quests for budget increases, calls for greater productivity through internal realloca-
tions and greater administrative efficiency, and a hold-the-line policy on growth
in the bureaucracy.

Upon receipt of the budget requests in early fall, the internal pace of analysis
and recommendation is brisk since briefings with the governor generally must
begin by November or early December if the budget is to be ready for the printers
in time to meet constitutional or statutory deadlines for submission to the legislature, usually timed to the beginning of the legislative session in January or February. Analysts have eight to ten weeks, at most, to prepare recommendations for
the governor's consideration. During this time the state budget office not only
reacts to agency requests but also may make recommendations for the governor's
consideration where no agency requests are made. To "get a jump" on the process, meetings with the governor may be held during the summer months to identify the major policy issues that need to be addressed in the budget development
process, as well as to get some preliminary policy direction from the governor.

The Legislative Fiscal Committee's Involvement

Upon completion of the executive budget, it is transmitted to the legislature.
Beyond the narrative material describing the executive budget—its priorities and
general outlines—the legislative leadership introduces one or more budget bills on
behalf of the administration. Twenty-one states consider only one comprehensive
budget bill containing all the executive budget-related appropriations. In the
other twenty-nine states, the number of associated appropriations bills varies from
two to as many as 450. Table 8.2 shows the considerable variation found among
the states.

The number of appropriations bills has implications for legislative decision
making as well as for executive-legislative relations. A higher number of appropriations bills tends to fragment the legislative decision-making process. Because ac-

TABLE 8.2. NUMBER OF BUDGET BILLS CONSIDERED

	Single Bill	More Than One Bill
Alabama		2 major; 608 minor
Alaska	x	
Arizona		4
Arkansas		450
California	x	
Colorado	x	
Connecticut	x	
Delaware	x	
Florida	x	
Georgia	x	
Hawaii	x	
Idaho		120
Illinois		150–200
Indiana		3–10

continued

TABLE 8.2., *continued*

	Single Bill	More Than One Bill
Iowa		10–15
Kansas		10–20
Kentucky		3
Louisiana		4
Maine		3
Maryland		3
Massachusetts		5
Michigan		17
Minnesota		6
Mississippi		225
Missouri		16–18
Montana	x	
Nebraska		5–8
Nevada		5–10
New Hampshire	x	
New Jersey	x	
New Mexico	x	
New York		10–30
North Carolina		2
North Dakota		82
Ohio		3–4
Oklahoma		90–100
Oregon		110
Pennsylvania		60
Rhode Island	x	
South Carolina	x	
South Dakota	x	
Tennessee	x	
Texas	x	
Utah	x	
Vermont	x	
Virginia	x	
Washington		2–3
West Virginia	x	
Wisconsin		3
Wyoming		6–10
Total	21	29

Source: Legislative Budget Procedures in the 50 States *(Denver, CO: National Conference of State Legislatures, 1983), p. 42.*

tion is taken on the bills at different times by a wide assortment of subcommittees, the legislative leadership is put in a difficult position, not only to exercise leadership of the process, but also simply to know what has occurred at any given time. Thus the existence of many appropriations bills greatly constrains the legislature's ability to come up with a comprehensive alternative to the governor's budget, which is drawn together and highlighted in the executive budget book.

Upon receipt from the governor, the budget is then immediately assigned to the legislative fiscal committee of the chamber into which the bill was introduced or to a joint fiscal committee if one exists in that state. The committee, in turn, reports out the amended budget to the legislative house to which the executive budget was first sent and introduced. In the process of the committee's review, committee members are assisted by staff members, who frequently prepare issue discussion papers and suggest alternatives, or even make recommendations, for the committee's consideration. When staff members do not make formal recommendations, the way in which issues are framed and alternatives are presented often structures the decision-making process and delimits the options that will be considered by the committee.

Committee deliberation can generally be divided into two phases. The first consists of formal hearings, at which the agency and state budget office representatives participate. The first hearing is generally attended by the committee as a whole. It focuses on the overall budget—its directions, costs, major policy initiatives, and position implications. Much of the hearing is of largely symbolic value, providing a widely publicized forum for a good deal of public and partisan staging.

The other, and more important, forum involves the subcommittee hearings. Subcommittees are organized most often along functional policy or state agency lines, with subcommittees frequently established for education, transportation, health and human services, natural resources, general government, and the like. Subcommittee staffs, who have developed expertise in these functional policy areas, prepare analyses of the executive budget recommendations in their assigned areas of responsibility and may present them to the subcommittee at the chairperson's or members' request. In addition, the state budget office representatives often attend and, upon invitation by the subcommittee, present the governor's recommendations and respond to questions. Agency representatives are also usually present and may be asked questions about the programmatic nature of the governor's request. They may also be put in the difficult position of being invited to express any concerns they may have with the executive budget for their agencies. This dilemma presents a clear problem for cabinet agencies whose heads serve at the governor's pleasure. How far can they go in indicating that their agencies' needs merit increased resources beyond what the governor recommended and, at the same time, still remain loyal to the governor and his or her budget directions? For noncabinet agencies, the problem is less direct; some may even welcome the opportunity to "take the governor on" in the public legislative arena.

Upon completion of subcommittee deliberation, votes are taken on motions to amend the executive budget. And successful motions, in turn, are referred to the full committee for action. Through subcommittee votes, members get an opportunity to hear the opinions of other members, and thus are able to size up the likely outcome when the vote of the full committee comes up.

Although the decision-making process can accommodate subcommittee strife, such is the exception. Subcommittees try to work out their differences before potentially divisive issues come to the full committee, and when this is successful, committee members of other subcommittees are more likely to go along with the group's recommendations. Reciprocity is an important element underpinning the full committee's decision making. Subcommittee recommendations often carry the entire committee with no or only few dissenters. Frequently, too, it is the chairs of other subcommittees who second motions for passage in the full committee. Discipline is maintained largely out of a recognition that if one subcommittee does not support the recommendations of others, it cannot expect to receive their support for its own recommendations.

Exceptions to the norm of reciprocity do occasionally occur, most frequently involving issues of financial aid to local units of government. Each committee member, after all, represents at least one municipality, county, and school district. Moreover, each committee member, through the aid of computer simulations, knows what various changes in formula and/or funding levels will mean for his or her district. Thus decisions governing local units are less easily contained within the subcommittee than are budget items dealing with state agency operations.

Illustrative of this distinction is the much broader attendance of committee members at subcommittees considering local aid issues. In fact, when major formula revisions are the subject of discussion, it is not uncommon for most, if not all, committee members to be present. Hence, in this environment, the committee chairperson attempts to come up with recommendations that redistribute aid in such a way that a clear majority of the entire committee members' districts are benefitted. Otherwise the chairperson cannot expect to receive the reciprocal support of other subcommittees. Local assistance items, then, may upset the generally accepted norm of reciprocity.

Upon completion of subcommittee work, the full committee reconvenes and takes up unresolved items, considers the aggregate spending package that the subcommittees have recommended, makes adjustments depending on revenue availability, and then reports out recommended amendments. The governor's budget may be amended in the form submitted by the governor or be submitted to the legislature as a complete substitute amendment.

Six states do not use appropriations subcommittees; committee work is done by the committee as a whole.[3] Wisconsin, one of those states, provides an alternative to the subcommittee—the "discussion group." The Joint Legislative Finance Committee is divided into discussion groups for the purpose of reviewing the budget. Each group reviews a different portion of the budget, assisted by staff members who are organized along functionally based discussion group divisions. Although no binding votes are taken at meetings, a "sense of the discussion group" emerges, giving observers a good indication of how the committee would probably vote on an issue. Just as with subcommittees in other states, the norm of reciprocity among discussion groups is strong. Discussion groups generally accede to the motions advanced by other groups in votes of the full committee.[4] (See Figures 8.2a and b.)

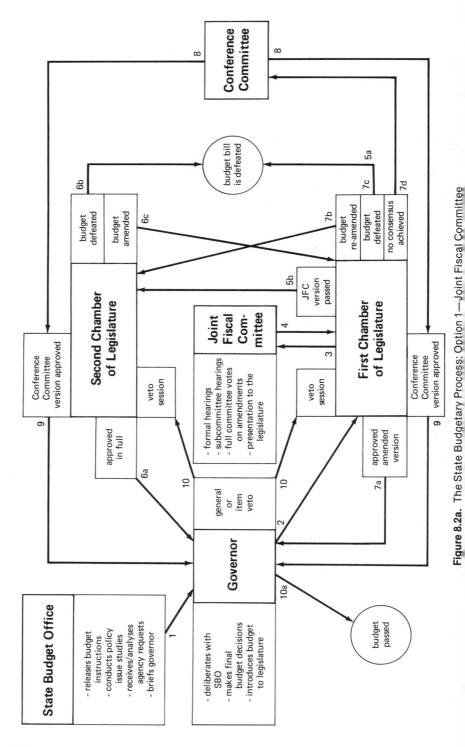

Figure 8.2a. The State Budgetary Process: Option 1—Joint Fiscal Committee

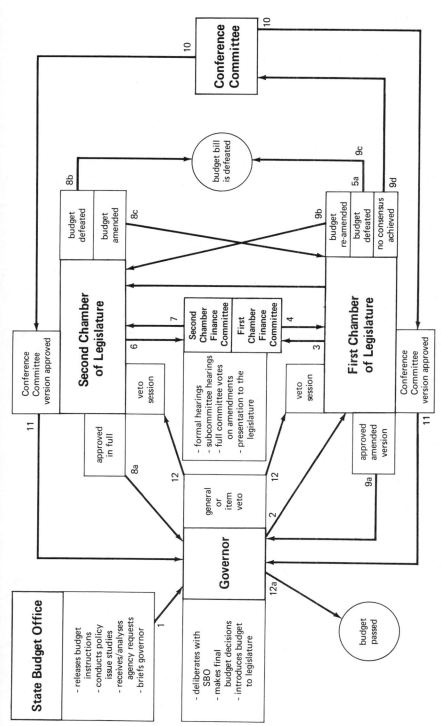

Figure 8.2b. The State Budgetary Process: Option 2—Separate Fiscal Committees

165

Action Shifting to the Legislative Chambers

After receiving the amended version of the executive budget from its fiscal committee, the first house of the legislature is allocated only about two to three weeks to complete its process of amendment from the floor. After clearing the first house, the budget bill is sent to the second house, where, similar to the process just discussed, it is referred to that chamber's fiscal committee. The ensuing process proceeds similarly to that described for the first house. Of course, in those states having a joint fiscal committee, the committee's recommendations are provided to both chambers simultaneously, even though each house deliberates on the executive budget separately, beginning with the house in which it was first introduced. If the second house cannot agree with the first, suggested changes are sent back to the first for its consideration. Modification may then be made, and again, that revised version is sent to the second house for review. The process continues until agreement is reached. Obviously, consistent lack of agreement can extend this phase of the process beyond the normal time frame.

If agreement cannot be reached, a conference committee may be appointed by the legislative leadership. The conference committee is normally allocated no more than two weeks to work out an agreed-upon version, which is then sent to both houses for a vote. Depending on the state, the conference report may or may not be amended by the legislature. In some states it must be voted up or down without amendment. Very seldom, however, is the conference report rejected altogether by one or both houses.

Debate on the floor characterizes the public arena for budget deliberations at this stage in the budgetary process. However, the more important arena for decision making is the partisan legislative caucus, which tends to be more extensively used for budget deliberation than for the single, substantive bill legislative process. Legislators advocate amendments and attempt to generate support for them in the caucus. At times "straw votes" are taken to gauge support for amendments. Frequently legislative staff directors and key staffs are invited, along with the caucus aides, to participate in the discussions. When the governor is of the same political party as the legislature, the state budget director may also be invited to attend and respond to questions.

In the caucus, members of the fiscal committee generally coalesce around the recommendations endorsed by the committee. A unified voice gives them considerable influence and contributes to preserving a budget that largely reflects the committee's work. However, the partisan caucus may become the battleground for those legislators who did not prevail during the committee's phase of budget deliberations.

In assessing the relationship of legislative leadership to the fiscal committee's endorsed budget, we must recall that the institutional role of the committee is to put together a fiscally responsible budget, which not only does not exceed revenues but also includes a basic cushion (generally at least 1 percent) to accommodate unforeseen events. Overall, this strategy is supported by the leadership, but support may break down on specific items. Also coalitions of maverick legislators may form in opposition to the leadership's position. Such coalitions try to gain a stranglehold on the entire budget by aggregating support for a broadly inclusive package of amendments not supported by the leadership. If they are successful in getting enough support so that a majority no longer exists in the majority party, these subcaucuses can hold the leadership hostage.

For the less broadly significant items that involve little cost and affect few other legislators' interests, a threat by a majority party caucus member not to vote for the budget unless his or her pet item is included may win a concession from the leadership if the final caucus vote looks to be marginal. On the other hand, for significant issues affecting a large number of caucus members, a much broader supportive coalition is needed to hold the leadership hostage.

Two features characterize this segment of the budgetary process. First, time constraints are the most severe of any phase. Thus legislators must be selective in their deliberations. Second, the agenda is less shaped by staff members at this stage than at any other stage in the process. Legislators bring their own distilled agenda to the caucuses, and the deliberation process is one of determining where consensus lies among the legislators themselves. Fiscal staff members may prepare fiscal notes and discussion papers on the major proposed amendments, but they generally exercise less influence at this stage than during committee deliberations. The emphasis in the caucuses is more on coalition building and less on policy analysis.

At the conclusion of the caucus sessions, the legislative leadership has a good sense of which amendments will receive sufficient support for passage on the floor. To the extent possible, the majority party leadership attempts to mobilize support to reject amendments that have not been approved in caucus.

The Governor's Chance Again: The Veto

After the budget clears the legislature, the governor again gets an opportunity to shape its final form. Governors in forty-three states possess item veto authority for appropriation bills, including the state budget.[5] (Figure 8.3 provides an example of an item veto.) Veto recommendations are generally made by the state budget office and may be supported by issue discussion papers. Agencies, interest groups, and individual legislators may also submit veto recommendations.

Although the state budget office normally plays a role in identifying sections of the budget bill for veto, it plays a less direct role during veto deliberation than during the earlier period of executive budget development. The decision-making process for veto deliberation is less self-contained and more subject to influences by forces outside of the governor's executive budget agency. Legislative leaders of the governor's political party are frequently brought in to discuss the politics of vetoes. An often-discussed question is, Can the vetoes be sustained? In addition, the governor and/or executive office staff members consult with those legislators who will be most affected by prospective vetoes. Their reaction to the vetoes, and

SECTION 977m. 49.19(11)(a)1.a of the statutes is amended to read: 49.19(11)(a)1.a. Monthly payments made under s.20.435(4)(d) and (p) to persons or to families with dependent children shall be based on family size and shall be at ~~85%~~ 8~~4~~.0~~4~~% of the total of the allowances under subds.2 and 4 plus the following standards of assistance for the period from ~~September 1, 1985~~ <u>the first day of the first month beginning at least 20 days after the effective date of this subd.1.a....[revisor inserts date]</u>, to ~~March 31, 1987.~~ <u>June 30, 1989.</u>

Vetoed in Part

```
In this item veto the governor lined out both
4s and the decimal point of 84.04%, to change
it to 80%, thus reducing welfare benefits by
five percent from current law. The
legislature had reduced benefits by only .96
of one percent from current law, and the
governor's item veto reduced benefits by an
additional 4.04 percent.

The governor explained his veto using the
following message:
```

Section 977m

This section amends current law to reduce the benefits paid under the Aid to Families with Dependent Children program by one percent during the 1987–89 biennium. I am partially vetoing this section in order to reduce the benefits by an additional five percent during this biennium.

With this veto, I am standing firm on my position that our efforts for welfare reform must be funded primarily through a redirection of a portion of the current expenditures for benefits. This veto accomplishes the first part of that objective. In addition, in making this veto I am reaffirming my commitment to using the savings from the reduction in benefits to fund programs to eliminate welfare dependency. I will introduce legislation in the fall, authorizing expenditures from these savings to further expand our welfare reform efforts.

Figure 8.3. Example of Line-Item Veto Reducing Welfare Costs

how hard they will work for override, are subjects of much conversation. Also, the governor's aides query interest group representatives to get their reaction to veto candidates.

In summary, then, input is considerably broader for veto consideration than is the case for executive budget development. Moreover, since vetoes represent a relatively small but controversial part of the budget, the governor personally takes a more focused, active part in the deliberations.

Legislative Review of Gubernatorial Vetoes

Legislative requirements for overriding budget vetoes, in whole or by line item, are the same as for other legislation. When considering attempts to override, legislative leaders once again use the partisan caucus. There, legislators put together an agenda of desired overrides. The leadership submits its recommendations, and other legislators attempt to generate enough caucus support to add or delete items from that list.

This period in the budgetary process is a time of intense lobbying on the part of the governor's staff, particularly with members of the governor's political party. "Political hardball," when needed, is the name of the game. Chips are called in, and promises of future benefits are made in return for cooperation. Gubernatorial vetoes often become highly publicized, and a governor's political reputation can depend upon his or her ability to get those vetoes sustained in the legislature. For if a governor is unable to win support from his or her own party, that inability sends signals to the opposition party, the media, and the public at large that the governor lacks the political strength required to lead the state effectively.

Legislative committee staffs play a much less direct role in the veto override session than in the earlier segments of the budgetary process. They may prepare analyses of the effects of veto overrides, but much of the staff's work at this stage is normally taken over by the partisan legislative caucus staffs. The emphasis, at this stage, becomes coalition building with strongly partisan solidarity.

The Process Recycles

The budget, after veto consideration, becomes the state's fiscal "blueprint" for the next year or two. Adjustments to the budget can be made through the enactment of legislation in the intervening period before the next budget bill is considered, if the legislature is in session. However, few such changes are made in normal times. When the legislature is not in session, the fiscal committee in some states is empowered to appropriate limited amounts of money from a contingency fund to cover emergencies or unforeseen events. The committee may also usually transfer funds from one appropriation to another.

The process then repeats itself. New administrations come into office; yet the essential characteristics of the process, as described, generally endure among the states.

Major Variations on a Theme

Although the process just described includes a clear distinction between the executive development and legislative review phases of the generic state budgetary process, that distinction is blurred in a few states. In Arkansas, North Carolina, South Carolina, and Texas the legislature becomes intimately involved in the actual development of the state budget. The responsibility for budget preparation, typically accorded to the governor, assisted by the state budget office, is shared with the legislative branch in these states. Thus the legislature is in a position not only to approve the state budget but also to shape its form prior to referral.[6]

This sharing of power takes various forms. In North Carolina the executive budget is developed by a twelve-member advisory budget commission, consisting of four gubernatorial appointees, four senators, and four representatives. It is staffed by the state budget office. The commission, which operates through committees, directly receives agency budget requests, holds public hearings, and makes formal recommendations on budget requests. It may also initiate budget recommendations where no agency request has been made. Although the commission's recommendations are advisory, the governor largely accepts them.[7]

In a similar vein, the South Carolina state budget control board incorporates both executive and legislative representation in the process of budget development. But in South Carolina, the governor's institutional influence over the content of the executive budget is even more diluted. In addition to legislative representatives sitting on the board, power is shared with two independently elected executive branch officials, the state treasurer and comptroller general.[8]

In Arkansas and Texas the governor is responsible for developing the executive budget but faces competition from the legislature. Although the governor's state budget office in Arkansas receives agency requests and puts together a recommended executive budget, that package is referred to the legislative council, which, in turn, under the supervision of legislative leadership, prepares the official state budget for referral to the legislature.[9] The governor's budget development prerogative is also shared with the legislature in Texas. The governor prepares one version of the executive budget, and the legislative budget board prepares another. Both present their budget recommendations independently to the legislature. However, it is the legislative version that most prominently serves as the benchmark for legislative deliberation.[10]

INSTITUTIONAL POLICY MAKING
VERSUS DIRECT DEMOCRACY

The preceding discussion portrays executive-legislative policy making at the institutional level. Individuals hold policy-making positions in state government, but they exercise the *institutional* authority associated with the positions they occupy. The legitimate authority does not arise from them as individuals, however talented they may be, but as institutional participants carrying out the functions, and performing the roles, associated with their institutional positions. The structure, functions, and roles of the governor, state budget office, state executive agencies, legislature, legislative committees, and partisan caucuses—and their patterns of interaction—make up the traditionally described state policy-making process. But as acknowledged at the beginning of this chapter, the legislative process is only one of several avenues of state policy making, although perhaps the most significant.

One notable variant, to be treated in the next chapter, departs from the traditional institutional framework. The processes of direct democracy, where available, permit state residents to take policy making into their own collective hands, not mediated by the institutions of representative government.

SUMMARY AND CONCLUSIONS

The political institutions of state government make public policy in a number of ways that significantly affect our lives. And they do so by using a number of distinct processes. This chapter has focused on the two processes of executive-legislative lawmaking, the substantive bill legislative process and the budgetary process, while recognizing that courts make policy in interpreting the law, that regulatory agencies make policy in promulgating regulations, and that citizens make policy directly through the initiative and popular referendum.

The two law-making processes share similarities in their patterns of executive and legislative involvement and interaction, but some significant differences can be noted. The budgetary process generally involves greater gubernatorial initiative and influence, and it also alters patterns of legislative involvement and influence associated with the substantive bill legislative process. The budgetary process narrows the scope of legislative involvement and shifts influence from the substantive standing committees to the appropriations committees and their subcommittees.

In addition, the budgetary process tends to "crowd out" the substantive bill legislative process, given the significance of the state budget as both a resource allocation and policy vehicle. And as governors and legislatures tend to put more policy into the budget, where permitted by state law, the state budgetary process will become even more central to state policy making.

REFERENCES

1. Alan Rosenthal, *Legislative Life* (New York: Harper & Row, 1981), pp. 256–72.
2. Ratings done by the executive director and former deputy director of the National Association of State Budget Officers, October 1986.
3. *Legislative Budget Procedures in the 50 States* (Denver, CO: National Conference of State Legislatures, 1983), pp. 24–25.
4. James J. Gosling, *The Wisconsin Budgetary Process: An Interpretive Description* (Madison, WI: The Robert M. La Follette Institute of Public Affairs, 1985), pp. 3–8.
5. *The Line-Item Veto: An Appraisal* (Washington, DC: Committee on the Budget, U.S. House of Representatives, 1984), p. 13.

6. *Budgetary Processes in the States* (Washington, DC: National Association of State Budget Officers, 1981), pp. 2–3.
7. Rosenthal, *Legislative Life,* pp. 286–87.
8. Ibid., p. 287.
9. Ibid.
10. Ibid.

CHAPTER 9

Direct Democracy

Citizens across the country influence state policy making in a number of ways. They elect several executive branch constitutional officers, judges, and state legislators. They appear before duly-constituted government bodies to urge that public officials pursue a recommended course of action. They may even picket and protest government action or lack thereof. And in several states they may directly make or change laws or amend the state constitution by a majority vote on ballot propositions. It is this last phenomenon, that of direct democracy, with which this chapter deals.

Direct democracy is most often identified with the *initiative,* the *recall,* and the *referendum.* Both the initiative and the recall allow citizens to act directly without any involvement of the governor or the state legislature. With the direct initiative, a required number of voters' signatures are needed to qualify proposed new laws, law changes, or constitutional amendments for placement on a statewide general election ballot, to be approved by a majority of those voting. The legislature plays no part in the electorate's decision, other than for individual legislators possibly to urge support or rejection of a given proposition. With the recall, after obtaining a specified number of signatures, citizens can vote to remove or keep a recalled official in office. Again, as with the initiative, the legislature plays no institutional role in the decision.

Conversely, the legislature is involved in the referendum, either indirectly or directly, depending on the particular form of referendum involved. The referendum can take one of three forms. In the first form, the *general* referendum, the state constitution may require the legislature to submit certain of its acts, such as proposed constitutional amendments or bond issues (which raise revenues for capital projects), to the voters for their concurrence or rejection. In the second form, a legislature may submit proposals to the voters for their advice on whether the legislature should pass specific legislation—a form commonly referred to as the *indirect* or *advisory* referendum. The third form, known as the *direct* or *popular* referendum, puts the impetus for action in the hands of the voters, who can decide within a specified time after the legislature's adjournment whether to reject a law passed in that legislative session. As with the initiative, the popular referendum requires the collection of a specified number of signatures for the referendum question to be put on the ballot, and then a majority of those voting is required for passage.

Direct democracy became an element in the political systems of the American states during the Progressive era at the beginning of this century, but its roots can be traced back to the New England town meeting, and further back to the Greek city-state. The Progressives believed that special interests corrupted politicians, political parties, and government institutions, undercutting the basis of representative government. Thus, to reduce the influence of organized interests and powerful elites, the Progressives initiated a set of devices designed to promote the direct involvement of voters in public policy making.

The philosophy behind direct democracy is similar today, although the emphasis on thwarting special interests is probably not as strong. The motivating concern today appears to focus more on the responsiveness of representative government. As the popular rhetoric goes, if elected representatives are not going to listen to what the people really want, citizens will take action into their own hands.

California's controversial Proposition 13, approved by the voters in 1978, provides a notable example of the "you've had your chance; now it's our turn" approach. The initiators of Proposition 13, Howard Jarvis and Paul Gann, argued that elected state officials were simply not in tune with the majority of Californians on the issue of taxes—property taxes in particular. The people were calling for lower taxes, but their elected representatives were doing nothing about it, in their view. Instead, taxes continued to rise. Something, Jarvis and Gann implored, had to be done; the people needed to take direct action. As a result of their initiative, the electorate voted by an overwhelming margin to cut local property taxes by 57 percent, or $7 billion.

Direct democracy has its advocates and its detractors. Advocates point out that the various mechanisms of direct democracy allow the public's interests to be translated directly into action. No "middleman" is needed. The underlying rationale is that individuals know what is best for themselves and will act when necessary. Another assumption is that voters possess sufficient intelligence and hunger for information to make the effort to inform themselves of what is at issue. Finally, when voters use the ballot for direct action, it is assumed that special interest groups will be the losers, since elected officials, on whom lobbyists descend, are effectively taken out of the picture. Thus, as the thinking goes, the people get what they want directly in an arena free from elected officials who readily bend to special interests' entreaties.

Detractors argue that prominent use of direct democracy will undermine the structures and institutions of representative democracy. Voters can take action into their own hands, prompted by whatever factors are motivating their choice. Political parties, accordingly, lose a great deal of their relevance and become weakened, as voters become less dependent on them for aggregating political interests. With direct democracy, the party label becomes largely irrelevant in providing cues that inform voters' choice.

Detractors further allege that petition signers and voters on ballot propositions often do not understand fully the proposals' substance or implications. And several research studies support that contention. Voters, when asked if they understand the measures before them, largely respond in the affirmative, but follow-up research suggests that their understanding is often incomplete or confused about the details.[1] Research also demonstrates that a direct relationship exists between educational level and the ability to identify the issues and implications associated with ballot questions.[2]

Finally, opponents argue that rather than reducing the impact of special interests on policy making, the devices of direct democracy have the contrary effect; they actually enhance the influence of organized interests, for special interests often have the financial capability to "buy" an initiative or referendum through advertising. If, as was assumed earlier, voters are not all that well informed about the complexities and intricacies of the propositions before them, but react according to images and/or preconceived ideas, advertising holds the promise of image and symbol manipulation, evoking a choice not necessarily based on substantive grounds.

Advocates might counter that it does not really matter on what basis individuals make public choices; the issue is whether citizens have a feel for what is in their own best interests and can relate those interests to the propositions before them. That is a different matter than being able to explain a proposition's substance. Nevertheless, there is still the risk that voters will base their choices on partial information, confusion, and even misunderstanding. But supporters see that risk as marking traditional electoral contests as well.

Detractors might respond that a capricious majority can play havoc with the rights of the minority and that representative government, not direct democracy, best protects minority interests. The process of partisan aggregation in a pluralist political system, together with separation of the executive and legislative branches, necessitates compromise and accommodation, helping to protect minority rights. In response, supporters of direct democracy might counter that if the initiative or referendum is alleged to abuse the minority unconstitutionally, the third branch of government, the courts, can correct the injustice upon petition.

THE INITIATIVE AND POPULAR REFERENDUM

Twenty-two states have the authority for both the initiative and the popular referendum. Of the twenty-three states having the initiative, all but one, Florida, also have authority for the popular referendum. Of the twenty-five states possessing authority for the popular referendum, only three have no authority for the initiative. (See Table 9.1.)

Direct legislation has its historical roots in the Upper Plains states and the West. South Dakota, in 1898, was the first state to institute both the initiative and the popular referendum, followed by Utah in 1900. By 1910, ten other states followed suit and authorized both reforms. Until recent times, 1918 marked the end of the spread of direct legislation devices among the states, with seven additional states assuming authority for the initiative and the popular referendum. During the first two decades of the twentieth century, Kentucky, Maryland, and New Mexico added only the popular referendum. Until modern times, there had been no case of a state approving the initiative alone, without the popular referendum, until Florida did in 1978—the most recent addition to the ranks of states having authority for direct legislation.

Besides Florida, four states adopted direct legislation mechanisms in recent

TABLE 9.1. AUTHORITY FOR THE INITIATIVE AND POPULAR REFERENDUM

State	Initiative	Popular Referendum
Alaska	x	x
Arizona	x	x
Arkansas	x	x
California	x	x
Colorado	x	x
Florida	x	
Idaho	x	x
Illinois	x	x
Kentucky		x
Maine	x	x
Maryland		x
Massachusetts	x	x
Michigan	x	x
Missouri	x	x
Montana	x	x
Nebraska	x	x
Nevada	x	x
New Mexico		x
North Dakota	x	x
Ohio	x	x
Oklahoma	x	x
Oregon	x	x
South Dakota	x	x
Utah	x	x
Washington	x	x
Wyoming	x	x

Source: David B. Magleby, Direct Legislation (Baltimore, MD: Johns Hopkins University Press, 1984), pp. 38–39.

decades: Alaska (the initiative and popular referendum in 1959), Wyoming (both in 1968), Illinois (both in 1970), and Montana (the initiative in 1972, added to the existing popular referendum). It is notable that forty-one years elapsed between Massachusetts' adoption of both devices in 1918 and Alaska's action upon its admission to statehood in 1959. Considering the time lag involved, it appeared in mid-century that interest among the states in direct democracy had come to an end.

But the experience of the 1980s shows that contemporary interest has been very much alive. Legislatures in several states not now possessing direct democracy have taken up the debate. However, voters in Minnesota (1980) and Rhode Island (1986) recently rejected measures that would have amended their constitutions to provide for the initiative and popular referendum, with the Rhode Island vote falling only three percentage points short of passage. In both states, organized labor and business led the opposition. Public employee unions, in particular, were worried about the proclivity of the electorate to make laws that would negatively affect their members' salaries and pensions. Business associations were concerned that the public might be more inclined to heighten state regulation of business practices beyond the limits that the state legislature would be willing to go.

This defeat in Rhode Island may hold significant implications for the prospects of future action in other states, particularly those in the eastern part of the nation. As Sue Thomas, a close observer of direct democracy, observed, "For many years, those who follow initiative politics have been convinced that if one eastern state adopted I&R others would soon follow. If this hypothesis is correct, the reverse must also be true. Therefore, it may well be that with the defeat of the initiative in Rhode Island, surrounding states will be less likely to embrace direct democracy."[3]

The recent experience of Minnesota and Rhode Island may call into question another popular assumption. Advocates of direct democracy have traditionally held that the process is so attractive to voters that, given the opportunity, they will jump at the chance to adopt it. The electoral response in Minnesota and Rhode Island suggests that voters may have other ideas about what represents their best interests.

Despite the recent two failures, several state legislatures continue to debate the relative merits of direct democracy. Contemporary issues of tax reduction, legalized gambling, and public morality (including abortion) have kept citizens' interest alive. Strongly held convictions on single-issue politics have prompted citizens to consider taking action into their own hands, particularly when they believe that their elected representatives are not pursuing these issues vigorously enough.

At the federal level, in the 1970s, Congress considered the merits of establishing a national initiative. However, no bill passed either congressional chamber. And in the 1980s, Congress did not devote serious attention to its adoption, obviously having a stake in the maintenance of representative government.

The initiative has been adopted in two forms among the states. The *direct* initiative represents the most common form, requiring no legislative involvement to place a proposal on the ballot. The *indirect* form requires that the petition, having garnered a specified number of signatures, be submitted to the legislature, which, in turn, can adopt the proposal as received, place it on the ballot unaltered, or modify the proposal before placing it on the ballot. Fifteen states possess the direct form alone, three have the indirect form alone, and five have the authority for both. (See Table 9.2.)

The common thread to the initiation and early spread of direct democracy has been its Progressive heritage. As introduced briefly earlier, the Progressives wanted government to be given back to the people. They believed that government was too beholden to special interests and operated too much behind closed doors. It had to be made more open to people directly—people not bound by traditional party politics or narrow representative government. In pursuing that philosophy, the Progressives devoted their attention not only to the instruments of direct democracy but to the direct primary as well. The underlying tenet was the same for both: that individuals were in the best position to decide things for themselves, whether that be laws or who will run in general elections. The Progressives viewed the electorate as basically able and well enough informed to judge

TABLE 9.2. CITIZENS' INITIATIVE

State	Constitutional	Statutory	Direct or Indirect*
Alaska		x	D
Arizona	x	x	D
Arkansas	x	x	D
California	x	x	D
Colorado	x	x	D
Florida	x		D
Idaho		x	D
Illinois	x		D
Maine		x	I
Massachusetts	x	x	I
Michigan	x	x	B
Missouri	x	x	D
Montana	x	x	D
Nebraska	x	x	D
Nevada	x	x	B
North Dakota	x	x	D
Ohio	x	x	B
Oklahoma	x	x	D
Oregon	x	x	D
South Dakota	x	x	D
Utah		x	B
Washington		x	B
Wyoming		x	I

*D = direct; I = indirect; B = both. (Source: David B. Magleby, Direct Legislation (Baltimore, MD: Johns Hopkins University Press, 1984), pp. 38–39.

what is in their best interest. In fact, Theodore Roosevelt was so enamored of direct democracy that he once proposed subjecting court decisions to popular review. Political leaders in several Progressive states pursued both reforms, but one strongly Progressive state, Wisconsin, was conspicuously absent. There, political leaders put their strong support exclusively behind the open direct primary—one of the many Progressive legacies of the Robert M. La Follette era. But the roots of representative government had been sunk too deep to be dislodged in favor of direct action.

The Petition

To initiate legislation through the initiative or popular referendum, citizens must be able to show that the proposal has a certain minimal level of support among the electorate. Evidence of support must take the form of signatures given by qualified voters; proponents must canvass the electorate and acquire a predetermined number of signatures. Minimal signature requirements have been established to ensure that the proposed legislation has a core level of support among the electorate, keeping frivolous or narrow initiatives off the ballot.

The basis among the states for calculating the required number of signatures is variously a prescribed percentage of the state's total population; the vote cast in the immediately preceding general election; or the vote cast in a designated election, either for governor or secretary of state. The required percentage may, and generally does, vary, depending on whether the initiative is intended to amend the state's constitution or create or change a law. Where a difference exists, the percentage requirement for the constitutional initiative is consistently higher.

Across the states, the most common requirement for the constitutional initiative is 10 percent of the vote cast in the most recent gubernatorial election, whereas it is 8 percent for the statutory initiative. In comparison, the average requirement for the popular referendum is 5 percent. This lower percentage can probably be attributed to the legislature's prior involvement: The issue is not new to the state's policy debate and is therefore less likely to catch an unwary electorate by surprise. But the actual percentage requirements vary considerably by state. On the more lenient end of the spectrum lies North Dakota, which requires signatures equal to 2 percent of the voting-age population. In contrast, Wyoming, on the more constrained side, requires 15 percent of the total votes cast in the preceding general election.[4]

To be counted as valid, signatures must be attested to by designated public officials. In most states this responsibility falls to local officials, most commonly either the county clerk or county registrar, who carry out their task under the general oversight of the secretary of state's office—an otherwise largely ceremonial agency at the state level, with primary responsibility for authenticating public records and legislation enacted by the legislature. The secretary of state generally accepts the local official's validation count but may intervene directly when allegations of wrongdoing are leveled against the local validation effort.

The administrative costs of local validation have become considerable. Not only do the counties incur costs with the validation process, but also several states, most notably California, face the added costs of publishing voter handbooks, which are mailed to the known addresses of registered voters. The handbooks contain a description of the propositions on the ballot as well as, in several states, arguments in support or opposition.

Before signatures can even be collected, most states require the organizers of the petition drive to file the complete text of the proposition with the secretary of state. Once done, the proposition is referred in several states to the attorney general, who gives it an official title. Then, after the text of the proposal is filed, it may not be subsequently changed prior to the election—a protection against voters signing the petition in one form, only to find it altered later in the process.

Initiators and supporters of initiative and popular referendum measures can go about seeking the required number of signatures in two ways. First, volunteers can be solicited—people who are willing to go out on the stump and seek voters' signatures because they believe strongly enough in the merits of the proposed measure. They not only contact individuals with whom they are acquainted and who they believe might support their cause but also may set up tables in large shopping malls—where permitted by law—hoping to convince strangers to lend their support and provide their signature. The contact in quest of signatures also provides an opportunity to seek financial contributions to help defray the costs associated with the development, preparation, and distribution of supportive written materials.

The obstacles facing a wholly volunteer organization are several. First, the sheer magnitude of the required number of signatures means that the volunteer organization has to be large and highly active. Second, the time limits placed on the signature drive greatly constrain the volunteer organization, which often has to spend considerable front-end time just getting itself organized and prepared to undertake the signature-gathering effort. Third, the organization has to develop a statewide network. A local group, with a largely local issue, faces the momentous task of broadening the issue base in a way that will expand the core of volunteers who will zealously carry the effort to areas beyond the base of origin.

Faced with these significant constraints, supporters have increasingly turned to paid signature gatherers, who often are compensated on a per signature basis. Interest groups, which feel strongly about an issue and are willing to dip into their pockets to help the cause, are the prime candidates to employ paid assistance. Paid signature collectors have traditionally sought out signatures in places where large numbers of people gather, such as shopping centers and malls, athletic events, and outside of churches on days of worship. But with the greatly enhanced capabilities of computers and information systems, direct-mail campaigns have largely come to replace person-to-person contact.

With clever ways of targeting audiences, computers and direct mail solicitation have enabled supporters to get tailored information to prospective signers. The core information may remain constant, but the tailored portion zeroes in on the respective sympathies of would-be adherents. Not only is this method effective in yielding signatures, but it also has proven successful in winning financial support—support that can, in turn, be used to expand initiative efforts. This is basically the way Howard Jarvis and Paul Gann were able to qualify Proposition 13 for the ballot and to continue to finance subsequent tax-limiting initiatives. In one subsequent direct mail campaign, the Jarvis letter contained the following postscript: ''This petition was made possible by a $12 contribution by Ms. Barbara Murphy of Vista. If you fail to return your petition, the Murphy family's contribution will have gone to waste. Mail it today.''[5] Of course, the clever appeal also invited the reader to become one of the ''fighting Murphys'' by including a check along with the signature.

The petition industry had its birth and growth in California, and has exported the phenomenon to other states. California petition firms have qualified initiatives in Arizona, Florida, Montana, and Oregon.[6] The price, however, is not cheap, ranging from several hundred thousand dollars to well over a million. Direct-mail campaigns tend to be priced on the higher side. The spending record in California goes to the Howard Jarvis-led ''Save 13'' Committee, which spent over $2.2 million, using largely a direct-mail campaign, to qualify Proposition 36 on the November 1984 ballot, despite its ultimate defeat.[7] The most expensive signature-gathering campaign on record in any state goes to the Florida Medical Society's efforts, using a California signature-collection firm, to qualify Proposition 9 for the ballot—an initiative that would have limited damage awards for ''pain and suffering'' to no more than $200,000. The implications for Florida physicians were readily apparent. Approval of the initiative would result in significantly reduced malpractice insurance costs. The measure was of sufficient interest to the Florida medical community that its members contributed nearly $3 million to finance the signature-collection efforts.[8] However, because of problems with an ambiguous ballot title and summary, the Florida Supreme Court ruled that the measure could not be placed on the ballot—a case of growing court intervention in the initiative process, which will be discussed more fully later in this chapter.

Signature collectors are usually paid between twenty cents and one dollar for each signature obtained, with the higher range paid to gatherers in tightly contested campaigns or where time is at a premium. Where direct mailings are used, most of the costs can be attributed to postage itself, followed by material and labor expenses.

The goal of paid signature campaigns is to gather the required number of *qualified* signatures. The goal of paid signature collectors is to maximize the number of signatures collected, and thereby maximize their income. Therefore, their incentive is to obtain the greatest number of qualified signatures with the least investment of time and effort. Such an incentive does not lead to voter education on the issues but to techniques that bring voter cooperation. In this vein, the executive director of California's Common Cause described the signature-gathering process as follows:

The people out front were salespeople—pitchmen—their commission was a signature, and the fewer words they had to use, the greater their commission.

Once at the table anyone who wished to read the document was ushered to the side and given a copy so as not to block the petition itself. Antagonists were ignored or asked to move on. . . . People with questions about the content were given information to read, but not discussion time from the workers. . . . The singular objective was 500,000 signatures in five months. Education on the issues will have to wait until after the measure was qualified.[9]

In responding to the question whether signers actually read what they signed, one close and long-time observer of the process responded "generally no," commenting that most people trust the petition circulator's description of the issue.[10]

Because of the possible abuse associated with paid signature collection, three states—Colorado, Massachusetts, and Nebraska—have prohibited its use, confining signature collection to the ranks of volunteers. However, in October 1986, a Colorado district court judge ruled the Colorado law prohibiting payments unconstitutional. On appeal, the Colorado Supreme Court sustained the ruling.

The Electoral Campaign

Once the petition becomes qualified for the ballot, both supporters and opponents attempt to convince the electorate how to vote on the proposition. Several forms of advertising can be employed to influence public opinion, among them television and radio spots, billboards, newspaper advertisements, bumper stickers, and direct-mail campaigns. Highly visible public figures and celebrities may be asked to provide endorsements in support of, or in opposition to, ballot propositions.

The costs of such efforts can be high, particularly when highly significant or controversial measures are before the voters. A study of California initiatives found nine recent campaigns that involved over $4 million in total spending. But the study also showed that the balance of spending bore only a modest relationship to success at the polls. Outspending the opponent was shown to be most effective when employed in opposition to a proposition, regardless of the margin of overspending.[11] This finding supports an earlier study of California propositions, which found that outspending opponents has been generally ineffective when in support of propositions but particularly effective when heavily one-sided (at least a 2:1 margin) in opposition to propositions.[12]

Recent Experience with the Initiative

The 1986 election cycle saw 227 initiatives filed and titled in twenty-three states. Of that number, forty-three, or 19 percent, garnered sufficient recognized signatures to be put on the ballots of fifteen states. That number can be compared to the experience of 1984, when forty-two measures appeared on state ballots out of 305 titled—a success rate of 14 percent.

Among the states, Oregon was clearly the most prolific, filing fifty-two measures, of which fifty-one were titled. Of that amount, twelve actually appeared on the ballot. California, the perennial leader in state initiative activity, both filed and qualified the second highest number of measures, getting six on the ballot out of thirty-five titled. Oregon's twelve initiatives represented the highest number before the electorate since 1914, the heyday of Oregonian progressivism. In contrast, California's 1986 experience constituted a downturn from the 1984 level, when sixty-four proposals were filed and titled and seven subsequently were put on the ballot.[13]

Table 9.3 provides a comparison of the relative success of initiative drives among the states for the 1982, 1984, and 1986 electoral periods, comparing measures titled, qualified, and actually placed on the ballot.

Of the forty-three measures on state ballots in 1986, tax and revenue proposals represented the greatest number, eleven. The most significant among them required that general and special purpose local tax increases be approved by a two-thirds vote of the electorate (California); that state and local tax increases be approved by a simple majority vote (Colorado); that the 7.5 percent surtax on the state personal income tax be phased out and that state revenue growth be limited to the level of growth in wages and salaries for the preceding calendar year (Massachusetts); that future growth of the property tax be limited to 2 percent annually (Oregon); that the income tax rate be reduced for low-income individuals and raised for those with higher incomes, allocating added net revenues as property tax relief (Oregon); and, the most radical fiscal proposal of all, that *all* real and personal property taxes be abolished (Montana).

Legalized gambling accounted for another five measures, including four to establish state lotteries (Florida, Idaho, North Dakota, and Oklahoma) and one proposing casino gambling (Florida).

Public morality issues also claimed a significant share of initiatives on the 1986 ballot. Two proposed to limit the use of public funds for abortions (Arkansas and Oregon). Another, which also might be categorized as a public health issue, but with overt moral overtones, provided for the quarantine and isolation of individuals having the AIDS virus (California).

Another proposal, and the only one with a truly national focus, called for Alaska's voters to support a "mutual and verifiable" nuclear weapons freeze. A second largely symbolic measure, Ballot Measure 16 in Oregon, would have created tax credits for businesses that voluntarily elected to make capital investments converting manufacturing plants from the production of nuclear weapons or parts to the manufacture of consumer products. It would also have made the manufacture of nuclear weapons or parts a civil offense subject to fines of up to $5,000 per day.

Table 9.4 shows changes in initiative ballot measures, by category, among the states over the most recent three electoral periods. Whereas those dealing with regulation of business and/or labor topped the list on 1982 ballots, they dropped to a tie for fourth place in 1986. Moreover, whereas only three measures pertained to issues of public morality in 1982, that number rose to nine in 1986. Measures posing national policy issues have fallen significantly over the past four years.

TABLE 9.3. COMPARISON OF SUCCESSFUL INITIATIVE DRIVES BY STATE

State	1982			1984			1986		
	Titled	No./Pct. Qualified	No./Pct. on Ballot	Titled	No./Pct. Qualified	No./Pct. on Ballot	Titled	No./Pct. Qualified	No./Pct. on Ballot
Alaska	4	4 100	3 75	4	2 50	1 25	5	2 40	2 40
Arizona	14	4 29	4 29	15	2 13	2 13	11	2 18	2 18
Arkansas	5	1 20	0 0	5	4 80	3 60	6	3 50	3 50
California	30	9 30	9 30	64	9 14	7 11	35	6 17	6 17
Colorado	13	3 31	3 31	10	3 30	3 30	3	1 33	1 33
District of Columbia	2	2 100	2 100	12	2 15	2 15	12	0 0	0 0
Florida	11	0 0	0 0	17	2 12	1 6	22	2 9	2 9
Idaho	6	3 50	3 50	11	1 9	1 9	2	1 50	1 50
Illinois	2	0 0	0 0	—	— —	— —	—	— —	— —
Maine	5	3 60	3 60	1	0 0	0 0	3	3 100	3 100
Massachusetts	14	1 7	1 7	20	1 5	0 0	10	5 50	3 50
Michigan	19	5 26	5 26	17	1 6	1 6	21	2 10	0 0
Missouri	9	2 22	2 22	3	1 33	2 66	1	0 0	0 0
Montana	10	4 40	4 40	10	3 30	2 20	5	4 80	4 80
Nebraska	2	1 50	1 50	6	0 0	0 0	5	1 20	0 0
Nevada	2	2 100	3 100	6	0 0	0 0	3	0 0	0 0
North Dakota	3	2 66	2 66	4	2 50	1 17	2	2 100	1 50
Ohio	4	1 25	1 25	1	2 50	2 50	1	0 0	0 0
Oklahoma	2	2 100	2 100	11	0 0	0 0	1	1 100	1 100
Oregon	27	4 15	4 15	57	8 14	8 14	51	12 24	12 24
South Dakota	4	1 25	1 25	4	3 75	3 75	3	1 33	1 33
Utah	4	0 0	0 0	6	1 17	1 17	3	1 33	0 0
Washington	31	3 10	3 10	17	3 18	3 18	20	2 10	1 5
Wyoming	2	0 0	0 0	4	0 0	0 0	2	1 50	0 0
Total	225	56 25	56 25	305	49 16	42 14	227	52 23	43 19

Source: Initiative Quarterly, Vol. 3, Issue 3 (1984) 9; Monthly Initiative Bulletin, Vol. 1, No. 1 (Sept. 1986), 11.

TABLE 9.4. INITIATIVE BALLOT MEASURES BY CATEGORY

Category	1982		1984		1986	
	No.	Pct.	No.	Pct.	No.	Pct.
Government/Political Reform	6	10	5	12	7	16
Public Morality Issues	3	5	9	21	9	21
Revenue/Taxes/Bonds	14	24	7	16	11	26
Regulation-Business/Labor	16	28	8	19	6	14
Health/Welfare/Housing	—	—	2	5	6	14
Civil Liberties/Rights	2	3	5	12	3	7
Environmental/Land Use	9	16	2	5	0	0
Education	—	—	2	5	0	0
National Policy Issues	8	14	2	5	1	2
Total	58	100	42	100	43	100

Source: Initiative Quarterly, *Vol. 3, Issue 3 (1984), 8;* Monthly Initiative Bulletin, *Vol. 1, No. 1 (Sept. 1986), 11.*

Eight appeared on state ballots in 1982, but that number dropped dramatically to a sole initiative only four years later. Taxes, revenues, and morality became the grist for direct public decision making in 1986.

Going Before the Voters

Of the forty-three initiatives on state ballots in November 1986, voters approved eighteen.[14] Political or government reform measures proved most successful. Arizonans approved a measure that would limit campaign contributions, Californians chose English as their official state language, Oregonians established a twenty-day preelection cutoff for voter registration, and South Dakotans shifted their state's Memorial Day observance to coincide with the federal observance.

Four tax and/or revenue-related measures were also adopted among the states. California voters gave themselves the opportunity to approve (by a two-thirds vote) or reject proposed local tax increases, voters in Arkansas gave the counties the authority to float county revenue bonds, Montanans froze local property taxes at current levels, and voters in Massachusetts phased out a temporary personal income tax surcharge and tied state revenue growth to the level of growth in state wages and salaries.

Public morality measures proved the next most popular, as three were approved nationally. Lotteries were approved in Florida and Idaho, and a measure limiting the use of public funds to pay for abortions barely squeaked by in Arkansas—a surprisingly close vote given the strength of Arkansas' religious fundamentalism.

Two measures each were approved in the remaining three categories of business and labor regulation, public health, and civil liberties. Voters in Maine and Oregon proscribed telephone companies from imposing mandatory local measured service rates on their customers, requiring that local flat rates be offered as an option; Californians placed restrictions on the discharge of toxins into state drinking water; Massachusetts residents called for a timely and effective cleanup at oil and hazardous material disposal sites; Oregonians reformed their criminal codes; and Montanans passed major tort reform.

Finally, on the only national policy issue before the electorate, Alaskans declared a nuclear weapons freeze to be state policy.

Along with the successes, several highly visible rejections were found among the states. Californians overwhelmingly defeated an AIDS proposal, by 71 percent of the vote, thereby not requiring that persons found to have the AIDS virus be subject to quarantine and isolation; and voters also rejected placing ceilings on state and local employees' salaries. Oregonians voted down a proposal to legalize marijuana use and plant growth by adults, rejected restrictions on the use of state tax dollars to fund abortions, defeated a property tax exemption and renters' relief initiative, and turned back efforts to restrict nuclear power-plant operations and to make Oregon a nuclear-free zone. Montanans turned down a proposal calling for abolition of all real estate and personal property taxes. Finally, among the more visible or controversial measures, Florida rejected the legalization of casino gambling.

A Closer Look at the More Controversial Propositions

Several highly visible and controversial measures appeared on state ballots in 1986.[15] They deserve closer scrutiny.

As has come to be expected, California had its share of the more sensational initiatives in that year. Proposition 61, controlling the salaries of public officials, received national attention. It was also the subject of extensive and costly lobbying by both proponents and opponents. The proposition, also commonly referred to as the ''Fair Pay Amendment,'' would have set a ceiling on the salaries that could be received by the governor, constitutional officers, and other elected or appointed state and local governmental officials. According to its provisions, the governor could not be paid more than $80,000, other constitutional officers $52,500, and the remaining state and local government officials $64,000 (80 percent of the governor's salary). This last limitation would also have affected the salaries of state agency heads and other appointed state government officials; higher-salaried classified employees; mayors and city administrators; and public university and college administrators, faculty, and clinical practitioners.

In addition to the limitations on salary, Proposition 61 also would have prohibited state (including university) and local government employees from carrying over unused sick leave or vacation days from one year to the next; all such accumulated days in any year would have to be used by the end of that year. It would also have prohibited state and local governments from hiring outside consultants at rates higher than $75 per hour.

Needless to say, Proposition 61 stirred up a proverbial hornets' nest among higher-paid government employees and public university administrators, senior staff, and faculty. Higher education officials in California painted the dire results of Proposition 61's passage, noting that over 4,500 employees would be affected. In certain fields, such as medicine, law, and engineering, deans at the University of California predicted that up to 90 percent of their faculty members would leave the university if the proposal passed.[16]

In response to the threat posed by Proposition 61, several higher education organizations joined a coalition of groups actively opposing the initiative. University staff and faculty even organized canvass campaigns to take their case directly to the voters across California. They received support in their opposition from a number of influential individuals and organizations throughout the state, among them Republican Governor George Deukmejian, the University of California Board of Regents, State Superintendent of Public Schools Bill Honig, the League of Women Voters, state employee associations, and the pro-business California Chamber of Commerce.

Champions of Proposition 61 notably included Paul Gann, of Jarvis and Gann Proposition 13 fame. The People's Advocate, a group led by Gann, gathered more than 900,000 signatures in qualifying the statewide proposition. Supporters argued that the only effective way to limit the "spiraling" salaries of public officials was to put a statutory lid on them. And they characterized opponents as trying to frighten the voters by painting the picture of a decimated University of California.

The opponent's efforts proved successful, as Proposition 61 was defeated at the polls by an almost 2:1 margin. This result, in the aftermath of Proposition 13, provided yet another recent demonstration that California voters will not automatically throw their support behind budget-cutting proposals. Instead, having witnessed the consequences of Proposition 13, they are assessing the likely consequences of broad-based spending-reduction devices.

Another highly visible and emotionally laced controversy surrounded Proposition 63, which would have designated English as California's official language. It would have required the legislature and state officials to "take all steps necessary to ensure that the role of English as the common language of the state is preserved and enhanced."[17] It further provided that any state resident or person doing business in California may sue the state to enforce the proposal's provisions.

The leadership for Proposition 63, like Proposition 61, came from an individual well known to the people of California. Its leader, S.I. Hayakawa, a former U.S. senator from California, rose to fame while president of San Francisco State University during the height of student protests against America's involvement in Vietnam. The picture of Hayakawa ripping the wires out of huge speakers, used by long-haired, unkempt protestors on the San Francisco campus, appeared on the front page of nearly every California newspaper in the early 1970s. The image of Hayakawa striking back at unruly college demonstrators was even on national television news, to the delight of many voters who had had enough of campus protest demonstrations. Nearly overnight, Hayakawa became a celebrity.

In supporting the proposal, Hayakawa and his colleagues argued that bilingual education had gone too far in California. Not only would the proposal save money in bilingual translation and printing costs, but also it would, according to its authors, keep English as the state's mainline language, the common fabric of a diverse, ethnically based state. They maintained that English is the "language of opportunity," and to participate in society one must be schooled in that language.

Opponents argued that Proposition 63 was culturally divisive, doing nothing to improve Spanish speakers' use of English. Instead, they charged that it would overtly discriminate against those who have not learned English, often through no fault of their own, hampering their education and ultimate prospects for advancement. Opponents also suggested that approval of the amendment would lead to the elimination of bilingual public services, such as emergency 911 telephone service requirements for bilingual police officers and firefighters. In voicing his opposition, Governor Deukmejian termed it "unnecessary, confusing, and counterproductive."[18]

Unlike the fate of Proposition 61, Proposition 63 passed overwhelmingly, by a 73 to 27 percent margin. Reacting to the results, opponents have threatened court action, arguing that the expected outcomes of the new law, when implemented, will deny the large Spanish-speaking contingent in California their constitutional rights.

Oregon had its own share of eye-catching initiatives on the November 1986 ballot. Ballot Measure 5, as propositions are called in Oregon, proposed legalization of marijuana use among adults and creation of a state marijuana control board. It would not only have legalized marijuana use by adults but also have allowed each adult resident to purchase a permit to grow up to three marijuana plants for personal use. Growth for profit or sale out of state would have become a felony offense, and revenues from permits would largely have gone back to local units of government as tax relief. A small percentage would have been devoted to drug education—a somewhat apparent paradoxical dedication. The measure, as expected, was defeated by a 3:1 margin.

Another Oregon initiative is worthy of note. Ballot Measure 14 would have prohibited nuclear power-plant operation until the Oregon Energy Facility Siting Council found that a federally licensed high-level radioactive waste-disposal site was available to accept plant waste for permanent disposal. In the absence of such finding, if the state legislature declared an emergency need for electricity not available from other sources, including conservation measures, any temporary suspension of the prohibition would have to be referred to the voters in a statewide referendum. Again, the voters handily rejected the proposal, by a vote of 65 to 35 percent.

The 1986 ballot results, in conclusion, provided a mixed bag. It would be difficult, in trying to summarize the results, to declare the electorate's response as a broad-based victory for either conservative or liberal interests.

A case could be made that conservative interests fared well. Tax-limitation measures passed in four states, Californians backed English as their official state language, Oregonians defeated the proposed legalization of marijuana, and voters in Arkansas restricted public funding of abortions.

On the other end of the spectrum, a case could also be made that liberal interests prevailed. California voters defeated a proposal aimed at quarantining AIDS victims, placed restrictions on toxic discharges into drinking water, and required notice of exposure to toxins; Oregonians chose not to restrict public funding of abortions; Alaskans supported a nuclear weapons freeze; Arizonans limited campaign contributions; and voters in Maine and Oregon prohibited mandatory local measured telephone service.

THE COURTS AND DIRECT DEMOCRACY

Supporters of the initiative and popular referendum, in attempting to get their measure enacted into law, first put their collective efforts into securing the required number of signatures to qualify a measure on the ballot. Then, for the election, they wage a campaign, generally based on mass appeal through media advertising, geared to get prospective voters to turn out and support their measure on election day.

Opponents, on the other hand, not only attempt to defeat the measure at the polls but also try to keep it off the ballot through legal challenges. Such litigation may challenge the constitutionality of the titled measure, its intent, or compliance with duly established process. The last category, dealing with specifics of the initiative process, such as provisions for titling, signature certification, and preparation of voter information, has increasingly been the subject of litigation. For example, the use of random sampling techniques in the signature-verification process has come under attack. Specifically, courts have taken issue with the standards of sample selection, the criteria for signature disqualification, and levels of statistical significance.[19]

Beyond the increased incidence of legal challenges, courts have shown a greater willingness to entertain them. Traditionally, state courts have upheld the general constitutionality of the initiative and popular referendum. They have also chosen to construe state law liberally as it relates to the states' handling of the initiative process. Recent practice has painted a different and less tolerant picture. At least four 1984 cases resulted in express definitions of the initiative, in which the rulings affirmed that the initiative process is intended to propose statutes or constitutional amendments. In California, Montana, and Nebraska cases, the courts refused to allow a "resolution" or "advisory" initiative to be considered by the voters. A Massachusetts court disqualified a measure, labeling it a "rule" rather than a law. In a separate process-centered case, the Michigan Supreme Court, in 1986, upheld the constitutionality of the state's limit on initiative petition circulation to 180 days from titling. The litigation was brought by opponents of a successful petition drive, who argued that the 180-day limitation was violated and that the state had not enforced its provisions. With the court's ruling, opponents effectively kept the measure off the ballot.

Recent court rulings in Florida illustrate an increasingly common pattern of courts intervening to disqualify initiatives. The Florida Supreme Court found ballot titles and summaries to be overly broad in three recent cases. In one such case, *Askew v. Florida,* 421 So. 2d 151 (Fla. 1982), the court found that the petition's wording misled the electorate because it failed to indicate that the proposed measure would replace even stricter requirements existing in the constitution, even though the proposal was presented as a "get-tough" initiative.[20] Another measure was removed from the ballot because it was found to violate Florida's "single-subject requirement" that each measure deal with only one discrete subject. The Florida Supreme Court found that the proposed 1984 amendment included "at least three subjects, each of which allows a separate existing function of government." The final disqualification dealt with deceptive labeling and summary information. Amendment 9 was officially titled "Citizens' Rights in Civil Actions," even though the purpose of the measure was to limit the amount of money that could be awarded in a malpractice suit.[21]

THE GENERAL REFERENDUM AND RECALL

Unlike the popular referendum, the *general* referendum does not permit citizens to petition the legislature directly on a legislative proposal. In states having the general referendum, the legislature has the authority to refer legislation to the voters; the voters are in a reactive posture, acting either to approve or disapprove the legislature's actions. Of the thirty-seven states possessing the general referendum, twelve do not provide for the popular form. Several states possess both.

The general referendum takes two forms: the *compulsory* and the *advisory* referendum. The compulsory referendum is used when a certain proposition, such as a constitutional amendment or bond issue, is required to be submitted to the electorate for approval or rejection. Nineteen states make use of the compulsory referendum. The advisory referendum gives the legislature the discretion of referring legislation to the voters. But the legislature may or may not be bound by the public's vote. Thirteen states make use of the advisory referendum.

The *recall* is both the least common and least used mechanism of direct democracy. Only fifteen state constitutions contain recall provisions.[22] Under recall, voters circulate petitions calling for the removal of a public official. Upon receipt of the required number of signatures, an election is scheduled at which the voters cast their vote on the issue of removal. If a majority of those voting approve removal, the elected official loses his or her public office.

Recall, compared to the initiative or popular referendum, requires a much higher percentage of voters' signatures, usually 25 percent of the most recent vote cast for the office in question. Again, as with the devices of direct legislation, recall is primarily used in the western states. And where permitted, it is disproportionately used against local elected officials. Only one governor in history has ever been recalled, and that happened in North Dakota in 1922.[23]

Recent experience in Michigan shows that the recall can still be a vital tool in the hands of a dissatisfied electorate. During that state's deep recession of the early 1980s, two state senators were recalled for voting in favor of a tax increase aimed at balancing the state's budget. Taxpayer groups argued that budget reductions were most in order, not tax increases. Two legislators, in a highly publicized and charged environment, paid the price of not acting in concert with the popular sentiment in their districts.

SUMMARY AND CONCLUSIONS

The character of direct democracy among the states has changed and will continue to change. The initiative process, the most widely used form of direct democracy, has become a big business in several states, particularly California. Most significantly, the use of professional signature-collection firms, employing paid signature gatherers, has nearly displaced volunteer efforts. Even the image of an army of paid workers hitting the shopping centers and malls is being reconstructed. Direct-mail campaigns, using computer-generated letters and sophisticated audience targeting techniques, have proven highly successful—both in terms of yielding signatures and in raising financial support.

But the costs of getting a measure on the ballot have risen accordingly. As noted earlier, recent campaigns in California and Florida have cost $2 million to $3 million. And although the costs of person-to-person solicitation are likely to continue to rise, direct-mail campaigns, taking advantage of the growing efficiencies arising from new developments in computer and information systems, may help to stabilize costs. Increased market competition may also restrain cost increases, as additional firms move in to capture a part of the action.

Although some state legislatures are considering legislation that would lower the percentage of registered voters needed to qualify petitions and allow for a longer circulation period, under the assumption that such actions would give citizens a greater opportunity to qualify measures through volunteer effort, the paid petition industry is likely to remain a vital participant in the process of citizen democracy.

The behavior of the courts is another factor that will increasingly influence the course of the initiative. It appears likely that state courts will continue to show interest in both the substantive issues and process of direct democracy. Not only will they consider the constitutionality of measures approved by the voters, but also they will increasingly act to keep misleading and ambiguous measures off the ballot itself. In exercising that judgment, they will in part be influenced by their own views of what constitutes desirable public policy.

In summary, although direct democracy shows no immediate signs of expanding its reach to additional states, neither does it appear to be waning in those states where the authority now exists. Direct democracy is alive and thriving. Popular use of the instruments of direct democracy has not meant the end of state legislatures as important policy-making bodies. Although ballot propositions have made a significant mark on public policy in several states, state legislatures continue regularly to shape public policy in those states. Flamboyant citizens' initiatives—a number having important substantive effects—will continue to capture the public's attention and attract widespread media coverage. Legislatures, nonetheless, will continue to leave their collective stamp on major state policy. Legislatures will enact state budgets, establishing state spending priorities; change state taxes; set and modify standards governing a wide range of state regulation; and reapportion their own legislative bodies. However, the mechanisms of direct democracy can serve, and have served, as a "release valve" for representative democracy. Through direct democracy, where available, citizens have a recourse if they believe that their elected representatives are not promoting their collective interests. Yet the majority can only go so far in legislating directly: The courts are available as a safeguard to protect minority rights from possible abuse at the hands of the majority. Overall, both direct democracy and representative government are generally alive and well.

DIRECT DEMOCRACY EXERCISE: SUPPORTING AND OPPOSING CITIZENS' INITIATIVES

Success in two phases is necessary for citizens to make laws directly through the initiative. The first entails obtaining the required number of signatures to get a proposition placed on the statewide ballot. The second involves securing the support of a majority of those voting. To be successful, each phase requires different, but related, resources and strategies.

The class should be divided into a series of teams, with equal numbers supporting and opposing selected propositions. The number of propositions employed will depend on the size of the class. Supporters should first try to get their proposition qualified on the ballot. Detractors should oppose the qualification effort. Then, assuming successful qualification, supporters should wage a campaign to ensure passage by the electorate. Opponents should work toward defeat of the proposition.

Areas of possible initiatives could include

1. Limiting the growth in state taxes to one-half the growth in state personal income
2. Legalizing wagering on dog races
3. Limiting the use of state funds for abortion only in cases of rape or incest
4. Legalizing the private use of marijuana
5. Quarantining those having the AIDS virus

In attempting to *qualify* a proposition on the statewide ballot, supporters need to develop strategies regarding (1) the actual wording of the proposition, (2) the identification of likely supporters, (3) the method of signature collection to be used, (4) the costs of the signature-collection campaign and the prospects of raising adequate revenues to support it, (5) the promotional methods to be adopted, (6) the concepts and symbols to be used to elicit mass support, and (7) the best ways to neutralize the opposition's efforts.

Opponents of qualification need to consider how to structure their campaign of opposition—the audience to be reached, the promotional methods to be adopted, the concepts and symbols to be used in rallying opposition, and the methods to be used to solicit financial support. Opponents have to convince prospective supporters not to sign the qualifying petition when asked.

Assuming successful qualification, supporters and opponents need to take their case to the electorate. After carefully identifying who are the likely primary core supporters and opponents, each side should develop a campaign strategy to maximize its chances of a favorable outcome on election day, paying particular attention to (1) optimally reaching *likely voters* who would most likely support a given side's position on the proposition; (2) structuring an appeal, using carefully selected images and symbols to evoke the support or opposition desired, including decisions about whether or not to attempt to discredit directly the appeals of the other side; (3) methods and sources of raising funds in support of one's efforts; and (4) whether or not to elicit public support from major political actors or celebrities in the publicity efforts, including an evaluation of their likely contribution and of any possible negative effects.

Each team should be prepared to discuss its strategies with the class as a whole. The class should note what differences it sees in the elements of campaigns in support and in opposition, depending on the type of issue in question. The class should then assess what it believes would be the likely outcome of each proposition considered. Finally, the class should generalize from each campaign the elements that appear to be most important to success in getting initiatives approved or defeated.

REFERENCES

1. See the extensive discussion provided by David Magleby, which cites and discusses the results of numerous studies. David B. Magleby, *Direct Legislation* (Baltimore, MD: Johns Hopkins University Press, 1984), pp. 127–44.
2. Ibid.
3. Sue Thomas, *Monthly Initiative Bulletin,* Vol. 1, No. 3 (Nov. 1986), 4.
4. Magleby, *Direct Legislation,* p. 43.
5. Maureen S. Fitzgerald, "Computer Democracy," in Thomas R. Hoeber and Charles M. Price, eds., *California Government and Politics Annual 1984–85* (Sacramento: California Journal Press), p. 98.
6. Charles M. Price, "Experts Explain the Business of Buying Signatures," in Thomas R. Hoeber and Charles M. Price, eds., *California Government and Politics Annual 1986–87* (Sacramento: California Journal Press), p. 87.
7. Greg Baradi, "A Record $2.2 Million," in ibid., p. 84.
8. Manning J. Dauer and Mark Sievers, "The Constitutional Initiative: Problems in Florida Politics," in Thad L. Beyle, ed., *State Government* (Washington, DC: Congressional Quarterly), p. 30.
9. Quoted in Magleby, *Direct Legislation,* p. 62.
10. Ibid.
11. John R. Owens and Larry L. Wade, "Campaign Spending on California Ballot Propositions, 1924–1984: Trends and Voting Effects," *Western Political Quarterly,* Vol. 39 (Dec. 1986), 681 and 684–85.
12. Daniel Lowenstein, "Campaign Spending and Ballot Propositions: Recent Experience, Public Choice Theory and the First Amendment," *UCLA Law Review,* Vol. 29 (Feb. 1982), 511.
13. *Monthly Initiative Bulletin,* Vol. 1, No. 1 (Sept. 1986), 12.

14. See *Monthly Initiative Bulletin,* Vol. 1, No. 3 (Nov. 1986).
15. The September 1986 issue of the *Monthly Initiative Bulletin* lists and describes the measures that qualified for the 1986 ballots among the states.
16. Scott Jaschik, "California Colleges Working to Defeat Pay-Cap Proposal," *The Chronicle of Higher Education,* Vol. 33, No. 6 (Oct. 8, 1986), 19.
17. *California Journal,* Vol. 17, No. 10 (Oct. 1986), 7.
18. Ibid.
19. Magleby, *Direct Legislation,* pp. 35–58; *Initiative Quarterly,* Vol. 3, Issue 3 (1984), 3–5.
20. Dauer and Sievers, "Constitutional Initiative," p. 30.
21. Ibid., p. 31; *Initiative Quarterly,* Vol. 3, Issue 3 (1984), 1–2.
22. Thad L. Beyle, "Direct Democracy: Introduction," in Beyle, ed., *State Government,* p. 17; Magleby, *Direct Legislation,* pp. 38–39.
23. David C. Saffell, *State Politics* (Reading, MA: Addison-Wesley, 1984), p. 152.

ISSUES OF CONTEMPORARY STATE POLICY MAKING

—————————— CHAPTER 10 ——————————

Educational Policy

Educational reform has been at the top of state policy agendas of the mid-to-late 1980s. Its effects have been felt not only at the elementary and secondary levels but within higher education as well. State policy makers have been calling for a restored emphasis on quality and demonstrated achievement. Governing boards, administrators, teachers, and students themselves have all come in for criticism, and all have been challenged to play their part in stopping what has been broadly perceived as an erosion of educational quality nationwide.

The reports of several prominent national commissions have shaped and reinforced this negative perception. One such report issued by an eighteen-member commission appointed by former federal Education Secretary T. H. Bell, entitled *A Nation at Risk,* received the most exposure, being cited by President Reagan in his call for educational improvements. Over 700 newspaper articles covered the report's findings and recommendations.[1] Other key reports—most notably *Making the Grade,* a report of a Twentieth Century Fund task force, and *Action for Excellence,* a report of an Education Commission of the States task force—were highly critical of current educational practices and recommended a number of measures designed to improve learning, instruction, curriculum content, and assessment standards.

Several similarities can be found in the policy debate over reform in primary, secondary, and postsecondary educational circles. Most important, the calls for reform have largely come from outside the organized educational establishment. It is the governors and state legislatures who have pressed the educational professionals to pursue reform. Educational policy has become politicized as in no time before. And the politics are largely played out in the state capitals. For it is the states, and not the federal government, that most significantly shape educational policy at all levels in this country. Nevertheless, because of some significant differences, it is probably best to treat each level of education separately.

PRIMARY AND SECONDARY EDUCATION

Historically, there has been a strong tradition of local control inherent in American educational policy. The local school district evolved as the central policy-making and administrative unit for primary and secondary education. Before the twentieth century, community control of education was almost absolute. Although state governments have had the authority to create school districts, state legislatures have traditionally followed the wishes of local communities in granting new district charters. It was not really until the post–World War II reformist period that the states exercised any meaningful discretion over the composition of local districts. Thus local districts have tended to be small in size and numerous. At the turn of this century, over 100,000 existed, but greater state interest and involvement prompted a move to consolidate adjacent districts, creating fewer but larger districts, and thereby expanding the core educational resources that each district could make available to students. Only about 15,000 districts remain today. Consolidation also had the effect of increasing the operating efficiency of local districts by greatly improving economies of scale. Politically, consolidation reduced the number of local school boards and, accordingly, the number of local residents who serve on these policy-making bodies. Although the principle of local control over educational policy remained intact, the schools became both more physically and more psychologically distant from their local communities.

Local school districts are at the center of educational policy making. District administrators, under policies developed by local governing boards, develop budgets and staffing plans, hire teachers, set school calendars and attendance requirements, select the curriculum to be used, and allocate resources among district schools. Governing boards determine tax levies for school purposes, approve operating budgets and capital construction projects, and establish compensation policies for district staffs.

This is not to suggest that local districts function autonomously. School districts are legally creatures of the state, with their authority both prescribed and proscribed by state constitutions and statutory law. State laws have been enacted among the states that constrain local districts' ability to tax, spend, or incur debt. State laws have also established minimal requirements to be met by all local districts in the areas of curriculum, school calendar and attendance, teacher certification, collective bargaining (often prescribing the use of binding arbitration of labor disputes in certain situations), and graduation. State control tends to be most pronounced in the southern states, where course curriculum and required texts are commonly mandated at the state level. In contrast, schools in New England appear to enjoy the greatest local autonomy. Moreover, beyond the states, the federal government has dictated policy requirements in the areas of desegregation, education of the handicapped, school discipline, and the equalization of state financial aid to local districts.

Changing Financial Arrangements

Both the states and the federal government have helped finance the costs of elementary and secondary education. Of the two, the states have been the major contributor by far. Today the states pay half the costs of public elementary and secondary education in the United States, compared to only about 17 percent at the turn of the century. Local revenues cover another 44 percent. The federal government provides the remaining 6 percent—a pittance compared to the federal contribution to social welfare and transportation.[2]

As Figure 10.1 shows, the states' share of financing elementary and secondary education increased dramatically from the Great Depression era through the Korean War period, directly displacing local tax support. But post–Korean War enrollment growth kept the pressure on local and state funding, as the costs of public elementary and secondary schools rose by 450 percent between 1952 and 1970.[3] Both local school districts and the states greatly increased their financial support of education during that period, but the state share remained at about 40 percent. It was not until the 1979–1980 fiscal year that the state share exceeded the local contribution.

The post–Korean War "baby boom" had much to do with the increase in state support. As pressures on the property tax mounted, local school officials, supported by state superintendents of public instruction, increasingly called on state governments for assistance. By the early 1970s, however, the rationale for increased state support became less based on responding to an enrollment boom,

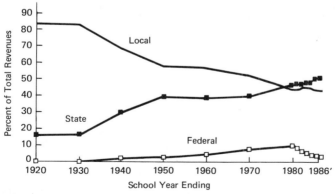

Figure 10.1. National Trends in Revenue Sources for Public Elementary and Secondary Education (Source: Center for Education Statistics, *The Condition of Education, 1986* [Washington, DC: U.S. Department of Education, 1986], p. 55.)

as primary enrollments began to fall and drops in secondary enrollments were forecast to follow. (See Figure 10.2.) Instead, during the 1970s and 1980s, supporters of continued increases in state financial aid emphasized the contribution that school aid makes toward local property tax relief. Moreover, during the 1980s, supporters increasingly tied the need for additional state aid to improvements that could be realized in educational quality.

Changing Orientations Toward Educational Policy

Orientations toward elementary and secondary education have changed over this century. Before World War II, education was not a priority on either the federal or state policy agendas. Largely confined to local concern, community efforts involved raising adequate funds to finance the necessary capital construction and operating budget requirements to accommodate the population growth that had occurred during the 1900s. Yet the growth curve of school-aged children allowed for manageable planning and revenue raising. That all changed with the mushrooming population growth following World War II and greatly accelerating during the post–Korean War years. Even beyond the enrollment growth and its associated challenges, other issues emerged to capture the public's attention over the decades following World War II. And there have been distinct patterns to their emergence.

1946–1964: An Era of Capacity Building. During the period from the close of World War II to the beginning of the Great Society, the emphasis in education had been placed on expanding the capacity of school districts to accommodate the large increases in enrollments because of postwar demographic changes. Faced with steadily rising enrollments, local districts turned to bond issues to pay for the new wave of school construction and to increases in the property tax to finance swollen operating budgets. With the rapid expansion came a concern that quality should not be sacrificed for growth's sake. The strong push for additional financial

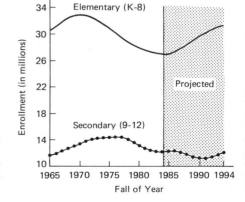

Figure 10.2. Public School Enrollment: 1965 to 1994 (Source: Center for Education Statistics, *The Condition of Education, 1986* [Washington, DC: U.S. Department of Education, 1986], p. 142.)

resources, beyond supporting capacity building, was also justified as necessary to maintain prized elements of the existing educational system, such as low student-teacher ratios and well-equipped facilities. In retrospect, the continuous increases in performance measures, most notably in the Educational Testing Service's SAT scores through 1965, suggest that quality did not suffer as a result of growth.

The Soviet Union's successful launch of the *Sputnik* satellite in 1957, in the face of unsuccessful U.S. attempts to beat the Soviets in space, shocked American society. For many, the Soviet success represented an American failure: The Soviets had the technical skill to get the job done, and we did not. Congressional supporters of an expanded role of the federal government in education used the development as an opportunity to press their case. The Russian success provided a prime symbolic wedge. In this context of public concern, heightened by extensive media coverage, Congress authorized federal funding to strengthen programs in science, mathematics, and foreign languages. Yet the fledgling federal role, associated with the National Defense Education Act of 1958, was still greatly limited in scope and financial resources.

1965–1977: Concern Over Equal Educational Opportunity. As the necessary resources were assembled to educate increasing numbers of children, the influence of President Lyndon Johnson's Great Society initiatives could be felt in primary and secondary education. The Great Society's emphasis on attacking the "cycle of poverty" accorded education a key role in breaking the vicious circle of poverty and welfare dependence, which entrapped the so-called permanent "underclass" in society. To help break the cycle, educational policy turned toward ensuring all children an *equal educational opportunity.*

The value of equal educational opportunity struck a responsive chord in most Americans. Our classic liberal heritage prizes individual choice and action. Individuals are to be free to pursue their own self-interests, to the best of their abilities, unhampered by artificial constraints. Thus Americans could readily agree that barriers beyond differences in ability and effort should not be allowed to keep the otherwise enterprising behind.

Thinking about educational opportunity was greatly affected by a federally supported research project that involved thousands of schools, teachers, and students throughout the country. This ambitious research effort, led by James Coleman, resulted in a 1966 report entitled *Equality of Educational Opportunity,* which analyzed the relationship between student achievement and educational inputs. The significance of the study lay in its conclusion that the family background of one's classroom peers proved to be the most important element in predicting student achievement—a conclusion that flew in the face of conventional wisdom. The study's findings contradicted the widely accepted belief that resource-related "inputs" such as per pupil expenditures, classroom size, available facilities, and teachers' salaries were most closely associated with student success. A reanalysis of the Coleman data by Thomas F. Pettigrew and others for the U.S. Civil Rights Commission found that educational achievement scores were significantly higher (up to two grade levels) for black students attending predominantly white schools than for those attending predominantly black schools.[4] The policy implications were readily apparent, and the Civil Rights Commission used the findings to advocate desegregation policies. The Coleman report was also used in the courts in support of forced busing to achieve school integration.

Despite the landmark U.S. Supreme Court decision in *Brown v. Board of Education* (1954)—which ruled that the Fourteenth Amendment's guarantees of equal opportunity were being abridged by policies based on race and that racially separate education was inherently unequal and therefore illegal—little of significance was done through 1964 to change the entrenched patterns of racial segregation in the schools. Although some progress in desegregation was made in a number of "border" states (especially Delaware, Kentucky, Maryland, Missouri, Oklahoma, and West Virginia), the states of the Deep South elected a policy of resistance to the Supreme Court's ruling. A "legislate and litigate" strategy was employed, involving the enactment of state anti-integration laws, going through the accompanying long and costly process of litigation, followed by the passage of new legislation when the former state laws were ruled unconstitutional by the federal courts.

The Civil Rights Act of 1964 gave some teeth to the federal government's desegregation policies, by providing that any recipients of federal financial assistance that practiced racial discrimination would have their federal funding terminated. Concomitantly, the Elementary and Secondary Act of 1965 greatly raised the costs of noncompliance through significant increases in federal funding for elementary and secondary public education. The act also gave the Department of Health, Education and Welfare (HEW) regulatory authority that required it to develop desegregation plans in cooperation with noncompliant districts.[5] By 1967, HEW had terminated funds to thirty-four school districts and was in the process of cutting off funds to 157 more. In addition, a federal district court ordered the state of Alabama to begin desegregation by the fall of 1967—the first time an entire state had been so ordered—based on the court's finding that state education officials had thwarted previous selected efforts at the local district level. Alabama was also ordered to establish remedial programs for black students in the newly integrated schools to make up for past discrimination. But by the late 1960s it became evident that school segregation had actually increased in many parts of the United States because of the emigration of whites from central city school districts and their displacement by blacks from rural areas.[6]

The traditional view of factors related to student achievement continued to influence educational policy, nevertheless. Professional educators had little self-interest in agreeing with the proposition that per student spending, the level of teachers' salaries, or the quality of facilities bore a scant relationship to learning. Administrators and teachers generally backed the call for equality of educational opportunity, but put it within the traditional context. Expanded public financial support and greater equity in its allocation became their preferred means toward the desired end of higher student achievement.

State financial aid to primary education increased by over 380 percent from 1964 to 1977.[7] Attentive to the growing national debate over educational opportunity during the mid-to-late 1960s, educational policy makers in several states began to pay far greater attention to how these mushrooming state funds were being allocated among school districts. Most commonly, state aid was shared with school districts on a per student basis. On that basis, the more students a district has, the more aid it receives. Thus poor and wealthy districts benefit alike. But they start from a quite different financial base. The wealthier districts are already able to provide a higher level of financial resources underlying each student's education. Districts with high property values can set their tax *rate* at a level well below that of poor districts and still yield considerably more tax revenue in support of their educational programs. Per student state aid tends to perpetuate the inequalities. Even with state aid, poorer districts have comparatively fewer resources to finance their students' educations than do the wealthier districts. Students in poorer districts can be said to be at a clear disadvantage; they are not accorded an equal opportunity for high-quality education. And traditional per student state-aid formulas did little to close the gap between the relatively wealthy and poor districts.

In the context of the growing national debate over equality of educational opportunity, both the governing boards of disadvantaged schools and parents of children attending them increasingly directed their concerns about inequitable treatment to the courts. In a landmark 1973 U.S. Supreme Court case, *San Antonio Independent School District v. Rodriguez,* the Court refused to equate inequities in property values and the resulting differences in per pupil expenditures with a violation of the equal protection clause of the Fourteenth Amendment to the U.S. Constitution. Nevertheless, the airing of the debate, which began years before the Court's decision, set off a national discussion among state educational policy makers. The state courts became the avenue for challenge since most state constitutions guarantee state residents the right to a high-quality, free education.

The first, and most significant, state court challenge resulted in the California State Supreme Court's decision in *Serrano v. Priest.* In that case the court ruled that quality education is a fundamental right guaranteed by California's constitution that ''cannot be a condition of the wealth of a child's parents or neighbors.''[8] Following the *Serrano* decision, fifty-two lawsuits were filed in thirty-one states in attempts to elicit similar rulings.[9] And although in only two instances, that of New Jersey and Connecticut, can a state court's decision in favor of the plaintiff be viewed as a *mandate* that the state legislature enact reform legislation, the very debate occasioned by the litigation in the other states, and what appeared to be the likelihood of court direction, prompted governors and legislatures to take up the call for reform. During the period from 1971 (the year of the *Serrano* decision) through 1977, twenty-five states reformed their systems of school finance.[10]

Beyond court action, or its likelihood, school finance reforms spread as do reforms in other policy areas. State policy makers, through national associations, become readily aware of reforms that have taken place in other states. National associations of state superintendents of public instruction, school boards, governors, and legislatures provide forums for communicating issues of emerging concern, court litigation, gubernatorial initiatives, and legislative enactments. And although policy learning is strongest among states of the same region, there are a few bellweather states to which others consistently look for innovations. As reforms spread, a nationwide agenda emerges. Such was the case with school finance reform.

School finance reform focused on the equalization of state school aid. Legislation enacted in twenty-four states required that state financial assistance to school districts be based on need and ability to pay. Based on this principle, allocation formulas were changed so that districts with relatively lower property wealth would receive disproportionately more state aid than would those with higher property value. Operationally, state legislation most often set a guaranteed level of property value behind each student in the state. Those school districts falling furthest from the guarantee would receive the greatest amount of aid in making up the difference. Conversely, those districts having a per student property value in excess of the guarantee would receive no state aid, being deemed to possess resources adequate to ensure a base-level financial equity.

One state, Wisconsin, took equalization a step further than its counterparts. There the state legislature, at the behest of Governor Patrick Lucey, passed legislation incorporating the concept of "negative school aid." Under its provision, not only would the wealthiest districts receive no state aid, but also they would be forced to contribute locally raised property tax revenue into a state-administered fund for redistribution to poorer districts. In Wisconsin, then, equalization was determined to involve the reallocation of local as well as state revenues. Under challenge by contributing districts, the Wisconsin State Supreme Court ruled the negative aid provision unconstitutional.

Other elements of reform have differentially adjusted state aid to address the unusually higher costs of some disadvantaged big-city school districts, with their higher-than-average special educational needs. To meet such problems, California, Florida, Michigan, and Washington have established formula adjustments to benefit urban school districts.[11]

1978 to the Present: Ensuring Educational Accountability. The late 1960s through the better part of the 1970s saw school costs rising faster than real estate valuations, creating a growing burden on the local property tax. With the spotlight on spending, governors and state legislators, along with taxpayers and parents of school-aged children, began to ask what they were getting educationally for their growing financial investment. They believed that they were getting less rather than more, and a 1975 College Board report that test scores had been in steady decline for a decade reinforced their more intuitive impressions. As the report showed, the mean verbal and mathematical scores of high school seniors taking the Scholastic Aptitude Test (SAT) had fallen each year since 1965 (and continued to fall until 1984). Moreover, the College Board's blue-ribbon panel, charged with investigating the drop, reported in 1977 that educational standards had declined in most areas nationally, as the school curriculum lost required courses in math, science, and language. The authors also noted that "less thoughtful and critical writing is now being demanded and done, and that careful writing has apparently gone out of style."[12]

Several national-level commissions were established in the early 1980s to assess the state of elementary and secondary education in this country. The popular perception was that educational performance was not improving, and that it was probably worsening; Gallup polls consistently showed that the general public only gave the public schools a C+ grade for performance.[13] Not only were the commissions charged with evaluating student learning and identifying apparent trends, but they were also given the more difficult task of accounting for any observed change. Counts will vary, but at least a dozen reports and books that were national in scope could be identified by 1983. They all pointed out significant problems meriting attention. The educational system was portrayed as failing in its essential task of grounding students in the "basics." Measures of student performance in the classroom and on nationally normed objective tests suggested a further erosion of competencies. The reports, in turn, called for strengthening of the curriculum. *A Nation at Risk,* the most nationally prominent report, identified "five new basics" that had to be shored up in high schools across the country: four years of English, three years of mathematics, three years of science, three years of social studies, and at least one course in computer science. This core curriculum was intended for all high school students, not just for those intending to go on to college. In addition, two years of a foreign language were recommended for the college bound. The other reports also offered similar formulations aimed at strengthening the core high school curriculum. Expanded homework was presented as an important corollary in the prescription for improvement in the basics.

Beyond focusing on the curriculum, the reports also dealt with the educational profession itself. The quality of teacher-education programs and of the teaching candidates themselves came in for recurrent criticism. The reports commonly exhorted schools of education to raise their admission standards and strengthen their curriculum. Two highly influential reports, *A Nation at Risk* and *Educating Students for the 21st Century* (which focused on science and math education), criticized the lack of qualifications of newly certified teachers in those fields. They also projected serious shortages of science and math teachers in the near future. The National Science Board, reflecting these concerns, recommended that the states assign top priority toward improving teacher education in science and math and toward providing special incentives for top students to enter teacher-training programs in these disciplines.[14]

Comparing all the reports and books on educational reform that emerged in the early 1980s, they had one bottom-line concern in common: the need for a recommitment to quality. That also became the watchword of legislative debate in the state capitals. The stubborn decline in quality, sensed by parents and educators alike, had to be reversed. State policy makers readily took up the banner of reform. They felt that, with the states' greatly increased financial commitment to education, they had the right to take the kinds of initiatives necessary to turn the educational record around. States acted quickly, and initiatives soon spread across state borders.

Two categories of reform initiatives could be commonly found among the states by the mid-1980s—those directed at student achievement and those aimed at teacher quality. Major state initiatives directed at the students included (1) the establishment of formal statewide course and credit requirements for high school graduation, (2) the imposition of statewide exit tests requiring successful completion as a condition of graduation, (3) the requirement of academic performance assessment tests conducted in selected elementary and secondary grades as a means of monitoring student performance over time, (4) the addition of core course hours in the curriculum, and (5) the institution of mandatory kindergarten. On the teacher side, state initiatives included (1) higher salary scales and entry-level pay, (2) required provisions for merit pay, (3) tests of subject matter competence, (4) higher educational school requirements, and (5) financial aid for teachers entering high-priority academic disciplines. Table 10.1 shows the incidence of such initiatives among the states.

TABLE 10.1. MAJOR STATE EDUCATIONAL INITIATIVES: NUMBER OF STATE ACTIVITIES, 1985

	Action	Under Consideration	Rejected
Student Achievement			
Graduation requirements	43	5	1
Increased college admission requirements	17	3	
Statewide assessment tests	37	6	
Promotional tests	8	3	
Exit test	15	4	
Class size reduction	13	7	2
Additional instruction time	13	7	3
No pass/no play	6	4	2
Mandatory kindergarten	5	2	7
Preschool opportunities	7	8	2
The Professions			
Salary increase/new minimum	18	17	2
Career ladder/merit pay	14	24	1
Certification changes	28	16	1
Teacher tests	29	10	1
Revised education school requirements	19	10	
Teacher loans, aid	24	13	2

Source: William Chance, The Best of Educations: Reforming America's Public Schools in the 1980's *(Chicago: The John D. and Catherine T. MacArthur Foundation, 1986), p. 113.*

A number of states led the nation in initiating educational reforms. Among them, California, Florida, and South Carolina merit special attention because of the comprehensiveness of their reforms.

The push for educational reform in California gained impetus as a result of the 1982 campaign for state superintendent of public instruction. Facing a three-term incumbent, the challenger, William Honig, presented himself to the electorate as the candidate of educational reform. The battle cry of Honig's campaign was "return to quality." In contrast, Honig's predecessor, Wilson Riles, had advanced an educational policy of equity, on which he championed programs directed at improving the educational performance of underprivileged children. That continued focus was not in harmony with the popular concerns of the 1980s. Honig, in contrast, preached the gloomy gospel of general educational decline. Students were characterized as having regressed in their basic academic skills. He further noted that class size had increased in response to cutbacks associated with Proposition 13, with California dropping from tenth to thirty-third within only four years of the revenue-reducing initiative. Honig also was able to enlist the support of the business community, which looked at education from an economic development perspective. Quality education was clearly associated with a competent future work force.

Honig regarded his victory at the polls as a mandate for his brand of reform, and he had every right to do so. The public debate over educational policy associated with the campaign for state superintendent spilled over into the campaign for governor, as well as the many campaigns for seats in the state legislature. Although education issues were not at the top of Governor Deukmejian's policy priorities, he got drawn into the debate as legislative leaders and the various competitors for legislative seats around the state raised the public profile of educational reform.[15]

The California reform package, wrapped into Senate Bill 813, which passed the legislature during its 1983 session, contained a number of the reforms recommended by the national commissions. Included in the act, and in other legislative actions that followed and were tied to the 1983 landmark legislation, were graduation requirements; model curriculum standards for the high school grades; the extension of assessment tests in science, mathematics, reading, and language arts to the eighth and tenth grades; an optional "Golden State's" achievement test for students wanting to earn honors; and financial bonuses available to districts that increased the number of instructional minutes in each school day. Regarding teachers, California reform initiatives included increased state appropriations to raise the level of teachers' salaries; changes in teacher-certification requirements, including beefed up in-service training requirements; and forgivable loans for education students who enter critical-need fields. But among all the reforms, it was the increased state appropriation for education—a billion dollars in 1983, followed by another billion dollars the next year—that mollified organized opposition to what teachers considered the less desirable elements of teacher reform.[16] As one Department of Education official observed, "The promise of money was what neutralized the unions. The unions felt they were giving up some things, such as longer days, for a pay raise. They saw goodies and calculated they could take care of the downside—dismissals, personnel things. They could water these things down through court suits and collective bargaining, and that is exactly what they've done.''[17]

Florida was among the first states to adopt minimal competency testing. Since its passage in 1976, Floridians already had five years of information on how well their children were performing in core educational areas. And the results did not look very good. In response to mounting public concern, Governor Robert Graham appointed a Commission on Secondary Education to study the problem and offer suggestions for improvement. The commission's report was submitted in late 1982, and its recommendations set the agenda for legislative proposals that had the support of both the governor and legislative leaders. Clearly, the governor's strategy of naming key legislative leaders from both chambers to the commission had paid dividends. As in California, political leaders were anxious to take the "high ground" on the issue of reform. As one legislator observed, "There had been a lot of discontent with the quality of graduates from the high schools. We heard for a long time from employers and some college and university sources that the kids couldn't read, and they couldn't write. The Governor appointed this commission to begin to take a look at what was wrong, with a combination of educators and legislators.''[18] Commenting on legislative leadership, another observer noted that "there was a great fervor of reform led by the speaker of the House and the president of the Senate, both of whom, at the same time (in my opinion a very dangerous thing to have happen) really almost had a contest to see who could create the most reform in education.''[19] Moreover, both the governor and legislative leaders held little hope that the state education department or local school districts across the state would do much on their own to turn the situation around.

The Florida reform package contained initiatives on a number of fronts. Most publicized among them were those directly affecting teachers. Of these, requirements for merit pay evoked the greatest controversy. Supporters argued that the best teachers should receive the highest pay increases, regardless of their tenure on the job. Other initiatives focused on teacher-training programs and built on an earlier reform (1978) that had established mandatory competency examinations for teachers—an action well ahead of its time. Under the new Florida requirements, teacher-training programs faced loss of their accreditation if 90 percent of their graduates failed the competency examination. Thus, whereas merit pay addressed the teachers themselves, the accreditation sanctions shared the responsibility for teachers' competency with higher education.

Regarding student achievement, Florida's "RAISE" legislation, as the reform package was popularly known, required the state education department to specify minimum performance standards for all grades, with testing to occur in grades three, five, eight, and eleven. The RAISE package also increased graduation requirements, mandating that high school students successfully complete four years of English, three years each of math and science, and two years of history before they could graduate. Students would also have to maintain at least a 1.5 grade point average, on a scale of 4.0, to remain eligible to participate in competitive athletics.[20]

California and Florida (at least within the South) have traditionally been viewed as progressive states; therefore it is not surprising that they should take a lead in educational innovations. Another reform leader, South Carolina, can hardly be included within the circle of innovating states. Traditionally, when compared with other states on nationally normed student test scores, South Carolina has consistently ranked in the bottom five. Yet South Carolina has recently been among the leaders in the current reform movement—an apparent paradox.

The South Carolina reform movement bears some similarities to California's. Passage of reform legislation was preceded by the election of a new governor and a new state superintendent. However, South Carolina's newly elected governor, Richard Riley, provided earlier and stronger leadership than did California's Governor George Deukmejian. As in California and Florida, the legislative leadership acted quickly to join the others leading the reform parade. But as in Florida, the 1983 reforms built on feedback from the early results of skills assessment scores made available as a result of the testing program put in place in the late 1970s. Again, as in Florida, the results fell below the expectations of parents and policy makers. A consensus emerged that something had to be done about it.

Faced with rising public awareness of the state's educational deficiencies, the governor and state superintendent each commissioned ad hoc task forces to look into the problem. The independent work of these groups led to interest in creating a formal commission to recommend specific proposals for change, much as had just recently been done in the nearby state of Florida. In an attempt to develop broad-based support for reform legislation, the governor appointed a Business/ Legislative Partnership Committee, chaired by himself, and co-chaired by the state superintendent. Legislators and business spokespersons filled out the body. In the debate over a tax increase to finance the so-called "Move to Quality" reform package, their joint involvement was an important element in its passage, even though the top legislative leadership did not initially support the proposed reforms and their associated penny sales tax increase. The joint endorsement of the governor and state superintendent, together with business' support, forced the leadership to come aboard. In addition, extensive media coverage of the legislative deliberations tended to mobilize public support for passage. In the end, the legislative leadership joined the governor and state superintendent in heralding the momentous passage of educational reform in their traditionally conservative state.[21]

South Carolina's reform package shared several similarities with those enacted in California and Florida. As in Florida, South Carolina's reforms were in significant part directed at teachers. One- to four-year probationary periods were instituted in place of six-month probations, and in addition, all teachers were to be evaluated at least once every three years. The school year was increased by five days. And finally, as had occurred earlier in Florida, a merit pay program was established. In return, teachers' salaries, which had lagged nationally, were raised to the midpoint of the other southeastern states.[22]

The Equity or Excellence Debate

More than half the states have changed their school aid allocation formulas since 1970 in order to achieve greater equity in districts' ability to provide equal educational opportunity to their students. Recent reforms, however, have focused primarily on promoting excellence in education. One educational expert, observing the changing contours of the national debate, predicts that it will be very difficult for local school districts, even with increased state financial help, to promote both ideals. Since the newer quality-improvement funds have largely been appropriated separately from existing equalization-based appropriations, the two have necessarily been placed in competition with each other for the scarce educational dollar.[23] Furthermore, as governors and state legislatures continue to turn their attention toward issues of quality in higher education (to be discussed later in this chapter), those pursuits will add a further element of competition with support for elementary and secondary education.

Some advocates of the excellence reform argue that America's preoccupation with equity in the 1960s and 1970s stifled educational quality, leading to a leveling of performance to the lowest common denominator. Such contemporary critics as Theodore Black advocate additional local district spending aimed at strengthening the core curriculum, adding advanced-level courses, and generally expanding opportunities for talented and gifted students, despite the fact that such increases in those districts best able to afford them will likely further enlarge the spending gaps between wealthy and poor districts. For the advocates of excellence, however, relative deprivation is not a sufficient reason to hold back districts that elect to excel.[24]

Advocates of quality reform also argue that educational policy makers have to look beyond interdistrict comparisons and begin to be more concerned about international comparisons. Such advocates see the United States increasingly falling behind in international economic competition, and comparative tests support that contention. (See Figure 10.3.) One contributing factor they identify is the inadequate academic preparation provided to graduates of American high schools, particularly in math and science. In their view, local districts and the states have no choice but to pay additional attention to quality, for the price of inaction is a worsened national competitive position.

With the growing concern about the "quality gap," some observers fear that tougher core curriculum and graduation requirements will create undue pressure on the marginal students, possibly prompting more to drop out. Others worry that the new reforms will squeeze out money for programs aimed at addressing the problems of "at-risk" students—the nearly twofold dropout rate for blacks and the limited resources available for non–English-speaking students and compensatory programs for the socially disadvantaged. In addition, academic professionals have voiced concerns that increased use of empirical assessment devices

Performance by 8th Grade Students on an International Test in Mathematics: 1982.

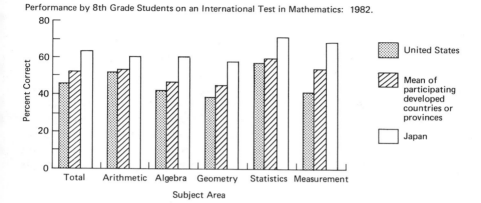

Performance by Advanced Mathematics Students in the 12th Grade on International Tests: 1982.

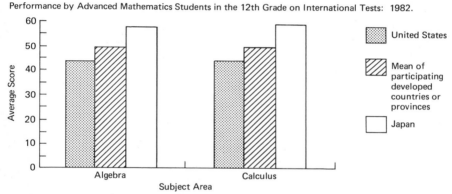

Figure 10.3. International Student Achievement (Source: Center for Education Statistics, *The Condition of Education, 1986, [Washington, DC: U.S. Department of Education, 1986], p. 35.)*

for measuring quality could have a number of negative educational side effects, including "teaching to tests," overuse of workbooks, memorization rather than reflection, and reduced creativity.[25]

Differing perspectives on the subject of testing teachers' competency can also be found. Supporters argue that such testing provides a needed element of quality control. They ask how students can be expected to make strides in an academic discipline when their teachers have not mastered the basic knowledge of that discipline. And the only reliable way for the public to know whether or not their children's teachers are academically competent, they argue, is regularly to test for that competence. Supporters of teacher testing express doubt that supervisory evaluation or peer review alone, where it exists, will identify incompetent teachers. Even where it does, they argue, administrators traditionally have a difficult time assembling a case for dismissal, especially in unionized environments. However, armed with consistent unsatisfactory test results, administrators and school boards can more tangibly press their case for dismissal. Thus, as the argument goes, quality can be better protected with testing.

Opponents of teacher testing, particularly the politically powerful teachers' unions, argue that some teachers may be expert in their subject matter but, at the same time, be poor teachers. Other teachers may not fare as well on subject-based examinations but still be extremely effective instructors, able to communicate well and effectively motivate students. Opponents of testing suggest that such qualities are not readily testable. But beyond the feasibility of testing for teachers' competence, detractors ask who is to decide what teachers in a given academic discipline should know. They want to know how substantively and procedurally this basic knowledge is to be identified.

HIGHER EDUCATION

Growth in higher education demographically followed the growth patterns seen in high schools. It follows logically: As more school-age children progress through elementary and secondary schools, increased enrollment pressure is felt on the educational institutions next in line. That would clearly be the case even if the percentage of high school graduates going on to higher education remained constant. But what happened was that, in addition to the increased size of the postsecondary age group associated with the demographic changes of the mid-1960s through the 1970s, a higher percentage of college-age youths elected to continue their educations. It was this double effect of increased base and self-selection that caused college enrollments during the 1960s and 1970s to skyrocket.

Policy makers in the early 1960s faced an imposing challenge: Not only did they have to accommodate the growing numbers of postsecondary students who were already at their doors, but they also had to plan for the period of certain accelerated growth that lay ahead. They had to expand existing colleges and universities by erecting new buildings, equipping them, and adding faculty to instruct the growing student population. In addition, new institutions had to be built from scratch. The combination of expansion and new construction placed a tremendous demand on existing universities to turn out students with advanced degrees who could join the ranks of new faculty members.

The job market for new Ph.D.s was clearly a seller's market. It was not uncommon at all in the mid-1960s for doctoral graduates from top universities in almost any field to receive multiple job offers. Accordingly, graduate programs were expanded at doctoral-granting institutions, and prospective postgraduate students swelled the ranks of applicants. Here, again, demographic factors were at work: An increased number of college graduates were coming out of the higher educational pipeline. Beyond the important demographic factor, America's expanding involvement in the Vietnam War represented a salient contributing social factor underlying the growth in graduate student enrollment. For male students, graduate education held out the promise of an educational deferment from military service. But for students of both sexes, the Vietnam experience prompted many to pursue professions that involved independent self-expression and helping others; in this light, the life of the professor looked appealing.

The growth in higher education was staggering. Between 1966 and 1985, 916 new institutions of higher education had been created. Faculties grew by 249,000 members—a 56 percent increase—and enrollments grew by 5.9 million students—a 92 percent increase. Although significant growth occurred in both public and private institutions, it was the public institutions that had the greatest enrollment pressures. Whereas private enrollments grew by about 40 percent over the twenty-year period, public enrollments increased by 116 percent during the same period.[26]

As Table 10.2 illustrates, expenditures for public higher educational institutions rose by an astonishing 720 percent during the same two decades. And major increases in state appropriations and student tuition and fees financed the greatly increased costs. State financial support grew by 934 percent, and tuition and fees were up by 856 percent, both offsetting reductions in the relative share of federal support over the same period.

TABLE 10.2. REVENUES AND EXPENDITURES OF PUBLIC HIGHER EDUCATIONAL INSTITUTIONS, SELECTED YEARS (IN $ BILLIONS)

Expenditures

Year	Amount
1965–1966	7.1
1969–1970	13.2
1974–1975	23.5
1978–1979	33.7
1981–1982	46.2
1984–1985	58.3

Revenues

Year	Total	State Support	Tuition and Fees
1965–1966	7.4	2.9	0.9
1969–1970	13.8	5.7	1.7
1974–1975	24.0	10.6	3.1
1978–1979	34.5	16.0	4.4
1981–1982	47.3	21.4	6.4
1984–1985	59.8	30.0	8.6

Sources: American Council on Education, 1986–1987 Fact Book on Higher Education (New York: Macmillan, 1987), pp. 46 and 52; Center for Education Statistics, Digest of Education Statistics 1987 (Washington, DC: U.S. Department of Education, 1987), pp. 229 and 238.

The Growing Politicization of Higher Educational
Policy Making

Governors and state legislators are taking a renewed interest in public higher educational policy making in their states. Some observers attribute their heightened interest to the increase in state appropriations financing public higher education. However, that explanation alone is not very satisfying, since state financial support has grown steadily over the past three decades. Something more is at issue. Two factors help to account for the growing government interest.

Governors and legislators have historically recommended and voted for increased state appropriations for higher education. They were of necessity in the business of expanding resources to meet a burgeoning popular demand for access. Because of demography, as discussed earlier, there were more students to be educated, providing a ready rationale for increased state financial support for public higher education. However, the demographic curve also led experts to project enrollment declines in the 1980s—declines that never materialized. Instead, enrollment growth continued, despite the relative downturn in the college-age cohort. College costs correspondingly continued to rise. The expected respite remained a phantom.

Considering that nearly one-third of high school graduates went on to higher education by 1987, up from less than one in four in 1960, state policy makers increasingly began asking if public higher education was trying to do too much. They inquired whether or not all who chose to go to college really belonged there. They worried about declining quality in the face of enrollment growth unaccompanied by commensurate increases in public funding. Yet they also expressed concern about the ability of state treasuries to meet the growing financial demands and still be able to accommodate public demands for tax cuts, property tax relief, and increased public spending in other policy areas. If they were to continue supporting increased appropriations for higher education after they had already met the demographically based demands for access, they had better be sure that public colleges and universities were not compromising their standards of quality in pursuit of continued enrollment growth—in essence spreading state support thinner and thinner.

The debate over quality in elementary and secondary education influenced policy makers' thinking about higher education. Many reasoned that, if it made sense to assess students' and teachers' competence in elementary and secondary schools, why should a similar approach not be applied to higher education? More theoretically, they asked how anyone—they or general members of the public—could know if higher education was doing its job. For example, the nation's governors, at their annual meeting in 1986, went on record that they "wanted to hold institutions accountable for the performance of their students."[27] Yet American colleges and universities have largely continued to utilize the traditional method of student assessment—individual evaluation of the student's performance by faculty members, based on exams, papers, and laboratory projects. Interest in alternative forms of performance evaluation is increasing, attested to by the growing number of national workshops held on the subject. Among them, one concept has received the greatest attention: value-added assessment. With this approach, students are assessed in terms of their general knowledge and skill level upon matriculation, and then again upon graduation. Students may also be tested in a given discipline when they declare their major and during their last semester or quarter of study. The measured difference in knowledge and skill level represents the value that has theoretically been added as a result of their higher educational experience.

Policy makers in the 1980s also appear to have become more pragmatic about higher education, expressing growing interest in the relationship between higher education and economic development. Their focus is not so much on economic development as a concept; it is more on the edge that strong institutions of higher education give a state in competition with other states, regionally and nationally, for development. As former Colorado Governor Richard Lamm put it, ''The state that is second best educationally will be second best economically.''[28] Spurred by the popular association of university education with economic development, state policy makers have increasingly provided funding to establish university-industry consortia at major state universities, strengthening and formalizing the university's role in applied research. In addition, entrepreneurship centers have recently sprung up at several universities with the goal of assisting would-be entrepreneurs in the creation of new business ventures and product lines. Although such developments probably provide solace to deans of engineering and business schools, with their applied orientations, they engender fear in the hearts of administrators and faculty in several liberal arts disciplines. Moreover, a growing emphasis on the university's role in economic development sets up increased competition for the scarce state dollar between the major universities' research and instruction functions.

State policy makers are also increasingly questioning the efficiency of higher educational operations. They are becoming more concerned about questions of program array and undue duplication among public institutions in the same state. These concerns have gotten them more interested in the different missions of a state's various public universities and colleges. The elected representatives' message to state college and university governing boards and administrators is clear: Be sure you know what your institution is about, and do it well; but do not try to be everything to everybody.

Such increased scrutiny on government's part has flown in the face of the well-established tradition of university autonomy and faculty governance. Legislatures have historically acted to insulate state universities and colleges from undue political interference in academic operational matters. In place of cabinet government, where state agency heads serve at the pleasure of the governor and are expected to pursue the chief executive's policy agenda, state university and college presidents are traditionally appointed by citizen boards and serve at their pleasure. Members of these distinguished governing bodies are generally appointed by the governor for staggered, fixed terms. With staggered terms, most often set between six and ten years, a first-term governor does not have an opportunity, under normal circumstances, to appoint a majority of the board. In any event, board members are expected to act foremost as trustees, representing the best interests of the institutions that they have been appointed to oversee.

Governing boards exercise responsibility for policy and administrative oversight, having the authority to approve legislative budget requests and annual operating budgets as well as the academic degree programs offered at each campus. This does not mean that the regents approve every course that is required as part of an academic major, but it does mean that the regents have to approve the addition of a new major or the creation of a new graduate-level degree program such as the masters of business administration (M.B.A.) at a given campus.

Aside from these matters of overall university direction, day-to-day operational governance is shared between the campus' chief executive officer and the faculty, under the broad policy guidance and budget allocations of the governing board. "Faculty governance" is an oft-evoked refrain on university and college campuses. And in fact, faculties exercise significant collective decision making. Faculties, organized by departments and schools (also often called colleges), establish the institution's curriculum within policies set by the board, evaluate scholarship, recommend faculty members to be hired or terminated during probationary periods, and advise the campus administration on policies ranging from the assignment of space and parking to the criteria governing sabbaticals. Faculty governance tends to be stronger on the more prestigious, research-oriented "flagship" campuses across the states. In California, for example, with two separate university systems, faculty governance is much more pronounced on the campuses of the University of California, particularly at Berkeley and Los Angeles, than at the State University campuses. In fact, faculty unionization at the latter institutions has eroded the role of faculty in university governance.

Despite the long traditions of university autonomy and faculty governance among the states, public college and university governing boards, administrators, and faculty have all expressed a growing concern about what they believe to be an unwelcomed intrusion on the part of governors and legislators into their institutions' internal affairs—one that they fear may threaten their special status among state agencies.

SUMMARY AND CONCLUSIONS

The public spotlight is currently on education across the states. With the enrollment pressures associated with the post–World War II baby boom behind us, and with public financial support for education reaching record heights, governors and state legislators are increasingly turning their attention to the educational product. They appear no longer willing to increase state aid without greater assurance that students are learning. The key concept of the day has become educational quality at both the lower and higher educational levels. State policy makers appear to be less preoccupied today with such concerns as assuring educational opportunity for the less advantaged than they were in previous decades. Instead, the watchwords of today have become competence and competitiveness. There has emerged a growing policy consensus that students' achievement needs to be raised if states are to be competitive in the growing interstate competition for economic development, and if the United States is to remain competitive internationally. In this pursuit for competitive quality, state policy makers have become less willing than in the past to leave the job of quality assurance largely to educational governing boards, administrators, and teachers. Governors and legislators are increasingly supporting and enacting legislation that toughens educational requirements and assesses educational performance. In addition, educational governing boards are embarking on reforms of their own, in anticipation of heightened government scrutiny. And the educational establishment is under scrutiny today as in no time in the past.

REFERENCES

1. Lorraine M. McDonnell and Susan Fuhrman, "The Political Context of School Reform," paper presented at the Annual Meeting of the Midwest Political Science Association, Chicago, April 1986, p. 19.
2. *Significant Features of Fiscal Federalism, 1987 Edition* (Washington, DC: Advisory Commission on Intergovernmental Relations, 1987), p. 37.
3. Center for Education Statistics, *Digest of Education Statistics 1987* (Washington, DC: U.S. Department of Education, 1987), p. 25.
4. Clark E. Cochran et al., *American Public Policy: An Introduction*, 2nd ed. (New York: St. Martin's Press, 1986), pp. 278–79.
5. Jennifer L. Hochschild, *The New American Dilemma: Liberal Democracy and School Desegregation* (New Haven, CT: Yale University Press, 1984), p. 27.
6. Harrel R. Rodgers and Charles S. Bullock, *Law and Social Change: Civil Rights Laws and Their Consequences* (New York: McGraw-Hill, 1972), pp. 81–88.
7. *Significant Features of Fiscal Federalism*, p. 59.
8. Cochran et al., *American Public Policy*, p. 275.
9. Ibid.
10. Leanna Stiefel and Robert Berne, "The Equity Effects of State School Finance Reforms: A Methodological Critique and New Evidence," *Policy Sciences*, Vol. 13 (1981), 92.
11. Michael W. Kirst, *The States' Role in Education Policy Innovation* (Palo Alto, CA: Institute for Research on Educational Finance and Governance, Stanford University, 1981), p. 305.
12. William Chance, *The Best of Educations: Reforming America's Public Schools in the 1980's* (Chicago: MacArthur Foundation, 1986), pp. 17–18.
13. Center for Education Statistics, *The Condition of Education, 1986* (Washington, DC: U.S. Department of Education, 1986), p. 91.
14. Chance, *Best of Educations*, pp. 179–87.
15. Ibid., pp. 37–47.
16. Ibid., pp. 115–51.
17. Ibid., p. 140.
18. Ibid., pp. 84–85.

19. Ibid., p. 85.
20. Ibid., pp. 115–51.
21. Ibid., pp. 48–57.
22. Ibid., pp. 138–51.
23. John Augenblick, "The Current Status of School Financing Reform in the States," in Van D. Mueller and Mary P. McKeown, eds., *The Fiscal, Legal, and Political Aspects of State Reform of Elementary and Secondary Education* (Cambridge, MA: Ballinger, 1985), pp. 12-16.
24. Theodore M. Black, *Straight Talk About American Education* (New York: Harcourt, Brace, Jovanovich, 1982).
25. H. Howe, "Giving Equity a Chance in the Excellence Game," *NASSP Bulletin* (Sept. 1984), 74–85.
26. American Council on Education, *1986–87 Fact Book on Higher Education* (New York: Macmillan, 1987), pp. 76–77; Center for Education Statistics, *Digest of Education Statistics,* pp. 123 and 126.
27. Quoted in Ernest L. Boyer, *College: The Undergraduate Experience in America* (New York: Harper & Row, 1987), p. 252.
28. Quoted in Frank Newman, *Choosing Quality: Reducing Conflict Between the State and the University* (Denver, CO: Education Commission of the States, 1987), p. 3.

CHAPTER 11

Social Welfare and Health Policy

It makes sense to look at social welfare and health policy together in the same chapter because they are closely related in several ways. As we shall see later in detail, the greatest share of state health expenditures goes to recipients of major public welfare programs. The two policy areas are intricately linked, as recipients of the two largest public assistance programs are also automatically eligible for publicly supported health care. As the state welfare rolls increase, so do public health-care costs. Moreover, in both welfare and health, state governments are heavily dependent on federal funding and are subject to detailed federal regulations. Thus state policy makers tend to view both types of programs in tandem. State cash assistance programs provide income support to the poor, elderly, and disabled; other programs offer various supportive social services to the same recipients; and medical assistance programs provide them with basic health care. Taken together, they make a statement about what states are doing for their needy residents.

Significant health policy issues also elicit the attention of state officials in their own right. States regulate the providers of medical services—physicians, nurses, and other medical assistants—as well as the hospitals in which the most expensive services are delivered. State governments pass laws defining medical malpractice and setting limits (if any) for liability. In addition, state legislatures around the country have passed laws directed at containing the rapidly rising costs of health care for all, not just that portion supported by taxpayers. And most recently, state policy makers are beginning to develop and support information and prevention programs aimed at stemming the rapid growth of AIDS cases and their associated deaths.

SOCIAL WELFARE POLICY

Government programs of social welfare at all levels can be grouped into four general categories:

1. *Income maintenance,* including Aid to Families with Dependent Children (AFDC), General Assistance, social security, Supplemental Security Income (SSI), and unemployment compensation
2. *Nutrition,* including food stamps, school breakfasts, and school lunches
3. *Social services,* including community mental health; legal services; and supportive social services such as child day care, adoption, homemaker guidance and counseling, and family planning, to list only the most prominent
4. *Health,* including Medicaid, Medicare, and various public health programs (to be discussed under Health Policy)

These programs serve different clientele and have different bases of funding. Some are organized as social insurance programs, in which the recipients of financial support or services, and/or their employers, pay into a segregated fund from which monies are drawn to cover program costs. General taxpayer support is not involved. Conversely, others can be grouped as public assistance programs, for which taxpayers largely foot the bill, although recipients may be required to pay some limited fees. The distinctions between social insurance and public assistance programs, however, are deeper than the differences in their sources of financial support and fund organization. Social differences are significant. Whereas public assistance programs are considered to be welfare, social insurance programs are viewed as draws on a prepaid account. Such different perceptions carry with them important social connotations that influence program content, conditions, and levels of financial and political support.

Social Insurance Programs

Social insurance programs are based on contributions by both employers and/or employees into a revolving account trust fund. Only individuals who have paid, or on whose behalf employers have paid, are eligible for benefits. Contributions support benefits; present contributors, in many instances, are paying for the benefits received by current recipients. Yet current contributions are co-mingled with carried-forward balances, and today's contributions will become part of future balances.

Social insurance benefits go to workers—those who have regularly been attached to the labor force and who have retired, become disabled or injured, or who have become temporarily unemployed—*regardless of financial need.* No income or asset requirements need be met for eligibility.

The major social insurance program in the country is Old Age Survivors Disability and Health Insurance (OASDHI), established in 1935, and most commonly referred to as *social security*. An *exclusively federal program,* and therefore one that will be dealt with only in passing, it covers over 90 percent of the working population. The primary exceptions include most federal employees and some state employees who are covered by their own separate retirement systems. Those who qualify for cash payments also qualify for Medicare health-insurance benefits, although the monies supporting each are kept in separate trust funds, with each component expected to be independently solvent. Benefits for both are paid out as legal entitlements, that is, the rights of those who qualify, regardless of the recipients' income or assets. Thus social security has come to serve foremost as a retirement program, providing financial support and medical care to all who qualify regardless of financial condition or social class. Although not considered a welfare program, its benefits to retirees may well be the only financial resource keeping some out of poverty. On the other hand, the social security check for the well-to-do represents only a modest supplement to their retirement income. For most Americans, social security is only one form of retirement income, accompanied by employer-provided retirement plans. Yet some employers, in designing retirement plans for their employees, look at these plans as supplements to social security, using projected social security benefits as the core retirement reserve.

A second major social insurance program, *unemployment compensation (UC),* is co-administered by the federal government and the states. The first unemployment compensation law in the United States was established by the Wisconsin legislature in 1932, and it served as the model for the current federal-state program. In the present partnership, the federal government sets program standards, but state legislatures determine their own tax and benefit levels. The regular program is financed solely from contributions made by employers into state accounts held by the federal government. Employers also pay a federal tax that finances program administration, both at the federal and state levels, as well as certain special wholly federally funded benefit programs. However, federal law allows employers to credit up to 90 percent of the state tax against the federal tax. The noncredited portion therefore becomes available to fund administration and the limited special programs. But as an inducement for states to enact UC programs meeting federal standards, the tax offset is available only to participating states—a good reason why all fifty states have established such programs.

As with social security, UC operates on a revolving fund basis, with contributions supporting benefit claims. Unlike social security, states collect the tax revenue, although it is held by the federal government in earmarked state accounts and released as states require the funds to meet benefit claims. States also maintain wage records, take claims, determine recipients' eligibility, and pay benefits. Also unlike social security, individual states can draw down their accounts to a negative balance, requiring them to borrow from the federal trust fund, with interest, to meet benefit claims. The states, in turn, are expected to enact legislation that will bring errant accounts into balance by increasing the UC tax on employers, reducing benefit levels, or by a combination of the two. Failure to do so can result in the federal government directly increasing its administrative tax on employers, without offset, thus recouping sufficient revenues to balance the account over a prescribed period.

In periods of especially high unemployment, Congress can approve the use of federal general revenues to supplement UC funds. "Extended benefits" kick in after an individual has exhausted his or her benefit entitlement, usually after twenty-six weeks, but that duration can also be extended by Congress. Federal general funds support extended benefits based on the philosophy that when exceptional levels of unemployment are reached, state accounts are not equipped to finance longer-term benefits. In addition, extended benefits recognize that very high, sustained unemployment must be viewed as a product of the national economy, and consequently, of direct national concern.

Like social security, the UC program carries no means-test requirements. Unemployment benefits are available as a matter of entitlement to unemployed workers who have met minimum requirements for previous work time and earnings. Unemployed workers receiving benefits must also be "ready, able, and willing to work" and be registered with a state job service office.

Another social insurance program found in all fifty states is *workers' compensation,* providing income support and medical services to workers who have been injured or disabled on the job, regardless of their personal financial condition. States administer the program in one of two ways. The first requires employers to provide proof of privately carried insurance to the state workers' compensation agency or to be qualified by the state agency as financially able to self-insure themselves. In both cases, the state sets program standards and prescribes minimum levels of coverage depending on the employers' size and type of enterprise. With the private insurance approach, the state workers' compensation agency works with insurance carriers to ensure that they honor all appropriate claims. Where contention exists, the agency, in most states, conducts administrative hearings and makes binding determinations, subject only to appeals to the courts. The same process applies to claims against self-insurers.

In eight states, however, commercial insurance is not allowed. Employers must insure with an exclusive state insurance fund or be qualified as self-insured. In another fourteen states, the state fund competes with commercial insurers. With this second variant, employers pay into a state-held and -administered revolving fund. As with unemployment compensation, claims are paid from the fund's available balance. Most states using this state insurance method tax employers on an "experience-rated" basis, in which employers having lower claims pay less than their comparably sized counterparts having higher claims.

Regardless of the method used, private employer coverage is mandatory in forty-seven states, excepting New Jersey, South Carolina, and Texas. In these three states, participation is elective. However, employers rejecting coverage waive their customary common law defenses against suits by injured employees.[1]

Public Assistance Programs

Public assistance programs, generally labeled as "welfare," are aimed at the needy in society. Prospective recipients must meet a means test, based on income and assets, to be eligible for benefits.

Two kinds of public assistance programs exist: cash and in-kind assistance. Cash assistance programs put money in recipients' pockets. They provide the income necessary to bring them out of poverty. In-kind programs, although not including cash, still provide something of tangible value to recipients, which if not provided, would entail still one more drain on an already tight budget or would not be afforded at all. Examples of in-kind assistance include medical care, food stamps, and public housing.

There are three major cash assistance programs available to the poor: Supplemental Security Income (SSI), directed at the aged, blind, and disabled—independent of social security; Aid to Families with Dependent Children (AFDC), the largest in terms of recipients and cost; and General Assistance, primarily a local program, providing aid to those who are poor but not eligible for any other form of governmental cash assistance.

The earliest cash assistance programs provided aid to the needy elderly. Even before the federal government got into the act, the states had established their own forms of assistance. Arizona created the first program in 1914; and by the time the federal government adopted the Social Security Act in 1935, thirty states had already established old-age assistance programs.[2]

Prior to enactment of the Social Security Act, assistance to the nonelderly poor was largely confined to private charity. Church-related organizations led the way. Local governments, most often in response to state laws passed during the first quarter of the twentieth century, established modest cash assistance programs to aid children whose fathers had died and left them without support. A few states extended coverage to children whose fathers had become disabled or who had deserted the family.

The Great Depression placed unprecedented challenges on both the private and the meager public assistance programs. With mounting unemployment, private welfare programs could not meet the cascading demands for assistance. Individuals and families were exhausting their personal resources and finding no place to turn for help. State general "relief" programs were formed to assist those who had pursued all other avenues. But the states, faced with severely declining tax resources, soon became unable to finance the required levels of assistance. In response, Congress passed the 1932 Emergency Relief and Construction Act, which, while providing funds for public works projects, also included $300 million in loans to the states for welfare purposes (none of which was repaid). However, unemployment continued to rise, and 14 million Americans were unemployed by the beginning of 1933. The federal government acted again by creating the Federal Emergency Relief Act of 1933, which authorized $500 million in "relief grants" to the states.[3] By 1935, with the passage of the Social Security Act, the federal government's role in public assistance became institutionalized, as programs were created to assist the needy elderly, the blind, and dependent children. In 1950, eligibility was broadened to include permanently and totally disabled needy adults. And these programs still exist, in modified form, today. General relief largely became the responsibility of local governments, aided by state financial assistance in some states.

Supplemental Security Income. In 1972, Congress, in response to the Nixon administration's recommendation, replaced the various categorical programs for the needy elderly, blind, and disabled—each having its own earmarked funding—with a unified program, entitled the *Supplemental Security Income (SSI)* program. Under the change, eligibility requirements and federal benefit payments were made uniform. Recipients, therefore, are now guaranteed the same *minimum* amount regardless of where they live. In addition, states may choose to supplement the federally provided minimum. They may also vary the amount of supplement by recipient category, by living arrangement, or by geographic area (recognizing different costs of living).

Although the basic SSI program is administered by the federal government, states may elect to administer the supplementation component. Most rely on federal administration. Table 11.1 shows the number of persons receiving assistance, by state and recipient category.

Aid to Families with Dependent Children. The *AFDC* program provides a matching grant-in-aid to the states to provide cash assistance to needy families with dependent children. As noted, the program began in 1935 as part of the Social Security Act and was originally entitled Aid to Dependent Children. In 1950, adult heads of families were also made eligible for assistance. In 1961, a new

TABLE 11.1. NUMBER OF PERSONS RECEIVING FEDERALLY ADMINISTERED
SSI PAYMENTS, JANUARY 1987

State	Total	Aged	Blind	Disabled
Alabama[2]	130,342	58,310	1,761	70,271
Alaska[2]	3,584	1,013	68	2,503
Arizona[2]	35,067	10,552	694	23,821
Arkansas	73,433	32,653	1,333	39,447
California	712,821	274,036	20,287	418,498
Colorado[2]	31,331	9,264	447	21,620
Connecticut[2]	28,128	6,454	516	21,158
Delaware	7,672	1,965	164	5,543
District of Columbia	16,200	3,875	216	12,109
Florida	188,552	77,918	3,052	107,582
Georgia	153,736	57,627	2,774	93,335
Hawaii	11,801	4,931	166	6,704

continued

TABLE 11.1., *continued*

State	Total	Aged	Blind	Disabled
Idaho[2]	8,667	2,037	136	6,494
Illinois[2]	145,086	30,379	2,362	112,345
Indiana[2]	50,672	11,130	1,227	38,315
Iowa	28,633	8,468	1,070	19,095
Kansas	21,770	5,637	354	15,779
Kentucky[2]	100,953	32,805	2,083	66,065
Louisiana	127,660	46,891	2,266	78,503
Maine	22,303	7,609	266	14,428
Maryland	52,955	14,263	782	37,910
Massachusetts	112,555	50,305	4,816	57,434
Michigan	126,711	28,249	2,101	96,361
Minnesota[2]	34,114	9,637	652	23,825
Mississippi	111,618	48,797	1,757	61,064
Missouri[2]	80,014	26,174	1,196	52,644
Montana	8,032	1,882	132	6,018
Nebraska[2]	14,072	3,825	248	9,999
Nevada	8,609	3,730	507	4,372
New Hampshire[2]	6,433	1,702	120	4,611
New Jersey	94,801	29,573	1,241	63,987
New Mexico[2]	27,370	9,269	507	17,594
New York	365,937	112,221	4,128	249,588
North Carolina[2]	139,771	52,825	2,805	84,141
North Dakota[2]	6,926	2,403	92	4,431
Ohio	133,865	25,248	2,493	106,124
Oklahoma[2]	58,942	23,365	948	34,629
Oregon[2]	26,771	6,428	596	19,747
Pennsylvania	169,181	44,279	3,064	121,838
Rhode Island	16,119	5,072	216	10,831
South Carolina[2]	87,051	32,469	1,878	52,704
South Dakota	8,730	2,980	140	5,610
Tennessee	128,915	47,364	2,021	79,530
Texas[3]	263,830	120,303	4,798	138,729
Utah[2]	9,212	1,798	212	7,202
Vermont	9,471	2,887	125	6,459
Virginia[2]	87,055	30,729	1,474	54,852
Washington	50,799	11,511	750	38,538
West Virginia[2]	43,409	10,275	701	32,433
Wisconsin	75,436	22,945	1,099	51,392
Wyoming[2]	2,473	695	52	1,726
Unknown	10	—	—	10
Northern Mariana Islands	598	292	18	288
Total[1]	4,260,196	1,467,049	82,911	2,710,236

[1]Includes persons with federal SSI payments and/or federally administered state supplementation, unless otherwise indicated.
[2]Data for federal SSI payments only. State has state-administered supplementation.
[3]Data for federal SSI payments only; state supplementary payments not made. *(Source:* Social Security Bulletin, *Vol. 50, No. 4 [Apr. 1987], 96.)*

program component was added, providing assistance to children if the principal wage earner in the family is unemployed and the required means test is otherwise met. This is an option, and only twenty-three states participate in the AFDC-UP program. In contrast, all fifty states participate in the basic AFDC program.[4]

The AFDC program is jointly administered by the federal government and the states. Using formula-based grants, the federal government matches state expenditures for assistance at a rate that varies by state. Wealthier states (as measured in terms of per capita income) receive relatively lower matching levels than do poorer states. The federal government also assists states with the costs of program administration. Overall, the federal government covers about two-thirds of the total cost and about 57 percent of the cost of benefits themselves. And the costs of benefits have risen by 185 percent since 1970, exceeding $14 billion by the mid-1980s.[5]

To receive federal aid, the states must comply with the following federal requirements:

1. Anyone wishing to apply for AFDC must be given the opportunity to do so regardless of race or age;
2. Assistance must be confined to those in need;
3. An applicant's income and assets must be considered in determining eligibility and payment levels;
4. An AFDC program must be administered by a single state agency and made available statewide; and
5. Prompt notice of, and the opportunity for, a hearing must be provided to anyone whose application is denied or whose payment is reduced or terminated.[6]

Within these requirements, states essentially have the option of determining who will receive assistance and at what amounts. In determining eligibility, states establish what is called a *needs standard,* which is a dollar amount set by state law and determined to be necessary to provide a minimum standard of living for a family. Although the dollar amount is usually based on a family of three, adjustments are made according to actual family size. However, no guarantee exists that recipients will actually receive a payment corresponding to the needs standard. State laws may set payment levels at only a fraction of the standard. Thus three factors can affect benefit levels among the states: varying standards of need; payment levels set at various percentages of the standard; and, indirectly, varying percentages of federal cost sharing. Benefit levels, once set, are increased by state law or not at all; cost of living increases are not prescribed in the federal program requirements.

As Table 11.2 illustrates, the maximum potential AFDC benefits for a one-parent family of three varied greatly among the states in 1987, from a low of $118 in Alabama to a high of $749 in Alaska. The median maximum AFDC grant in 1987 amounted to $354 nationally. Looking at the array of benefit levels, several observations can be made. First, benefit levels tend to be considerably lower in the southern states. In fact, the ten lowest benefit levels in the nation can be

TABLE 11.2. MAXIMUM MONTHLY POTENTIAL BENEFITS, AFDC
& FOOD STAMPS, ONE-PARENT FAMILY OF THREE PERSONS, JANUARY 1985

State and Region	Maximum AFDC Grant	Food Stamp Benefit	Combined Benefits
Median state	$354	$182	$536
New England			
Connecticut	590	111	701
Maine	405	166	571
Massachusetts	491	141	632
New Hampshire	397	169	566
Rhode Island	503	175	678
Vermont	572	116	688
Mideast			
Delaware	310	195	505
Washington, DC	364	179	543
Maryland	345	202	547
New York (New York City)	497	155	652
New York (Suffolk Co.)	602	123	725
New Jersey	404	174	578
Pennsylvania	382	173	555
Great Lakes			
Illinois	342	191	533
Indiana	256	211	467
Michigan (Washtenaw Co.)	503	151	654
Michigan (Wayne Co.)	473	160	633
Ohio	302	202	504
Wisconsin	544	125	669
Plains			
Iowa	381	174	555
Kansas	403	170	573
Minnesota	532	128	660
Missouri	279	204	483
Nebraska	350	183	533
North Dakota	371	177	548
South Dakota	366	178	544
Southeast			
Alabama	118	214	332
Arkansas	192	214	406
Florida	264	209	473
Georgia	256	211	467
Kentucky	197	214	411
Louisiana	190	214	404
Mississippi	120	214	334
North Carolina	259	210	469
South Carolina	199	214	413
Tennessee	155	214	369
Virginia	354	182	536
West Virginia	249	213	462

continued

TABLE 11.2., *continued*

State and Region	Maximum AFDC Grant	Food Stamp Benefit	Combined Benefits
Southwest			
Arizona	293	200	493
New Mexico	258	211	469
Oklahoma	310	195	505
Texas	184	214	398
Rocky Mountain			
Colorado	346	184	530
Idaho	304	197	501
Montana	354	182	536
Utah	376	175	551
Wyoming	360	180	540
Far West			
California	617	103	720
Nevada	285	202	487
Oregon	397	204	601
Washington	492	154	646
Alaska	749	197	946
Hawaii	468	301	769

Source: Significant Features of Fiscal Federalism, 1987 Edition *(Washington, DC: Advisory Commission on Intergovernmental Relations, June 1987), p. 126.*

found in the South, reflecting not only a comparatively low cost of living but also a tradition of relatively low public support for human services programs rooted in political conservatism; an aversion to high taxes; and, historically, racism. The top ten benefit-level states are dispersed among three regions of the country: the Far West, the Midwest, and the Northeast. But focusing on AFDC benefits in isolation provides only a partial picture of what the states are doing for their poor residents. To get a more complete picture, the value of food stamps should also be taken into account since food stamps can be used much like cash to purchase food and certain other necessities.

Table 11.2 also illustrates the value of food stamps, by state. Whereas the southern states trail the nation in AFDC benefit levels, they are consistently among the top in food stamp benefits, exceeding the $182 median value. However, that seeming disparity might be partially accounted for by the fact that the federal government pays the entire cost of the food stamps themselves, whereas the states, on the average, pick up over 40 percent of the costs of AFDC benefits. But even in combined benefits, it is still the southern states that provide relatively lower levels of total assistance.

Who Are the Poor?

Across the states, approximately one in every three children lives in a household receiving a means-tested benefit; about one in four receive free or reduced-price meals in school, and about one in seven live in a family receiving AFDC and/or food stamps.[7] Poverty is clearly not an isolated phenomenon in America. Although more whites are poor than blacks and Hispanics nationally, blacks are three times more *likely* to be poor than are whites. Hispanics are nearly two and one-half times more likely to be poor than are whites. In addition, regardless of race or ethnicity, female-headed households with children are five times more likely to be poor than are married-couple families, illustrating what has become the *feminization of poverty* in America.[8] Families headed by black and Hispanic women are two times again more likely to be poor compared to those headed by white women.[9] Poor minorities not only have low income and limited resources but also face the increased prospects of discrimination in employment and housing.

Two Contrasting Views of Poverty and Welfare

The More Conservative Critique. America's intellectual and cultural inheritance has preconditioned us to look at social phenomena and public problems in certain ways. We believe in the value of the individual: that each person should be free to pursue what he or she believes to be in his or her best self-interest, as long as that pursuit does not unduly infringe on the rights of others. Out of this belief in the individual comes a sense of "rugged individualism," which suggests that individuals are best left to their own devices in pursuit of their self-interest. Individuals should not be discriminated against or otherwise artificially held back in those efforts, but neither should they be advantaged. In this view, government's role is at best a limited one.

There is an economic corollary to our emphasis on the individual, and that relates both to our belief in the value of the marketplace and in the Protestant work ethic. We believe that capitalism provides an environment in which, through hard work, we can better ourselves economically. And we judge ourselves and others in terms of this kind of success. Work is an integrally important element in individual advancement. But even beyond success, work itself becomes bound up with human dignity.

In contrast, this world view looks at poverty as an aberration, as a failure of sorts. Not only have the poor been unable to succeed in an environment providing unlimited individual potential, but also because they have become dependent on others, they have lost an essential element of human dignity that is associated with work. Within an intellectual and cultural inheritance that prizes self-help, those who have become dependent on government assistance do not fully measure up. The poor themselves become suspect. They become branded as the "losers" in life, who may even have become comfortable relying on the support of others. To extend this way of thinking, it may be the very public assistance that engenders such dependency, that suppresses the "natural" drive to compete in the survival of the fittest. For welfare critic George Gilder, public assistance programs are problematic because they "break the psychological link between effort and reward."[10]

The contemporary conservative criticism of welfare includes concerns about its rising costs and potential for fraud, but its most basic criticism is that public assistance may be helping to maintain or even expand poverty by undermining the natural incentive for the poor to seek jobs. Here the criticism is heaped not so much on the poor as on the structure of the welfare system itself. Critics see the benefit structure as rewarding greater dependency since benefit payments rise if additional dependent children are added to a family's size. A part-time job, although it will bring in extra revenue, also often results in reduced public assistance benefits. A full-time job at subsistence wages may result in the elimination of AFDC benefits and, at the same time, yield comparatively less family income than did welfare. The income of an older child may have the same effects.

Another criticism of welfare is that it contributes to the breakup of traditional families. Fathers may live apart from their families in order to maintain their family's eligibility for AFDC benefits. Critics also argue that the AFDC law encourages males to live with a mother and her dependent children *outside of marriage* so that benefits will not be affected. Although this perception remains real, research suggests that welfare programs, in themselves, have little or no effect on family instability beyond that of poverty itself. In the broader social context of the changing American family—away from the traditional conception of the nuclear family—there is little evidence that "family disintegration is any more extensive among welfare families than in the population at large, and conversely, the factors that contribute to the development of alternative forms of family life in the larger society are equally influential among families receiving welfare."[11] But the perception persists nonetheless.

Conservatives, and society in general, make a distinction between the deserving and the not-so-deserving poor. Those who become poor because of something that has happened to them *beyond their control,* such as becoming blind or disabled, tend to be viewed differently from AFDC mothers. Society does not generally begrudge public financial support of the blind or disabled; they are viewed as being forced into dependency *against their will.* The aged are the subject of similar public sympathy, but a qualitative difference between the two can be detected. The elderly poor who do not have adequate social security benefits might be willingly accorded government aid because they are indeed old and unable to be gainfully employed; but at the same time, they are not accorded the same degree of benevolence extended to the blind or disabled because the noninsured elderly poor can be suspect for not preparing for their future. When they had the chance, so the argument goes, they were not attached to the labor force sufficiently to qualify for social security benefits. In that way, they may be viewed as irresponsible. Nevertheless, they are old and poor and not now able to help themselves. Conversely, the welfare mother may be viewed as young and able-bodied, capable of providing for herself and her family if only she had the drive.

The More Liberal Critique. The more liberal perspective sees welfare as meeting a real need. Families with dependent children do not choose to be on welfare; they are on welfare because of their need. If given the opportunity, welfare recipients would choose to work, deeply appreciating the association between employment and a sense of human dignity. People become unemployed and without income (beyond the expiration of unemployment compensation benefits) most often through no fault of their own. During these temporary setbacks, they have a right to public assistance. Others just seem to "fall through the cracks" of economic prosperity. They are often poorly educated and unskilled, who have difficulty finding a job even during periods of relatively low unemployment. They appear to be caught in the proverbial "cycle of poverty," not having available any means to escape. Young single-parent mothers with infants and toddlers at home find it a difficult choice to leave their children while working or seeking work, believing that a mother should be at home with her children during their early, formative years.

A recent University of Michigan study provides two ways of looking at the relative dependence of the poor on welfare. Between 1969 and 1978, those who were on the welfare rolls for eight or more of the ten years constituted only 17.5 percent of the welfare recipients over the entire period, apparently providing evidence in support of the temporary nature of welfare dependence. In other words, from this statistic it appears that recipients are largely receiving support to get them through a personally atypical, temporary need—supporting the liberal contention. But these same recipients were found to make up about half of the overall welfare population at any one time during the period, a statistic that suggests the more enduring nature of welfare dependence.[12] However, even taking the latter perspective, it appears that at any time long-termers and short-termers make up nearly equal segments of those receiving public assistance.

Liberals may also argue that the welfare system has worked. Since poverty statistics began to be kept in 1959, the number of persons living in poverty has declined by nearly 15 million.[13] Welfare is meeting a need, helping to provide the necessities to those who would have to go without them in the absence of public support. Yet the contemporary welfare system fails to escape criticism. For liberals, the state-federal partnership breeds inequality. Benefit levels are viewed as inequitable among the states and not in fact related to actual need. For many liberals, however, the real problem is not welfare; it is the broader social "system," which tolerates an underclass in society. And from the liberals' perspective, changes in the educational system have to come first. Education, for them, holds the greatest promise of breaking the cycle of poverty.

Calls for Welfare Reform

Virtually every major study of public assistance programs has called for significant reform of the present welfare system, whether coming from a more conservative or liberal perspective. Reform proposals tend to fall into one of two categories, either incremental or comprehensive.

Incrementalists accept the present collection of diverse categorical assistance programs. They look to improve them, "fill in the gaps," and make them more efficient administratively. Reform initiatives are often recommended as solutions to specific problems. Examples abound in the AFDC program. One often-advanced proposal has been directed at greater benefit equality among the states, calling for the federal government to require states to meet certain benefit standards in order to receive matching support. As a variant to this basic proposal, other recommendations have called on the federal government to increase its matching share. But as pointed out in response, a state like Mississippi, which has the lowest benefit payment nationally, now only pays 17 percent of its benefit costs.[14] A high percentage of federal sharing has already failed to elicit increased benefits. Recognizing this problem, another variant has called on the federal government to finance fully the minimum benefit level, with the states left to supplement it as they see fit.

Welfare Reform and Work. Comprehensive reforms range from restructuring the relationship between public assistance and work to establishing a cash-based income maintenance system. The first category, comprising the so-called "work-relief" programs, is built on three goals: to ensure adequate benefits for those in need but unable to work; to focus benefits on those in greatest need; and to minimize disincentives against work, or actually require work in exchange for public assistance. In an effort to minimize disincentives against work, Congress in 1967 passed the *work incentive (WIN)* program. The WIN program, now defunct, included the reformist "thirty plus one-third" provision, whereby the first thirty dollars of earned income each month, plus one-third of the remainder, would not be counted as offsets against AFDC benefits, thus making remunerative work more financially attractive. In addition, state welfare agencies were awarded federal funds to provide working AFDC mothers with day care and selected job-training services. These recipients were also required to register for employment referral with state job-service offices.

Several evaluations of the WIN program suggest that it failed to realize its promise. A U.S. Congress Joint Economic Committee report noted that during its first six years in existence only 138,000 persons were claimed to have obtained employment as a result of the WIN program. The report goes on to suggest that this figure might be inflated by as much as 40 percent.[15] Henry Levin challenges the efficacy of WIN job placements by suggesting that the program "creamed" off the best employment prospects, those with better educations and work records, who were already more likely to find a job.[16] Irene Laurice adds that the costs involved in marketing poorly trained and educated AFDC mothers in a highly competitive labor market far exceeded the benefits, whether benefits are measured as reduced AFDC benefit costs or increased family earnings.[17] In explaining the program's lackluster performance, critics generally agree that, even with job training and placement services, welfare recipients are at a distinct disadvantage in the job market. With only so many jobs available, employers are drawn not only to the best prepared prospective workers but also to those who have a stable "track record" of work.

The Reagan administration, in rejecting the WIN program, did not give up on the concept of work. The orientation has changed. Rather than attempting to place those few AFDC recipients who are the most employable, with or without additional job training or other supportive services, whereas the remainder collect benefits without working, the Reagan administration's *workfare* program requires all able-bodied recipients to work for their benefits. Under workfare, welfare recipients are required to work a specified number of hours at a calculated minimum wage to "earn" the value of their benefits. The prescribed work is often of the public service variety, involving such tasks as snow shoveling, trash clean-up, and routine clerical tasks. Here the emphasis is not so much on employability as on the value of the work ethic itself.

Although President Reagan's proposal for a mandatory workfare program was rejected by Congress in 1981, Congress enacted the Tax Equity and Fiscal Responsibility Act of 1982 (TEFRA), which provided incentives for the states to enact workfarelike programs. In response, more than half the states now require able-bodied welfare recipients to work for their benefits. Yet several states, most notably California and Massachusetts, have resorted to forced public service work only after welfare recipients undergo an initial, intensive period of employability preparation and job search—in parts, reminiscent of the WIN program.

The California program, known as GAIN (Greater Avenues to Independence), requires two-parent welfare households (permitted under California's AFDC-UP program) and single-parent households with no children under age six to meet with a social worker and develop an "individualized employment plan." That plan may include language training for non-English speakers, coaching on job search and interviewing techniques for those already possessing marketable job skills and a recent employment record, or job training for those lacking such skills. In addition, child-care services are provided to mothers during their periods of job search or job training. Welfare recipients who remain unemployed after having been through job training or a "job club" work search are then required to work for the state, for no more than a year, to put off their welfare benefits. The state jobs are valued at the same hourly rate as the lowest-paid classified state employee. The concept is that meaningful work gets done, and in the process, welfare recipients get needed employment experience.

An evaluation of the workfare program in San Diego County showed mixed results. Local officials boasted that almost half the workfare participants found jobs, a seemingly impressive result and one that was used in the state legislature as justification for statewide workfare. In comparison, however, nearly four-fifths as many nonenrolled AFDC recipients were able to find jobs on their own. Supporters of the program claimed a savings of $2.50 for every dollar spent, but detractors questioned the value of the work product. As David Kirp noted, "It is the recipients, not the taxpayers, who are better off. Only by placing a fairly high value on the product of workfare, the better-swept streets and better-organized government files, can society be regarded as benefitting, on the basis of the evidence at hand."[18]

A variant of workfare is Wisconsin's *learnfare* program, which requires school-age children of families receiving AFDC to attend school or have their families face the loss of benefits. Wisconsin welfare officials look at the pilot program as an effort to break the cycle of poverty through education, creating a financial incentive for parents to keep their children in school. The pilot is based on the premise that dropping out of school constitutes a key ingredient in perpetuating welfare dependency across generations.

Reform by Dismantling the Welfare Bureaucracy. Another alternative, which dramatically breaks from the present system of welfare in the United States, is the so-called *family allowance.* With this approach, used widely in western European nations, all families are given a monthly benefit check from the government. It is generally employed in conjunction with a steep progressive income tax. The poor pay no tax on the allowance income, whereas the affluent pay a heavy tax. But every family of comparable size receives the same level of benefit regardless of income. Thus the stigma associated with welfare is removed. The allowance level is also set at a bare minimum level of support, encouraging families to find other income supplements. And because of the high progressivity of taxation, the poor pay little or no tax on supplementary income, up to a point. The family allowance system therefore carries with it little disincentive for the unemployed poor to seek employment.

If adopted in the United States, such a system would probably be fully federalized, with the federal government picking up the sizable costs and using the Internal Revenue Service to administer the program. The allowance amounts could be the same for comparably sized families across the nation, or allowances could be tied to cost of living differences among the states or even within states. Another approach would find the federal government and the states sharing both the costs and administration of a family allowance program. The states could process the allowance checks and keep the records, and the federal government, through reimbursement, could share in the costs of allowances and administration.

Another alternative, commonly known as the *negative income tax,* associated with conservative economist Milton Friedman, would work on a similar principle of guaranteed minimum income, but families would not receive a monthly allowance from the government. Instead, the federal government would set annual minimum guaranteed levels of income for families of various sizes. Again, as with family allowances, the amounts could be made uniform among the states or varied according to the cost of living. All families would file federal income tax statements, and those with incomes above the guaranteed income levels would pay taxes on those amounts, as usual. However, those whose incomes fell below the recognized floors would not only pay no tax at all but would also receive a check in the mail from the federal government at an amount necessary to bring them up to the guaranteed minimum.

A variation on this theme would find the federal government setting both an income floor and a ceiling for participation. Needy families would then receive a specified percentage of the difference between their earned income and the ceiling. To illustrate how this would work, assume that the floor for a family of three was set at $7,000 a year and that the ceiling was set at $14,000. Under this formulation, the family with no additional earned income would receive $7,000 a year from the federal government. The same family earning $9,000 through employment would receive an additional $2,500 (or one-half of the difference between $9,000 and $14,000) at a 50 percent disregard level. On the other hand, a family of three earning $14,000 or more, in this example, would receive nothing additional from the federal government. Obviously, such an earned income provision encourages beneficiaries to seek additional income.

The underlying concept behind the negative income tax is that those whose incomes fall below the guarantees would have unused exemptions or deductions available to be turned into cash. In comparison to family allowances, the negative income tax would be easier to administer and would involve far less money that would have to be collected as taxes and then be disbursed as expenditures.

Beyond getting money into needy people's pockets, supporters of both options see them as agents for dismantling the present welfare system and its so-called "social welfare-poverty complex." In their view, the government welfare bureaucracy has become a largely unnecessary appendage, and their proposal would greatly decimate both the government bureaucracy and the vast network of social service suppliers. Under a guaranteed income program, the poor would become empowered, within the limits of their available income, to decide how to spend their money, including decisions about what social services they might want to purchase. Social workers would have no role to play in those essentially private decisions.

Although a dismantling of the contemporary welfare system is attractive to political conservatives, one conservative school of thought views the guaranteed minimum income with distaste, seeing it as a violation of the self-help principle. To put it baldly, the commonly voiced objection is that people would be paid to do nothing to improve their less-than-desirable life-styles. Others take the position that, although some beneficiaries will accept their minimum income alone, the vast majority will pursue additional earned income as long as tax rates do not remove such a natural inclination to do so. This school of thought is premised on the belief that people want to work—to get ahead—and will seek to rise above that very minimum standard of living for their family's benefit.

This variety of welfare reform received serious consideration in response to a proposal offered by the Nixon administration in 1969. It was defeated in the Senate by a coalition of liberals and conservatives. Liberal senators argued that the benefits were too low, and the conservatives objected ideologically to the concept of a guaranteed family income, viewing it as too radical a departure from America's traditional work-reward ethic.

Reducing Welfare Fraud and Error

Popular stereotypes include that of the welfare cheat. In one study of attitudes about the poor, approximately 40 percent of the respondents expressed the opinion that welfare recipients lie in order to receive welfare.[19] A recent highly publicized case of Dorothy Mae Parker, labeled California's "welfare queen," has reinforced that perception. She was convicted of having defrauded the state out of more than $350,000 in welfare benefits, using nine aliases to file claims for herself and thirty-eight nonexistent children.[20] Nevertheless, the actual incidence of fraud is estimated to involve only about 4 percent of all cases.[21]

Beyond the wasted resources associated with fraud, others are dissipated as a result of administrative error resulting from caseworker miscalculation, from failure to apply complex guidelines properly, and from the sheer volume of paperwork. In an effort to reduce error, Congress passed an amendment in 1981 that, beginning in 1983, penalized states having AFDC error rates in excess of 4 percent of their total caseload—a level about the same as that of suspected recipient fraud. Two years later that permissible level of error was dropped to 3 percent. Yet despite their increased efforts, states have had difficulty complying. On behalf of the states, the American Public Welfare Association, representing state welfare administrators, argues that the welfare program error rates are not at all high when compared to other federal programs. Moreover, the association notes that states are now spending up to one-fifth of their AFDC administrative budgets on monitoring activities.[22]

Cutting Costs by Restricting Access to Welfare

Historically, although the federal government has acted to expand the poor's access to AFDC benefits, Reagan administration initiatives have tended to reduce access as a means of reducing rising program expenditures. The historic and controversial Omnibus Budget Reconciliation Act (OBRA) of 1981 served as the vehicle for such changes.

To reduce access, and thereby costs, the 1981 act lowered the age ceiling, from twenty-one to nineteen, at which the federal government shares in the costs of AFDC benefits. States would thereafter have to pick up the costs totally on their own if they wished to continue benefits for twenty and twenty-one-year-olds. The act also reduced federal reimbursement for aid to pregnant mothers for only those pregnancies continuing beyond six months. But other Reagan initiatives cut more broadly into the previously eligible AFDC population.

Prior to the act, states, in determining eligibility, could disregard five dollars per month of income from any source and any income set aside to cover the "future identifiable needs of a child." The OBRA eliminated both areas of state direction. It also tightened up other disregard provisions. Until 1981, working recipients could deduct reasonable work-related expenses for day care, taxes, required clothing, and other enumerated categories from their gross earned income for eligibility purposes. The act put dollar limits on each category of work-related expense. Very significantly, it also rendered ineligible any family with an income of more than 150 percent of the state's need standard, regardless of that family's aggregate level of disregarded income. With all these changes, the federal government limited the state discretion that had existed.

Preliminary evidence suggests that these initiatives have indeed restricted access, as intended by the Reagan administration. Initial estimates indicate that between 10 and 14 percent of the caseload was dropped from the AFDC rolls during the first year following the change.[23] Even progressive states such as Wisconsin and Minnesota have tightened welfare eligibility restrictions in response to the Reagan administration's reforms.

HEALTH POLICY

The poor generally have a greater need for health care than do their fellow Americans. The poor often have a bigger backlog of unmet medical needs, and inadequate nutrition often complicates matters. But the poor also face barriers in getting their health needs met. One barrier to access is economic. Public supported health care addresses this constraint to a certain extent but does not eliminate it. About 30 percent of those deemed to be living in poverty among the states are considered to be poor enough to qualify for state medical assistance.[24] In fact, it is the "marginal poor" who face the most significant barriers to access. Their incomes and/or assets may render them ineligible for publicly financed medical services, but they are the very ones most affected by the rapidly rising costs of medical care. Often lacking private health insurance, the marginal poor may find it impossible to come up with sufficient financial means to pay hospital bills covering even routine diagnostic services or surgical procedures.

Even beyond economic factors, social conditions limit the poor's access to health care. The poor may be less socially conditioned than the middle class to seek out care and demand satisfactory follow-up. They may also find it more difficult to get to health-care providers, finding themselves more reliant on public transportation than those economically better off. Finally, for the working poor, a visit to the doctor usually entails lost wages since most low-income workers are employed on an hourly compensation basis.

Publicly Supported Health Care

Compared to other industrial nations, health care in the United States is still largely in the private domain. Outside of the United States, government's involvement in health care usually takes one of two forms. In the first, government itself operates a national health service, and health-care providers, including physicians and nurses, are public employees. Countries in this category include Great Britain and Israel, among democratic nations, and most totalitarian nations including the Soviet Union and East European bloc countries. In the second form, the government mandates universal insurance coverage through employers, and government policies are available to those unable to obtain the private insurance. Countries following this form include most West European nations. In the United States, government subsidies for health care are available only to the poor, the elderly, or the disabled, in addition to care provided to military veterans at federal Veteran's Administration hospitals around the country.

Two major programs support the bulk of government-financed medical care in the United States: Medicare and Medicaid. In addition, state and county hospitals may provide care to the poor who have no other means of receiving care under an indigent patient program. In these cases, the taxpayers pick up the cost of care.

Medicare. *Medicare* is not a health-care program for the poor. Instead, as with social security, it is a federally administered social insurance program, financed by contributions from employers and employees alike. Nor is it a medical care program for the elderly per se. It is a program providing benefits only to those who have qualified for social security or railroad retirement benefits, by having been attached to the labor force for a certain period, and who have made minimally required contributions into the fund. Others who have reached age sixty-five, but who do not qualify, may receive hospitalization coverage but must pay a high monthly premium for the federal insurance. The premium amount is adjusted annually in relation to changes in hospital costs, amounting to $226 per month in 1987.

The Social Security Amendments of 1965, part of Lyndon Johnson's Great Society initiatives, established two related contributory health-insurance plans: a basic *compulsory* program of hospital insurance (HI) and a *voluntary* program of supplementary medical insurance (SMI). Hospital insurance covers the following:

1. Inpatient hospital services are covered for up to ninety days. If hospitalized, the patient pays a one-time deductible amount, recalculated annually (amounting to $520 in 1987). If hospitalization exceeds sixty days, an additional co-insurance payment of one-fourth the deductible amount is assessed each day up to ninety days. Beyond ninety days, the co-insurance payment rises to one-half of the deductible per day. The inescapable conclusion to be drawn is that long-term hospitalization can be expensive, even with Medicare coverage.
2. Nursing-home care following hospitalization is also covered. Persons who have been hospitalized at least three days are eligible for follow-up care in a skilled nursing facility. But after the first twenty days, patients are required to make co-payments at an amount equal to 12.5 percent of the hospital deductible per day.
3. Home health services are also covered, including nursing visits and physical therapy. No co-payments are required.
4. Hospice care is covered for the terminally ill with a life expectancy of six months or less. As with home care, no co-payment is required.

Supplementary medical insurance is available to Medicare eligibles at a monthly premium ($17.90 in 1987), which is deducted from their benefit check. The SMI covers the costs of various nonhospitalization costs, most prominently including physicians' and surgeons' fees, outpatient diagnostic tests, physical therapy, and prosthetic devices prescribed by physicians. A $75 annual deductible is charged for some of the services.[25]

Although Medicare greatly limits the costs that the elderly or disabled would otherwise have to pay for medical services, it should be clear that its medical insurance protection is far from free. Major medical problems can significantly cut into the savings of the Medicare-eligible patient. Then again, Medicare was not designed as a program for the poor; it was developed as an insurance program for all Americans, and Congress, in adding deductibles and co-payments, has operated on the assumption that the vast majority of Americans have the financial resources to pay the added charges.

Medicaid. Medicaid was enacted along with Medicare in 1965. Unlike Medicare, Medicaid is a joint federal-state program limited to the needy. All states participate except Arizona. In twenty-two states, only AFDC and SSI recipients are eligible; the remaining states open the program up to other "medically needy" individuals who fail to meet AFDC or SSI eligibility standards. To participate in the latter category, individuals cannot have income over one-third higher than the AFDC cash payment for a similar-sized family, with only marginal exceptions made for those with low income and extraordinarily high medical bills.

Over 21 million persons receive Medicaid benefits annually. (Table 11.3 shows the categories of recipients.)

The federal government is the major financial supporter of the program, contributing 55 percent of the $41.3 billion cost of benefits and administration. States, based on their per capita income, are reimbursed from between 50 and 83 percent of their actual program expenditures.[26] To receive federal reimbursement, states must provide the following basic medical services to patients:

- Physicians' services
- Inpatient and outpatient hospital services
- Laboratory and x-ray services
- Skilled-nursing care for adults
- Home health services
- Rural health clinic services
- Screening, diagnostic, and treatment service for children
- Family planning services and supplies
- Nurse/midwife services

TABLE 11.3. MEDICAID RECIPIENTS 1985

Aged 65 or older	3,061,000
Blind	80,000
Permanently and totally disabled	2,936,000
Dependent children younger than age 21	9,752,000
Adults in families with dependent children	5,518,000
Other	461,000
Total	21,808,000

Source: Social Security Bulletin, *Vol. 50, No. 4 (Apr. 1987),* 59.

Additionally, states, at their option, may provide other services and still receive federal reimbursement for those costs. Such services might include chiropractic care, dental care, physical therapy, prescription medicines, and eyeglasses. Seventeen different optional services qualify.

The Medicaid program also complements the Medicare program. Medicaid can be used to pay the premiums for SMI and the deductible and co-insurance costs for social security recipients who do not have the financial means to meet Medicare's contributory requirements.

Although AFDC families make up two-thirds of Medicaid beneficiaries, their medical bills account for only about one-fourth of all Medicaid expenditures. Presently about two-thirds of Medicaid spending goes to care for the elderly and mentally retarded who are institutionalized in skilled nursing homes and state institutions. In states with large elderly populations, the percentage can reach 80 percent. The corresponding cost of institutional care has also increased steadily; today Medicaid pays an average of $21,000 a year for a nursing-home resident and $36,000 a year for a mentally retarded resident of a state institution. However, nursing-home costs are increasing at a higher annual rate.[27]

Containing the Rising Costs of Health Care

Medical-care costs have risen one-fifth faster than inflation over the past two decades. During the same period, the cost of hospitalization has more than doubled the general rate of inflation.[28] These rapidly rising costs are being met primarily by third-party payers, which alone pay approximately 70 percent of all medical costs and over 90 percent of hospital expenses.[29] Third-party payers can be either public, as in the case of Medicare and Medicaid, or private, represented by insurance companies such as Blue Cross/Blue Shield or American Family.

Individuals covered by third-party payer arrangements may have little personal incentive to control the costs of medical care. Where all or a majority of the costs are covered by the government or by insurance, patients will be most concerned about having their medical needs met, as they see them, and will most dearly value the quality and comprehensiveness of service, regardless of its cost. With public third-party payers, patients may feel that they themselves are not paying for the services. They may not realize that greatly increasing costs could bring with them pressures for cuts in benefits or increased taxes (if they even pay taxes). With private insurance, patients may feel that they should be "getting their money's worth" by being well-served, not fully recognizing that rising costs can bring with them increases in their insurance premiums.

Health-care providers may also have little incentive to restrain costs. If physicians and hospitals are liberally reimbursed for the various services that they render, there is scant economic reason that "the more, the better" philosophy should not prevail. This does not mean that providers will necessarily provide unneeded services, but some evidence suggests that this has been the case. Instead, providers are more likely to "err" on the side of service inclusion in cases of marginal need. Further, if providers are reimbursed on a fee-for-service basis, charging the "usual, customary, and reasonable'' rate prevailing in a given location, they have a built-in incentive collectively to increase fees.

Managed Health Care—HMOs. In 1984, Congress, at the behest of the Reagan administration, gave the states greater freedom to pursue a number of cost-cutting alternatives in the Medicaid program, which were aimed at replacing the existing system of incentives. Of these, use of primary care case management *(PCCM)* and health-maintenance organizations *(HMO)* for Medicaid patients have become the most popular approaches adopted by the states. Currently, thirty states offer some form of managed health care to their Medicaid beneficiaries. In addition, the same federal legislation allows Medicare patients to participate in HMOs. With managed health care, a primary physician takes responsibility for a patient's complete medical care. When the patient becomes ill, the patient first sees his or her primary physician. Normally, the primary physician treats the problem; but if the care of a specialist is required, *in the primary physician's judgment,* a referral is made. The primary physician, not the patient, seeks out supplementary medical services.

With HMOs as a prominent form of managed care, physicians and other medical practitioners form a prepaid group practice. Subscribers pay a monthly or annual fee for medical care, and all services are covered by that fee. Because medical care is prepaid, physicians have no financial incentive to overtreat patients. For the same reason, hospital care is used only when absolutely necessary, and financial incentives prompt stays to be kept as short as is medically prudent. Moreover, managed health care has been employed to discourage the use of emergency rooms as primary sources of medical care for the poor, with its attendant higher costs. Advocates also argue that an assigned primary physician encourages greater preventive health care and more continuity of care. Critics, on the other hand, argue that the comprehensiveness of care might suffer. Since most HMOs are operated for profit, financial incentives exist for the medical profession to underserve patients, providing them with a bare-bones service. Critics also suggest that it is the poor who will probably be less served than other elements in society, for the poor are less accustomed and equipped to press their demands for high-quality and comprehensive health care.

Prospective Hospital Reimbursement. To address the fastest-growing component of health-care costs, hospital charges, Congress, also in 1984, passed legislation creating a prospective payment system for the hospitalization of Medicare and Medicaid patients. With a system called Diagnosis Related Groups, or *DRG,* hospitals began to be reimbursed on a fixed scale for treating 467 specified ailments, instead of for the "customary costs" of each separate service, as was the previous practice. As with the philosophy underlying managed physician care, hospitals had a new incentive to provide only necessary services. If the actual cost of services to treat an illness should exceed the DRG prepayment, the hospital loses. Conversely, if the actual cost of services can be kept below the prepayment level, the hospital keeps the difference. As might be expected, the arguments in support of, and in opposition to, DRGs are similar to those directed at HMOs.

Cost Control Through Regulation. As noted earlier, hospital costs have grown faster than any other component of the health-care system. The per day costs of hospitalization have exceeded the general rate of inflation, but so have the costs of specialized medical services, particularly sophisticated diagnostic services. To address these rising costs, Congress enacted the 1974 Health Planning Act, reauthorized in 1979, which created a number of local planning agencies, coordinated at the state level, to review and comment on the need for additional health facilities within a designated geographical area. The act also provided incentives for states to pass laws that establish criteria governing the needs that have to be documented before health-care facilities (primarily hospitals) can be constructed or augmented. Also covered is capital equipment valued in excess of $150,000, such as CAT scanners and prenatal diagnostic equipment.

These so-called *certificate-of-need* laws have been enacted on the premise that excess capacity leads to higher costs because fixed costs have to be spread among lower than optimal levels of utilization. All states, except Louisiana, have passed such legislation.

The regulatory approach to cost control has recently been downplayed by the Reagan administration. Instead, prospective payment programs and ailment-based reimbursement initiatives have come to displace regulation as the most prized policy vehicles of cost containment.

The Growing Specter of AIDS as a Health-Care Problem

The growing problem of Acquired Immunodeficiency Syndrome, better known as *AIDS,* has assumed a significant position on most state public health agendas. As of early 1987, nearly 31,000 AIDS cases have been *reported* in the United States, producing over 17,000 deaths. But beyond the development of AIDS cases, it is estimated that $1\frac{1}{2}$ million Americans carry the AIDS-producing Human Immunodeficiency Virus (HIV) and could develop AIDS itself. The factors that determine the progression from an HIV infection to the actual development are largely unknown. Yet the Public Health Service estimates that approximately one-fourth of all persons infected with HIV will develop AIDS—a staggering number. Accordingly, AIDS-related deaths are conservatively projected to increase to about 150,000 by 1991.[30]

AIDS cases and related deaths are no longer isolated phenomena. Although the greatest incidence of AIDS cases can be found in the major metropolitan population centers, they are not limited there; Table 11.4 shows that AIDS cases have appeared in every state. Yet the two highest-risk categories, homosexual or bisexual males and intravenous drug abusers, are found disproportionately in major metropolitan areas. It is not surprising to find the New York, San Francisco, and Los Angeles areas heading the list.

In response to the growth and expected further increase in AIDS cases, state

TABLE 11.4. ALL CUMULATIVE AIDS CASES PER MILLION POPULATION
BY STANDARD METROPOLITAN STATISTICAL AREA (SMSA)
OF RESIDENCE

Metropolitan Area	Population	Cumulative Total
New York, NY	9.12	8,762
San Francisco, CA	3.25	3,140
Los Angeles, CA	7.48	2,649
Washington, DC	3.06	880
Miami, FL	1.63	916
Houston, TX	2.91	934
Newark, NJ	1.97	735
Chicago, IL	7.10	681
Philadelphia, PA	4.72	572
Atlanta, GA	2.03	468
Boston, MA	2.76	476
Dallas, TX	2.97	497
Jersey City, NJ	0.56	339
Fort Lauderdale, FL	1.02	346
Nassau–Suffolk, NY	2.61	375
Rest of United States	176.93	9,069
Total United States	230.11	30,839

Source: State of Wisconsin Department of Health and Social Services, Summary Report: Public Health Task Force on Acquired Immunodeficiency Syndrome (AIDS), Appendix A, Table 5, March 1987.

legislatures have begun to consider and pass AIDS-related legislation. Five categories of legislation have generated the greatest attention among the states: third-party access to AIDS antibody test results, medical personnel's right to information that they are treating AIDS patients, the specification of test procedures, criminalization of falsifying blood donation information on the part of those carrying the AIDS virus, and the creation of public education programs aimed at reducing the risk factors associated with AIDS transmission.[31]

SUMMARY AND CONCLUSIONS

Social welfare and health policy are closely linked. Poor people receiving public assistance have above-average health-care needs. They also lack the personal financial resources necessary to purchase the required medical care. Thus medical care for the needy has become a public responsibility, with its attendant costs. In fact, concerns about rising costs have greatly marked the public debate over welfare and health policies. Reforms in both areas have largely been premised on cost containment. Economy and efficiency have become the privileged criteria used to evaluate what constitutes good public welfare and health policy. Current emphasis is on cutting costs and restoring personal responsibility: the responsibility of those on public assistance to work for a living; the responsibility of government to provide incentives to, and assist, the poor to find jobs or to create them; the responsibility of physicians and hospital administrators to act "rationally" (primarily in terms of economic rationality) in managing health care; and the responsibility of government to create those incentives necessary to elicit that responsible behavior. The Reagan administration has provided incentives and constraints for the states to enact legislation along these lines, and many have done so.

REFERENCES

1. *Social Security Bulletin,* Vol. 50, No. 4 (Apr. 1987), 31–39.
2. Diana M. DiNitto and Thomas R. Dye, *Social Welfare: Politics and Public Policy* (Englewood Cliffs, NJ: Prentice-Hall, 1987), p. 89.
3. *Social Security Bulletin,* p. 53.
4. Ibid., p. 57.
5. Ibid., p. 102.
6. Ibid., p. 56.
7. U.S. Bureau of the Census, "Money, Income and Poverty Status of Families and Persons in the United States: 1984," *Current Population Reports* (July 1984).
8. U.S. Bureau of the Census, "Money, Income and Poverty Status of Families and Persons in the United States: 1984," *Current Population Reports* (August 1985).
9. DiNitto and Dye, *Social Welfare,* p. 53.
10. George Gilder, *Wealth and Poverty* (New York: Bantam Books, 1981).
11. Andrew W. Dobelstein, *Politics, Economics, and Public Welfare* (Englewood Cliffs, NJ: Prentice-Hall, 1980), p. 134.
12. Cited in David L. Kirp, "The California Work/Welfare Scheme," *The Public Interest,* No. 83 (Spring 1986), 45.
13. U.S. Bureau of the Census, "Money, Income and Poverty Status of Families and Persons in the United States: 1984," *Current Population Reports* (February 1985).
14. Mark D. Worthington and Lawrence E. Lynn, Jr., "American Welfare Strategies: Three Programs Under the Social Security Act," in Ellen E. Paul and Philip A. Russo, Jr., eds., *Public Policy: Issues, Analysis, and Ideology* (Chatham, NJ: Chatham House Publishers, 1982), p. 17.
15. U.S. Congress, Joint Economic Committee, *Handbook of Public Income Transfer Payments,* Paper 20, 1974.
16. Henry M. Levin, "A Decade of Policy Developments in Improving Education and Training for Low Income Populations," in Robert H. Haveman, ed., *A Decade of Federal Antipoverty Programs* (New York: Academic Press, 1977).
17. Irene Laurice, "Work Requirements in Income-Conditional Transfer Programs," *Social Service Review,* Vol. 52 (Dec. 1978), 551–66.
18. Kirp, "California Work/Welfare," p. 44.
19. Cited in John R. Tropman, "American Welfare Strategies: Three Programs Under the Social Security Act," in Paul and Russo, eds., *Public Policy,* p. 91.
20. Jeffrey R. Henig, *Public Policy and Federalism: Issues in State and Local Politics* (New York: St. Martin's Press, 1985), pp. 106–7.
21. Tropman, "American Welfare Strategies," p. 91.
22. Mary H. Cooper and Sandra Stencel, "Rising Cost of Health Care" in Hoyt Gimlin,

ed., *America's Needy: Care and Cutbacks* (Washington, DC: Congressional Quarterly, 1984), pp. 43–45.

23. Tom Joe and Cheryl Rogers, *By the Few for the Few* (Lexington, MA: Lexington Books, 1984), p. 95.

24. Guy Peters, *American Public Policy: Promise and Performance* (Chatham, NJ: Chatham House Publishers, 1986), p. 186.

25. *Social Security Bulletin,* pp. 22–24.

26. *Social Security Bulletin,* p. 59.

27. Donald N. Muse, "States Not Protected from Medicaid Growth," *State Government News* (February 1986), pp. 12–14.

28. Peters, *American Public Policy,* pp. 187–88.

29. Ibid., p. 189.

30. Wisconsin Department of Health and Social Services, *Summary Report: Public Health Task Force on Acquired Immunodeficiency Syndrome (AIDS)* (Madison, WI: Department of Health and Social Services, Nov. 1986), p. 1.

31. Michelle Polchow, "AIDS Legislation Reaches Beyond Public Health Issues," *State Legislatures* (January 1986), 7–8.

_____CHAPTER 12_____

Transportation Policy

Our daily lives are greatly affected by transportation policy. If we drive a motor vehicle, that vehicle has to be registered with the state in which we live. We, as drivers, have to be licensed by the state to operate a motor vehicle legally. Speed laws, set by the state and local governments, prescribe how fast we may legally drive. If we exceed those limits, a state or local police officer may arrest us for speeding. In addition, the interstate and state highways on which we drive are largely designed, built, and maintained under federal and state standards and are financially supported by state and federal funds. Local roads and streets, although under the jurisdiction of local governments, are built and maintained through a combination of federal, state, and local funds. Figure 12.1 shows the jurisdictional control of U.S. highways, roads, and streets.

We, as users of public highways, roads, and streets, pay fees and taxes for that privilege. Not only do we pay state fees for operator licensing and vehicle registration, but also every gallon of motor fuel that we purchase is taxed by both the federal and state governments. We may also have to pay a local registration fee, commonly called a "wheel tax," to a city or county government. Moreover, in areas where air pollution levels exceed acceptable air quality standards, we must have our vehicles regularly inspected and have deficiencies corrected, up to a specified maximum cost.

We may also take a bus or subway to work or school, or for shopping or entertainment. That vehicle has probably been purchased with a combination of state, local, and federal funds. In fact, the fare we pay would, on the average, have been almost three times higher if it had not been subsidized by state, local, or federal financial support.[1]

Whenever we fly on a commercial airline we pay a federal tax, which is redistributed to state and local governments to help pay for airport construction and improvements. If we have the good fortune to fly our own plane, we pay a registra-

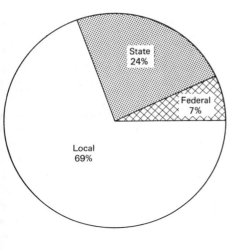

Figure 12.1. Jurisdictional Control of Roads and Streets in the United States. (Source: Federal Highway Administration, *Our Nation's Highways: Selected Facts and Figures* [Washington, DC: U.S. Department of Transportation, 1984], p. 4.)

tion fee to the state and an aviation gas tax to both state and federal governments. Either as a pilot or passenger, our air trip comes under the authority of the U.S. Department of Transportation, and federal air traffic controllers guide our flight through reserved airspace.

Even as consumers, we are affected by state and federal transportation policy. Federal deregulation of commercial air travel may mean lower fares for transcontinental and hub-to-hub flights, but it may also mean higher fares and less service for the least profitable routes. With deregulation, airlines are no longer forced to serve unprofitable routes to obtain the right to compete in the more profitable markets. The prospects for profit now exclusively motivate competition.

Deregulation of rail transport may permit railroads to rationalize their routes, but the profit motive may mean that certain lines will be abandoned altogether. Faced with increasing abandonments, several states have established programs to subsidize lines facing the likely prospect of abandonment or to provide financial support to local rail commissions established to continue operation on a particular shortline segment of an otherwise abandoned line.

Truck deregulation carries with it similar advantages and drawbacks. Greater competition and route efficiency may well lower costs to transporters and, ultimately, to consumers, where business prospects warrant increased market entry. Yet for less profitable hauls in nonmajor metropolitan areas, deregulation may result in higher costs to both transporters and consumers.

But just as transportation policy affects our daily lives, transportation policy may affect, and be affected by, other policy decisions. A policy that relies heavily on new highway construction to address the problem of congestion on urban freeways may have implications for energy, land use, and environmental policies. New freeways, or the expansion of existing ones, may help to relieve rush-hour congestion but at the price of creating higher levels of air pollution. New urban highways may cut through communities in ways that break up neighborhoods and reduce land values. New freeways may also be located through marsh or wetland areas displacing natural habitat harboring animal and fish life.

Conversely, transportation policy may be an instrument for achieving non-transportation policy objectives. The objective of greater energy self-sufficiency has prompted the federal government to require newly manufactured automobiles to meet fleet standards for fuel efficiency. That same objective has led some states and the federal government to subsidize the production of ethanol or methanol out of American-grown corn or grain, which, when mixed with gasoline, produces gasohol, resulting in up to a 10 percent savings of gasoline per gallon of gasohol. In addition, the 55 mph speed limit, besides being justified as an instrument of highway safety, was instituted as an important fuel conservation measure. But as fuel prices dropped sharply in the mid-1980s as a result of an international oil glut, and subsequently leveled off, energy conservation as a rationale for that speed limit lost much of its currency. In its place, drawing on the adage that "time is money," arguments in support of raising the speed limit to 65 mph emphasized the greater economic efficiency of faster highway travel.

In a similar vein, increased state and federal financial support for mass transit, although rationalized in transportation terms—that is, helping to provide mobility for those not having access to other forms of transportation or as a means of reducing urban congestion—has also been supported as a means of reducing energy consumption and air pollution.

THE PROPER ROLE OF GOVERNMENT: THE IMPORTANCE OF VALUES

What is the proper role of government in transportation policy? And are there grounds for distinguishing the appropriate roles of state, local, and federal governments? These two questions are at the heart of much of the contemporary transportation policy debate at all levels of government.

An extreme position would suggest that government has no role to play; mutual adjustment alone will resolve problems. Take the problem of congestion, for example. In situations of high congestion, individuals will make rational choices about what level of congestion they will tolerate on major urban and suburban arteries. They will compete with others on a crowded highway or street until a point at which they no longer find the situation tolerable. Then they will pursue alternatives, such as using other freer-flowing but less direct routes, making trips earlier or later than the competition, or utilizing an alternative transportation mode such as mass transit or rail (even though this alternative may involve a trade-off of higher transportation costs for savings of time and frustration).

This line of thinking assumes that economic self-interest will prompt private interests, seeing an opportunity for profit, to step in and provide alternatives to automobile travel during congested periods. But in order for that to happen, private entrepreneurs have to believe that operating revenues will be sufficient to retire high up-front capital investment costs while still returning an acceptable operating profit. Facing severe peak-travel congestion in many urban areas, motorists might theoretically be willing to pay the going rate for a viable transportation alternative. Several factors, however, mitigate the prospects of success.

First, Americans, as one prominent defender of the automobile's place in the U.S. social and economic fabric has observed, have a love affair with the automobile.[2] And it is the personal freedom and self-contained flexibility provided by the automobile that cements that love relationship. As Figure 12.2 illustrates, the number of registered motor vehicles in the United States grew steadily from 30 million in 1944 to over 164 million by 1983. Automobiles account for 76 percent of that growth. The populace, in overwhelmingly turning to the automobile for personal mobility, has done so not as part of any planned scheme but as the product of aggregated individual choice. It is this deep personal affection for the private auto that works against increased use of urban mass transit as a viable, thriving alternative.

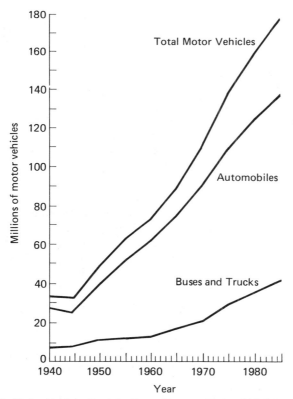

Figure 12.2. Motor Vehicle Registrations. (Source: Federal Highway Administration, *Our Nation's Highways: Selected Facts and Figures* [Washington, DC: U.S. Department of Transportation, 1984], p. 8.)

Another factor that mitigates private sector solutions to urban transportation problems is the level of unsubsidized user fees that would be necessary to undergird a profitable mass transit investment. Would an unsubsidized fee price too large a proportion of users out of the market? It might fall especially hard on those most dependent on mass transit but least able to pay the going rate—the elderly, the young, and the poor. Moreover, if prices get too high, those who are financially able might be willing to stay with the auto and endure the increased travel time and the frustration that accompanies its use in congested urban areas. Individual interest, focused on one's personal pocketbook and the attendant flexibility that accompanies automobile use, might well prompt one to stay with the automobile.

How does one go about evaluating the relative "goodness" or "badness" of such a personal decision? After all, if the individual believes that it represents the best choice, the alternative most in one's personal interest, why should it not be pursued? Yet the aggregation of individual choice might bode badly for society as a whole. Even if individuals are willing to endure long and congested commutes, is it in the public interest to allow them to do so? What if commuter traffic swells to the point of collectively producing unacceptable levels of air pollution? What if patterns of individual choice promise to deplete long-term supplies of domestic petroleum? What if the underclass and elderly of society have no viable transportation alternative to the automobile?

In these situations, government may intervene in the marketplace of individual choice and act in the so-called public interest. Such government involvement may take many forms. If mass transit operations are not economically viable for private enterprise, government may operate mass transit directly, using public employees or contract labor; or it may financially subsidize service provision by other public or private entities.

Of these two options, government subsidy has been the most prevalent practice. As an illustration, whereas local property taxes may supplement user fees at the local level, states and the federal government provide additional financial support to local mass transit operations. They do so for many of the same reasons that local governments devote their own-source revenues: to ensure broadened personal mobility, to relieve metropolitan congestion, to reduce air pollution, to save energy, to encourage regional development, and often from a more municipal perspective, to revitalize downtown areas.

Government may also attempt to bias individual choice by constraining the options available to people. A municipality—on its own or at the behest of the state or federal government—may greatly increase the price of parking downtown in order to reduce traffic congestion and encourage the use of mass transit. Special traffic lanes for mass transit vehicles and automobiles carrying a specified minimum number of passengers may be set up on state and local roads to encourage the use of mass transit or car pooling. These measures are aimed at enticing the operator of the single-passenger vehicle to choose other transportation options.

Such biasing of options against unbridled use of the private automobile has been part of the fabric of European public policy for decades. European policy largely treats the private automobile as an expensive luxury, not as a necessity of daily life. Urban roads and streets in most European nations were designed for the traffic of earlier eras, and the compact nature of most central cities holds the promise of immobilizing congestion and unacceptably high pollution accompanying unbridled use of the automobile. The costs of congestion and pollution in relation to the flexibility of personal mobility have been given greater weight in Europe than in the United States, where the scale seems to be tipped in the other direction.[3]

Government policy has made the cost of owning an automobile considerably greater in Europe than in the United States. One study has shown that, because of much higher taxation, the cost of gasoline in European countries compared to the United States has ranged from 92 percent higher in Britain to 247 percent higher in Italy.[4] Registration fees are also substantially higher in European nations and are predominantly based on either vehicle weight or engine displacement— a policy that disproportionately taxes less fuel-efficient vehicles.

A second constraint on automobile ownership in European countries is outright prohibition against driving or parking in certain downtown areas or the imposition of artificially high parking rates. With use of the private automobile in European urban areas treated as a luxury and not an unalienable right, the populace is charged a premium for exercise of that discretion, where it is permitted at all. Conversely, through government subsidy, mass transit fares in Europe have been kept about one-third lower than in the United States.[5]

Another nontransportation objective of capital and operating subsidies is to provide property tax relief. Contributing to local property tax relief might be viewed as an appropriate objective of public policy at the state level, but not necessarily at the federal level. Property tax relief might be viewed by the federal government as a matter of purely local or, at best, state interest. Similarly, mass transit itself, serving predominantly intrametropolitan travel, might also be acknowledged by the federal government as disproportionately of local concern.

This view of the appropriate role of government supports federal noninvolvement in mass transit at the outset or, given the existing partnership, provides a rationale for devolving federal responsibilities back to state and local governments. However, if the key issue is perceived as not just personal mobility but as energy conservation and/or air quality, national policy might well support federal involvement. Conserving limited petroleum resources or improving the quality of the nation's air could serve as a rationale for federal financial involvement in transit. It all depends on how one defines government interest and the nature of the problem.

Different levels of government may also have differing views of what constitutes appropriate involvement in highway policy. For the federal government, legitimate involvement might be confined narrowly to the interstate highway system. As a next level, the national federal-aid primary system might be added—a highway network of major state highways providing intrastate routes and limited interstate corridors. Federal responsibility might also be extended further to include highways and roads serving urban and localized rural areas within a state.

If the primary objective of federal financial support is to improve the quality of this country's overall highway infrastructure, a broadly defined federal responsibility follows. However, if it is to ensure a quality of highway infrastructure that permits *interstate* movement of people, manufactured goods, and commodities, the range of perceived appropriate federal participation narrows.

THE CONTEMPORARY FEDERAL-STATE RELATIONSHIP

These issues of the appropriate role of government in transportation policy, in general, and of the various levels of government, in particular, are central to the current public debate over transportation policy. The Reagan administration's broad-brush policy of reduced domestic spending and selective extrication of current federal responsibilities in many policy areas includes transportation. President Reagan's New Federalism initiatives, as they relate to changes in the federal-state-local financial partnership, have created an atmosphere of concern and uncertainty among state and local policy makers. It now appears that New Federalism in transportation policy has moved away from its original emphasis on reaching an agreed-upon package of swaps with the states. Under the original proposal for highways, for example, the federal government would retain only an administrative and financial interest in the interstate highway system. In turn, state and local governments would assume the exclusive responsibility for designing and financing the construction and repair of all other roads.

The proposal also called for returning half the federal motor fuel tax to the states to assist them in assuming the greater financial burden. The states could then raise any additionally required revenue directly. Presumably, states would share some of the revenues with local governments.

However, since these early discussions, the Reagan administration's tack increasingly appeared to have shifted away from consensual devolution and toward financial retrenchment. Support for highway construction and repair became tied to the administration's and Congress' efforts to reduce domestic spending and thereby cut the federal deficit. And obligation limits became the tool to restrain federal spending. Obligation limits control federal expenditures by restricting the amount of contract authority that can be apportioned to the states in any given year, even though higher levels of spending may have been previously authorized by Congress. To illustrate the impact of obligation limits, $20.9 billion was available for release to the states in FY 1987. In comparison, the president's budget proposal for FY 1987 included an obligation limit of $12.4 billion, only approximately 60 percent of the available authority.

From the states' perspective, federal financial support for highways was held hostage to deficit reduction. Federal revenues paid by highway users were sitting in the federal treasury, earning interest, and were not being used to meet the states' real highway improvement needs. Faced with the prospect that obligation limits would continue at the 1987 level, as indicated by the administration, state policy leaders voiced concern that they would be spending less for highway improvements in 1990 than they did in 1983, not counting lost purchasing power because of inflation, even though travel is projected to increase by almost 40 percent over that seven-year period.[6]

For transit, the federal posture has been to get out of the operating subsidy business altogether, leaving state and local governments to decide whether or not to fill the void based on their own relative state and local priorities. The federal government would retain only a limited role in financing transit rail development and bus acquisitions under the Reagan administration's policy. Congress, however, although approving reductions in transit operating subsidies, has not been willing to go as far as the president has recommended. Yet the $3.5 billion approved by Congress for FY 1987 was about $1 billion below the $4.5 billion level approved for FY 1983.

CHANGING PATTERNS OF TRANSPORTATION FINANCE

The present federal policy of budget retrenchment stands in marked contrast to the financial support given transportation earlier in the 1980s. Tax and fee increases at both the state and federal level had been necessitated largely by the failure of revenues to keep pace with the rising costs of highway construction and repair. The higher fuel efficiency of both automobiles and trucks, in response to federally imposed vehicle fuel efficiency standards and the changing market demand occasioned by rapid increases in the price of motor fuel, resulted in markedly reduced motor fuel consumption across the nation in the late 1970s and early 1980s. (See Figure 12.3.) Reduced fuel consumption directly resulted in lowered tax revenues flowing into the federal government's and the states' segregated highway or transportation funds. This environment of relative scarcity can be contrasted to the fiscally comfortable 1960s and most of the 1970s, when the number of motor vehicles on the road and the miles driven rose steadily, enriching federal and state transportation coffers without the necessity of tax rate hikes.

Recent experience, however, suggests that the 1978–1982 period might have been an aberration from a longer-term trend. The public has apparently returned to its behavioral pattern of earlier years. Individuals are again driving more miles and consuming increasing volumes of motor fuel. Furthermore, the steep rate of increase in vehicle fuel efficiency realized in the late 1970s and early 1980s has leveled off somewhat, as the popular movement to subcompact cars has apparently reached its zenith. The environment of rapidly rising gasoline prices and spot shortages of fuel now appears as a phenomenon consigned to history.

The experience of the late 1970s and early 1980s illustrates the interpenetration of policy areas. The rising cost of petroleum-based products, related to reductions in the availability of foreign oil, together with widespread forecasts of contin-

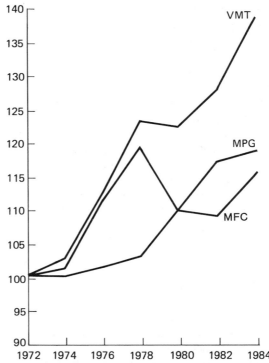

Figure 12.3. Vehicle-Miles of Travel, Motor Fuel Consumption, and Miles-Per-Gallon of Fuel for All Vehicles (Source: Federal Highway Administration, *Our Nation's Highways: Selected Facts and Figures* [Washington, DC: U.S. Department of Transportation, 1984], p. 14.)

ued foreseeable sharp price increases, pushed the costs of highway construction well above anticipated levels. Double-digit inflation, spurred in significant part by the sharply increased cost of oil, provided a ready justification for increased compensation adjustments in both the private and public sectors, directly affecting the labor costs of highway construction and maintenance. Costs were pushed up at the very time that income dropped in real-dollar terms.

As a consequence, states were forced to cut back on their highway construction plans. As Figure 12.4 shows, not only were revenues insufficient to support new construction projects, but they even fell short of meeting the escalating costs of improving and maintaining existing highways and roads. And in those states where mass transit subsidies were appropriated out of the highway trust fund or a unified transportation fund, the rising costs of mass transit operation and vehicle construction exacerbated an already difficult financial situation. The pressures of rising costs and reduced revenues quickly dissipated comfortable balances inherited from earlier decades. A crisis atmosphere soon pervaded transportation policy. Tax and fee increases appeared inescapable.

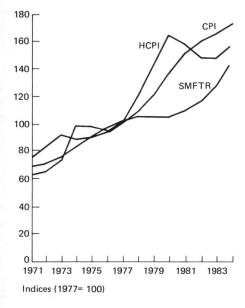

Figure 12.4. State Motor Fuel Tax Receipts, Highway Construction Price Index, and Consumer Price Index. (Source: Federal Highway Administration, *Our Nation's Highways: Selected Facts and Figures* [Washington, DC: U.S. Department of Transportation, 1983], p. 19; Federal Highway Administration, *Highway Statistics* [Washington, DC: U.S. Department of Transportation, Annually, 1971–1983]).

Support for revenue increases brought together a broad collection of interests. Initiatives to address the problem were proposed by state highway and transportation officials; road builder associations; local government officials; the U.S. Department of Transportation (with the belated support of President Reagan, prompted by the strong urging of then-Secretary Drew Lewis); and, yes, even mass transit operators, who hoped to get a share of revenue increases at the federal level and in those states where transit assistance competes for state transportation fund revenues.

In response to what looked like a very real public problem, and in light of broad-based support for a viable solution rather than a temporary "fix," the Congress and state legislatures responded by enacting motor fuel and vehicle registration revenue increases. Congress, in January 1983, enacted a five-cent-per-gallon increase in the motor fuel tax, the first federal motor fuel tax increase since 1956. Of the five-cent increase, four cents go to highway construction and improvement, and the other cent is devoted exclusively to mass transit construction and vehicle procurement. (The remainder of federal financial support for transit comes from the general fund.) Subsequently, in July 1984, the federal tax on diesel fuel was increased by six cents per gallon. In a similar vein, states that had not increased their motor fuel tax since the 1960s raised their rate at least once during the four-year period between 1979 and 1983, with some states increasing taxes as many as three different times during that short period. During the following three years, states that had held off increasing their motor fuel taxes were compelled to act, and some of those that had earlier increased taxes went to the well again, as the previous increase—although what the political market could bear—proved inadequate to close the financial gap. (See Table 12.1.)

Faced with projections of further increases in the price of motor fuel and continued conservation efforts, several states began to index their motor fuel tax as a way of providing some measure of revenue stability. The first states to index, such as Kentucky, Indiana, and Massachusetts, tied the tax to the pump price of motor fuel. But to their chagrin, the much-touted prophecies that gasoline would break the two-dollar-per-gallon mark by the end of 1983 never materialized. With hindsight, we know that an increased worldwide supply of oil not only stopped the inflationary spiral but reversed it as well. States that had indexed to price found motor fuel taxes falling far short of expectations. In response, those states have eliminated the index provision altogether, established tax floors, or changed the basis for indexation.

Another form of indexation—used in Michigan, Ohio, and Wisconsin—couples tax increases to motor fuel consumption and the cost of highway repair. As consumption decreases and highway costs increase, the motor fuel tax is automatically increased at established intervals. All three states enacted a statutory cap on the amount of increase permitted during any given period.

In addition to motor fuel tax increases, the federal government and several states acted to increase registration and other highway user fees. The U.S. Congress, as part of a revenue package to ensure that heavy trucks pay their "fair" share of highway construction and repair costs, enacted legislation in July 1984 that greatly increased user fees for vehicles in excess of 55,000 pounds. States also resorted to registration fee increases for autos and trucks, but with less frequency than the motor fuel tax.

The government clearly responded to a widely perceived public problem, enacting tax and fee increases to meet the rapidly rising costs of highway and transportation programs. The breadth of federal and state action is striking. Chief executives and legislators at all levels of government share an antipathy toward tax increases. Yet the reality of the earlier half of the 1980s flies in the face of this conventional wisdom. Why was this the case? First, there was the wide acceptance of the dilemma to be faced. Second, political pressure to arrive at a solution was

TABLE 12.1. STATE TAX ON GASOLINE (PER GALLON RATE IN CENTS*)

State	1979	1983	1986
Alabama	7	11	13
Alaska	8	8	8
Arizona	8	12	16
Arkansas	9.5	9.5	13.5
California	7	14.3	15
Colorado	7	12	18
Connecticut	11	14	17

continued

TABLE 12.1., *continued*

State	1979	1983	1986
Delaware	9	11	11
District of Columbia	10	14	15.5
Florida	8	9.6	9.7
Georgia	7.5	10.8	10.5
Hawaii	8.5	13.3	15
Idaho	9.5	14.5	14.5
Illinois	7.5	12.8	19
Indiana	8	15.4	19
Iowa	10	13	16
Kansas	8	10	11
Kentucky	9	10	15
Louisiana	8	8	16
Maine	9	14	14
Maryland	9	13.5	13.5
Massachusetts	8.5	11	11
Michigan	11	17.2	19
Minnesota	9	16	17
Mississippi	9	14.4	15
Missouri	7	7	7
Montana	9	15	15
Nebraska	10.5	13.9	19
Nevada	6	12	13
New Hampshire	11	14	14
New Jersey	8	8	8
New Mexico	7	11	11
New York	8	12.3	14.75
North Carolina	9	12	12.25
North Dakota	8	13	13
Ohio	7	12	12
Oklahoma	6.5	6.58	10
Oregon	7	8	11
Pennsylvania	11	14.5	18
Rhode Island	10	11	15
South Carolina	11	13	13
South Dakota	9	13	13
Tennessee	7	9	17
Texas	5	5	10
Utah	9	11	14
Vermont	9	13	13
Virginia	9	14.2	15
Washington	12	16	18
West Virginia	10.5	15.6	15.35
Wisconsin	7	13	17.5
Wyoming	8	8	8

*Includes motor fuel tax and any sales tax (expressed in cents per gallon) applied to motor fuel.
(Source: Federal Highway Administration, Highway Statistics 1979 *[Washington, DC: U.S. Department of Transportation, 1980], p. 60;* State Funding Methods *[Washington, DC: The Road Information Program, 1983], pp. 27–29;* State Motor Fuel Tax Rates *[Washington, DC: Highway Users Federation, 1986], Mimeograph.)*

great. A board coalition supported the need for additional revenues—a case even championed by the large, geographically dispersed, and well-organized interest that stood to bear disproportionately the burden of increased taxation: the trucking industry. The trucking industry argued that there was no viable alternative to revenue increases. The aging interstate and primary highways, largely built in the 1950s and 1960s, were badly in need of repair. Their deteriorated condition was portrayed by the trucking industry as a burden on interstate commerce, one that raised the costs of transport beyond the relative costs of increased taxation. A third factor is related to the relative low visibility of transportation tax and fee increases in the eyes of the general public. The trucking industry was certainly aware of, and officially supported, increased motor fuel taxes. The general public, on the other hand, knew that the price of gasoline was rising, but increases could be popularly attributed to exogenous factors such as inflation or greedy Arab nations. Fuel tax increases became hidden in the regular and rapid price increases at the pump. The public became accustomed to frequent jumps in the price of fuel, so a cent or two for the government became almost indiscernible.

This factor of "hidden" tax increases can also work in an environment of falling fuel prices, characteristic of the mid-1980s. As the price of motor fuel quickly drops, a half-cent or cent increase—the level commonly associated with indexation—is hardly noticeable. The public appreciates the fact that the price is dropping. That becomes the news, not a mere one-half-cent or one-cent tax increase.

Registration fee increases, on the other hand, are much more visible. The vehicle owner receives a bill that clearly discloses the increase. An individual accustomed to writing a fifty-dollar check for auto registration notices the need to fill in a new value of seventy-five dollars. Such heightened political visibility might go far toward explaining the considerably lower incidence of automobile registration increases compared to motor fuel tax increases.

Broad acceptance of the user-fee principle, which dictates that one should pay according to one's incidence of use, may also help to account for the greater willingness of executives and legislators to support motor fuel tax increases over registration fee increases. The motor fuel tax is elastic in relation to highway facility use. In general, the more miles driven, the more fuel consumed, and the higher the tax paid. In addition, heavier vehicles are less fuel efficient than their lighter counterparts, further contributing to higher consumption.

Registration fees are not based on the incidence of use. A fee is paid to operate a vehicle on public roads regardless of the miles driven. Registration fees, however, may be graduate according to vehicle weight, with higher fees assessed for heavier vehicles. The principle underlying weight-based fees is not use but costs incurred. Heavier vehicles do more damage than lighter vehicles, particularly at the heaviest weights. Accordingly, the cost-based principle dictates that they should pay more to help finance the higher costs of repair that they have caused.

Toward better untangling the relationship of highway damage and vehicle weights, both the federal government and several states have conducted highway cost allocation studies to identify the costs occasioned by different classes of highway vehicles. A 1982 federal study showed that, of all vehicles on the road, heavy trucks were underpaying the most. Whereas cars and light trucks were found to be paying 110 percent and 108 percent, respectively, of the repair costs attributable to them, heavy trucks were paying only 45 percent.[7] This comparison and an earlier finding that it takes 9,600 autos to equal the road damage of one maximally axle-loaded 80,000-pound truck[8] were used as justification in support of increased federal and state truck use and registration fees.

A continuation of Congress' current policy of returning only about 60 percent of available federal highway funds to the states will again put the states in the position of having to enact significant highway user tax and fee increases if states are to carry out planned highway improvement projects premised on the higher availability of federal funding. Then, once again, state policy makers will have to deal with the issue of how the increased tax burden should be apportioned among highway users.

Similar decisions will have to be made for mass transit. Where transit assistance at the state level comes out of a unified state transportation fund, its prospective state support necessarily competes with that for highways. Where transit aid is funded out of the state's general fund, it competes with the vast majority of state government programs. Faced with level federal support, at best, state legislatures have to decide if they are willing to increase their support to offset the lost purchasing power due to inflation. Local governments, in turn, confronting a combination of reduced federal and state support, have to decide if they are willing to increase local general tax support, cut the current levels of service, or pass more of the costs on to the riders.

This last option raises a number of social and economic concerns for local government officials. Socially, significant increases in fares may price transit out of the financial reach of the disadvantaged—the very population that is disproportionately dependent on transit for mobility. It is one thing for the middle-class professional to reach a little deeper to pay for higher fares on commuter bus or light rail routes, but it is quite another for the single welfare mother to obtain the extra cash. This consideration necessarily draws policy makers back to a consideration of to what extent mass transit should be considered a "public good" and to what extent it should be viewed as a fee-based service of particularistic benefit. Economically, local officials are also concerned with the elasticity of fee increases, fearing that fare increases may reach a point of diminishing return, cutting into ridership. Recent evidence suggests that such a concern is well founded. Between 1980 and 1983, fare revenues increased by 24 percent, and ridership declined by about 4 percent.[9] And that drop in ridership occurred during the very time that steeply rising fuel prices should have provided an incentive for some motorists to abandon their private vehicles in favor of mass transit; at least that is what the economists would suggest.

Other policy considerations might prompt local elected officials to opt for general tax increases over fare increases as they consider the prospects of declining ridership. One might be a desire to retain transit's financial incentive to limit the number of automobiles that come into downtown areas, with their associated air pollution and urban congestion. Here, other policy objectives—clear air and reduced congestion—come to influence transportation policy choice.

REGULATION

In addition to financing and administering state highway construction and maintenance, as well as subsidizing transit and other modal operations, states also play a significant regulatory role in transportation. State regulation is more pervasive for commercial transportation carriers than for private operators, but private operators still come under state jurisdiction. State agencies register private automobiles, license drivers, and enforce the rules of the road on state highways. The average citizen comes into only limited contact with the state on transportation matters. That historically, however, has not been the case for commercial transportation operators, who have had frequent interaction with regulatory agencies.

Both the states and the federal government have been involved in regulating commercial trucking, airline, rail, and bus operations. A division of labor has prevailed: The federal government has exercised authority over interstate operations, whereas the states have overseen intrastate operations. But Congress, under the urging of the Carter administration and subsequently under the Reagan administration, largely deregulated interstate commercial operations. And following the federal lead, a number of states deregulated intrastate carriage.

Government regulation of transportation operators can be divided into two categories, economic and noneconomic regulation. With economic regulation, the government controls who may provide transportation services, over what routes, and within what rates or prices. Noneconomic regulation involves such matters as taxation, vehicle characteristics, safety, and hazardous materials transport.

Federal deregulation all but eliminated economic regulation of interstate trucking, airline, rail, and bus operations. Not only did federal law greatly reduce federal regulation in these areas, but also it prohibited the states from stepping in and regulating interstate commerce in the federal government's absence. In retrospect, the effects of federal deregulation on the states have varied by transportation mode.

Although the states have historically been little involved in interstate airline and rail regulation, they still have felt the effects of federal deregulation. Prior to deregulation, the airlines and railroads were not free to compete openly in the marketplace. Instead, they were obliged to provide service to nonprofitable locations in exchange for the authority to serve profitable ones. Whereas several airlines might have had the authority to compete over heavily traveled routes, a single carrier may have been given the responsibility to provide service on a sparsely traveled route. Railroads were similarly obliged to provide service on nonprofitable routes. With deregulation, the airlines and railroads became relatively free to abandon service on nonprofitable routes and to concentrate their competition on potentially profitable ones. For the airlines this meant acquiring landing rights and facilities at the more desirable airports and relocating aircraft there. For the railroads it meant abandoning track. As a consequence, service was lost to a number of previously served communities.

The loss of local rail service has proven to be a greater hardship than the loss of air service to many local communities. The cessation of air service often meant that passengers would have to travel farther by car to another airport than, for convenience, they would otherwise choose. For commercial cargo service it meant that freight would have to be carried farther by truck to and from the nearest airport providing such service. But the loss of local rail service was of another magnitude. Plants that were previously served by rail had to turn to truck service upon abandonment, but often at a significantly increased price. And for certain bulky and heavy freight, truck transportation failed to provide a viable alternative at all. In this environment, several states intervened and established rail "short-line" assistance programs—either operating key abandoned stretches directly or assisting local governments or nonprofit locally affiliated corporations to do so. These programs most often involved state loans for track and equipment acquisition as well as state-provided operating subsidies. The resulting shortline operations filled important gaps in rail service, connecting suppliers and manufacturing plants. The shortline service, where it connected with a mainline, also provided access to markets for finished products.

Although not the case in air and rail, the states have traditionally exercised considerable regulatory authority over the motor carrier industry. Both state and federal governments were heavily involved in economic regulation within their respective jurisdictions, providing grants of authority to carriers that enabled them to haul a certain type of commodity between specified points of commerce. Prior to deregulation, the federal Interstate Commerce Commission (ICC) had jurisdiction over interstate trucking. Thus a common carrier wishing to haul a certain type of goods on a regular basis from Cincinnati to Chicago, for example, would have to apply for that authority from the ICC. The ICC, in turn, would determine if the carrier should be certified as "fit, willing, and able" to meet its obligations to shippers. Considerations included the financial standing of the carrier, its past record of performance, the experience of its personnel, and its insurance coverage. A favorable determination might not necessarily mean that the requested authority would be granted since the ICC, in making the decision, also considered whether existing carriers could adequately meet shippers' demands as well as the competitive impact that such a new entry would have on existing providers. Moreover, even if the new entrant obtained authority to haul the specified goods over the Cincinnati to Chicago route, that same carrier would not necessarily have secured the authority to haul like or different goods on a return run from Chicago to Cincinnati. A separate determination would have to be made by the ICC, and the service and competitive factors might look somewhat different to the federal regulators. When such return trip authority could not be secured, the truck often had to return empty, unless it had the authority to transport a different load from

Chicago to another destination. Nor was the trucker free to lease the rig to another operator who possessed the necessary authority for the return trip.

With federal deregulation, the preexisting restrictions on operating authority and backhaul leasing have been eliminated for all practical purposes. Carriers were given broad operating authority in the geographic territory to be served and the commodities to be carried. Many even received nationwide authority to carry general freight on an irregular basis. In addition, the ICC greatly liberalized rate regulation, approving virtually all rate reduction proposals, including even those naming only a single beneficiary—a practice unheard of prior to deregulation. Interstate carriers, therefore, are now much freer to compete for carriage, deciding on economic grounds which commodities to carry over which routes.

Several state legislatures followed Congress' lead and enacted laws deregulating intrastate trucking, with the most significant deregulation occurring in Arizona, Florida, Maine, Vermont, and Wisconsin.[10] Yet most states continued their existing forms of economic regulation. Beyond economic regulation, however, all states continued to exercise other forms of regulation for all motor carriers, including intrastate operators. Noneconomic state regulation can be categorized into operating requirements and revenue-producing requirements. Operating requirements apply to truck size and weight, speed, and safety restrictions established and enforced by the states. (However, the federal government recently preempted the traditional right of the states to set maximum truck size and weight limits for operation on interstate and other federally designated four-lane highways.) Revenue-producing requirements include vehicle registration; fuel taxes; and the so-called third-structure taxes, that is, taxes other than registration fees and fuel taxes, most prominently including taxes based on the weight of the load carried and the distance traveled.

Each of these areas of operating and revenue-producing requirements has associated administrative procedures. The trucking industry often finds itself dealing with several different state agencies, each having its own procedural and record-keeping requirements. In the typical state, truckers must deal with the motor vehicle department on registration matters, the revenue department on fuel tax and third-structure taxes, the highway department for vehicle size and weight permits, the highway patrol for safety and hazardous materials enforcement, and state utility commissions for intrastate regulation where still in place. Motor carriers, looking at federal deregulation and its promise of relieving burdens on interstate commerce, point to the remaining state regulation as perpetuating an undue and costly burden on commerce. Accordingly, the trucking industry has called on the U.S. Department of Transportation and Congress to prompt states to adopt greater uniformity in the filing, reporting, and record-keeping requirements employed to administer the various forms of noneconomic regulation. But should the states collectively not be able to simplify compliance with these requirements, the trucking industry may demand federal preemption of state motor carrier regulation, arguing that greatly disparate requirements present an inappropriate state burden on interstate commerce.

Under federal preemption of current state noneconomic regulation, the U.S. Department of Transportation would assume responsibility for truck registration nationally; an expanded federal fuel tax would displace existing state fuel taxes, with fuel being taxed at the pump; and no reports could be required by any state. Faced with the possibility of federal preemption, state policy makers are working with representatives of the trucking industry, the National Governors' Association, and the U.S. Department of Transportation to minimize the effects of disparate state regulation. For the states the stakes are high: Not only would they lose their present ability to set the level of transportation taxes and fees, but also they would probably become dependent on the federal government to share the federally collected revenues with the states—not an inviting proposition from the states' perspective, given the recent record of the federal financial partner.

SHORT-TERM DIRECTIONS IN TRANSPORTATION POLICY

Transportation policy in the near future will continue to be the subject of different, and often clashing, perspectives. The dominant perspective will view transportation in terms of personal mobility and the efficiency of transit and transport operations. The signs of the times are everywhere: The 55 mph speed limit was recently raised on interstate highways in large part to allow private motorists and commercial operators to save time in getting to their destinations. Truck, bus, rail, and air transport have been deregulated to improve the efficiency and "rationality" of transport operations, and thereby improve the profitability of the most efficient service providers. The increased competition resulting from deregulation, it is suggested, will benefit operators, shippers, consumers, and passengers. Truckers and bus operators will continue to be able to operate more freely over new routes, carry more diverse commodities, give up unprofitable operations, and compete on the basis of price. Railroads will continue to scrutinize the economic viability of their routes, abandoning those that appear hopelessly unprofitable and entering into cooperative operating agreements with other lines when such cooperation appears mutually beneficial. Airlines will increasingly compete for passengers on profitable routes and will continue to abandon the unredeemable losers.

Advocates of this more openly competitive environment suggest that not only will transportation decision making become more rational, and transportation systems more efficient, but also transportation users will benefit as increased competition brings down prices and offers greater flexibility in the choice of service providers. Skeptics, on the other hand, point to the prospect of growing gaps in service as economically rational operator choices lead to service reductions or outright elimination in parts of the country. And they are the ones who are increasingly calling on the states to intervene and subsidize otherwise unprofitable service in all the transportation modes. For the advocates of subsidy, the availability of service is the bottom line, whether that be air, bus, or rail service to shippers or passengers. In the trucking area, there is less concern about the unavailability of service because it can still be obtained statewide, but at a much dearer price.

Concerns over efficiency have also influenced policies governing mass transit. Transit operators, faced with declining ridership and reductions in federal aid, are being forced to "rationalize" transit operations, raising fares, cutting back on lower-density routes, and reducing the frequency of service. Critics, in turn, view these measures as eroding a necessary public service and constituting an infringement on the basic right of individuals for mobility, one that hits hardest on those economically most dependent on public transportation: the young, the elderly, and the poor.

All these contemporary directions are likely to continue in the near future because the criterion of economic efficiency remains a motivating force in transportation choice. The objectives of energy conservation and air quality no longer appear to guide transportation policy making as they did in the 1970s. Current signs suggest that these relative priorities will probably continue into the near future.

SUMMARY AND CONCLUSIONS

Although the crisis among the states precipitated by the major transportation revenue shortfalls of the early 1980s, also a time of rapidly rising motor fuel prices and transportation labor costs, is now consigned to history, transportation policy issues remain high on state policy makers' agendas. The promise of significantly expanded federal financial assistance has not been realized in practice. In fact, federal aid to transportation has been held hostage to the Reagan administration's policy of reducing the federal deficit through cuts in domestic spending. Both states and local governments are feeling the fiscal pinch, and the states are being called on to do more to fill the gap.

The states, faced with federal obligation limits that restrict the tapping of available federal highway fund revenues, will continue to be pressured by highway interests to raise state transportation taxes and user fees high enough to finance state highway improvement and maintenance plans. Moreover, as federal budget reductions affect local units of government, especially in mass transit assistance and support for rural secondary and urban roads, county and municipal officials will continue to look to the states for financial help.

State policy makers will also continue to be faced with the decision of whether to create new programs or expand existing ones to subsidize those services eliminated or significantly reduced as a result of federal economic deregulation of rail and air operations. Moreover, as additional states follow the federal government's lead and deregulate intrastate trucking, legislative interest in deregulation is likely to grow in currently regulated states. At the same time, all states will continue to face pressure, under the threat of federal preemption, to create greater uniformity in their administration of motor carrier taxation, safety, and highway access as the trucking industry advances its case that such nonuniform state regulation constitutes an undue restraint on interstate commerce.

REFERENCES

1. *Transit Fact Book 1985* (Washington, DC: American Public Transit Association, 1985), p. 14.
2. B. Bruce-Briggs, *The War Against the Automobile* (New York: Dutton, 1977).
3. For a discussion comparing European and American transportation policies, see James A. Dunn, Jr., *Miles to Go: European and American Transportation Policies* (Cambridge, MA: MIT Press, 1981).
4. Irving B. Kravis et al., *A System of International Comparisons of Gross Product and Purchasing Power* (Baltimore, MD: Johns Hopkins University Press, 1975), cited in Dunn, *Miles to Go*, p. 152.
5. Dunn, *Miles to Go*, p. 152.
6. Lester P. Lamm, Statement Before the Subcommittee on Transportation, Committee on Environment and Public Works, United States Senate, May 20, 1986 (Washington, DC: Highway Users Federation, 1986).
7. *Our Highways* (Washington, DC: American Association of State Highway and Transportation Officials, Subcommittee on Highway Transport, 1984), p. 13.
8. Highway Research Board, *AASHTO Road Test*, Special Report 61 (Washington, DC: National Academy of Sciences, 1962), cited in *Our Highways*, p. 7.
9. *Transit Fact Book 1985*, pp. 18 and 30.
10. National Association of Regulatory Commissions, telephone interview, Oct. 20, 1987.

_____ CHAPTER 13 _____

Taxation and Economic Development

In stark contrast to businesses, state governments seek to decrease revenues and increase expenditures. Businesses, of course, aim to increase their revenues and keep their expenses low. Business leaders who are successful at earning much more than they are spending are cited as models to be followed by others. Elected officials who accumulate large surpluses in the public treasury, however, are not congratulated; they are condemned for collecting more than they need.

The major political forces on governors and legislators are to lower taxes and at the same time to increase the services and benefits enjoyed by various special-interest groups and by the public generally. The favorite tax cut for most taxpayers always seems to be the next one. The favorite cut in spending is always someone else's program.

One way of responding to the contradictory pressures for tax cuts and spending increases is to promote economic growth and development in a state. As a general principle, a lower tax rate on a larger base can generate more revenue and less political opposition than a higher tax rate on a smaller base. For example, a state with a personal income tax with a top rate of 7 percent gets more money as the number of people within the state who are earning a moderate to high income increases. In this situation, state government might get just as much or more revenue if it lowered its top income rate to 6 percent if that decrease attracted more wealthy people to the state. One might take this line of reasoning one step further and argue that a state might lower its tax rates as a strategy to induce economic development. Lower tax rates might not only attract more businesses to move to the state but also those already in the state could invest more of their own money for economic expansion, rather than pay that money in taxes.

Taxation and economic development are, in short, inextricably intertwined.

These two subjects, at the same time, are each distinct. Taxation policies include more concerns than the interaction between state revenues and economic growth. Likewise, the strategies that state governments use to promote economic development include more than tax reform. This chapter will first discuss taxation, then consider approaches to economic development, and conclude by showing how the two are and are not linked.

TAXATION

State governments get revenue from three major sources: the federal government provides about 23 percent of the funds spent by state governments, specific charges and user fees (like state park entrance fees, public university tuition, and motor vehicle licenses) generate another 15 percent, and the remaining 60 percent comes from taxes levied by state governments. The exact mix, of course, changes from one state to another.[1]

Like other levels of government, state governments have grown in size and scope and have raised revenues accordingly. One way of measuring this growth is to identify the relative place of government in the national economy, expressed in terms of the gross national product (GNP). In 1950, state governments were 3 percent of the GNP, local governments were 4.8 percent, and the federal government was 15.1 percent. By 1975, state governments had grown to 6 percent, local governments to 8.9 percent, and the federal government to 19.6 percent.[2]

Not surprisingly, this growth pattern prompted concern. The most visible and dramatic expression of concern about increases in state and local government spending and taxing was the passage, in 1978, of Proposition 13 in California, as discussed in Chapter 2. Voters in California, through the direct initiative, changed their state constitution to restrict the growth in local property taxes and to limit the growth in state expenditures by the rate of change in inflation and population. Between 1978 and 1983, eighteen other states placed constitutional and statutory limits on the growth of state government. Fourteen focused on expenditures and four on revenues, although since states must balance their budgets, the consequence of either approach is to limit taxation. The most common approach was to tie state government increases in revenue or expenditure to personal income per capita within the state.[3] States that did not adopt general formulas for limits on growth joined in the retrenchment pattern nonetheless.

In Chapter 1 we discussed patterns of state tax increases in the 1980s, and Chapter 2 includes an analysis of the links between state budget balances and tax increases and decreases. Here we note that the net effect of these changes was, as intended, to reduce state governments' collective share of the national economy. By 1983, state governments had declined from 6 percent (1975) to 5.3 percent of the GNP, and local governments went from 8.9 percent to 7.8 percent. The federal government, in contrast, rose from 19.6 percent to 22.4 percent during the same period. Increases in defense spending and interest on the growing national debt offset cuts in domestic spending and led to federal government expansion.[4]

The level of taxation is a visible and somewhat simple target of concern. The fiscal policies of state governments are more complex than an effort simply to generate revenue. As explained at the outset, the incentives are actually to cut taxes and minimize revenue collection. The criteria for how to tax, whom to tax, and what to tax include political and policy concerns as well as fiscal ones.

Criteria for Evaluating Taxes

State governments rely on the sales tax more than any other. (See Figure 13.1.) Personal income taxes and corporate income taxes are also common among the states. Those states with oil, coal, or minerals rely heavily on a severance tax, that is, a tax on the energy source or mineral leaving their state. Virtually every state levies a tax on gasoline, alcoholic beverages, and tobacco. (The last two are fondly referred to as "sin taxes.") (See Table 13.1.) Although local governments rely on property taxes much more than do state governments, the latter are so involved in regulating that tax and trying to relieve property tax burdens that we will include this form of taxation in our discussion.

State governments can use any of these taxes and more. The U.S. Constitu-

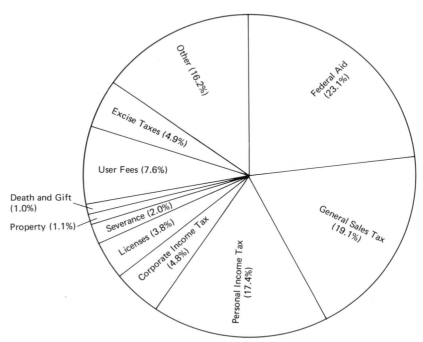

Figure 13.1. Sources of State Government Revenue (1985). (Sources: *The Book of the States, 1986–87* [Lexington, KY: Council of State Governments, 1987], pp. 265–66; *Significant Features of Fiscal Federalism, 1987* [Washington, DC: Advisory Commission on Intergovernmental Relations, 1987], p. 47.)

tion prohibits state taxation only of exports and imports and requires only that tax policies and tax administration not violate equal protection clauses. As states decide what mix of taxes to adopt and what reforms to make, they confront a number of value choices:

1. *Will the tax generate very much money?* A primary purpose of a tax is to secure funds. A tax on outdoor swimming pools may make sense in California and Florida, but it won't do much for the treasury of Alaska.
2. *Is the tax stable?* A tax that is highly dependent on the condition of the economy or on a particular activity can put state revenues on a veritable roller coaster. A lack of predictability causes management and political problems for elected officials, who may need to establish new or increased taxes to cover projected revenue shortfalls.
3. *Can the tax be administered?* Some taxes are difficult to collect because of the lack of valid and reliable information. Even an income tax and a sales tax are difficult to administer when money changes hands informally, outside visible commercial channels.
4. *Is the tax fair?* The major standard of fairness applied to taxation is whether it is based on ability to pay. The poor should pay less and the rich more.
5. *Is the tax politically acceptable?* A tax that meets all the preceding criteria but is politically unpopular is not likely to be adopted. Taxes are not enjoyed, but they must at least be tolerated.

Major forms of taxation can be discussed by applying the preceding criteria.

Sales Tax

A sales tax is a levy that is made whenever someone buys a good or a service. The tax is a set percentage of the sales price. It is paid by the purchaser and collected by the seller.

Will the Tax Generate Very Much Money? Every state except for Alaska, Delaware, Montana, New Hampshire, and Oregon levies a tax on the sale of goods and services. This tax is the major source of revenue for state governments. In 1985, for example, 19.1 percent of the total revenue (including federal aid) of the fifty state governments was from sales taxes. Individuals, on the average, spend slightly more than 2 percent of their incomes on state sales taxes. The next largest revenue source was the personal income tax, which accounted for 17.4 percent. State income taxes constituted 1.8 percent of average personal income.[5] The sales tax, in short, meets the first criterion and generates considerable revenue for state governments.

Is the Tax Stable? Although the amount of revenue earned by a sales tax obviously varies according to how much people spend, it constitutes a relatively stable source of funds. People incur expenses even in the worst of economic times, and so a

TABLE 13.1. STATE GOVERNMENT USE OF REVENUE SOURCES

State	General Sales	Personal Income	Corporate Income	Excise on Motor Fuel	Excise on Cigarettes and Alcohol	Property	Death and Gift	User Fees	Severance
Alabama	x	x	x	x	x(a)	x	x	x	Oil, gas, iron ore, timber
Alaska			x	x	x	x	x	x	Oil, gas, fish
Arizona	x	x	x	x	x	x	x	x	Minerals, timber
Arkansas	x	x	x	x	x	x	x	x	Oil, gas, minerals
California	x	x	x	x	x	x	x	x	Oil, gas
Colorado	x	x	x	x	x	x	x	x	Oil, gas, minerals
Connecticut	x	x	x	x	x		x	x	
Delaware			x	x	x		x	x	Oil, gas, minerals
Florida	x		x	x	x	x	x	x	Phosphates
Georgia	x	x	x	x	x		x	x	
Hawaii	x	x	x	x	x		x	x	
Idaho	x	x	x	x	x (a)	x	x	x	Oil, gas, minerals
Illinois	x	x	x	x	x	x	x	x	Timber
Indiana	x	x	x	x	x (a)		x	x	Refined petroleum
Iowa	x	x	x	x	x		x	x	
Kansas	x	x	x	x	x	x	x	x	Oil, gas, minerals
Kentucky	x	x	x	x	x	x	x	x	Oil, coal
Louisiana	x	x	x	x	x (a)		x	x	General
Maine	x	x	x	x	x		x	x	Minerals
Maryland	x	x	x	x	x	x	x	x	
Massachusetts	x	x	x	x	x (a)	x	x	x	Coal, minerals
Michigan	x	x	x	x	x (a)	x	x	x	Oil, gas

268

State								Severance tax items
Minnesota	x	x	x		x	x	x	Minerals
Mississippi	x	x	x	x	x (a)	x	x	Oil, gas, timber, salt
Missouri	x	x	x		x	x	x	Coal
Montana	x	x	x	x	x (a)	x	x	Oil, gas, coal, minerals, cement
Nebraska	x	x	x	x	x	x	x	Oil, gas, uranium
Nevada	x		x	x	x		x	Oil, gas
New Hampshire	x	x	x	x	x (a)	x	x	Refined petroleum
New Jersey	x	x	x	x	x	x	x	
New Mexico	x	x	x	x	x	x	x	Oil, gas, minerals
New York	x	x	x	x	x	x	x	
North Carolina	x	x	x	x	x (a)	x	x	Oil, gas, timber
North Dakota	x	x	x	x	x	x	x	Oil, gas, coal
Ohio	x	x	x	x	x (a)	x	x	Oil, gas, coal, cement
Oklahoma	x		x	x	x	x	x	Oil, gas, minerals
Oregon	x	x	x		x (a)		x	Oil, gas, timber
Pennsylvania	x	x	x		x (a)	x	x	
Rhode Island	x	x	x		x	x	x	
South Carolina	x	x	x		x	x	x	
South Dakota	x		x		x	x	x	Minerals
Tennessee	x	x	x	x	x	x	x	Oil, gas, coal
Texas	x		x		x	x	x	Oil, gas, cement
Utah	x	x	x	x	x (a)	x	x	Oil, gas, minerals
Vermont	x	x	x	x	x (a)	x	x	
Virginia	x	x	x	x	x (a)	x	x	Coal, oil, timber
Washington	x		x		x (a)	x	x	Uranium, fish
West Virginia	x	x	x	x	x (a)		x	Minerals
Wisconsin	x	x	x		x	x	x	Minerals
Wyoming	x		x		x (a)	x	x	Oil, gas, minerals

Note: (a) Excise tax on cigarettes, but not alcoholic beverages. (Sources: Council of State Governments, Book of the States, 1986–87 [Lexington, KY: Council of State Governments, 1987], pp. 251, 252, 258–60; U.S. Bureau of Census, 1987, pp. 265, and 266; and Advisory Commission on Intergovernmental Relations, Significant Features of Fiscal Federalism, 1987 [Washington, DC: ACIR, 1987], p. 47.)

sales tax will always provide state governments with money. In periods of recession and high unemployment, however, many people will postpone large purchases of appliances, vehicles, and the like. The resulting loss of sales tax revenue is especially harsh because it comes at a time when states must spend more on welfare, unemployment compensation, and other programs designed to reduce the hardships associated with economic downturns.

Can the Tax Be Administered? A sales tax is easy to administer. The key mechanism is to require merchants and providers of taxable services to collect the tax whenever they make a sale, to keep a record of their sales, and to give the state revenue department both the taxes collected and the records. Some states make modest payments to businesses to help defray the costs of sales tax collection. With cash registers that can be programmed to calculate the taxes due and that keep accurate records, the burden of administering the sales tax is reduced considerably.

When economic activity occurs outside the realm of formal record keeping, the sales tax is very difficult to administer. Vendors of goods on roadsides, for example, do not always charge a sales tax and keep records. Rummage sales and other forums for the selling of second-hand items also escape the purview of those monitoring the collection of sales taxes. We do not know, of course, exactly how much that which should be covered by taxation goes unnoticed.

Is the Tax Fair? In general, a sales tax is not fair because it is not based on ability to pay. A sales tax is a regressive tax, which means that it places a relatively larger burden on those with a low income and a lighter burden on the wealthy. Lower- and middle-income individuals—and families—spend a larger share of their earnings than do those with a high income. As Table 13.2 shows, to reduce the extent to which the sales tax is regressive, some states do not tax food or medicine.

Is the Tax Politically Acceptable? Even though the sales tax is basically regressive and constitutes the largest source of revenue for state governments, it is generally accepted by the public. The Advisory Commission on Intergovernmental Relations has conducted annual surveys on public attitudes toward government and taxes since 1972. When those surveyed are asked to rank the federal income tax, state income tax, state sales tax, and local property tax as "the worst tax—that is, the least fair," consistently only 14 to 20 percent rank the state sales tax as the worst. (See Table 13.3.) A major reason for public acceptance of the sales tax is that it is (sometimes literally) paid in pennies and nickels, a little at a time. Consumers simply perceive the sales tax as part of the cost of a particular item.

Income Tax

The second largest source of revenue for state governments is the personal income tax. Income tax rates are set as percentages of income, with certain deductions allowed. Wisconsin, in 1911, was the first jurisdiction to levy a tax on income. The federal government followed two years later. Both the federal government

TABLE 13.2. FOOD AND DRUG SALES TAX EXEMPTIONS (AS OF JANUARY 1, 1986)

State	Tax Rate	Exemptions Food	Exemptions Prescription Drugs
Alabama	4		X
Arizona	5	X	X
Arkansas	4		X
California	4.75	X	X
Colorado	3	X	X
Connecticut	7.5	X	X
Florida	5	X	X
Georgia	3		X
Hawaii	4		
Idaho	4		X
Illinois	5	X	X
Indiana	5	X	X
Iowa	4	X	X
Kansas	3		X
Kentucky	5	X	X
Louisiana	4	X	X
Maine	5	X	X
Maryland	5	X	X
Massachusetts	5	X	X
Michigan	4	X	X
Minnesota	6	X	X
Mississippi	6		X
Missouri	4.225		X
Nebraska	3.5	X	X
Nevada	5.75	X	X
New Jersey	6	X	X
New Mexico	3.75		
New York	4	X	X
North Carolina	3		X
North Dakota	4	X	X
Ohio	5	X	X
Oklahoma	3.25		X
Pennsylvania	6	X	X
Rhode Island	6	X	X
South Carolina	5		X
South Dakota	4		X
Tennessee	5.5		X
Texas	4.125	X	X
Utah	4.625		X
Vermont	4	X	X
Virginia	3		X
Washington	6.5	X	X
West Virginia	6	X	X
Wisconsin	5	X	X
Wyoming	3		X

Source: Council of State Governments, Book of the States, 1986–87 *(Lexington, KY: Council of State Governments, 1987), p. 253,* from Federation of Tax Administrators, 1987.

TABLE 13.3. PUBLIC RANKING OF WORST (LEAST FAIR) TAX (PERCENT OF U.S. PUBLIC)

	1972	1974	1976	1978	1980	1982	1984	1986
Federal Income Tax	19	30	28	30	36	36	36	37
Local Property Tax	45	28	33	32	25	30	29	28
State Sales Tax	13	20	17	18	19	14	15	17
State Income Tax	13	10	11	11	10	11	10	8
Don't Know	11	14	11	10	10	9	10	10

Source: Significant Features of Fiscal Federalism, 1987 (Washington, DC: Advisory Commission on Intergovernmental Relations, 1987), p. 111.

and state governments have found this to be a good well from which to draw revenue.

Will the Tax Generate Very Much Money? Increasingly, states are relying on income taxes. In 1957, only 17.6 percent of all revenues collected directly by states (excluding federal aid) was from income taxes. In 1985, income taxes accounted for 36.7 percent. In eighteen states, income taxes now generate more revenue than sales taxes.[6] Forty-three states levy a personal income tax, and forty-six levy a tax on corporate profits. Like the sales tax, states can always count on a substantial amount of revenue from income taxes.

Is the Tax Stable? The amount of revenue earned from income taxes varies with the economy and how much people in a state are earning. But that amount will change and is not entirely predictable. Also, like the sales tax, the income tax will tend to produce less revenue in those circumstances in which state welfare expenses go up, that is, during downturns in the economy.

Income taxes, even more than sales taxes, can produce more revenue even when the economy is not strong and growing. This is most apt to happen during periods of inflation, when people are earning more money but the value of their purchasing power is, at the same time, decreasing. During the mid- and late 1970s, for example, the inflation rate was high, ranging from 9 to 12 percent a year. People's salaries would go up primarily because of inflation, putting taxpayers in a bracket with a higher rate. This, of course, represented a tax increase, even when "real income" was not increasing. To illustrate, let us suppose that the Jones family increases its taxable income at the rate of inflation, which is 10 percent. Their annual income rises from $30,000 to $33,000. The tax structure taxes incomes from $20,001 to $30,000 at a 5 percent rate, and incomes from $30,001 to $50,000 at 6 percent. The Jones family, in other words, has its state income taxes increased from $1,500 to $1,980, or 32 percent, simply because of the effects of inflation (which was 10 percent). In response to this phenomenon, ten states between 1977 and 1982 indexed to the rate of inflation the tax categories or brackets that determined when tax rates changed.[7] In the case of the Jones family, they would continue to compute their taxes at the 5 percent rate. Their taxes, like inflation, would go up 10 percent.

Is the Tax Fair? The income tax scores the best on the third criterion—fairness. As with the federal income tax, state rates are graduated according to the ability to pay. Individuals below a certain level of income owe no tax at all. Rates increase as income increases. The more you earn, the more you pay—both in dollar amounts and in percentage of income. A tax that increases with ability to pay is considered progressive.

Personal income tax systems typically include another progressive feature; that is, taxes are reduced for every person who is financially dependent on an income earner. The basic concept behind this provision is that the ability to pay is a function not only of the level of income but also of how many are supported by that income.

Other ways in which personal income taxes are lowered are more the result of who won in a legislative battle or what other public policies a state government is pursuing through income taxes. Generally, the concept of achieving nonrevenue goals through tax systems is known as ''tax expenditures.'' For example, when a government reduces taxes of people who make their homes more energy efficient, it is as if the government is ''spending'' money on energy conservation. Tax expenditures take two forms: deductions and credits. *Deductions* are made on the income used to calculate the taxes owed. If we return to the Jones family, we can illustrate the impact of a deduction. Let us suppose that their state allows deductions for charitable contributions and interest payments on home mortgages, and the Jones family spent $3,500 on these two items combined. In the example given, where income tax rates change at $30,000, this deduction would reduce the amount used to calculate the tax owed from $33,000 to $29,500 and would lower the tax rate from 6 percent to 5 percent. *Credits*, in contrast to deductions, are subtracted from the taxes owed. Some states give credit, up to a limit, for money contributed to political campaigns. If the Jones family owes $1,475 in income taxes ($29,500 × 5 percent) and they contributed $75 to political candidates, the total tax bill would be $1,400. Credits, unlike deductions, do not affect the tax rates that apply, but credits are more directly effective in reducing taxes. A dollar credit is a dollar in tax reduction, whereas a dollar deduction must be multiplied times the applicable tax rate before the taxpayer knows how much it is worth.

Is the Tax Politically Acceptable? As evident in Table 13.3, the state income tax is generally accepted by citizens. It is regarded as fair and is collected from most people in a relatively invisible and painless way, that is, through withholding from wages an amount estimated to be what a person will owe. The amount withheld for state, like federal, income taxes is based on the level of the wage and the information provided by the employee about how many dependents he or she has.

Property Tax

Property taxes are not a major source of state revenue, as demonstrated in Figure 13.1. The most significant property taxes are levied by local governments—cities, counties, school boards, and some special districts. Nonetheless, state governments are centrally involved in property taxes. Local governments exist and are empowered because of state government action. Thus state governments can and do control how property taxes can be calculated and levied. State governments are under constant pressure to relieve the burden property taxes place on individuals. Property taxes are the most despised form of taxation (see Table 13.3). States can set limits on the level of these taxes, as was done with Proposition 13 in California. States can also relieve the property tax burden by providing financial aid to school districts, counties, and the like, so that these governments do not have to generate all their own revenue.

Will the Tax Generate Very Much Money? Property taxes are the major source of revenue for almost all local governments. For those for which this is not true, the major source is aid from state government and/or the federal government. The tax is calculated as follows:

$$\text{tax due} = \text{value of property} \times \text{mill rate}$$

The mill rate, the tax per $1,000 worth of property, is set by local governments within whatever state limitations that might apply. Typically, a local government, like a school district, will establish its budget for the next year so that it knows how much money it needs. From this amount, the school board will subtract what it anticipates in aid from the federal and state governments. The value of the property within the district is known, so the school board will set the mill rate at the figure it needs. A school district, for example, may establish a budget with $20 million of expenditures. This district anticipates $7 million in aid from the state and $1 million in aid from the federal government. The value of property that can be taxed in the district may be $1 billion. Thus, to get the $12 million that the school district must raise itself, the mill rate must be 0.12 (or $12 of taxes for every $1,000 of property). In short, property taxes can be structured so that local governments can get whatever amount they need to meet their costs.

Is the Tax Stable? No matter what the state of the economy, there will be property to tax. Property values can move with the rest of the economy, but not like sales and income taxes. Periods of inflation and recession typically mean significant increases and decreases, accordingly, in the price of land and buildings. A community that is undergoing change, either growth or decline, will see its property values rise or fall accordingly.

With the exception of peanut and tobacco growers in the Southeast, farmers in states throughout the nation had severe financial difficulties during most of the 1980s. Part of the crisis was a sharp decline in agricultural land values, which in turn made it more difficult for farmers to use land as security to get loans. From 1985 to early 1986, farm real estate values dropped 12 percent, on the average. The decline in Minnesota was 26 percent, and Colorado and New Mexico 18 percent.[8] Property taxes did not necessarily decline with land values, however. School districts and local governments still needed revenue. Some needed more revenue, ironically, to provide assistance to hard-hit farmers. These jurisdictions either used old land values or raised mill rates to generate the funds they needed. Some jurisdictions were able to shift the relative tax burden from farmers to town dwellers. In short, the basic property tax formula allows governments to collect what they need, but changes in property values can have significant effects on individual taxpayers.

Can the Tax Be Administered? Property taxes in some states used to be a nightmare to administer. Property in these states included everything an individual or a company owned. Imagine ascertaining the value of cars, jewelry, furniture, clothing, and so on for everyone. Today, property is synonymous with real estate (land and dwelling) for individuals and with real estate plus production machinery and equipment for corporations. The limited definition of property allows for fair and efficient administration of the tax.

The major challenge in administering the property tax is, nonetheless, in the assessment of values. Formulas are used, often computer-assisted, that include size, age of structures and equipment, and market prices as measured by actual sales in the community. Disputes emerge within communities about whether the formulas are "right" (Should half bathrooms be appraised at half the value of full bathrooms or is their real value some other percentage?) and about whether the formulas are being applied consistently (Is the north side of town being treated more favorably than the south side?). At the state level, the disputes often concern whether the formulas used by various communities are fair and consistent on a statewide basis. Since assessors and the formulas they use are locally determined, state concerns about equity among communities become an issue of local prerogatives and state controls.

Is the Tax Fair? An initial impression may be to regard property taxes as fair because they increase with the value of the property. However, the value of someone's home is not always a good indicator of the owner's ability to pay. This is particularly true for the elderly, who may have purchased a home when they were earning more than they get in social security and retirement benefits and when the home itself cost less. Most agree that it would be insensitive to place these people in the dilemma of having to use the home to get a loan to pay property taxes or, even worse, to sell the home in order to meet their tax obligation.

Another dilemma is whether a community should give businesses a break in property taxes so that the community will be better able to compete with other communities in enticing or keeping businesses. Such a policy, of course, means that other property owners will shoulder a heavier share of the property tax burden. But if the business or industry would actually locate elsewhere because of property taxes, others may very well have a heavier tax burden over the short- and long-term anyhow. The criteria of fairness (ability to pay) and economic development may be inconsistent.

Is the Tax Politically Acceptable? As pointed out, the property tax is disliked more than any other state or local form of taxation. The major focus of the so-called taxpayer revolt of the 1970s and 1980s was the property tax. The response of both state and local officials has been to seek to ease the burden and make this tax more acceptable.[9] No one has seriously proposed abolishing the property tax altogether.

Excise Tax

Excise taxes are often referred to as "sin taxes" or "luxury taxes." An excise tax is very much like a sales tax, but it refers to a special tax on selected items like alcoholic beverages, cigarettes and tobacco products, jewelry, and leather goods. Where applicable, one pays both an excise tax and a general sales tax on the same item.

Will the Tax Generate Very Much Money? This is not a major source of revenue for state governments. Excise taxes in the 1980s have accounted for slightly less than 5 percent of the total revenues collected by state governments. In the 1940s, over 11 percent of state revenues came from excise taxes—the highest relative level. It is instructive to note that it was at this point that state governments expanded and needed more money.[10] The revenue that can be generated from alcohol, cigarettes, and so on is very limited. Thus states turned more to income taxes and general sales taxes, and excise taxes decreased in importance.

Is the Tax Stable? Despite campaigns against smoking and alcohol abuse, consumption of these and other items subjected to excise taxes remains fairly constant. Moreover, people tend to smoke and drink regardless of whether the general economy is doing well or not. Excise taxes are based on the volume of alcohol and on packages of cigarettes, rather than on the prices. The key issue from the standpoint of taxation is the amount consumed rather than the effects of inflation or recession on prices. From the standpoint of getting needed revenues, it is fortunate that efforts to reduce consumption have had only limited effects.

Can the Tax Be Administered? American lore includes colorful and sometimes dramatic stories about moonshining, the production and sale of alcoholic beverages outside the purview of tax collectors. Most of the economic activity associated with items subject to excise taxes is, however, legitimate, visible, and taxed. Administration is not complex and difficult.

Is the Tax Fair? A study conducted by the Congressional Budget Office (CBO) as part of the federal government's deliberations about federal excise taxes noted that "sin taxes" are regressive. Based on an examination of consumer expenditure surveys, the CBO concluded that people with lower income spend a higher percentage of their income on alcohol and cigarettes than do people in middle- and higher-income brackets. Those earning under $5,000 a year, for example, spend, on the average, .37 percent of their income on excise taxes for beer, whereas those in the $20,000 to $30,000 range spend .07 percent, and those earning over $50,000 spend .04 percent. Likewise, those in the lowest-income category spend 1.05 percent on their income for excise taxes on cigarettes, those in the middle category spend .21 percent, and those in the highest category spend .07 percent.[11] Thus excise taxes pose a heavier burden on poorer people than on the more well-to-do.

Is the Tax Politically Acceptable? Because excise taxes are on products that people can (and maybe should) live without, these taxes are very acceptable. In fact, there is in part a moral justification for these taxes, conveyed in the label "sin taxes."

Inheritance Tax

An old adage states, "You can't take it with you." Most state governments might add, "And you can't leave it all behind." One source of revenue for state governments is the money and assets that individuals' inherit. A justification for this tax is that an inheritance constitutes an income for the recipient that is not earned in the same sense that money is earned through work or even through returns on investment decisions. Those opposing inheritance taxes point out that taxes presumably were paid by the person leaving the estate while he or she was earning a living.

Will the Tax Generate Very Much Money? Inheritance taxes constitute slightly less than 1 percent of all revenues collected by state governments. As of 1988, twenty-one states levy an inheritance tax. Seven of these states exempt surviving spouses. Rates of taxation often depend on the relationship of the recipient of the inheritance to the deceased, and of course, rates of taxation vary among states.[12] A common pattern is for states to tax only amounts above a certain figure (often set at $100,000).

Is the Tax Stable? The amount of money involved is relatively low and so stability is not all that consequential.

Can the Tax Be Administered? This tax is very easy to administer. Wills must be probated in state courts. The records of court actions enable states to levy inheritance taxes on fairly accurate and systematic information. The way to avoid inheritance taxes is to give one's possessions away before dying or to move to a state where there is no inheritance tax. Often, neither of these options is practical. Besides, most states levy a tax on gifts over a certain amount.

Is the Tax Fair? Despite the debate regarding whether taxes have in a sense already been paid on what is being inherited, the inheritance tax does meet the standard of fairness considered as ability to pay. The sudden windfall of an inheritance almost by definition enables someone to pay a portion to the government. Moreover, the greater the inheritance received, the higher the tax that must be paid.

Is the Tax Politically Acceptable? Although the inheritance tax does not generate the opposition and resentment of the property tax, and although it does not generate the funds earned by income or sales taxes, considerable symbolic importance is attached to this tax. Those who regard an estate as part of a family's resources or as part of a friendship resent sharing with the government. Those who will never inherit anything nonetheless fantasize about some long-lost, rich aunt or uncle and identify with the sentiments of those for whom inheritance is, or will be, a reality.

Other Taxes and Fees

Taxes, at least in theory, can be levied on almost anything. States that have a significant tourist industry can generate revenue by taxing hotel and motel rooms and by charging extra fees to nonresidents for the use of parks and harbors. Those states that have oil, coal, natural gas, or other material that they export can place a severance tax on these items as they leave the state. States like Alaska, Louisiana, Texas, and Oklahoma, in fact, rely heavily on severance taxes for their state treasuries. Licenses, tuition, motor vehicle registrations, and permits are all sources of revenue and can all be measured against the criteria applied to the taxes just discussed.

TAX REFORM

Taxes are important symbolically as well as substantively. They represent government presence and evoke all the feelings of wanting to be free of the burdens imposed by government. Those feelings have been a part of the fabric of politics in the United States since the Boston Tea Party, the first taxpayer revolt. Taxes do impose burdens. As pointed out, except for the income tax and, to some extent, the inheritance tax, the burdens tend to fall disproportionately on lower- and middle-income people.

Taxes are also essential to finance the services and protections that the public expects from government. States must be concerned about an adequate and stable source of revenue. Elected officials are obviously sensitive to the political acceptability of taxation policies.

With these concerns in mind, state legislatures and governors have enacted considerable and significant tax reforms since 1959. States, as a whole, have most noticeably diversified and broadened their sources of revenue. In 1959, only thirty-three states had a general sales tax, and thirty had personal income taxes. By the late 1970s, as Table 13.4 demonstrates, forty-five had adopted a sales tax and forty-three a personal income tax. Only Alaska and New Hampshire have neither a sales nor an income tax. In contrast, thirty-seven states have both.[13]

As Table 13.4 shows, except for the peak of the tax revolt (1978–1980) states have increased sales and personal income taxes to increase their revenues. Heavier reliance on income and sales taxes and reduced reliance on excise taxes has meant a link to a more lucrative source of funds for state governments. As pointed out,

TABLE 13.4. STATE PERSONAL INCOME AND SALES TAX LEGISLATION

	1959–1977 Real State-Local Growth	1978–1980 Tax Revolt	1981–1983 Recession	1984–1985 Mixed Bag
New Tax Adoptions				
Personal income tax	13	—	—	—
Sales tax	12	—	—	—
Tax Increases				
Personal income tax	75	2	28	5
Sales tax	76	6	30	14
Tax Decreases				
Personal income tax	n.a.	35	2	25
Sales tax	n.a.	19	1	7

Source: Adapted from John Shannon and Robert J. Kleine, "Characteristics of a 'Balanced' State-Local Tax System," Thad L. Beyle, ed., State Government *(Washington, DC: Congressional Quarterly, 1986), p. 159.*

excise taxes are based on the amount consumed rather than the price paid. Thus the amount of revenue earned is going to be fairly constant since consumption patterns for cigarettes, alcohol, and the like tend to be fairly constant.

Receipts from income and sales taxes also increased with economic growth and inflation. Thus, between 1978 and 1982, a period of high inflation, state revenues grew in absolute dollars, even though states tended to decrease taxes, state income taxes as a proportion of personal income stayed the same, and state sales taxes as a proportion of personal income actually declined (from 2.17 percent to 2.01 percent).[14] State and local government taxes, as a whole, declined between 1978 and 1985 in every state except Alaska, New Jersey, North Dakota, Oklahoma, West Virginia, and Wyoming. In 1978, state and local taxes were 12.8 percent of personal income, and in 1985 the level was down to 11.5 percent.[15]

States relying heavily on severance taxes on oil and gas suffered a major blow as world oil prices declined in 1986. Table 13.5 shows the effects on state revenues when oil prices drop. The general response was to cut expenditures, draw on reserves from previous budget surpluses, and avoid major overhauls in tax systems. Texas, for example, shunned the adoption of an income tax but joined Louisiana in raising sales taxes. Alaska, as mentioned, still has neither a sales tax nor a personal income tax.

In part, the changes in taxes and tax burdens are a response to cross-pressures from the business community, on the one hand, and local officials and teachers, on the other. In a study of the politics of tax reform, Richard Bingham, Brett Hawkins, and F. Ted Hebert found that the most active interest groups were individual businesses and business associations, who consistently opposed tax increases but especially focused on corporate and personal income tax increases. Those who advocated tax increases were municipal officials' and teachers' associations, and

TABLE 13.5. STATES RELYING ON OIL SEVERANCE REVENUES

State	Revenue Loss for Each $1 Drop in Oil Price ($ Millions)	Severance Tax Revenues as Percentage of Total State Taxes*
Alaska	150	71
Louisiana	33	25
Montana	3	25
New Mexico	7	27
North Dakota	6	29
Oklahoma	11	26
Texas	70	23
Wyoming	4	48

*Includes all severance tax collections, from oil, natural gas, and coal. Revenue loss based on 1986 data; percentages calculated using FY 1984 tax base. (Source: Governors Weekly Bulletin, Vol. 86, No. 10 (Mar. 7, 1986), 1.

they focused primarily on sales taxes.[16] In addition, states have reacted to the general taxpayer sentiment associated with California's Proposition 13. This reaction is clearest in the nineteen states that have placed limits on spending and taxation, usually through statutory mandates tying increases in state spending to increases in the cost of living. In a more general sense, states seem to be more cautious in their growth since Proposition 13.

Lotteries and Other Forms of Gambling

Legalized gambling used to be associated with Nevada. As other states have reacted to the general message of Proposition 13 to reduce taxes or at least to control tax increases, they have increasingly accepted the strategy of generating money through gambling. With almost enthusiastic support from the general public, state governments have sponsored lotteries, in which about half of the money paid for tickets goes to prizes for those playing, 10 percent goes for administrative expenses, and the rest goes to the public treasury. A state lottery is not a tax, although opponents note the remote chances of someone winning and call lotteries a "tax on stupidity." Taxes are mandatory, whereas participation in a lottery is voluntary. A lottery has a kind of entertainment value and quite simply offers the prospect of making money.

Lotteries do not generate much revenue for state governments. For the seventeen states that had a lottery in operation in 1985, net proceeds contributed less than 6 percent of the revenue collected by state governments. A typical state with a population of about 5 million garnered about $138 million per year, or about $26 per person. Those who play in a lottery are primarily in the low- to middle-income brackets.[17]

Although lotteries have been the most popular new source of revenue, states are increasingly turning toward other forms of gambling for funds, such as parimutuel betting on dog and horse racing. Sometimes the revenue earned is earmarked for special purposes, like property tax relief or school financing, and at other times the money is available for any purpose.

Income Tax Simplification

Tax reform efforts in the 1980s have also included the simplification of income tax laws and forms. In response to particular concerns and pressures over the last several decades, income tax codes have included a wide array of special provisions, benefits, and rules. Even those who make careers out of helping individuals and businesses file income tax returns found their work too complex. The complaints were hurled at the federal government as well as at state governments. The federal government responded with the Tax Reform Act of 1986, a major change that, given state reliance on the federal income tax form and code, had major implications for state tax systems.

Tax Capacity and Tax Effort

The federal Advisory Commission on Intergovernmental Relations (ACIR), which consists of federal, state, and local government officials who direct a staff of researchers to report on various matters, has developed measures of the capacity of states to tax and the efforts made by states to collect revenue. Tax capacity is calculated by applying the average tax rate used by states to twenty-six different indicators (such as personal income, agricultural production, industrial production, and employment rate) of economic conditions. The basic question, in other words, is how much money could a state raise, given its economic base, if it taxed at an average rate. Tax effort measures whether, given a state's economic situation, it is taxing at average rates or above or below those rates.[18] Table 13.6 shows tax capacity and tax effort scores for each state, using 100 as the score for average.

The pressure in some states is to match capacity and effort. This pressure comes from social service and education advocates, in particular, when a state has an effort below its capacity and from business when a state taxes above its capacity. One might debate the methodology used by ACIR and whether the twenty-six indicators of economic conditions are the right ones. Indeed, debates occur within ACIR, and occasionally the methodology is revised. Nonetheless, the concepts of tax capacity and tax effort, the measures and the methodology, and ACIR itself have acquired considerable credibility. Those engaged in tax reform efforts feel advantaged when they are able to bolster their arguments with an ACIR analysis.

The concerns of policy makers are not only with the level but also with the forms of taxation. When, for example, the United States was essentially an agrarian and frontier society, a personal income tax would have been difficult to administer and probably inappropriate for other reasons as well. With the industrial revolution, our economy became wage-based. A personal income tax seemed appropriate, and it could be administered in large part by withholding from paychecks an amount estimated to be owed in taxes. Economists predict significant changes in the nature of the U.S. economy. The economy of tomorrow may be more reliant on high technology, and jobs are likely to be primarily in the service

**TABLE 13.6. STATE TAX CAPACITY
AND TAX EFFORT (1984)**

	Tax Capacity	Tax Effort
Alabama	73	90
Alaska	250	141
Arizona	99	95
Arkansas	75	87
California	119	93
Colorado	121	82
Connecticut	124	99
Delaware	123	77
Florida	105	74
Georgia	89	89
Hawaii	118	99
Idaho	78	91
Illinois	97	110
Indiana	87	95
Iowa	87	112
Kansas	100	95
Kentucky	77	89
Louisiana	102	81
Maine	88	105
Maryland	105	100
Massachusetts	111	105
Michigan	93	129
Minnesota	101	124
Mississippi	70	95
Missouri	89	85
Montana	95	101
Nebraska	93	99
Nevada	146	65
New Hampshire	110	69
New Jersey	114	109
New Mexico	103	85
New York	98	158
North Carolina	87	89
North Dakota	106	93
Ohio	90	105
Oklahoma	113	76
Oregon	94	103
Pennsylvania	88	105
Rhode Island	86	123
South Carolina	77	95
South Dakota	83	87
Tennessee	81	81
Texas	117	69
Utah	81	106
Vermont	95	94
Virginia	96	88

continued

TABLE 13.6., continued

	Tax Capacity	Tax Effort
Washington	99	103
West Virginia	79	100
Wisconsin	89	133
Wyoming	181	105

Source: Measuring State Fiscal Capacity: Alternative Methods and Their Uses (Washington, DC: Advisory Commission on Intergovernmental Relations, 1986).

sector.[19] Perhaps corporate taxes and sales taxes will be more important than personal income taxes and property taxes.

The consideration of tax policies is likely to be especially important for state governments in the near future because of the consequences of the dramatic rise in the national debt between 1981 and 1987. The federal government is likely to focus on national taxation and national spending, to the neglect of state concerns with welfare and economic development. State government responsibilities and activities are likely to grow. It will be important to be certain that states have an adequate treasury for these activities and that taxes are fair in their impacts.

ECONOMIC DEVELOPMENT

Economic development includes but is not limited to business growth or manufacturing expansion. Economic development also includes other sectors and activities, such as service, mining, agriculture, and tourism. The role of the federal government in economic development is primarily in its monetary policies and macro activities, designed to address inflation, recession, and interest rates. States are uniquely positioned to affect economic growth in specific communities and yet retain regional perspectives. States can more effectively target efforts to particular activities and specific geographic areas.

As states develop policies to ensure health and growth for their economies, they compete with one another. The most visible instances of competition are when major companies decide where to locate a particular operation or whether to relocate an existing activity. Chrysler's decision, for example, concerning where to locate its new Saturn operation (Kentucky was the winner) set off vigorous competition among nine states. Each tried to outdo the other in providing tax exemption incentives; publicly financed job-training programs; provision of roads, sewerage facilities, and other infrastructures; and reminders about low crime rates, recreation opportunities, and other quality-of-life issues. The attraction of the Saturn plant was primarily jobs.

Similarly, Sematech, the consortium of computer companies formed to promote research and development, was wined and dined by twelve states (Texas was the winner). Here the issue was not so much the number of employees who would be directly hired as it was that those who did work would be highly paid, and both their spending and the operations of Sematech itself would prompt other economic activities in the community.

The attraction of major employers is important for symbolic as well as substantive reasons. About 5 percent of job growth in a typical state comes from major, highly visible projects like Saturn and Sematech.[20] Five percent is not inconsequential, but the publicity surrounding these decisions loses sight of the importance of the job growth that comes from small businesses already in the state (40 percent), the public sector (10 percent), and medium to large businesses already in the state (45 percent). The visible entrance or departure of a major employer does, however, have political importance. Governors, in particular, are judged in part on perceptions about whether a state is attracting new economic activities or chasing businesses to other parts of the country.

The term *business climate* is used to refer to the policies of state government related to economic development and to the competitive position of a state vis-à-vis other states. The term is fundamentally based on perceptions, and it is an important component of the political arsenal of the business community. There is no single measure of whether a state is a good or bad place in which to conduct business, and there is no consensus on a set of measures. Table 13.7 presents different ranking systems, with the state ranked highest and the state ranked lowest for each system. Note that each system identifies different states as ''the best'' and ''the worst.'' The major reason for the different rankings is the variation in importance, or weight, given to different concerns. The Grant Thornton rankings, which are announced each June, are the oldest and are cited by those seeking low taxes for businesses. *Inc.* magazine started its own ranking system to emphasize the criterion of primary interest to its readers, that is, programs to assist small businesses. The Corporation for Enterprise Development is a private

TABLE 13.7. COMPARISON OF BUSINESS CLIMATE RANKINGS

	Ranking System		
	Grant Thornton	Inc.	Corporation for Enterprise Development
Emphasis in Ranking	Low business taxes	Help for small businesses	Equitable income distribution; unemployment
State Ranked Best	South Dakota	Arizona	Massachusetts
State Ranked Worst	Michigan	Wyoming	Louisiana

consulting group that, with support from businesses, labor organizations, and foundations, developed a ranking system that weights heavily equal distribution of income, low unemployment, and public support for education. In short, "business climate" is almost anything you want it to be.

Financial Approaches to Economic Development

To varying degrees, state governments pursue the following strategies that involve financial assistance to firms deemed important to economic development in a state.

Tax Abatements. States offer certain businesses a temporary or long-term tax break to help them out. This might be a tax holiday, in which, for example, they would be exempt from a corporate income tax for a certain period. Another form of this strategy would be to exempt certain property from a property tax.

Loans. States have an ability to borrow money that is not always available to businesses. Because a state government can usually be counted on to repay its debts, it can secure funds through a bond (borrowing) or general tax revenues and then lend the money at little or no interest to risky businesses or overextended farmers.[21] Although a bank may not make such loans, state governments may determine that public interest is served by either making the loans themselves or guaranteeing the loan to a commercial lender.

Infrastructure. Physical facilities, accompanied by access to transportation networks, power sources, and waste disposal, are key areas where state governments can and do provide assistance. Sometimes states can help make existing facilities available and more suitable. At other times it is a matter of ensuring the timely completion of infrastructure construction.

Service Approaches to Economic Development

Besides providing financial help, state governments can perform their traditional functions of providing services and regulation in ways that can help business development.

Education and Training. Education is a major responsibility of state governments, as pointed out in Chapter 10. Those states that over the years have established and maintained high-quality educational systems, kindergarten through university, find themselves in advantageous positions as the country's economy relies increasingly on high technology. In addition, states have traditionally provided technical and vocational education. The use or adaptation of these programs and facilities can be vital in helping new or existing businesses hire and develop work forces with the skills necessary for their particular industry.

Research. Major public universities have a history of contributing to economic development in their respective states and in the country as a whole through both applied and basic research. Wisconsin is a dramatic illustration of this point. This state had relied almost entirely on wheat until breakthroughs were made at the University of Wisconsin in breeding productive milk cows and in processing milk products. Within a six-year period the state's farmers abandoned wheat almost entirely and made the state well known for its dairy industry. In the 1980s, state governments and state businesses turned to their universities for assistance in developing robotics, computer technologies, and genetic engineering. The Research Triangle in North Carolina and the Ben Franklin Partnership program in Pennsylvania are noted examples of the utilization of university research capabilities for economic development.[22]

Regulations.   Although deregulation is usually touted as the most useful approach governments might take to promote economic development, it is too simplistic to think that the demise of government regulations is a panacea. Indeed, government regulations regarding land use, occupational licensing, consumer protection, and the like can sometimes be an obstacle to economic growth. At other times, however, businesses invite governments to issue regulations. One illustration of this point is the legislation in many states that regulates the hostile takeover of a company. Rules regarding public notice, compensation, the need for new permits, and the like are at the request of state businesses seeking protection and what they regard as fair compensation.

State governments have a responsibility, of course, to pursue economic development strategies in ways that do not lose sight of other goals and public policies. The general public cannot be expected to subsidize businesses indefinitely in the name of economic development. Regulations intended to protect consumers and preserve the environmental resources cannot be abandoned in order to allow a business to make an attractive profit. And when in the final analysis businesses fail, state governments have—whether they want it or not—the responsibility to help the individuals and the communities who have been adversely affected. Unemployment compensation and job-training programs exist not only for economic development but also, as pointed out in Chapter 11, for social and individual welfare.

SUMMARY AND CONCLUSIONS

Like many policy areas, taxation and economic development involve multiple objectives and diverse political pressures. State governments need revenue in order to fulfill their responsibilities. The collection of that revenue must be as fair as possible, and it has to tap major sources of money without destroying the economy. Economic development is key to individual and societal welfare. State governments and businesses sometimes see each other suspiciously as rivals. Yet they need one another and they must work together, both for their own interests and for the interest of the general public. The need for striking a balance is obvious.

The way to strike a balance is not always obvious, and the efforts to do so are the stuff of state politics.

TAXATION EXERCISE: TAX POLICY ANALYSIS

Suppose that you are on the staff of the governor of Alaska. You have just received a report from respected energy economists that the price of oil and gas will drop precipitously in two years. You recognize that Alaska relies almost entirely on its severance tax for state revenues. Alaska is one of only a few states without an income tax or a sales tax.

The governor wants a paper that suggests what she might do. The paper is to emphasize concepts and strategies, not numbers. The governor intends to run for reelection three years from now.

Write the paper for the governor, using the information and the concerns discussed in this chapter.

REFERENCES

1. U.S. Census Bureau, *State Government Finances, 1987* (Washington, DC: U.S. Government Printing Office, 1987).
2. *Significant Features of Fiscal Federalism, 1980–81* (Washington, DC: Advisory Commission on Intergovernmental Relations, 1981), p. 64.
3. John L. Mikesell, "The Path of the Tax Revolt: Statewide Expenditure and Tax Control Referenda since Proposition 13," *State and Local Government Review*, Vol. 18, No. 1 (Winter 1986), 5–7.
4. *Significant Features of Fiscal Federalism, 1983-84* (Washington, DC: Advisory Commission on Intergovernmental Relations, 1984), p. 57.
5. *State Policy Reports,* Vol. 5, No. 10 (May 30, 1987), 6.
6. *The Book of the States, 1986-87* (Lexington, KY: Council of State Governments, 1982), p. 401.
7. Steven D. Gold, "Recent Developments in State Finances," *National Tax Journal,* Vol. 36, No. 1 (Mar. 1983), 1–29.
8. *State Budget and Tax News,* Vol. 5, No. 20 (Oct. 21, 1986), 12.
9. J. Richard Aronson and John L. Hilley, *Financing State and Local Governments,* 4th ed. (Washington, DC: Brookings Institution, 1986), pp. 134–41.
10. U.S. Census Bureau, *Historical Statistics of the United States: Colonial Times to 1957* (Washington, DC: U.S. Government Printing Office, 1960), pp. 727–28; and U.S. Census Bureau, *State Government Finances in 1984* (Washington, DC: U.S. Government Printing Office, 1985), Table 6.
11. Congressional Budget Office, *The Distributional Effects of an Increase in Federal Excise Taxes* (Washington, DC: U.S. Government Printing Office, 1987).
12. Aronson and Hilley, *Financing Governments,* pp. 115 and 116.
13. Gold, "Recent Developments," 7.
14. Ibid., 8.

15. U.S. Census Bureau, *Government Finances in 1984-85* (Washington, DC: U.S. Government Printing Office, 1986), p. 23.
16. Richard Bingham, Brett Hawkins, and F. Ted Hebert, "The Revenue Decision Process," in Marilyn Gittell, ed., *State Politics and the New Federalism* (New York: Longman, 1986), pp. 343–51.
17. Steven D. Gold, "Lotteries in 1985: Is the Gamble Paying Off?" *State Legislatures*, Vol. 12, No. 4 (Spring 1986), 28.
18. *Fiscal Survey of the States, September, 1987* (Washington, DC: National Association of State Budget Officers, 1987), p. 3.
19. Carol E. Cohen, "1984 State Tax Wealth: Preview of the RTS Estimates," *Intergovernmental Perspective*, (Summer 1986), pp. 24 and 25.
20. Enid F. Beaumont and Astrid E. Merget, "State Revenue Prospects: Reforms Versus Reaction," in Gittell, ed., *State Politics*, pp. 352–68.
21. Robert Vaugh et al., *The Wealth of the States* (Washington, DC: Council of State Planning Agencies, 1984), p. v.
22. Hugh O'Neill, *Creating Opportunity* (Washington, DC: Council of State Planning Agencies, 1985), pp. 93–110.

THE STATE AS REGULATOR

CHAPTER 14

Finding the Appropriate Regulatory Balance

We, as Americans, take justifiable pride in our country as a home of freedom, individual liberty, and free enterprise. We value our opportunity to live, individually and collectively, unfettered from rules, controls, and regulations by government.

Yet we are outraged when a private company sells children's clothing made of highly flammable material or a gas and electric company shuts off service in the middle of winter to poor people who have not been able to pay utility bills. We recognize the right of a chemical company to exist and to make a profit, but we reject the notion that efforts to minimize costs might include dumping hazardous waste directly into a nearby stream. Members of professions support the concept that individuals should be able to pursue whatever occupation suits them, but they do not want people calling themselves doctors, lawyers, architects, real estate agents, or accountants simply because they think they can do the work.

We treasure individual freedom, but we also need protection. To protect ourselves from those who, intentionally or unintentionally, would sell harmful products, pollute water, or work in a field for which they lack qualifications, we call upon government. The pressures for government regulations come from almost every possible source. Businesses seek protection from what they regard as unfair competitive practices, especially from those establishing monopolies. Labor asks government to make certain that collective bargaining occurs in a fair and orderly manner. Consumers, environmentalists, farmers, stockholders, minority groups, and others pursue their objectives through government regulation.

WHAT IS GOVERNMENT REGULATION?

Alan Stone defines a regulation as a government-imposed "limitation on the discretion that may be exercised by individuals or organizations, which is supported by the threat of sanction."[1] Regulations are mandates or prohibitions that are fairly specific and distinct from criminal law, which deals with murder, assault, robbery, and other violations of persons and property. Regulations are laws, although they typically are in the form of rules promulgated by an administrative agency rather than statutes passed by a legislature. The usual pattern is that legislative bodies respond to a concern for regulation by passing a law that establishes an agency with a general mission and with the authority to issue regulations consistent with that mission. The regulations themselves have the force of law.

The most visible examples of regulatory agencies are part of the federal government. They include the Environmental Protection Agency, which regulates activity that might pollute or destroy the environment and which supports and regulates efforts to improve the environment; the Food and Drug Administration, which regulates the substances that can be put into food and medicinal drugs; and the Federal Communications Commission, which licenses radio and television stations and regulates what can be broadcast. Although the federal government is obviously and clearly involved in regulation, the role of state governments as regulators is at least as important.

DEVELOPMENT OF STATE GOVERNMENT
AS A REGULATOR

State-level actions defining standards of fairness in the marketplace began during the colonial period.[2] For the first century of the Republic's existence, states were the primary actors in regulation. States passed laws and established agencies to incorporate businesses; to license certain occupations; and to regulate banking, transportation, insurance, and utilities. Industrial states adopted regulations ensuring the safety and health of workers in factories. Illinois, in 1874, led the way in regulating food and drugs.

The construction of an interstate railroad system prompted a major change in the role of the federal government in regulation and, concomitantly, in the role of states. Railway transportation became a major feature of the economy. Railroad companies were in an obviously enviable position. They were also suspect. Customers, sometimes with good reason, questioned price structures and service schedules. Community leaders raised concerns about what they regarded as the public interest.

State governments responded with investigations and regulations. States in the Northeast created advisory commissions to consider the many and conflicting interests associated with railroad development. In the 1870s, states in the Midwest created regulatory commissions that set rates and prohibited prices that would discriminate against any particular region or economic group.

The railroad companies, not surprisingly, feared continued state action. They could imagine high administrative and financial costs as they sought to comply with the variety of regulations coming out of each state. To avoid this, the railroad companies advocated regulation by the federal government. Their efforts led to the passage of the Interstate Commerce Act in 1887, which established the first major federal regulatory agency, the Interstate Commerce Commission (ICC).[3]

This action by the federal government did not mean the demise of regulation by state governments. Some states recognized that they were preempted by the ICC, but they promulgated additional rules to apply to the railroads when they did not feel the ICC fully addressed certain issues. States continued to be active in other policy areas. States under the leadership of the Progressives, in particular, strengthened antitrust regulations, established restrictions on banks, stipulated how water power would be used, and promulgated rules to preserve wildlife areas.

The regulation of public utilities by state governments took form during the turn of the century and followed a pattern parallel to that of the railways. Electric companies were initially dependent on municipal governments for franchises and licenses. For some companies, this meant cooperating with the bosses of political machines. Executives considered their options. They did not relish continuing to work with municipalities, for they feared another option: public ownership by municipalities. They rejected federal government regulation primarily because, unlike railways, utilities are more regionally based and national standards are not likely to be sensitive to the unique needs and circumstances of local areas. State governments appeared the most feasible level of government. Governors Robert M. La Follette of Wisconsin, Charles Evans Hughes of New York, Woodrow Wilson of New Jersey, and Hiram Johnson of California were, consistent with their Progressive philosophy and their desire to destroy political machines, eager to assert a state role in utility regulation. The convergence of political and business objectives first led to laws establishing public utility commissions in Wisconsin and New York (1907). Within six years, two-thirds of the states followed suit.[4]

Both the states and the federal government have been active in regulation in the twentieth century. In some areas, such as occupational licensing and regulation, states have been the sole actors. In other areas, such as utilities, where the state public utility commissions and the federal Nuclear Regulatory Commission are both relevant regulators, there is some overlap and even redundancy. As will be discussed later, another pattern is for the federal government to make general policies and then rely on state regulations and procedures for implementation.

Regulatory policies, both in state governments and in the federal government, focused primarily on economic activities until the 1960s. The scope has since broadened to include concerns about the environment, general health hazards, and social issues such as discrimination. The instrumental value of governing through regulations has accordingly been enhanced and complicated.

REASONS FOR REGULATION

As with the convergence of different interests that led to the establishment of public service or public utility commissions, any single regulation or regulatory policy can be based on several justifications. Sometimes one particular justification can be identified as most important. The significance of a reason is likely to be an important determinant of how a particular regulation actually operates. It is, therefore, useful to discuss the major reasons for having government regulations.

Surrogate for Market Forces

A traditional concern that has prompted government regulations is the need to prevent monopolies, in the absence of competition, from charging confiscatory fees for services that meet basic public needs. A utility company, for example, typically is a monopoly in a given region. That company could exploit the dependence of other businesses and of residences on the utility and charge very high prices. Presumably, there is no meaningful incentive for providing good or equitable service. The company could have a very short-term perspective and not do planning or research and development for the future. To avoid these problems, government regulations can set prices based on giving owners a reasonable return on their investments. Public service commissions can set standards for service delivery and require medium and long-term planning. In a very real sense, government regulations force businesses in this situation to behave as if there were competitive market forces in operation.

Protection

Although it is natural to think of the need for government regulations to protect consumers from unscrupulous businesses, consumers are not the only ones seeking protection. As pointed out, businesses also pursue protection through government regulation. The antitrust laws, both state and federal, were in large part a response to the concerns of some firms that they might be put out of business by ruthless and unfair practices by a major competitor. In the 1980s, states adopted regulations that would apply to firms that bought a controlling interest in another business against the wishes of the board of directors. The intent was to protect businesses—especially those located in the state—against hostile takeovers.

Government regulations can also be used as protection against bad public relations. Next time you fly with a commercial airline, listen to the standard speech about smoking and about putting carry-on baggage under the seat in front of you. Why these restrictions? Federal regulations! In fact, the Federal Aviation Agency promulgated these rules with the support of the airline industry. Nonetheless, should a passenger object, the stewardess or steward can conveniently blame the government. Similarly, state regulations are blamed when customers complain about the space that must be reserved in a building for elevators and about the specifications of design and materials, even though builders and architects usually play a major role in drafting those regulations.

Professions and occupations protect themselves through the use of state licensing boards. Investigations in 1986 suggested that as many as 10,000 people were practicing medicine as physicians or hospital residents with fraudulent degrees and licenses.[5] Licensing requirements are, with few exceptions, established by those already in the profession, rather than in some arbitrary manner by some faceless state official. Individuals appointed to state licensing boards, with few exceptions, are members of the occupation that is being regulated. The requirements set by these boards make it illegal for someone to practice medicine, cut hair, sell real estate, or embalm a body unless the person meets the standards of that profession or occupation.

Likewise, the revocation of a license or some other sanction is done by state boards. This is another way for the profession to police and protect itself through the use of government authority. It also offers reassurance and protection to those who must rely on licensed practitioners but who are not in a position to judge personal qualifications.

Protection of the public can be invoked as a justification for almost any government regulation. In part, this justification is so readily available because "the public" is a vague and ambiguous concept. Monopolies and hostile takeovers can be opposed on behalf of consumers as well as current owners and stockholders.[6] Unqualified professionals imply poor and even dangerous service. These are, of course, genuine concerns, whether or not they are the primary reason for a regulation. Food and drug regulations and consumer protection regulations, at both the state and federal levels, are very direct attempts to protect members of the public from unscrupulous businesses. This protection is especially important with the increasingly complex technology that is now part of so many goods and services.

Externalities

The example of the chemical company that dumps its waste and pollutes a nearby stream illustrates the need for government regulation because of an externality. The fundamental transaction for the chemical company is producing and selling a product to a customer. The waste produced is external to this transaction, and the issue created by the waste is, thus, called an "externality." In this example, the waste, unfortunately, becomes a central concern for the community. The implications of polluted water necessarily prompt government action. The federal government and state governments have established regulatory agencies (like the Environmental Protection Agency) to promulgate and enforce rules that foster and preserve a healthy environment.

Safety

Safety is not always a value around which a consensus readily forms. Proposals to require motorcyclists to wear a helmet and those in a car to wear seat belts have been met with impassioned pleas to uphold the principle of individual freedom in our country. State governments have traditionally regulated for safety reasons. Public health rules, for example, determine what must be done when someone has a contagious disease. Public health concerns are responsible for state rules on the production, storage, transportation, processing, and serving of food. The federal government and some states regulate tools, machinery, and general working environments to ensure safety for workers.

Equity

Although the most visible example of a regulatory agency promoting equity is the federal Equal Employment Opportunity Commission, states, too, are active in this area. Some state regulations overlap federal ones: Others provide more protection (beyond employment, e.g.) than offered by the federal government. In the 1960s, states were generally considered laggards in the fight against discrimination. In the 1980s, states—particularly on both coasts and in the Midwest—pioneered efforts to prohibit discrimination based on sexual orientation and to ensure adherence to the principles of pay equity.

REGULATION AND FEDERALISM

Several points have already been made about the relationships between federalism and regulation. It was noted, for example, that there is overlap between some federal and state regulatory agencies. The historical background included instances in which states initiated regulation of a particular activity and then the federal government adopted the state model. Over the years, distinct patterns of state and federal involvement in regulation have emerged. (See table 14.1.)

Sole Responsibility. The regulation and licensing of occupations is an example of where states act and the federal government is not involved at all. Another exam-

TABLE 14.1. MAJOR INTERGOVERNMENTAL REGULATORY STATUTES

Water Quality Act	1965
Highway Beautification Act	1965
Wholesome Meat Act	1967
Wholesome Poultry Products Act	1968
National Environmental Policy Act	1969
Occupational Safety and Health Act	1970
Clean Air Act	1970
Coastal Zone Management Act	1972
Endangered Species Act	1973
Safe Drinking Water Act	1974
Resource Conservation and Recovery Act	1976
Toxic Substances Control Act	1976
Surface Mining Control and Reclamation Act	1977
Public Utility Regulatory Policy Act	1978
Comprehensive Environmental Response, Compensation and Liability Act	1980
Nuclear Waste Policy Act	1982

ple is the regulation of the insurance industry. Interestingly, shortly after the Supreme Court ruled that the federal government had the constitutional authority to regulate insurance, Congress passed the McCarran Act of 1945, which provided for state government jurisdiction over this industry.

Federal Government Has Sole Responsibility. The Securities and Exchange Commission, which regulates the stock market, and the Federal Communications Commission, which regulates radio and television broadcasting, are the only regulatory agencies having oversight of these industries.

Parallel: Federal Preemption. The preceding description of the Interstate Commerce Commission illustrates this pattern. The federal government and many state governments have agencies that establish regulations that must be followed by the railroads. Wherever federal and state regulations conflict, the federal rules prevail. State regulations, then, supplement those of the federal government.

Parallel: Federal Partial Preemption. This has become the most common pattern.[7] The federal government assumes responsibility in a particular policy area, thus potentially displacing conflicting regulations issued by states. However, the federal government then on a compulsory or voluntary basis hands responsibility to state governments. The Clean Air Act of 1970 is an example of a mandatory program of partial preemption. States must submit their own air pollution regulations to the federal government for review. Minimum standards must be met. More commonly, the pattern is voluntary, as with the Occupational Safety and Health Act (OSHA) of 1970. The federal government encourages state participation through the provision of authority and financial support. If states do not promulgate their own regulations, the federal rules apply. By the mid-1980s, twenty-one states had acted on their own in the occupational safety and health field. State governments do not always take advantage of a federal offer to assume responsibility because the states eagerly support regulating a particular activity. Some states appeared to take advantage of the OSHA partial preemption by enforcing their regulation less seriously than was done by the federal government.[8]

State Veto. In a few instances, the federal government has assumed responsibility for regulating in a particular area and then has allowed individual states to veto the application of those regulations. Two examples of this are the Coastal Zone Management Act of 1972, which regulates drilling for oil in outer continental shelf areas, and the Nuclear Waste Policy Act of 1982, which governs the siting of permanent depositories of high-level radioactive waste and spent nuclear fuel. In both of these acts, the vetoes of states can be set aside by a complicated process that the U.S. Congress would follow (probably unsuccessfully).[9]

States retain considerable authority and autonomy in issuing regulations, even when the federal government is active. States do not necessarily celebrate this independence. When states are competing with one another for the location of economic enterprises, they do not enjoy being unique in promulgating new regulations. Whatever sound policy objectives support the new regulations, states tend to avoid the image of having an overbearing government. It is sometimes preferable, from this standpoint, for the federal government to mandate that everyone follow the same (hopefully, good) policy.

THE REGULATORY PROCESS

Formal Process

The formal process of government regulation starts with the passage of a law that authorizes an agency (new or existing) to regulate a certain activity. Let us suppose that a state legislature is concerned about the sale of dangerous firecrackers. The legislature knows that new firecrackers are being developed each year, and it would not be effective to pass a law banning those that are currently deemed dangerous

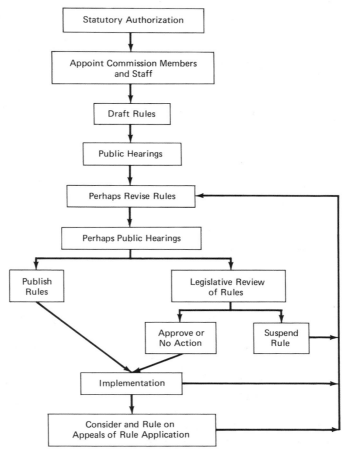

Figure 14.1. The Regulatory Process

since that presumably would not cover ones that are still on the drawing boards. The legislature does not, however, want to pass a law banning all firecrackers. Instead, it passes a law establishing a Firecracker Control Commission to regulate the sale of firecrackers, with the specific intent to prohibit the sale of those regarded as dangerous to people, whether spectators or operators, and/or to property. The law stipulates that the governor will appoint five persons to the commission, each serving a five-year, staggered term. Appointments must be approved by the state senate. The commission is given funds and authorization to hire a staff to provide legal, expert, and clerical support.

The standard process for the commission to promulgate rules that specify criteria for banning a type of firecracker, penalties for violating regulations, requirements for dealers to report what they are selling, and the like begins with a draft from the staff. Then public hearings are scheduled to allow comment from manufacturers, dealers, and other interested parties. The draft may be revised and there might be more hearings.

When the commission is satisfied, the regulations are published and sent to a legislative committee, where, in most states, it has an opportunity to object to rules, suspend for a limited time the implementation of those rules, and seek the submission of a more acceptable rule from the commission. The legislature, in accordance with the doctrine of separation of powers between the branches, cannot itself revise a rule. If a legislature faces a recalcitrant commission, it can argue in the courts that legislative intent is being violated in some way or it can pass a new law. Statutes supersede rules. Although it rarely happens, the legislature could specify its wish in statutory form or it could even abolish the commission.

The implementation of the firecracker regulations includes gathering information on enforcement and on the development of new firecracker technology. The commission and its staff are also responsible for being certain that information about the regulations is disseminated, both by answering questions as well as publicizing the commission's work. While completing these tasks, it is likely that new or revised rules will emerge, primarily in response to technical information and to administrative problems.

Those penalized for not conforming to the regulations have a chance in most states to appeal. Sometimes the appeal is made to the commission, and at other times it is heard by a separate body of administrative law judges or hearing examiners. Besides being sure that the penalty is justified, appeals provide another opportunity for reaction to what the commission is doing. One result of an appeal is the revision of some of the existing regulations. In the course of an appeal, for example, information might be presented that changes the commission's evaluation of a chemical, a casing, or an ignition system.

Informal Process

Political scientists have examined the regulatory process—primarily at the federal level—and, perhaps not surprisingly, have found that the formal process is only part of the picture. Several competing theories have emerged from studies of what happens informally.

Capture Theory. One theory holds that over time the regulatory agencies are captured by the very industries they were supposed to control.[10] Expertise and interest are the major elements of capture. It stands to reason that the issues and solutions considered by our Firecracker Control Commission will increasingly be framed by the firecracker industry. They are the ones, after all, who are developing the new technologies and thus are a natural source of expertise for evaluating relevant technologies. Their level of interest in the commission is obviously going to be high. Not only might the industry convince the commissioners that firecracker manufacturers are responsible and need little external control, but also the issues might change. Industry spokespersons might protect themselves against new competitors by suggesting safety problems with their rivals' products. Concerns that on the surface seem to be ensuring a sales system that can be monitored easily may in fact become an effort to ensure more sales by favored dealers.

The capture theory aptly describes the dynamics for some agencies. The Interstate Commerce Commission is probably the most notable illustration. However, James Q. Wilson assembled a group of scholars to test the application of this model more generally and concluded that although independent regulatory agencies were rarely fully independent, they were not universally captured by the industries they were established to regulate.[11] William Gormley suggests that although the capture theory may apply to some of the initial economic agencies in which the concerned industries were clearly prominent, it does not apply to the newer agencies established to protect the environment or ensure health and safety.[12]

Interest-Group Theory. Another perspective considers regulatory agencies as the arenas for interest-group politics.[13] According to this model, the way to predict policy outcomes for the Firecracker Control Commission would be to identify those groups interested in the subject of the commission and then assess the influence they wield and the strategies they pursue. Presumably manufacturers, dealers, organizers of festive occasions, concerned parents, and children would feel they have something at stake in the decisions of the commission. Probably the most powerful groups are the manufacturers and the dealers, especially if they join together. A major limitation of this model is that it is rarely possible to identify all the actors and even rarer to assess meaningfully their relative power.

Representation Theory. Yet another way of understanding why regulatory commissions make the decisions they do is to consider who is making the decisions.[14] A commissioner who used to be a dealer in firecrackers might be expected to foster the interests of dealers. A key staff member who wrote a law review article while a student arguing for limiting the discretion of regulatory commissions would be expected to pursue that interest. An individual or group designated to represent concerned parents and the welfare of children presumably would satisfy its charge. As with interest-group theory, it is not always possible to get the information needed to apply this model. Also, individuals are complex and do not consistently adhere to one value or one experience.

REGULATORY REFORM

The 1970s and 1980s have been characterized by a concern that if government regulations have accomplished noble purposes, we might have too much of a good thing. Regulations, along with the size of government budgets, the size of the public sector work force, the tax increases, were all considered indicators of a government that was too big. A successful political strategy of candidates was to run for office, ironically, by running against government, promising to cut back on taxes, budgets, employees, and regulations.

The frustration for government officials was that although public sentiment was against regulations generally, opinion polls also showed widespread support for specific regulations. Surveys in 1987 by NBC News and the Gallup Organization, for example, showed that whereas 55 percent of the respondents agreed and only 34 percent disagreed that government regulation of business usually does more harm than good, only 6 percent thought there should be less regulation of the environment and on-the-job health and safety. Fifty percent thought there should be more regulation of on-the-job health and safety, and 41 percent thought current regulations were adequate. Sixty-one percent favored more environmental regulation and 29 percent thought we already had the right amount.[15] Granted, governments were not trusted, but few thought it desirable to allow businesses to act without limitations. The general wish to eliminate or reduce regulations did not extend to water or air pollution, to licenses for physicians, or to dangerous chemical substances in food and drugs.[16]

Perhaps because of the lack of focus in public sentiment, there was a lot of reform activity in state governments and the federal government, but efforts were general and procedural. The catalog of initiatives included a wide array of institutional reforms and the elimination of some regulations. Sunset laws were the most popular institutional reform at the state level. Thirty-five states passed statutes that specified the elimination of agencies and regulations at a specific time unless the legislature was convinced they should be renewed. Typically, however, renewal was almost automatic and not based on serious reviews.[17] Another common approach (twenty-six of thirty-seven states) was to reorganize regulatory agencies, putting them administratively within a single umbrella department. The intent was to provide more effective supervision and more efficient staff services. Also, thirty-six states adopted the formal procedures described above, complete with the opportunity for legislative review and rule suspension.[18] The few instances of deregulation include the elimination of some minor licensing boards and the deregulation of intrastate transportation in Arizona, Florida, Maine, Vermont, and Wisconsin.

Some deregulation advocates had second thoughts as the 1980s came to a close. In the early 1970s, for example, states and the federal government lifted restrictions on financial institutions, letting competition determine whether savings and loan associations should also provide checking accounts and whether banks should offer their customers services and investment opportunities that had once been allowed only to savings and loan associations. Fourteen states (Florida, Hawaii, Idaho, Illinois, Iowa, Maine, Maryland, New Hampshire, New Jersey, Ohio, Oklahoma, Rhode Island, South Carolina, and Wisconsin) reported to the National Association of State Savings and Loan Supervisors that they had not only eliminated some of their regulations but also were not examining financial institutions as frequently as was mandated by their own state laws.[19] With the decrease in regulations and oversight came a dramatic increase in bank failures, bankruptcy of savings and loan associations, and scandalous frauds. The federal government, through the Federal Savings and Loan Insurance Corporation and the Federal Deposit Insurance Corporation, insures the customers of financial institutions when there is a failure, either because of fraud or because of poor business decisions. Federal insurers had to spend over $50 billion to handle just the failures of savings and loan associations between 1983 and 1987. Most of the losses were in Texas and California. To minimize further failures and the need for more payments, the federal government increased its regulatory activity, prompting a call by bankers and state officials alike to reverse inactivity by states.[20] As with other areas, state regulation is preferred to allow for response to unique regional needs and opportunities.

It may appear that reformers were not serious and were engaged in symbolic action only. That may be true, although it is just as likely that state governments set out to reduce regulation but ran into all the special concerns that provided support for specific rules and agencies.

SUMMARY AND CONCLUSIONS

This chapter explores the institutions and issues of government regulation. State government regulation includes formal processes and informal relationships. Sometimes the target of regulation actually is dominant over the regulatory agencies. Federal-state relationships between regulators are increasingly characterized by more state discretion. For those who must comply, the diversity among states can be burdensome.

This chapter also includes brief descriptions of theoretical perspectives used by scholars to describe the political dynamics of regulation. Scholars lack consensus. That thoughtful and careful scholars differ on the perspective they find most useful is more a reflection of the diversity of regulatory agencies than a criticism of the scholars. Few of the subjects covered in this text lend themselves so neatly to a presentation of alternative schools of thought. The discussion of regulation provides an opportunity to remind readers of the contributions of scholarship as well as the policies of state government. If no single theory explains all regulatory agencies, it is unlikely that a single theory can usefully be applied to all institutions and processes and policy areas of state government.

REFERENCES

1. Alan Stone, *Regulation and Its Alternatives* (Washington, DC: Congressional Quarterly Press, 1982), 10.
2. Jonathan R. Hughes. *Social Control in the Colonial Economy* (Charlottesville: University of Virginia Press, 1976).
3. Gabriel Kolko, *Railroads and Regulation, 1877–1916* (Princeton, NJ: Princeton University Press, 1965), 217–21.
4. Douglas D. Anderson, "State Regulation of Electric Utilities," in James Q. Wilson, ed., *The Politics of Regulation* (New York: Basic Books, 1980), pp. 5–16.
5. *The Book of the States, 1986-87* (Lexington, KY: Council of State Governments, 1987), p. 380.
6. Michael D. Reagan, *Regulation. The Politics of Policy* (Boston: Little, Brown, 1987), pp. 20–22.
7. Ibid., p. 191.
8. Frank J. Thompson and Michael J. Scicchitano, "State Implementation Effort and Federal Regulatory Policy: The Case of Occupational Safety and Health," *Journal of Politics*, Vol. 47, No. 4 (1985), 689.
9. Reagan, *Regulation*, pp. 191–92.
10. Samuel Huntington, "The Marasmus of the ICC: The Commission, the Railroads and the Public Interest," *Yale Law Journal* (Apr. 1952), 467–509; Marver Bernstein, *Regulating Business by Independent Commission* (Princeton, NJ: Princeton University Press, 1955).
11. Wilson, ed., *Politics of Regulation*.
12. William T. Gormley, Jr., *The Politics of Public Utility Regulation* (Pittsburgh: University of Pittsburgh Press, 1983).
13. Erwin G. Krasnow and Lawrence D. Longley, *The Politics of Broadcast Regulation* (New York: St. Martin's Press, 1973).
14. *Serving Two Masters* (Washington, DC: Common Cause, 1976); Gormley, *Public Utility Regulation*; and Paul Quirk, *Industry Influence in Federal Regulatory Agencies* (Princeton, NJ: Princeton University Press, 1981).
15. Surveys by the Gallup Organization, Apr. 25–May 10, 1987, and NBC News/*Wall Street Journal*, Mar. 15–17 and Oct. 25–27, 1987, cited in James A. Barnes, "Government as Villain. Has the Era Ended?" *Government Executive*, (Jan. 1988), 15.
16. "Regulators and the Polls," *Regulation*, Nov./Dec. 1978, pp. 10–12, 54.
17. Robert P. Behn, "False Dawn of the Sunset Laws," *Public Interest*, Vol. 49 (Fall 1977), 103–18.
18. John T. Scholz, "State Regulatory Reform and Federal Regulation," in *Regulation*, Vol. 10 (May/June, 1986), 347–59.
19. Bill Bancroft, "Banking on Deregulation Can Be Hazardous to Your State's Financial Institutions," *Governing*, (Jan. 1988), 47.
20. Ibid., pp. 44–49.

MANAGING THE STATE

CHAPTER 15

Budgeting and Financial Management

Budgets clearly represent programmed resource commitments. They respond to the old adage, "Put your money where your mouth is." Budgets cut through rhetoric and depict real fiscal priorities. Besides being fiscal plans, budgets are also "political scorecards,"[1] separating winners from losers; for if politics is really concerned with who gets what, when, and how, as Harold Lasswell[2] has suggested, budgets show the results in concrete terms. That is not to suggest that the political contest does not continue after the budget is enacted into law, for it definitely does. Budget participants will seek as much latitude as possible to see that the budget is executed in ways that are most consistent with their interests. But that latitude is constrained by the budget's structure and composition as well as by expressions of legislative intent. Funds are appropriate for limited purposes, and budget controls exist to ensure that they are employed as approved. This chapter looks at the relationship between budget making and budget control and examines several issues related to sound state financial management.

THE STATE BUDGET

If you ask a number of different state officials what the size of their state budget is, you might get different answers. One answer might refer to the general fund budget, and the other to the all-funds budget. The *general fund* budget includes all the budgeted expenditures that are financed from general-purpose state revenues, derived primarily in most states from the sales tax, the personal income tax, and the corporate income tax. The general fund budget excludes budgeted expenditures financed from segregated revenues. Major examples of the latter include motor fuel tax revenues and vehicle registration fees, which are deposited in a segregated highway fund, and boat registration or hunting and fishing license fees, which are deposited in a conservation fund. In the former example, the revenues must be used exclusively to finance highway construction and maintenance; in the latter, they can be used only for natural resource and conservation purposes. In both cases, segregated revenues may not be used for any nondesignated general purpose, such as for paying higher salaries to university professors or increasing the level of state aid to local school districts. Such expenditures would have to be covered by general fund revenues and be authorized by *appropriations* (grants of legislative authority for government to spend up to a specific dollar amount for a specified purpose).

Segregated funds are usually based on the user fee principle, that those who derive the benefits from government services should pay for them. A motorist pays an excise tax when purchasing motor fuel, which, in turn, is dedicated to road repair. As the theory goes, the general taxpayer who does not own a motor vehicle should not be expected to finance others' highway use. Likewise, people who do not hunt or fish should not be expected to pay for the wildlife stocking and conservation services provided by state natural resources staffs.

The general and segregated fund accounts are kept separately on the state's budget information system and financial operations ledger. Budgeted appropriations authorized for a given fiscal year from one fund, if unspent, lapse back into the balance of that fund. For example, if highway construction costs are much lower than expected in a given year, allowing all the planned work to be completed at a lower than expected cost, the resulting unspent appropriation would carry forward in the fund's balance, to be drawn against for next year's approved expenditures. The unspent appropriation for highway construction could not be used for any other general purpose, unless the legislature officially transferred the balance from the highway fund to the general fund. Then it would be available for appropriation to a nonhighway use.

Appropriations are identified with a specific fund. Four appropriation types are commonly found among the states: general purpose revenue (GPR), segregated revenue, federal revenue, and program revenue. The GPR appropriations are deposited in and drawn against the general fund, and segregated appropriations are deposited in and drawn against the appropriate segregated fund. But federal appropriations can be drawn against either the general fund or a segregated fund, depending on the way they were deposited. For example, grant funds from the Federal Highway Administration are deposited in the state highway fund, to be dedicated to highway work, and become part of that segregated fund. On the other hand, federal revenues for nonsegregated purposes are deposited in the general fund. Examples include federal financial support for the large Medicaid and AFDC programs. In both cases the state revenues are kept track of separately from the federal revenues deposited in the fund. Similarly, program revenues can be deposited in different funds. Program revenues usually consist of receipts from the sale of goods or services by state government agencies. For example, a general services agency may auction used fleet vehicles. The proceeds of that sale are usually treated as program revenue and deposited in the general fund. But if the state highway vehicles are sold, the proceeds would be applied to the segregated highway fund.

Some states, as an exception to general practice, further break out such revolving service accounts from the general fund, establishing separate special funds to cover enterprise operations (such as prison industries or state vehicle fleets) or internal service operations (such as general stores, central duplicating services, or central computing services). In addition, states can also establish special funds to segregate debt-service accounts and those devoted to trust bequests. Again, however, the usual practice is to keep such operations as separate accounts within the general fund or the appropriate revenue-based segregated fund.

Budget comparisons among the states most often use general fund budget figures, exclusive of federally funded budgeted expenditures. State general fund budgets involve large sums of money, ranging from $396 million in South Dakota to $32.7 billion in California for the 1987–1988 fiscal year. (See Table 15.1.)

Governors, legislators, and their fiscal staffs worry most about bringing the general fund into balance—a legal requirement in all states except Vermont. In some states, however, a "temporary" deficit is technically allowable in a given year if extenuating circumstances make it unavoidable, but the deficit must be corrected in the immediately following year. Failure to match revenues and expenditures requires a tax increase, expenditure reduction, or a combination of the two. General fund-based tax increases are politically worrisome because their major revenue sources come from the highly visible personal income and sales taxes, as was discussed in detail in Chapter 13. On the other hand, if governors and legislators foreswear tax increases, and the prospective revenue shortfall is large, major reductions in budgeted expenditures may be required—an action inviting political opposition from supporters of the programs identified for reduction.

TABLE 15.1. FY 1988 STATE GENERAL FUND BUDGETS (IN $ MILLIONS)

State	Budget Amount	Ending Balance
Alabama	2,694	0
Alaska	2,077	(270)
Arizona	2,610	14
Arkansas	1,558	0
California	32,772	1,086
Colorado	2,107	131
Connecticut	4,917	0
Delaware	1,041	37

continued

TABLE 15.1., continued

State	Budget Amount	Ending Balance
Florida	8,629	0
Georgia	5,782	0
Hawaii*	1,860	121
Idaho	657	0
Illinois	10,552	200
Indiana	3,623	169
Iowa	2,372	14
Kansas	1,866	160
Kentucky	3,217	13
Louisiana*	3,866	(372)
Maine	1,164	20
Maryland	4,872	18
Massachusetts	7,067	43
Michigan	6,464	14
Minnesota*	5,446	181
Mississippi	1,613	1
Missouri*	3,625	0
Montana	372	11
Nebraska	917	62
Nevada*	586	12
New Hampshire	546	42
New Jersey	10,087	269
New Mexico	1,514	77
New York	25,275	185
North Carolina	5,978	0
North Dakota*	518	6
Ohio	10,904	156
Oklahoma	2,203	117
Oregon*	1,792	81
Pennsylvania	10,461	1
Rhode Island	1,245	26
South Carolina*	2,864	0
South Dakota	396	13
Tennessee	3,032	76
Texas	8,672	0
Utah	1,371	0
Vermont	490	29
Virginia	5,046	2
Washington	4,984	136
West Virginia	1,520	(22)
Wisconsin	5,308	124
Wyoming	426	8
Total	228,958	2,991

*Budget Stabilization Fund is included with ending balance.
(Source: Fiscal Survey of the States [Washington, DC: National Association of State Budget Officers, Sept. 1987], p. 32.)

The Budget Bill

In the preceding section we discussed the various ways of looking at what constitutes the state budget. But we still do not have a feel for what the budget is or how it is organized. We normally speak of the *executive budget* or the governor's budget. Such references connote "oneness," as if there is one document presented to the legislature by the governor. We also speak of the governor's "budget book," further reinforcing that idea. However, just as there are several different ways of conceptualizing what constitutes the state budget, there are a number of different documents that describe its contents.

Like any other legislative proposal, the executive budget has to be reduced to bill form if it is to be enacted into law. And, as was discussed in Chapter 8, only legislators or legislative committees can introduce bills. Thus the budget bill or bills must be introduced by the legislative leadership or by the respective fiscal committee, either as a constitutional or statutory requirement or as a customary courtesy to the governor where no such legal requirement exists.

What does a budget bill look like? Its appearance is variously shaped by state law and administrative practice. In those states where the budget bill is limited to appropriations exclusively, the bill consists of a series of appropriations schedules, with totals summed along organizational or program lines. Table 15.2 provides an example of such an appropriations schedule. In this example, Correctional Services represents a program within the Department of Correction's budget structure. As is the case with many state executive budgets, the program structure follows the agency's organizational structure. The correctional program, in this example, is divided into four subprograms, each paralleling the department's divisional structure, including adult institutions, juvenile institutions, parole supervision, and general administration. (See Figure 15.1.) However, the appropriations, in this case, are identified only at the program level.

The alpha characters, at the far left of Table 15.2, represent designations of the various distinct appropriations through which the department receives its spending authority. The second column includes a brief narrative description of each appropriation, and the third column indicates its source of revenue. Notice that (a) through (f) are General Purpose Revenue (GPR) appropriations; (g) through (j) are program revenue (fee or extramural support); (k) is devoted to revolving fund accounts (program revenue service); and (m) through (o) are devoted to federally financed expenditures. In addition, though not shown in this example, an appropriation can be designated as a segregated revenue appropriation, whether the revenue source is state or federal. The fourth column indicates the appropriation type, denoting the duration of the appropriation. *A* indicates that the temporal limitation on the appropriation is *annual*—that the appropriation is made for a single fiscal year and that any amounts remaining in the appropriation at the year's end lapse back to the general fund. *B* signifies that the appropriation is *biennial,* for the two-year biennial period. And as with annual appropriations, unspent balances lapse at the end of the fiscal period, in this case the biennium. *S* signifies *sum sufficient,* that the state treasury will make good whatever amounts are required to meet program costs. With sum sufficients (analogous to entitlements in the federal budget), the appropriation figures are only estimates of expected spending and are not treated as binding sum-certain appropriations. When employed among the states, they are most often used to cover debt service or public utility costs. Finally, C stands for *continuing appropriation,* meaning that the amounts available in the appropriation continue to roll forward without any temporal limitation, most frequently the case with federal appropriations.

As is apparent from the example, general correctional operations make up by far the largest share of state GPR included in the budget for the Department of Corrections. The (a) appropriation is labeled "General Program Operations," and its funds can be used for just any purpose related to correctional operations. Appropriation (dd), however, can only be used to pay for "special living arrangements" for prisoners placed on work release in metropolitan areas, and agencies are legally proscribed from spending monies for purposes other than those designated in the appropriation authority. Nor can agencies transfer resources from one appropriation to another; that is usually the legislature's legal prerogative, although the legislature may delegate that authority to its fiscal committee(s) when the full legislature is not in session.

As noted previously, the (a) appropriation covers all the department's general program operations not covered by any of the other appropriations in the schedule. However, as also discussed earlier, the correctional program has four distinct subprograms. An alternative way of organizing the appropriations structure would have been to establish a separate general program operations appropriation to coincide with the subprogram structure, namely, one each for adult institutions, juvenile institutions, parole supervision, and general departmental administration. Had this approach been followed, the appropriations may have been designated (aa), (ab), (ac), and (ad). (But as is apparent from the schedule, alpha designations do not have to follow a strict subalphabetical sequence.) Following this alternative approach would limit the flexibility now enjoyed by the department, by segmenting appropriations for adult and juvenile operations, and thereby limiting the agency's ability to reprogram spending authority.

Beyond an appropriations schedule, the budget bill may contain specific prescriptions and proscriptions regarding agency spending. As an example of prescription, the legislature might designate that a certain bridge be replaced, using appropriated highway funds. By including such a specific designation in the budget bill, the legislature is limiting the highway department's discretion to select the projects that will be financed by appropriated funds. The department may replace other bridges during the fiscal year if the appropriations stretch that far; but given the clear expression of legislative intent, the department would be required to include the legislatively directed bridge project among them. Proscription, on the other hand, might involve a legislative mandate that no funds be spent on an expanded job-training program until the state labor agency submits a report to the legislature evaluating the results of a pilot program.

TABLE 15.2. SAMPLE APPROPRIATIONS SCHEDULE

Statute, Agency, and Purpose		Source	Type	1987–1988	1988–1989
20.435(1)	Correctional Services				
(a)	General program operations	GPR	A	101,663,900	108,625,200
(af)	Institutional repair and maintenance	GPR	A	941,600	1,055,400
(ag)	Intergovernmental corrections agreements	GPR	A	6,045,500	1,641,800
(b)	Juvenile correctional services	GPR	A	276,500	276,500
(c)	Reimbursement claims of counties containing state institutions	GPR	S	106,100	106,100
(d)	Purchased services for offenders	GPR	A	891,000	1,351,800
(dd)	Special living arrangements	GPR	A	1,873,500	2,334,000
(e)	Principal repayment and interest	GPR	S	14,579,400	19,155,900
(ef)	Lease rental payments	GPR	S	271,500	271,500
(f)	Utilities and heating	GPR	A	4,556,400	5,762,700
(g)	Probationer and parolee loan fund	PR	A	26,400	27,000
(h)	Administration of restitution	PR	A	137,200	137,900
(hm)	Juvenile correctional services	PR	A	14,800,200	14,904,100
(ho)	Foster care	PR	A	2,476,000	2,577,700
(i)	Gifts and grants	PR	C	22,300	23,400

(jp)	Correctional officer training	PR	A	608,700	606,500
(kk)	Institutional operations and charges	PR-S	A	3,885,400	3,984,100
(km)	Prison industries	PR-S	A	6,861,100	8,063,100
(ko)	Prison industries principal and interest	PR-S	S	10,100	90,000
(kx)	Interagency and intraagency programs	PR-S	C	1,296,900	1,458,900
(ky)	Interagency and Intraagency aids	PR-S	C	3,500	3,600
(kz)	Interagency and intraagency local assistance	PR-S	C	0	0
(m)	Federal project operations	FED	C	1,110,000	0
(n)	Federal program operations	FED	C	2,650,000	2,800,000
(o)	Federal aid; foster care	FED	C	282,200	297,800

(3) Program Totals

General purpose revenues	131,205,400	140,580,900
Program revenue	30,409,900	32,174,100
Other	18,070,800	18,276,600
Service	12,056,900	13,599,700
Federal revenue	4,042,200	3,097,800

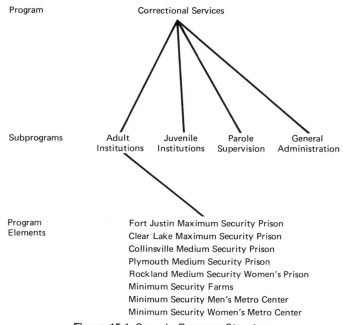

Program   Correctional Services

Subprograms   Adult   Juvenile   Parole   General
                  Institutions   Institutions Supervision Administration

Program   Fort Justin Maximum Security Prison
Elements   Clear Lake Maximum Security Prison
                         Collinsville Medium Security Prison
                         Plymouth Medium Security Prison
                         Rockland Medium Security Women's Prison
                         Minimum Security Farms
                         Minimum Security Men's Metro Center
                         Minimum Security Women's Metro Center

Figure 15.1 Sample Program Structure

The Executive Budget Book

Budget bills themselves are not the documents most commonly turned to by members of the public trying to unravel the executive budget's content. Instead the executive budget book is the most widely used budget guide. Although its form varies among the states, the executive budget book has several consistent elements. It usually contains tables providing summary information for the budget as a whole, including the total dollars and positions requested and/or recommended by source of funds for each state agency. State law in several states requires that the budget book specifically include all agency requests and their associated gubernatorial recommendations. In most states, however, only the governor's endorsed budget need be included in the executive budget. In either case, it is still the job of the state budget office to organize the contents of the executive budget book and to decide how much and what kinds of information to include.

As Table 15.3 shows, most state budget offices include the governor's budget message as part of the budget book, although it is distributed as a separate document in twelve states. The budget book also often includes brief justification for the governor's recommendations, but more detailed supporting information can variously be found in separately issued executive budget policy papers, which are published as a companion to the budget book itself. Where employed, these papers—often bound in a single volume—discuss the major policy issues raised by the governor's recommendations and may contain assessments of competing alternatives.

The state budget office may also prepare a more condensed budget-in-brief. The budget-in-brief, rather than providing detailed descriptions of budget recommendations on an agency-by-agency basis, is written to give an overview of the governor's budget. It contains summary information on the budget as a whole and may also include brief summaries by agency. In addition, not only does it often include the governor's budget message, but also it highlights the major emphasis and policy priorities underlying the governor's recommendations. In many respects it is a public relations document, placing the executive budget in a perspective most favorable to the administration.

The budget-in-brief, produced in much greater volume than the larger budget book, usually serves as the most popular summary of the governor's executive budget. It is frequently what gets sent to individuals or organizations who request a copy of the "governor's budget." In contrast, the executive budget book serves as a more detailed reference for those who are intimately involved in the budgetary process. Top agency officials, state budget office staffs, gubernatorial aides, legislators and their staffs, and interest group representatives—all who work at a greater level of detail—tend to rely on the executive budget book.

Other Executive Budget Summaries

In addition to documents prepared by the executive branch, legislative staff agencies usually prepare their own summaries of the governor's recommendations. They can range from descriptive summaries of these recommendations, essentially paralleling the information in, and organization of, the executive budget book, to analyses of budget alternatives. In fifteen states, legislative fiscal staffs actually formulate a suggested alternative legislative budget.[3]

Legislative staffs also often produce ongoing summaries of the changes to the executive budget made at each step in the process of legislative budget review. These documents usually contain brief narrative descriptions of the legislative changes, along with identification of their fiscal effects.

Interest groups frequently produce their own formal written analyses of the executive budget. Their focus is generally parochial, emphasizing how the budget will affect their organizational interests. In so doing, the authors may attempt to show how their treatment relates to the overall priorities of the governor's recommendations. As an example, the teachers' lobby, often organized into a state "educational association," will probably concentrate its attention on how the executive budget affects public instruction, most broadly, and teachers' benefits, more narrowly. Primary emphasis might well be given to how the executive budget affects state aid to local school districts because increased state school aid helps to take pressure off the local property tax, creating an environment in which local district officials might feel less constrained in negotiating contract agreements relatively favorable to teachers' unions. Therefore, in either supporting the governor's recommendations or calling for increased state support, the association's argu-

TABLE 15.3. BUDGET BOOK CONTENT

State	Governor's Message	Budget Summary			Narrative		
		General Fund	Other State Funds	Federal Funds	Program Description	Justification	Position Information
Alabama	X	X	X	A	X	X	—
Alaska	N/R	N/R	N/R	N/R	N/R	N/R	N/R
Arizona	—	X	X	N/A	X	X	X
Arkansas	X	X	X	A	X	X	X
California	X	X	X	A/NA	X	X	X
Colorado	X	X	X	A/NA	X	X	X
Connecticut	X	X	X	A	X	—	X
Delaware	N/R	N/R	N/R	N/R	N/R	N/R	N/R
Florida	X	X	X	A/NA	X	X	X
Georgia	—	X	X	A	X	X	X
Hawaii	X	X	X	A	X	X	X
Idaho	X	X	X	A/NA	X	X	X
Illinois	—	X	X	A	X	—	—
Indiana	—	X	X	NA	—	—	—
Iowa	—	X	X	A/NA	X	—	X
Kansas	—	X	X	A/NA	X	X	X
Kentucky	X	X	X	A	X	—	—
Louisiana	X	X	X	A	X	X	X
Maine	X	X	X	NA	X	X	—
Maryland	X	X	X	A	X	—	X
Massachusetts	X	X	X	NA	X	—	X
Michigan	X	X	X	A	X	X	X
Minnesota	X	X	X	A/NA	X	X	X
Mississippi	N/R	N/R	N/R	N/R	N/R	N/R	N/R
Missouri	X	X	X	A	X	X	X

State						
Montana	X	X	A	X	X	X
Nebraska	X	X	A	—	—	—
Nevada	—	—	—	X	X	X
New Hampshire	N/R	N/R	N/R	N/R	N/R	N/R
New Jersey	X	X	A/NA	X	—	X
New Mexico	N/R	N/R	N/R	N/R	N/R	N/R
New York	X	X	NA	X	—	X
North Carolina	—	X	A	X	—	—
North Dakota	X	X	A	X	X	—
Ohio	—	X	A	X	—	X
Oklahoma	X	X	—	X	—	X
Oregon	X	X	A	X	X	—
Pennsylvania	X	X	A/NA	X	X	X
Rhode Island	X	X	A/NA	X	—	X
South Carolina	—	—	NA	X	X	X
South Dakota	X	X	A	X	—	X
Tennessee	—	X	A	X	—	X
Texas	X	X	A	—	—	X
Utah	X	X	A	X	X	X
Vermont	X	X	A	X	—	X
Virginia	X	X	A	X	X	X
Washington	X	X	A/NA	X	X	X
West Virginia	X	X	A/NA	X	X	X
Wisconsin	—	X	NA	X	X	X
Wyoming	X	X	A	—	—	—

Code: X   = Yes
A   = Appropriated Federal Funds Only
NA = Nonappropriated Federal Funds Only
N/R = No Response

Source: Budgetary Processes in the States (Washington, DC: National Association of State Budget Officers, 1981), pp. 16–17.

ments might be cast in terms of both the resulting educational benefits of improved financial support and the benefits of property tax relief. On the other hand, if the executive budget emphasized income tax relief, resulting in lower than hoped-for increases in state school aid, the teachers' union might press its case that the governor's recommendations are misguided—that high property taxes pose a greater public problem than does the current income tax level. These budget analyses thus are used not only to inform members about how the proposed state budget relates to their interests but also often to provide members with arguments that can be used in contacting their elected representatives.

For those who wish to be informed, ample summaries of the executive budget recommendations are available, ranging from comprehensive reviews to narrowly focused snapshots. But once the budget is enacted into law, it is the budget bill that holds the greatest prominence because it serves as the basis for budget execution.

BUDGET EXECUTION
AND FINANCIAL MANAGEMENT

Once the budget has been enacted into law, the execution phase of the budgetary process begins. After final legislative approval of the budget, the state budget office informs each agency of its authorized budget for the coming fiscal year. State agencies in most states then have the opportunity to make adjustments to the legislatively approved budget as they develop their *operating budgets*. However, laws in most states prohibit the executive branch from transferring funds between appropriations without legislative approval. Allowable adjustments characteristically involve transfers between program elements and objects of expenditure. In our corrections example, transfers between program elements might involve the reallocation of expenditure authority from one state prison to another within the same adult institutions subprogram, reflecting recent changes in prison populations. An example of a transfer between objects of expenditure might include the movement of expenditure authority from the salary line to the supplies and services line. Most frequently used major objects include salaries, fringe benefits, supplies and services, and capital equipment.

Once approved by the state budget office, agency operating budgets become the basis for allotments. *Allotments* give state agencies the authority to spend up to a certain amount, in designated budget categories, within a specified period. They may cover the entire fiscal year or may be broken down into quarters. Quarterly allotments allow the state budget office to apportion spending authority in ways that conserve the appropriated resources, for example, by limiting would-be heavy agency spending at the end of the fiscal year designed to prevent the lapse of unspent authority.

When requested operating budget transfers stray from the routine, the state budget office assesses whether they are consistent with legislative intent. When they are, the state budget office normally approves them. However, when serious questions about legislative intent arise, top executive budget officials commonly consult with legislative leaders before granting approval. When it appears that approval would be in clear conflict with documented legislative intent, the state budget office usually demurs.

Once budget authority is allotted, the agencies are restricted in their ability to move budgeted funds around. Even with the more flexible appropriations structure shown in Table 15.2, laws in many states prohibit transfers between subprograms (adult prisons to parole supervision in the corrections example) without legislative approval. Legislative approval can take one of two forms: The entire legislature must approve such transfers, or that authority can be delegated to the legislature's fiscal committee. In those states where the executive branch is legally empowered to make transfers between subprograms, that authority may still be restricted by law, as transfers may be permitted only up to a certain percentage of the appropriation amount, most often 5 or 10 percent; above that level, legislative approval becomes necessary. The legislature may delegate its midyear approval authority to the governor, to the state budget office, or to the agencies themselves. Yet where the governor is given the authority, its actual exercise is usually delegated to the state budget office. In a few states the legislature gives the agencies the authority to make transfers directly, and they only have to report transfers to the state budget office retrospectively.

In all these cases in which controls are placed on intersubprogram transfers, there needs to be some way of breaking down and keeping track of budgeted subprogram amounts, even though the legislatively approved appropriations schedule is structured at the program level. To meet this need, the state budget office commonly requires that agencies apportion all program-level appropriations across subprogram lines both in their development of budget requests and in subsequent operating budgets. One way of keeping track of the subprogram detail is to assign numeric designations to the subprogram appropriations breakdowns.

Again, as an illustration, the $101 million appropriated for general program operations may be broken down as follows: $51 million for adult institutions, $22 million for juvenile institutions, $13 million for parole supervision, and $15 million for general administrative overhead. Following a common numbering sequence, the amount for adult institutions might be designated 101; the amount for juvenile, 201; the amount for parole supervision, 301; and the amount for general administration, 401. In this schema, the first digit provides a numerical reference to each of the four subprograms, and the last two digits, 01, indicate a tie to the (a) appropriation. Thus, throughout the budgetary process, the numeric framework serves as the basis for tracking appropriation changes, right up to the final approved appropriation levels. As an illustration, should the legislature reduce the governor's recommendation for corrections and specify that all the reduction should come out of adult corrections, the (a) appropriation would be reduced by the full amount of the legislative change, but all the reduction would be taken from the 101 numeric subdivision. Then, during the fiscal year, the agency might elect to request a transfer of funds from another subprogram if it believed that insufficient resources remained in the adult institutions' budget to support program requirements.

Here again we get into the often thorny issue of legislative intent. The legislature, in this example, specifically directed the nature of the reduction from the governor's recommendations. Obviously, the legislature can subsequently reverse that decision by amending the budget act. But it gets a little more tricky when the authority to approve midyear subprogram transfers is delegated to a committee of the legislature or to the state budget office. In the former case, although the committee possesses the legal authority to approve such a transfer and thereby modify the full legislature's expression of intent, the committee may be disinclined to do so if the issue is at all controversial, fearing a backlash among legislators at large. At least, in such instances, the committee chairperson would probably want to consult with the chamber's leadership. Likewise, where the state budget office has been delegated approval authority by law, it might put itself on thin ice with the legislature if it were to permit the transfer. If it does, the legislature might next time include a restriction on such administrative transfer right into the appropriations bill itself (assuming that state statutes permit such narrative restrictions in the appropriations bill, and most do). Then the state budget office's hands would be tied. Moreover, frequent use of such prohibitions written into appropriations acts would tend to undermine the state budget office's authority for budget control.

Preaudit Controls

Upon legislative approval of the state budget, unless agencies are forced to live within its terms, the entire budget review and approval process would become meaningless. If agencies can overspend appropriations and ignore other spending constraints related to subprograms and objects of expenditure, the legislature would have no assurance that the budget would be executed as approved. Therefore, in addition to the procedures established for the review and approval of budget adjustments within the fiscal year, controls are designed to ensure that the actual expenditure of funds is consistent with the approved budget. And where expenditures are not consistent, a means has to exist to prevent them from being executed.

Thus even after allotments have been granted to state agencies, giving them the general authority to commit funds up to the appropriated level, the agency must submit requests to spend the resources. The requests are compared to the agency's approved budget to ensure that the proposed expenditures are authorized and that sufficient funds are available in the agency's budget. If the requests are approved, encumbrances are entered into the agency's computerized financial books to indicate that the previous total is no longer available for commitment.

Oversight of the preaudit function is normally an exclusive executive branch function, but it is not often the state budget office's responsibility. Although that office develops the executive budget and often exercises the authority to approve designated budget transfers during the course of the fiscal year, the preaudit function is usually carried out by a separate executive branch office. That office, however, might be part of the same department that houses the state budget office. An example would be an umbrella state administration department organizationally comprising budget, financial operations, purchasing, and state facilities management. In that arrangement, the preaudit function is usually found within the division or bureau of financial operations—the state's central accounting operation. Several states follow such an organizational pattern. In other states, independently elected controllers or auditors may be responsible for preaudit, alone or as an independent check on the executive branch. The rationale in the latter case is that electoral independence might better situate the auditor to protect the public purse, free from the direct authority of the governor or a gubernatorial appointee.

In practice, however, the state's central accounting agency may delegate the preaudit function to the larger and administratively sophisticated state agencies. The central audit authority then conducts selective reviews of how that delegated authority has been exercised, and if serious deficiencies are found, it can pull back the delegation.

Postaudit Controls

After the fiscal year's close, another set of audits are conducted. Their purpose is to ensure that budgeted funds were committed consistent with appropriations authority and legislative intent. These postaudits make up the final phase of budgeting. After the fiscal year has ended, the issue becomes one of determining whether agency activities were duly authorized and funds were expended within the approved limits. This focus requires an audit of the actual financial transactions completed within the fiscal year. But since an audit of every single transaction would be an overwhelming task, postauditors rely on samples.

Auditors may base their samples on a number of factors. They may regularly look at the most costly state programs; rely on indicators from computerized audits, when proportional relationships do not square with expectations; or rely on tips, when irregularities are alleged. But beyond the audit of individual transactions, postauditors also concern themselves with the nature of the accounting system itself—whether it conforms to prescribed accounting standards.

The administrative responsibility for postaudit is variously located among the states. It may be an executive or legislative responsibility, or both branches may be involved.

In addition to the traditional financial postaudit, state auditors—particularly those of the legislative branch—have increasingly become engaged in so-called *performance auditing*. Instead of focusing on actual expenditures and the adequacy of financial control procedures, performance auditing looks at how well state programs are accomplishing their prescribed goals and objectives. Is the legislature, which appropriated the funds, getting its money's worth? Are programs accomplishing what agency and gubernatorial representatives claimed they would? Are they being managed and operated efficiently? As such, performance auditing has largely become an activity of the legislative branch. Legislative audit shops comprise thirty-eight, or 57 percent, of the sixty-seven postaudit agencies among the states (counting those reporting directly or indirectly to the governor, to the legislature, or to an independently elected state official). However, looking only at the thirty-one agencies that conduct performance audits, legislative audit operations comprise twenty-six, or 84 percent, of the total.[4]

Performance auditing has become another tool of the legislature in competing with the executive branch over state policy making. As with financial postaudits, it represents a natural culmination of the process of budget making and execution. Given the size of the state budget, it is reasonable that the legislature would ask how things went according to the budget plan. Although it is the executive branch that largely controls budget execution during the course of the fiscal year, it is increasingly the legislature that assesses whether the promised "goods" have been delivered, and with what degree of efficiency. The audit reports, then, are made available to executive line agencies, state budget reviewers, and legislative fiscal committees and their staffs, where they may become significant input into the next budget cycle.

ISSUES IN BUDGETING AND FINANCIAL MANAGEMENT

Several issues confront state budgeteers and financial managers; some are perennial, whereas others are a product of current times. But they are all issues that today must be addressed as state policy makers chart the fiscal course of the state, reconciling revenue and spending policies, managing the public purse, and ensuring that budgets are executed consistent with legislative intent.

Estimating Revenues and Expenditures

The state budget is a spending plan for a fiscal year or biennium. As discussed, it shows both the amounts and purposes of the budgeted expenditures over those periods. It also *presumes* the availability of revenues to finance the planned expenditures. Obviously, the amount of planned spending is constrained by the size of expected available revenue. Revenue estimating and budget planning go hand in hand.

State budget office staffs begin the expenditure-estimating process by working with state agencies to project the costs of continuing the existing state general fund budget, with no policy changes assumed. In that process they project likely changes in cost associated with inflation, employees' pay increases, debt service requirements, formula-driven local assistance payments, and changing numbers of public-assistance recipients.

At about the same time, usually in mid-fall, the state budget office or state revenue department—depending on the division of administrative responsibilities—projects the amount of revenues that can be expected in the coming fiscal period *without* any change in tax policy. Then, in comparing the cost-to-continue expenditure projections with estimated available revenues, the state budget director and the governor can get a picture of how much spending latitude they can expect. The difference between projected revenues and expenditures tells them what fiscal room may exist to fund new gubernatorial initiatives, reduce taxes, or pursue both objectives. However, in a deteriorating economy the projected balance can run into the red, pointing to the need for the governor to recommend budget cuts.

Accuracy is important in these projections, both on the expenditure and revenue sides. Errors of overestimate can create situations in which actual revenues prove to be insufficient to cover budgeted expenditures, necessitating subsequent budget cuts or tax increases *during* the course of the fiscal year or biennium. Or conversely, with underestimation, governors and legislators can find themselves in the position of sitting on unexpectedly high revenue balances, having lost the opportunity to initiate new programs or expand existing high-priority programs.

The degree of sophistication employed in making these projections varies among the states. Most states today rely on multiple regression or econometric modeling to project revenues. Multiple regression models project the expected effects that changes in such independent variables as gross domestic product, personal income, and unemployment will have on state tax revenues. Economic models tend to be more sophisticated, involving efforts to model the national economy, adjusting national economic projections to the state level, and accounting for the interactive effects of often several hundred indicators on state revenues.

Cost-to-continue projections generally rely on less sophisticated approaches, although economic models may be used to estimate changes in public-assistance caseloads and unemployment compensation claims. Often, however, state budget office staffs themselves estimate the increased costs of those programs to which they are assigned. They may apply standard inflationary factors or use commodity-specific factors. For compensation adjustments, the budget director may use a reasonably expected "plug" figure for the first pass; then, after getting a better sense of what the likely "no tax increase/cost-to-continue" balance looks like, employee, compensation can be scaled back or increased, depending on the political climate at that time.

Revenue and expenditure projections can be a precarious business, especially on the revenue side. One thing is known for sure from the start: Revenue projects are always going to be in error; it is just a matter of to what extent they will miss the mark. Given the time between initial revenue estimates, which serve as the basis for the governor's executive budget recommendations, and the end of the prospective fiscal period, nineteen to thirty-one months will have elapsed, depending on whether the state is on an annual or biennial budget. A lot can happen to the economy during the intervening period that can significantly alter the revenue and expenditure picture.

Because of the time dimensions involved, another revenue projection is usually made while the state budget is being considered by the legislature, but that reprojection puts the estimate only a few months closer to the start of the fiscal year. This time-lag problem is particularly acute with biennial budgeting, frequently requiring the legislature to make adjustments for the second year.

Revenue and expenditure estimating can be employed as a tool of political strategy. An administration that wants to hold the line on public spending might estimate revenues conservatively. Similarly, that administration might also project the costs of budget continuation on the high side, leaving little room for the legislature to pursue new spending initiatives.

Legislatures, however, have also gotten into the revenue-estimating business. To achieve some independence from the executive branch's forecasts, legislative staffs in thirty states make separate revenue estimates.[5] Most also make independent assessments of the costs of budget continuation. Legislatures, like governors, can use revenue estimates to their political advantage. They can come in with initial estimates lower than the administration's, inviting the governor to be a little more careful about spending; then, after the budget is in the legislative arena, subsequent estimates may "find" additional revenues that can be used to finance new legislative spending.

Managing Cash Flow

Revenue collection and expenditures do not coincide with each other during the course of the fiscal year. In managing state fiscal resources, executive branch financial administrators have to make sure that there is enough cash available to pay the bills when they become due. On the other hand, they do not want to have too much cash on hand in excess of what they need to meet their financial obligations, for cash accounts yield lower rates of return than do other less liquid investments as bonds and stocks. The key for financial managers is to increase investment yields to the maximum extent possible, while ensuring that just enough cash is available to pay the bills.

The optimal strategy to increase revenue yield involves speeding up tax and other revenue collections and slowing cash outflows to the extent feasible and appropriate. But if state payments are too slow in coming, private vendors, clients, and other units of government can be quick to voice their displeasure, even taking their case to their state legislator. Such pressures for timely payment have prompted several state legislatures to pass laws stipulating maximum time limits for the payment of state agency-incurred debts. In addition, state statutes often specify payment dates for major local assistance payments such as state revenue sharing, school aid, and transportation aid. Since these payments are most often made quarterly, state cash managers know in advance when funds have to be available. Hence they can anticipate the need to move funds out of higher interest-bearing investments into a cash account for payment.

Besides implementing an investment strategy that optimally mixes high yield with necessary liquidity, financial managers also want to ensure that payments received by the state earn as much interest as possible. Two factors relate to interest yield: the timeliness of deposit and the rate of interest earned. Regarding the former, states have increasingly adopted the practice of using *lock-box* deposits, whereby those owing the state money remit their payments not to a state agency office but directly to the state's bank account. There bank employees, for a fee, open the envelopes, deposit any enclosed checks, and enter the payment data at the same time. Then, after the funds have been deposited, bank employees send the payment records to the appropriate state agencies for posting. This method of direct payment eliminates the time traditionally required for agencies to handle the correspondence, update their records, and send the remittances to the central finance office, and for that office to transmit the checks to the state's bank account, thereby greatly reducing the period in which receipts generate no interest.

States have addressed the second factor, the *rate* of return, by pooling financial resources, across funds, for investment purposes and using these larger cash reservoirs to obtain higher bids or negotiated interest rates. With this practice fewer banks get a piece of a state's investment action, but yields are maximized.

Determining an Acceptable Budget Balance

In putting together a budget that balances revenues and expenditures, state budget makers must decide what constitutes an acceptable and affordable year-end general fund balance. Given the potential volatility of revenue and expenditure fluctuations, governors and legislatures commonly retain a limited revenue cushion as a hedge against normal uncertainty. But what constitutes an appropriate balance? According to Wall Street bond analysts, it is over 5 percent of budgeted general fund expenditures.[6] At that level, the bond industry feels comfortable that states have adequate fiscal flexibility to deal with most unforeseen economic downturns and thereby protect their bondholders' interests. Most states, however, have considerably lower balances today.

The average appropriated general fund balance stood at only 1.3 percent of expenditures for the 1987–1988 fiscal year. As Table 15.4 illustrates, that level can be compared to 9 percent just eight years earlier—a drop that can be attributed in part to the taxpayer revolt that spread from the cities to the states in the early 1980s. Faced with mounting pressures over taxation and government spending— the very forces that swept Reagan into power at the national level—governors and legislatures in the 1980s became cautious about leaving too much cash in the kitty. They responded to the public's admonition that "if you don't need it, don't take it from us in the first place." For FY 1988, twenty-four states appropriated less than a 1 percent general fund balance, and only eight met the over 5 percent guideline.[7]

In addition to having year-end balances on which to rely, thirty-six states have created *budget stabilization,* or "rainy-day," funds.[8] These special funds are intended to provide a reserve that can be drawn against during unexpectedly bad economic times—situations for which normal budget balances provide an inadequate cushion. Budget stabilization funds are also intended to be cumulative, with legislatures socking revenues away each good year or biennium, to be accu-

TABLE 15.4. SIZE OF GENERAL FUND YEAR-END BALANCES FISCAL 1978 TO 1988*

Fiscal Year	Year-End Balances ($ in Billions)	Balance as a Percent of Expenditure
1988 est.	$3.0	1.3%
1987 est.	3.5	1.6
1986	5.4	2.6
1985	8.0	4.3
1984	5.6	3.3
1983	2.0	1.3
1982	4.5	3.0
1981	6.5	4.4
1980	11.8	9.0
1979	11.2	8.7
1978	8.9	8.6

*Does not include balances from budget stabilization funds. *(Source:* Fiscal Survey of the States *[Washington, DC: National Governors' Association and National Association of State Budget Officers, Sept. 1987], p. 22.)*

mulated and used in fiscal emergencies. But for rainy-day funds to function as intended, they need to build to amounts that can provide an effective margin of safety. In this respect they have not accomplished their objective.

For FY 1987, budget stabilization funds amounted to less than 1 percent of budgeted expenditures, and seven of the states creating such funds have yet to put any money into them. Both lingering taxpayer suspicion about overtaxation and economic slumps in several states have mitigated the use of rainy-day funds.

For a few states, however, budget stabilization funds have proven a godsend, helping to cushion them from major economic downturns. Alaska withdrew in FY 1987 $436 million from its stabilization fund, which was accumulated during the period of rising energy prices and associated taxes in the early 1980s, to augment its later declining energy tax revenues. Louisiana transferred $53 million into its general fund for the 1987–1988 fiscal year, also to replace lower than expected energy tax revenues. On the other hand, states enjoying comparatively better economic times have added to their stabilization funds, including Florida ($425 million for the 1987–1989 biennium), Connecticut ($122 million for FY 1987), Ohio ($108 million for FY 1988), and Massachusetts ($102 million for FY 1987). Yet on the whole, rainy-day funds still only averaged about 1 percent of expenditures for FY 1988.[9]

Capital Budgeting and Debt Management
States do not pay for all their expenses with current revenues. Major capital projects, such as the construction of university buildings, prisons, and major nonfeder-

ally aided highway or bridge projects, are usually funded from bond revenues. Bond purchasers in effect lend states the necessary funds to pay for these types of projects up front. The states, in turn, pledge to pay back to the bondholders the principal amount of the loan plus a guaranteed rate of interest.

States commonly use two forms of financing to pay off bondholders. The first, *general obligation bonds,* draws on general purpose revenues of the general fund. With this device, states pledge their "full faith and credit" behind their promise to pay off bondholders. Not only do states commit general purpose revenues to retire bonded indebtedness, but they also stipulate that bondholders will have "first claim" to available revenues. And because of the security that this commitment affords, prospective bond purchasers are willing to accept lower rates of return than they could get from less secure investments.

States also issue what are referred to as *revenue bonds.* Unlike general obligation bonds, the state treasury does not stand behind revenue bonds. Instead, future earmarked revenues are committed to debt retirement, to the extent that they are expected to be available. For example, a state may garner sufficient funds, through the sale of bonds, to construct a new toll road in a highly congested urban corridor. But rather than paying back the bondholders with general revenues, the state pledges the expected future toll receipts. No other revenue source is available as a backup should actual toll revenues fall significantly short of projections. The state, to attract investors, has to make a strong case that the toll revenue forecasts are so sound that prospective investors have little to worry about in making the investment. Because of this higher element of risk, revenue bonds carry higher rates of return than do general obligation bonds; but they also cost the states more in interest.

States can increase the security of revenue bonds by pledging other earmarked revenues in case user fees prove insufficient to retire the debt fully. Using the toll road example, the state might commit revenues from its segregated highway fund as an available contingency reserve. Bondholders then have the added assurance that even if fewer motorists use the tollway than estimated, the fund's motor fuel tax and vehicle registration revenues are available, if needed, to meet repayment obligations. Such improved security would surely reduce the bonds' yield and its corresponding costs to the state.

The interest rates that states have to pay in the bond market are very much influenced by bond ratings made by two major private Wall Street corporations: Moody's Investors Services and Standard and Poor's Corporation. In rating major bond offerings nationwide, the two corporations make judgments on their relative security. For general obligation bonds the raters look at the basic financial condition of the state as well as the relative quality of its financial management systems. For revenue bonds they assess the probability that sufficient revenues will be generated and available to repay the bondholders on schedule. Ratings range from AAA for the most secure bonds to C for the least secure. States with an AAA rating will pay the lowest interest rates and be best able to attract investors compared to those with lower ratings. As a rule of thumb, general obligation bonds usually win higher ratings than do revenue bonds, but very strong revenue bonds can carry higher ratings than general obligation bonds offered by a state deep in economic trouble.

The actual interest rates that bonds carry are determined either by public sale or by negotiation. Public sales involve would-be buyers who submit sealed bids, with the state selecting the most favorable offer. Negotiated sales begin with the state establishing a rate that it is willing to pay, then negotiating that rate with one or a few prospective buyers. Often with negotiated sales, large investment firms acquire the bonds and then resell them to smaller investors at a slightly lower rate of return.[10]

According to the principles of finance, long-term debt (ten to twenty-five years) is appropriately employed as an instrument to finance the acquisition of fixed assets whose useful lives extend well beyond the upcoming fiscal year or biennium. As the theory goes, future generations who will benefit from a capital project should help pay for it by contributing to the debt service costs. A new university complex, for example, will benefit the state and future students for years to come; therefore, in financing its construction with long-term general obligation bonds, future taxpayers (and students, through their tuition payments into the general fund) share the financial obligations.

Most states, thirty-seven to be exact, have a distinct capital budget.[11] Although the capital budget is commonly assembled by an executive agency, several states employ a joint executive-legislative committee, frequently chaired by the governor, that makes recommendations to the legislature on the amount and types of bonding that should be authorized in a given legislative session. In other states the governor makes recommendations to the legislature directly. Ultimately, in approving bond issues, the legislature makes decisions on the overall size of debt that the state is willing to undertake in the coming fiscal period, as well as on the specific projects that will be financed by the bonds.

In contrast to the bond authorization process, the legislature uses the standard budgetary process to appropriate funds to pay back bondholders for both new issues and outstanding obligations. Moreover, funds to maintain the facilities and equipment financed by bonding also must be appropriated through that same process. Thus state budgeteers have to be alert to the added operating costs associated with capital acquisition. Conversely, capital budget planners have to keep well informed on policy and program changes that are considered in the operating budget or in separate legislation. For example, if the governor recommends major modifications in parole eligibility laws, such changes could markedly affect future prison populations and therefore be an important element in the state's decision about whether to build a new correctional facility.

In addition to incurring long-term bonded indebtedness, states may go into debt through short-term borrowing, usually for one year or less. State financial managers normally resort to short-term borrowing only to cover unanticipated emergencies or temporary inability to meet statutorily required payment dates because of cash flow problems.

Short-term borrowing increased by only about 2 percent between FY 1970 and 1984, accounting for less than 2 percent of all state debt in FY 1984, down from 8 percent in 1970. In contrast, state long-term debt grew by 371 percent over the same fifteen-year period, rising from $38.9 billion to $183.2 billion, as Table 15.5 shows. The greatest share of the increase can be accounted for by growth in debts falling outside of the state's full faith and credit guarantee. General fund guaranteed debt rose by 223 percent between 1970 and 1984, but other long-term debt increased by over twice that rate, at 494 percent. Looking at relative debt proportions, although full faith and credit obligations made up 46 percent of all long-term debt in FY 1970, that relative percentage dropped to 31 percent in FY 1984.

Historically, state constitutions and state laws have placed limitations on guaranteed debt. But since those limitations most often apply to full faith and credit debt exclusively, state officials have increasingly turned to revenue bonds, which are not covered by the limits. In addition, many states have created special authorities primarily responsible for capital facilities construction to issue guaranteed bonds that state courts have held are not subject to constitutionally imposed debt ceilings. One state using such an administrative vehicle is Pennsylvania, where the state constitution imposes a $1 million debt limit on a $10.5 billion annual budget.[12]

No widely accepted standards exist among the states for what constitutes imprudent or excessive debt. Defaults at the state level remain exceptionally rare, and the interest paid on debt is still comparatively small, at only 3 percent of expenditures.[13] However, the bond market itself may exert a practical constraint on a state's appetite for borrowing. Too much "bond paper" offered by a state in a given year, or even over a few years, may prompt rating firms and investors to worry about the state's longer-term ability to manage its increased debt service requirements.

The debt load among the states varies greatly. New York, at $29.4 billion, has over twice California's debt level of $13.6 billion. At the other end of the spectrum lie Kansas and North Dakota with $356 million and $445 million of outstanding debt, respectively. Population and budget size appear to be related to state indebtedness, but several states prove to be exceptions to that generalization. Looking at per capita total debt, Alaska, Delaware, Oregon, and Hawaii top the list. At the bottom fall Kansas, Arizona, Iowa, and Texas. Relative state tax effort appears to account best for the variant cases. Comparing tax effort, the former four states tax at a much higher level, in relation to their ability to pay, than do the latter four. Perhaps the higher-taxing states are broadly utilizing bonding in an effort to shift as many costs as can be put under the capital umbrella and thus limit the would-be size of their operating budgets, correspondingly keeping taxes from growing even higher.

TABLE 15.5. OUTSTANDING STATE DEBT: FYs 1970 AND 1984 (IN $ THOUSANDS)

	Full Faith and Credit		Other	
	1970	*1984*	*1970*	*1984*
All States	17,736,092	57,349,274	21,167,087	125,858,950
Alabama	86,630	713,175	655,994	2,183,539
Alaska	133,794	1,648,823	69,916	3,880,849
Arizona	—	0	90,929	607,720
Arkansas	12,016	0	88,694	683,344
California	4,642,660	4,355,073	681,179	9,157,550
Colorado	—	0	122,861	1,256,257
Connecticut	1,260,560	2,208,981	298,295	3,192,602
Delaware	331,644	563,515	86,330	1,229,389
Florida	—	1,095,934	891,039	2,813,632
Georgia	16	999,556	870,174	842,566
Hawaii	342,329	1,641,695	170,787	807,262
Idaho	456	345	32,646	574,014
Illinois	265,600	3,329,500	1,007,560	5,026,632
Indiana	—	0	536,758	1,391,471
Iowa	9,100	0	88,899	651,311
Kansas	17,780	27,800	205,655	328,336
Kentucky	264,445	206,600	918,422	3,177,583
Louisiana	449,901	2,624,006	411,401	3,893,574
Maine	166,005	294,584	66,317	899,814
Maryland	568,977	2,325,688	575,832	2,365,416
Massachusetts	1,119,202	3,481,225	640,070	4,981,741
Michigan	69,350	691,315	831,069	4,529,598
Minnesota	393,662	1,072,643	68,850	2,067,830
Mississippi	321,691	617,845	130,320	407,377
Missouri	35,320	225,920	106,232	2,555,083
Montana	395	107,541	80,945	549,455
Nebraska	—	0	73,535	606,139
Nevada	22,838	275,440	11,273	589,059
New Hampshire	102,269	374,431	2,830	1,338,473
New Jersey	696,776	2,421,332	992,235	9,122,584
New Mexico	17,196	12,641	103,498	1,135,502
New York	2,260,806	4,154,255	3,551,582	24,628,782
North Carolina	326,122	886,042	100,429	992,787
North Dakota	—	5,807	37,324	438,074
Ohio	301,570	2,439,125	900,418	4,127,894
Oklahoma	164,525	135,964	573,441	2,894,266
Oregon	689,672	5,617,356	8	660,338
Pennsylvania	741,041	4,000,290	2,467,547	2,595,969
Rhode Island	238,883	241,150	76,377	1,995,036
South Carolina	212,283	624,544	134,969	2,482,223
South Dakota	—	0	29,932	917,295
Tennessee	265,920	604,750	68,558	963,759
Texas	460,095	1,290,661	552,957	2,718,387
Utah	50,500	271,940	52,589	928,156
Vermont	188,674	296,468	31,495	513,288
Virginia	81,373	391,554	241,601	2,430,756
Washington	88,326	2,314,678	631,398	583,481
West Virginia	208,080	771,912	346,516	861,480
Wisconsin	127,610	1,987,170	408,310	1,564,957
Wyoming	—	—	51,091	716,320

Source: The Book of the States, 1972–73, *p. 202;* The Book of the States, 1986–87, *p. 245 (Lexington, KY: Council of State Governments, 1972, 1986).*

	Total		Short-Term		Total	
	1970	*1984*	*1970*	*1984*	*1970*	*1984*
38,903,179	183,208,224	3,104,485	3,168,672	42,007,664	186,376,896
742,624	2,896,714	247	0	742,871	2,896,714
203,710	5,529,672	18,545	0	222,255	5,529,672
90,929	607,720	—	0	90,929	607,720
100,710	683,344	100	20,000	100,810	703,344
5,323,839	13,512,623	10,698	41,200	5,334,537	13,553,823
122,861	1,256,257	1,491	0	124,352	1,256,257
1,558,855	5,401,583	360,600	68,200	1,919,455	5,469,783
417,974	1,792,904	2,945	16,099	420,919	1,809,003
891,039	3,909,566	—	0	891,039	3,909,566
870,190	1,842,122	—	0	870,190	1,842,122
513,116	2,448,957	15,059	63,136	528,175	2,512,093
33,102	574,359	—	0	33,102	574,359
1,273,160	8,356,132	32,782	280,412	1,305,942	8,636,544
536,758	1,391,471	47,065	171,800	583,823	1,563,271
97,999	651,311	—	0	97,999	651,311
223,435	356,136	155	0	223,590	356,136
1,182,867	3,384,183	41,211	0	1,224,078	3,384,183
861,302	6,517,580	3,685	398	864,987	6,517,978
232,322	1,194,398	—	1,012	232,322	1,195,410
1,144,809	4,691,104	1,070	70,078	1,145,879	4,761,182
1,759,272	8,462,966	102,494	402,189	1,861,766	8,865,155
900,419	5,220,913	58,042	1,567	958,461	5,222,480
462,512	3,140,473	—	248,395	462,512	3,388,868
452,011	1,025,222	3,175	0	455,186	1,025,222
141,552	2,781,003	370	50,235	141,922	2,831,238
81,340	656,996	446	39,075	81,786	696,071
73,535	606,139	—	115	73,535	606,254
34,111	864,499	—	21	34,111	864,520
105,099	1,712,904	52,850	21,429	157,949	1,734,333
1,689,011	11,543,916	73,757	98	1,762,768	11,544,014
120,694	1,148,143	—	2,741	120,694	1,150,884
5,812,388	28,783,037	1,575,448	607,676	7,387,836	29,390,713
426,551	1,878,829	115,000	7,100	541,551	1,885,929
37,324	443,881	—	875	37,324	444,756
1,201,988	6,567,019	429,910	97,302	1,631,898	6,664,321
737,966	3,030,230	1,646	11,514	739,612	3,041,744
689,680	6,277,694	—	267,000	689,680	6,544,694
3,208,588	6,596,259	11,850	41,565	3,220,438	6,637,824
315,260	2,236,186	57,940	55,519	373,200	2,291,705
347,252	3,106,767	3,200	135,047	350,452	3,241,814
29,932	917,295	—	267	29,932	917,562
334,478	1,568,509	81,750	166,800	416,228	1,735,309
1,013,052	4,009,048	—	0	1,013,052	4,009,048
103,089	1,200,096	—	0	103,089	1,200,096
220,169	809,756	434	145	220,603	809,901
322,974	2,822,310	220	79,602	323,194	2,901,912
719,724	2,898,159	—	200,060	719,724	3,098,219
554,596	1,633,392	—	0	554,596	1,633,392
535,920	3,552,127	300	0	536,220	3,552,127
51,091	716,320	—	0	51,091	716,320

SUMMARY AND CONCLUSIONS

Legislatures appropriate funds for a broad array of public purposes, and budget controls exist to ensure that state agencies commit those funds in line with legislative intent. The state budget serves as a state's fiscal game plan for a fiscal year or biennium. It is structured in such a way that appropriated amounts are identified by source of funds, program, and type of expenditure.

Two types of documents provide information on the budget and serve as the basis for budget execution. The budget bill, as enacted into law, provides the legal framework for budget execution and is the document on which expenditures are controlled. It contains details on legislative appropriations, including information on the program purposes to which they are committed, the amounts involved, the source of revenue financing the appropriation, and the duration over which they may be used. The budget bill may also contain specific expressions of legislative intent, at times restricting spending purposes beyond the limits included in the appropriation authorizations themselves. Such restrictions may be either prescriptive or proscriptive, requiring that funds be used for a designated purpose or, conversely, prohibiting their use in certain ways.

The executive budget book provides descriptive information on the governor's state budget recommendations. It not only includes summary, tabular information on the amounts recommended by agency, program, and source of funds but also contains justifications for the governor's recommendations. In addition, the legislature may produce its own budget summary documents, ranging from analyses of the governor's recommendations to summaries of legislative changes. Interest groups also often develop their own budget summaries, tailored to the special interests of their selective audiences.

Once the budget becomes law, the execution phase of the budgetary process begins. The focus turns from budget making to budget control. Toward that end, the state budget office processes allotments to state agencies, which give the agencies the authority to spend the appropriated resources. The state budget office commonly has the discretion to permit limited transfers of funds across budget categories, but major shifts—such as between appropriations—usually require legislative approval. Once funds are allotted, preaudit controls ensure that the actual expenditures are consistent with the approved budget and that the agency does not exceed its available appropriation limits.

Beyond exercising budget and expenditure controls, state financial managers face other significant challenges, including accurately estimating revenues and expenditures, retaining adequate year-end contingency balances, and prudently managing cash flow and debt. All are important elements of sound budget and financial management, aimed at ensuring that public monies are not only used as the people's representatives intend but managed wisely as well.

BUDGET EXCERCISE: FUNDING SERVICES FOR SENIOR CITIZENS

A CASE STUDY IN PUBLIC BUDGETING

This case study has been designed to portray, in a realistic manner, the complexity of state budgeting. It includes a substantial number of concerns and data which are pertinent to the program under consideration. These data and facts could be expected to be available in dealing with a problem of this nature. Some of the information is relevant and some is not.

Assuming your assigned role as budget analyst in the state budget office, you should prepare a policy analysis that culminates in a recommendation to the governor that best solves the budget problem before you. The policy paper should be the product of a careful analysis that *defines the problem, assesses* the merits of *alternative* possible solutions, and provides a well-reasoned rationale in *support* of the *recommendation*. In resolving the problem, you should remember that many of the solutions could create additional problems, some of which could be more severe than the one at hand.

Your analysis should be limited to seven pages double-spaced. The use of tables for illustrations is encouraged.

Background

You are located in the state of Confusion, USA. The state ranks twentieth in the country in land area and eighteenth in population. There are five metropolitan areas of over 150,000, one of which exceeds three-fourths of a million. Even so, the state's population is dominated by rural and suburban elements, and the mainstays of its economy are agriculture and related agribusiness. Heavy equipment manufacturing comprises a significant share of the state's industry. Support for public policies over the years reveals a curious mixture of ultra-conservatism and surprising progressiveness. Thus, for example, one observes adherence to Sunday "Blue Laws," on the one hand, and strong affirmative action and comparable worth programs, on the other.

In the provision of human services supported by state funds, one notes a similar checkered pattern. As an illustration, the state ranks sixth nationally in per capita expenditure for AFDC recipients but only thirty-sixth in the per capita level of effort expended in support of elementary and secondary public education.

The current administration has been in office for a little over two years of a four-year term. It assumed office following a popular, two-term governor who could not succeed himself. The present governor's primary campaign involved four strong candidates and a runoff that saw the losing candidate garner 47 percent of the vote. In the general election, the present governor won by only 4 percent of the vote. Both candidates in the general election had platforms that included the need to increase state aid for primary and secondary education while otherwise holding the line on state spending. The winning candidate, however, alone categorically pledged not to raise taxes. The losing candidate acknowledged that a tax increase might prove to be necessary unless the economy greatly improved.

The Budget Situation

Slightly over one year ago, the governor submitted to the legislature the first budget completely prepared by his administration. In general, the process of legislative review was characterized by numerous episodes of bickering about the details of particular programs. However, no significant changes were made in the governor's recommendations, with the sole major exception that the legislature increased school aid, leaving the state's general fund balance at one-half of 1 percent.

The administration's first budgetary crisis occurred in August, just after the start of this fiscal year. At that time it was found that the state funds in the budget for the Department of Transportation (DOT) were insufficient to match Federal Highway Trust Fund appropriations recently provided by the federal government. These new monies, requiring a state match of 30 percent, were totally unanticipated. The DOT is financed primarily by the proceeds from a cent-per-gallon motor fuel tax, and the highway construction and maintenance program has suffered because of more fuel-efficient vehicles and increased conservation measures. With no increase in state funds likely in the future, the governor felt that he had no choice but to secure the federal funds while they were available.

The strategy chosen was to call the legislature into special session and pass an emergency appropriation. Ultimately, this move captured the federal funds but carried with it political costs. The opposition party painted a picture of the administration in broad strokes of ineptitude for not anticipating and providing for such a contingency. In addition, much was made of the costs to the state ($450,000) of financing a special session. *Questions were also raised about what might occur next to illustrate further the flaws in the administration's handling of the budget.*

As part of that session, the legislature also passed a law that set aside $3 million in a contingency fund, to be released by the Joint Budget Committee, when the full legislature is not in session, to provide a source for appropriation supplements needed during the fiscal year. The contingency appropriation was approved as a base-level resource, meaning that it would be available each future fiscal year as well.

Economic Outlook

Although the economy of the nation (and that of Confusion) had come out of a recession about two years ago, resulting in a modest surplus, recent problems in agriculture have reduced current revenues and greatly cut into the state's surplus. Given recent revenue projections, the surplus could be all but gone at fiscal year's end. No one seems quite certain what will happen beyond that point. To complicate matters, an influential state taxpayers' association has joined hands with the state business association in pushing hard for tax *decreases* or, if unsuccessful, for state spending limits, to improve Confusion's economic development climate.

The Dilemma

The current 1988–89 fiscal year was little more than half over when the secretary of the state Department of Health and Human Services dropped this problem on the Budget Director's desk.

1. The participation rates in two programs administered under the Older Americans Act—namely, Title III, social services, and Title VII, nutrition—had already exceeded the level anticipated in formulating the budget.

2. Based on current data, if the participation rate is maintained at the current level there will be a shortfall of about $2.25 million in state general fund appropriations for both programs combined. If participation is not administratively controlled and continues to grow, the general fund deficit could go as high as $4 million during the remaining six months of the fiscal year.

Because of the sensitivity of the issue, and the need for immediate action, the governor was advised at once. He, in turn, notified the chairperson of the Joint Legislative Budget Committee—a member of his own political party.

Older Americans Act

The Older Americans Act (OAA) of 1965 and its subsequent amendments were established to promote and secure an acceptable quality of life for the elderly population of the United States. Through the OAA, Congress sought to assure the elderly adequate income, health care regardless of ability to pay, appropriate housing, employment opportunities, dignified retirement, meaningful activities, efficient community services, and independence. To achieve these goals, Congress developed a multifaceted program. Those services most familiar to the general public are the Area Planning and Social Service Programs (Title III) and the Nutrition Program (Title VII).

There are several layers involved in the process, including the federal, state, and local governments, as well as private sector service providers. (See Exhibit 1.) Such multiparty involvement accounts in a major way for the high cost of administering the program, and it probably has much to do with the unmanageability of the program, which has consistently been a point of administrative and legislative concern. The responsibility for administering these programs at the state level is vested in the Bureau of Aging Services within the Department of Health and Human Services.

Title III

Congress and the Federal Administration on Aging have chosen to define social services in the broadest possible terms. Activities funded under this title include transportation and access; education; health and long-term care counseling; housing repair; escort service; shopping service; legal, tax and general counseling; homemaker and home-care assistance; and general referral service.

The Legislative Fiscal Bureau's (staff to the Joint Legislative Budget Committee) recommendations express concern over the lack of coordination of service delivery and the high cost of program administration. However, because of the sensitivity of the clientele (senior citizens) and a united front by carefully organized Area Agencies on Aging (AAA), little attention has been paid to staff recommendations, which advocate the following changes:

1. Local governing authorities should finance a portion of Title III programs in very much the same fashion as they finance part of the costs of operating local health units. It is the belief of the legislative staff analysts that local governments would provide funds rather than see the program cut back; but until the state calls their bluff, the locals are volunteering absolutely nothing. The contribution rate generally agreed upon to be reasonable for the localities is one-fifth of the nonfederal share.

   For example, suppose the federal ceiling on Title III for next year was set at $4 million. The federal-state match is 80/20 overall, so to receive the $4 million federal grant, the state must come up with $1 million. Under this proposal, the state would put up $800,000, and the local governing authorities would come up with $200,000.

2. Administrative costs could be reduced by 4 percent by eliminating two highly paid unclassified positions and upgrading the jobs of two classified deputy-level positions in the Bureau of Aging Services. The two positions to be eliminated are (a) the coordinator of field services, who worked hard in the campaigns of both

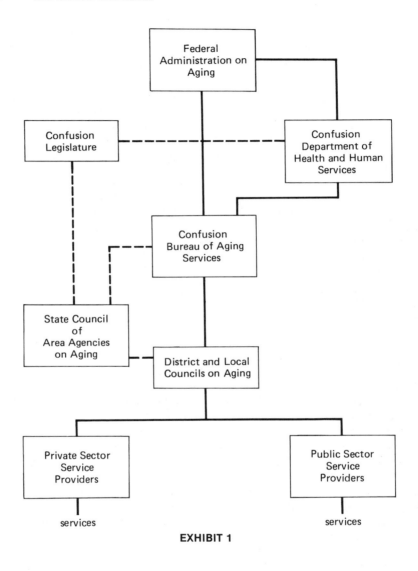

EXHIBIT 1

the former and current governor; and (b) the Bureau of Aging Services planning director, who made the transition between administrations because of strong ties to extremely influential legislators. But it is the deputies who actually provide oversight of the bureau's day-to-day operations.

In addition, the bureau has failed to spend an average of $20,000 in its LTE line over the past two years, monies that have lapsed into the state's general funds. The same thing is expected to happen again this year.

3. Program costs could be reduced by 3 percent if agency field service personnel would require strict adherence to eligibility criteria. As it stands now, many services

EXHIBIT 2. TITLE III—BUDGET (IN THOUSANDS)

Year	State Funds	Federal Funds	Total Budget
1985–86	$1,796	$2,275	$4,071
1986–87	4,123	5,153	9,276
1987–88	5,248	6,712	11,960
1988–89	5,879	7,821	13,700

Title III funds are available on a 80/20 match, up to a ceiling established for each state. The federal funds in this table represent the maximum available to the state in each year. The excess in state funding above the match reflects an expansion of the program financed entirely with state funds.

are administered on a first-come, first-served basis, with little or no eligibility screening.

The Exhibits 2 and 3 reflects the increase in popularity of this program indicated by the rise in the unmatched state support for the program (i.e., state funds above the 20 percent required to match available federal funds) from $1,227,250 in 1985–86 to $3,923,750 in 1988–89. This growth in part reflects the results of a promotional outreach effort funded in 1986–87, which was successful in increasing the awareness of services available under Title III. This outreach was not recommended for continued funding by the executive branch in the 1987–88 budget; however, through effective lobbying on the part of the area agencies on aging, it was included as a line-item add-on to the general appropriations bill. The line-item amendment was not supported by the governor. However, because of the sensitivity of the issue, he did not veto the amendment. A contract for the balance remaining in the appropriation ($220,000) has been negotiated with the advertising firm that handled the governor's recent campaign and has been sent to the Budget Office for its approval.

Title VII—Nutrition
The objective of the program is to provide meals to senior citizens sixty years or older, giving preference to low-income individuals and persons with specific problems that affect their eating habits. (See Exhibits 4–7.)

EXHIBIT 3. TITLE III—COMPARISON OF ADMINISTRATION AND PROGRAM COSTS (IN THOUSANDS)

Year	Administration Dollars	%	Program Dollars	%	Total Cost
1985–86 (actual)	$448	11	$3,623	89	$4,071
1986–87 (actual)	1,577	17	7,699	83	9,276
1987–88 (actual)	2,512	21	9,448	79	11,960
1988–89 (estimated)	2,968	22	10,732	78	13,700
*1988–89	1,522	22	5,394	78	6,916

*These figures represent the first six months' operation of the current fiscal year.

EXHIBIT 4. TITLE VII—BUDGET (IN THOUSANDS)

Year	State Funds	Federal Funds	Total Budget
1985–86	$3,571	$10,266	$13,837
1986–87	4,505	14,430	18,936
1987–88	5,478	18,095	23,573
1988–89	5,773	19,005	24,778

Title VII funds are also available on an 80/20 match of federal to state funds up to a ceiling established for each state. This chart tracks a rapid expansion of the program mainly because of the federal ceiling being raised significantly from 1983–1984 to 1986–1987. The excess in state funding above the required match reflects that portion of the program financed entirely with state general fund revenues.

Perhaps because this program is so visible or maybe because it appears to lend itself so well to a graphic analysis, it is one of the most controversial ones in the legislature.

As Exhibit 7 shows, meals are served at both congregate centers and, to a lesser extent, at the homes of recipients. But the meals-on-wheels program has proven considerably more costly, calculated at 1.6 times the cost, per meal, of those served in centers. And as the figures show, at-home meal service has recently grown nearly twice as fast as in-center service.

A recent evaluation of this program by a team from the state Budget Office revealed:

1. On average, two meals a day are served in both the congregate and in-home settings.
2. Women are the primary recipients of Title VII services, comprising 65 percent of the participants.
3. Sixty-eight percent of the participants are white, 30 percent black, 2 percent other.

EXHIBIT 5. TITLE VII—COMPARISON OF ADMINISTRATION AND PROGRAM COSTS (IN THOUSANDS)

Year	Administration		Program		Total Cost
	Dollars	%	Dollars	%	
1985–86 (actual)	$1,522	11	$12,315	89	$13,837
1986–87 (actual)	3,219	17	15,717	83	18,936
*1987–88 (actual)	3,536	15	20,037	85	23,573
1988–89 (estimated)	3,927	16	20,851	84	24,788
†1988–89	2,555	19	10,893	81	13,448

*The administrative cost was restricted to 15 percent by a session law amendment to the general appropriations bill. An attempt in the 1987–1988 budget-making process to add the same language a second time was unsuccessful.
†First six months.

EXHIBIT 6. TITLE III—SOCIAL SERVICES

Year	Client Service Visits
1985–86	362,300
1986–87	702,800
1987–88	761,100
*1988–89	430,000

*Operations for first six months of fiscal year.

4. The mean age of participants is 71 years.
5. Fifty-three percent of the clients are widowed. Adding to that the percentage who are divorced, separated, or single, 72 percent of the clients have no spouse.
6. Eighty-six percent of the clients surveyed indicated they were satisfied with the meals at nutrition sites at least four days each week. Fifty-four percent could suggest no ways in which meals could be improved.
7. Two percent of the persons surveyed statewide were ineligible for services because they were not sixty years old or not married to an eligible participant.

The information on the Title VII program was made available to the budget director and the director of the Legislative Fiscal Bureau in the regular reporting process.

The administrator of the Bureau of Aging Services has completely avoided the issue of the unusually high ratio of administrative to program costs.

The executive budget recommendations for this program in 1988–89 called for a 2 percent increase reflecting only one-half of the expected increase associated with inflation. The Legislative Fiscal Bureau's recommendations provided for *no increase* in the level of state support because the agency would not respond to queries from staff regarding information related to the request. The legislature, responding to active lobbying, approved a 5.4 percent increase.

Additional Facts about Confusion's Budgetary System
1. The State of Confusion is on an annual budget.
2. The fiscal year runs from July 1 to June 30.
3. The governor is required by the constitution to keep the budget in balance.
4. Agency heads are bound under penalty of law not to exceed appropriations.
5. Departments may transfer up to 5 percent of their state appropriations from one program to another with the approval of the Joint Legislative Budget Committee. Consequently, state dollars can be moved from the Title III to the Title VII pro-

EXHIBIT 7. TITLE VII—NUTRITION

Year	Meals Served	(At Centers)	(At Homes)
1985–86	2,463,000	1,799,000	664,000
1986–87	2,911,000	2,081,000	830,000
1987–88	3,312,000	2,318,000	994,000
*1988–89	1,921,000		

*Operations for first six months of fiscal year.

gram—or vice versa—but sufficient state funds must remain to meet the required state match for federal funds in each agency.

6. Self-generated revenues (user fees) may be added to appropriations with the approval of the state Budget Office.

7. The Joint Legislative Budget Committee is authorized by statute to provide a supplementary appropriation from a reserve fund (totaling just $3 million for the fiscal year) when a "fiscal emergency" exists. The committee decides what constitutes a fiscal emergency.

Some Assumptions

1. A changed sharing relationship (such as local governments paying a portion of the nonfederal share) would require a change in state law, requiring approval by the legislature—not just the Joint Legislative Budget Committee.

2. Federal regulations require *at least* one meal per day.

3. Your policy paper is a *public document.* Therefore, you could see your analysis and conclusions quoted in metropolitan newspapers.

REFERENCES

1. This concept comes from S. Kenneth Howard, *Changing State Budgeting* (Lexington, KY: Council of State Governments, 1973), p. 12.

2. Harold D. Lasswell, *Politics: Who Gets What, When and How* (New York: McGraw-Hill, 1936).

3. *Legislative Budget Procedures in the 50 States* (Denver, CO: National Conference of State Legislatures, 1983), p. 76.

4. *Auditing and the States* (Lexington, KY: National Association of State Auditors, Comptrollers, and Treasurers, 1986), pp. 44–45.

5. *Legislative Budget Procedures,* p. 118.

6. *Fiscal Survey of the States, September 1987* (Washington, DC: National Association of State Budget Officers, 1987), p. 21.

7. Ibid., p. 23.

8. Ibid.

9. Ibid.

10. Robert D. Lee, Jr., and Ronald W. Johnson, *Public Budgeting Systems,* 3rd ed. (Baltimore, MD: University Park Press, 1983), pp. 271–72.

11. *Budget Issues: Capital Budgeting Practices in the States* (Washington, DC: U.S. General Accounting Office, 1986), p. 2.

12. Lee and Johnson, *Public Budgeting Systems,* p. 265; *Fiscal Survey of the States,* p. 32.

13. Lee and Johnson, *Public Budgeting Systems,* p. 263.

CHAPTER 16

Personnel Management

State governments are labor-intensive enterprises. The quality and productivity of their personnel are critical to their functioning. Public policy making depends not only on the politics and processes described in chapters on elections, the legislature, governors, the bureaucracy, and the like, but also on state employees who make and implement decisions on a daily basis.

Personnel management concerns the hiring, treatment, and firing of employees. The number of employees in state governments ranges from about 12,000 in Vermont to 320,000 in California. In most states, 88 percent of the employees work on a full-time basis.[1] (Chapter 5 includes state-by-state figures on state government workers.) States hire people in a wide variety of occupations, including engineers, game wardens, accountants, clericals, doctors, nurses, librarians, computer programmers, building maintenance people, prison guards, social workers, budget analysts, car mechanics, professors, purchasing agents, investment analysts, and attorneys.

How state government personnel are managed is essential to how policies are formulated and implemented. State governments, like other employers, seek employees who are talented and who will work hard, based on the assumption that such a work force will provide the best service at the lowest cost. This assumption has some empirical support.[2] A state, for example, with competent and enthusiastic environmental engineers is likely to have innovative and effective programs for controlling pollution and maintaining clean air and water if those employees get the support they need. A state with low-paid, poorly trained, and poorly supervised highway troopers, on the other hand, invites corruption at worst and rude treatment of the public at best. States hiring incompetent and/or too few tax auditors probably will not collect as much revenue as they could if they had more and better auditors to identify mistakes and cheating that deprives the state of revenue.

Personnel management also does more than hire good people and give them incentives to work hard. Personnel management embodies public policies. Whether out of a sense of responsibility or in order to comply with laws, like other employers, state governments do not hire children for most jobs; allow employees a certain number of sick days; and make sure that those doing the hiring do not discriminate on the basis of religion, race, or gender. State governments generally pursue the following policies in managing their work forces:

Competence. States are concerned that they hire people able to do the assigned work. States typically, however, do not make very aggressive efforts to entice highly qualified individuals away from their current employers. Instead, state governments advertise and let those interested come to them.

Social Representation. As public employers and as fair employers, state governments seek to have their employees reflect the ethnic, gender, and other social background diversity of the general population. States differ on how intensely they pursue this policy and how they define their social representation goals, but they all do something in this regard.

Partisan Neutrality. States insist that most state employees have no or only limited involvement in partisan politics so that no matter which party wins control of the legislature or the governorship, they will have available to them a corps of professional and experienced state workers. This policy also intends to protect state government employees from harassment and intimidation that might force them to work in the campaigns of certain candidates.

Accountability. The preceding policy notwithstanding, a democratic form of government requires that government employees work for the electorate, through those officials voted into office. Public personnel management systems are obliged to incorporate mechanisms that allow for the exercise of political leadership over state agencies.

Productivity. To run a state government well, the right combination of directives, incentives, rewards, and sanctions must exist to prompt employees to be productive. Productivity results from hard effort and skill channeled into jobs designed to meet the state's needs. Translating that general formula into specifics is not an obvious or easy task.

Fairness. A good employer is, among other things, a fair employer. Employees should be compensated, disciplined, promoted, and generally treated in ways that are consistent and that are grounded in job-related reasons.

These policies reflect different concerns and embody different perspectives. Although they do not necessarily lead to different or conflicting conclusions, each policy may be given different relative weight from one state to another and from one time to another. The alteration of the emphasis given to a policy can raise fears of excess. Efforts to diversify the ethnic and gender backgrounds of state employees might, for example, be viewed as abandoning a concern for competence. A move to enhance accountability by providing a governor with more positions to fill with his or her own loyalists is vulnerable to charges of patronage and spoils.

EVOLUTION OF CURRENT PERSONNEL MANAGEMENT PRACTICES

Merit System

The assassination of President James Garfield on July 2, 1881, led to the adoption of the merit system, a basic component of current public personnel management policies. Charles Guiteau worked hard for the Republican party machine in order to receive an appointment to the U.S. Consulate in Paris. When President Garfield refused, Guiteau shot and killed him. Those who sought to destroy political machines and the patronage appointments they fed on used this dramatic incident to link spoils with evil. In January 1883, President Chester A. Arthur, who as vice president succeeded Garfield, signed the Pendleton Act and replaced the spoils system with the merit system.

The fundamental principles of the merit system are as follows:

1. Partisan identity or loyalty cannot be used as a criterion for hiring or firing employees.
2. Appointments will be based on qualification through examinations open to all.
3. Employees may retain their jobs as long as they perform satisfactorily.
4. A nonpartisan Civil Service Commission will act as a watchdog to prevent abuses.

Although most people today credit the merit system with emphasizing the policy goal of competence, it is more accurate to identify the Pendleton Act with the goal of partisan neutrality. The orientation was primarily negative, that is, antimachine and antipatronage, rather than a concern for hiring the best available people.

The main impetus for the adoption of the merit system was at the state and local levels of government, even though the federal government was the first to adopt such a law. Civil service reform groups fought machines primarily in the cities and states of the Northeast, where bloc voting and spoils involving new, non–English-speaking immigrants altered significantly the distribution of political power.[3] Bolstered by progress in the federal government, Theodore Roosevelt (as a member of the New York State Assembly) and Grover Cleveland (as New York's governor) secured adoption of the merit system by New York in May 1883. Massachusetts followed the next year. Both state laws covered municipal and state governments.[4]

Progressives battling machines generated the next flurry of state government activity. Wisconsin and Illinois adopted merit system laws in 1905, Colorado in 1907, New Jersey in 1908, and Ohio in 1912. Other states needed prodding from the federal government. In 1939, the federal government required state and local governments to use merit systems to hire any of their employees who had even partial support from federal funds to help administer their unemployment compensation and social security programs. Since 1939, this requirement has become a common feature of federal grant-in-aid requirements. All fifty states thus have at least some of their employees covered under a merit system. Five states operate two personnel systems: one for those employees whose salaries are at least partially funded by federal dollars and one for all others. The latter are not covered by the restrictions or the protections of the merit system.

Scientific Management

As civil service reformers at the turn of the century were fighting machines and installing merit systems, social scientists were developing an approach toward work in organizations that had an important impact on public personnel management. Led by Frederick Taylor, the intellectual parent of industrial engineers posited that it was possible to determine the single most efficient and effective way of accomplishing any objective. Taylor and his disciples further argued that once that way was identified, work could be defined in terms of discrete and separate jobs and these jobs could be orchestrated and coordinated in a way to meet the overall objective. This approach was labeled "scientific management," and it contributed significantly to assembly-line technologies and assembly-line organizations.[5]

The lesson for governments was that if politics could be isolated from the work of public employees, then government, like auto companies and makers of refrigerators, could be highly efficient and productive. In a seminal essay, Woodrow Wilson, as professor and civil service reformer, argued for this separation of politics and administration. In addition to providing additional support for merit system legislation, this line of thinking led to the Hatch Acts of 1939 and 1940 and to the adoption of job-classification systems. The Hatch Acts prohibited government employees from participating in active and visible ways in partisan politics. The 1939 act applied to federal employees, and the act of 1940 applied to state and local employees funded at least in part by the federal government. After 1940, all fifty states passed "Little Hatch Acts" that apply to all state civil servants.

Job classification was adopted earlier. The federal government and almost all state governments established job-classification systems in the 1920s.[6] In part out of a concern for fairness and in part to respond to the prescriptions of scientific management for efficiency, governments developed fairly precise definitions of their various jobs and then grouped together all similar jobs. Jobs were, in other words, defined in accordance with the work that had to be done. People would be hired to do predefined tasks, rather than because they were of good character or because they had a friend in the right place. By grouping similar jobs into a common classification, governments could pay all people doing the same work the same wage. This would treat employees in a consistent manner and avoid the significant differences that had existed in pay for the same position as one went from one agency to another. Prior to common classification, agencies were in a sense bidding with one another for the same employees and, in the process, driving salaries up.

Social Representation

The civil rights movement of the 1950s and 1960s forced a reexamination of public and private sector employment practices. The main concern was imbalance in social representation and a variety of discriminatory practices in employment opportunities. Besides addressing issues of social representation and fairness, in a way that is often not fully appreciated, personnel management changes had an impact on work force competence.

Landmark legislation that resulted from the civil rights movement included the 1964 Civil Rights Act. Initially this act did not apply to state governments. In 1972, however, an amendment passed that required state governments to comply with the provisions of Title VII of the act, which mandates equal employment opportunities, and to abide by the rules promulgated by the Equal Employment Opportunity Commission. One of the immediate effects of this law was for states to collect and analyze data on their own work forces to determine the number of women and minorities in various job categories and the number of women and minority applicants for jobs. Invariably, the profiles that emerged found minorities clustered in low-skilled and low-paying jobs and women in a limited number of low-paying, even though sometimes highly skilled, positions.[7] Like other major employers, state governments began designing affirmative action plans to correct imbalances and get women and minorities into all job categories.

One result of the 1964 Civil Rights Act and subsequent court litigation was that the personnel management profession redesigned the examinations and processes used to select individuals for jobs.[8] The key legal defense that an employer could offer when women and minorities were not hired for particular jobs was that the examinations and selection processes were job-related and the women and minority applicants simply were not as qualified as those selected. Extraneous biases that screened out women and/or minorities on criteria not related to job requirements had to be eliminated. In short, the equal employment opportunity requirements improved the relationship between examinations and jobs, important for ensuring competence as well as eliminating discrimination.

Unionization

Public employees in the United States did not have the right to form unions and negotiate contracts with their employers until 1959, when Wisconsin provided this right to local government employees. Wisconsin also pioneered the right of

state workers to bargain collectively when it authorized this process for its employees in 1967. The idea spread rapidly. By 1977, twenty-two states recognized the
right of their employees to unionize, and another four provided for a "meet and
confer"—nonbinding negotiation—process. The American Federation of State,
County and Municipal Employees, a public employees' union that started in Wisconsin and spread throughout the United States and Canada, became the largest
single union within the American Federation of Labor and the Congress of Industrial Organizations (AFL-CIO). Growth in the 1980s has been slower, but public
employees' unions are now major features of the public personnel management
landscape in state governments.

The major impact of unionization has been that individual employees now
have an advocate for their rights. It is difficult to determine whether unions have
secured higher wages or benefits for their employees.[9] In the federal government
and in thirty-five states it is illegal to bargain over wages. Public employees' wages
are set primarily in response to a combination of wage settlements in the private
sector, fiscal conditions in a jurisdiction, and increases in the cost of living. What
is common to all collective bargaining agreements is the process established for
raising and resolving complaints about poor and arbitrary management. Employees who feel mistreated by their bosses can get union assistance in pursuing their
grievance and can get a third party (an arbitrator) to settle the dispute.

Accountability and Productivity

The thrust of many of the preceding developments is negative. The merit system
says, "Thou shalt *not* use partisan identity as a qualification for government employment." The 1964 Civil Rights Act says, "Thou shalt *not* discriminate on the
basis of race or gender." The union contracts say, "Thou shalt *not* treat employees
in an arbitrary and capricious manner." Civil service reform efforts of the mid-
and late 1970s tried to balance these prohibitions with positive mandates, that is,
"Thou shalt work with elected officials" and "Thou shalt work hard and creat-
ively."

The states of California, Florida, Oregon, and Wisconsin led the way. Based
on comprehensive studies of their personnel management systems, these state governments adopted reform packages that emphasized competence, social representation, collective bargaining rights, managerial accountability, and productivity.
Accountability was approached by making more senior policy and management
positions available to governors for their own leadership teams. Approaches to
improving productivity varied from more serious and systematic performance evaluations, and the corresponding awarding of salary bonuses for exceptional work,
to employees' suggestion boxes.

President Jimmy Carter introduced major changes in the federal civil service
system in order to improve personnel management and to prevent repetitions of
some of the abuses that characterized the presidency of Richard Nixon. President
Carter proposed that the federal government adopt the same basic changes being
made by some state governments. The passage of the Carter reforms in 1978, in

turn, provided a model and some momentum for further reform efforts by other state governments. The major professional association of public personnel managers, the International Personnel Management Association, also subscribed to the reforms and played a role in encouraging change. By 1980, all but two states adopted some reforms, and twenty-nine states made comprehensive changes in their personnel management systems.[10]

PUBLIC PERSONNEL MANAGEMENT POLICIES AND PRACTICES

One result of the reform activities of the late 1970s is that there is now a general model of how states manage their work force. As with any model, specific instances will vary somewhat. The following is what one might expect in each of the fifty states, modified by individual traditions and needs.[11]

Job Classification and Evaluation

A fundamental task of personnel management is to make appropriate matches between people and jobs. In the United States generally and in state governments specifically, the approach has been to emphasize getting people to fill predefined jobs, rather than shaping jobs to fit individual persons. State agency heads must define the duties and responsibilities of each position they have or would like to have in their agency. Each position is then evaluated by a common set of criteria and classified so that similar positions might be treated the same.

Job classifications determine whether the same examination can be used for filling a number of positions. If several positions are classified as entry-level accountant, for example, agencies can hire the accountants they need from a ranking of applicants who took the same examination. Likewise, job classifications determine whether an employee can transfer from one job to another and how layoffs will occur, for example, by seniority within classifications. Pay ranges also depend on job classifications, so that people doing the same kind of work for a state government get paid the same, regardless of which agency they might work for.

Selection

One of the first decisions after a position has been created, evaluated, and classified is how it will be filled. Positions that involve senior-level policy making or management, or sensitive assistance to such a position, can be filled through political appointment. These positions are usually referred to as "exempt" or "unclassified." With such positions individuals serve at the pleasure of the governor or a cabinet member, or they might serve for a fixed term. The intent behind exempt or unclassified positions is to provide for accountability to the electorate. Leadership and sensitive staff positions should be filled by people who share the philosophy and the goals of those elected to office in order to link the bureaucracy with the dynamics of democracy.

Positions that are more important for their expertise than their political loyalty, on the other hand, are considered part of the classified civil service and are covered under the strictures of the merit system. To be appointed to one of these positions, one must take an examination and receive one of the top scores. All states allow veterans some points (usually five, and ten if disabled) that are added to their examination scores, giving them an advantage over nonveterans. Agency heads must hire from among those with scores in the top 3 or 5 or 10 percent (depending on the state). Thus, the effects of the 1964 Civil Rights Act in making examinations job-related and not discriminatory, and the effects of veterans preference points are very important. Agency heads have very little discretion over whom they may hire.

Some positions may, of course, be filled by current employees who might be transferred or promoted into a vacancy. Union contracts can be critical here. If the position is part of a job classification covered by a union contract, chances are high that before any new employee can be hired, transfers, promotions, and the recall of recently laid-off employees may have to occur. A resignation or retirement at one level, in other words, may precipitate a number of job shifts before a new person is hired. Transfers and promotions are important for the career advancement of current employees, but they also provide some limits on managerial discretion and flexibility.

Compensation

Market and fairness are the two key principles guiding compensation. State governments must, of course, pay at least at the level of other employers hiring in the same fields. Otherwise, qualified people will not apply for state jobs. However, state governments are the only employers or the major employers in many occupations, such as prison guards, drivers' license examiners, game wardens, and welfare administrators. Fair pay for these jobs has to be judged by internal standards. Positions evaluated to be at the same level in the state's classification system generally are paid the same.

Like employers in the private sector, state governments evaluate and rank jobs according to the level of difficulty and complexity in their duties, responsibilities, and working conditions in order to set pay in a fair and systematic way.[12] A major concern of the 1980s has been to apply the principles and techniques of job evaluation to correct for the effects of past practices, such as designating some jobs as appropriate for women and then paying those women less than if the jobs had been held by men. The issue is referred to as "comparable worth" or "pay equity," and state governments have taken the lead in addressing it.

At the time of the Civil War, 97.5 percent of all clerical workers in the United States were men. The library profession likewise was filled predominantly by men. In response to labor shortages and the advent of the typewriter, the federal government took the lead in consciously hiring women for these jobs and paying them less than men. As an illustration, the annual salary in 1869 for male clerks was $1,200, but female clerks were paid only $600. Male librarians were paid between $1,600 and $1,800, but female librarians earned only $1,000.[13] The assumption was that these differentials were appropriate because women needed less money;

that is, they worked only because they were single and supporting themselves or because they were supplementing their husband's salary. By the 1920s, these two occupations were filled almost entirely by women and paid at the "female" salary level, whether the incumbent was male or female.

Although the 1964 Civil Rights Act made it illegal to bar women from being hired in various occupations, it did not immediately correct the legacy of the pay practices for those jobs that had traditionally been filled predominantly by women. The corrective measure commonly used is to pay traditionally female-dominated jobs in accordance with their ranking with the job evaluation and classification system rather than in accordance with market rates. The assumption behind this practice is that the market rates continue to incorporate the effects of past discriminatory practices. As of 1988, all but seven states had begun studies or taken some other action to correct the pay equity or comparable worth problem, and fourteen states had actually made adjustments in salaries to establish or begin establishing a gender-neutral compensation system.[14]

A more difficult concept for state governments to adopt has been the provision of salary increases or bonuses because of individual merit. Unions strongly prefer increases based on seniority, unless there is documented evidence of unsatisfactory performance. Unions, like some managers, have little faith in the ability of supervisors to measure objectively the performance of employees. Those states that do have merit awards tend to give modest sums on a one-time basis, without any long-term effects on an employee's salary.

Employee Development

Public employees rank training and development programs just below retirement and health insurance as a benefit they value highly.[15] Ideally, supervisors would send employees for training not only as a benefit but also in response to weaknesses and strengths identified in performance evaluations. In practice, the typical response of state governments is to praise but not support employee training and professional development. Certainly state governments are not in the same league as major private sector employers in encouraging and providing employee development.[16] The predominant perspective is that employee training programs benefit employees more than they benefit state governments. Thus, when budgets must be cut, training seems like a nonessential that can be eliminated.

Individual agencies are the primary source of whatever training does exist. The unusually supportive agency head will, in addition, encourage and facilitate the assertive individuals who seek training through their professional associations and through nearby colleges and universities. On the whole, however, state governments do not make major efforts to train and develop their employees.

Workplace

State governments can foster fairness, productivity, and health by providing good workplaces for their employees. Public employers are not usually identified with dangerous or unhealthy working conditions. Prisons and hospitals, however, can certainly be dangerous. Highway police officers and inspectors of hazardous waste-disposal sites can encounter danger. Officials tracking down those who owe payments on student loans and even state university professors may have to deal with hostile people. More recently we have become aware of the risks of building materials in offices, hazards associated with video display terminals and computer keyboards, and discomfort due to temperatures and humidity in offices. Likewise, research indicates that breathing air filled with the tobacco smoke of others is, like smoking itself, dangerous to one's health.

Attention to the health and safety needs of its employees contributes to productivity since effort and effectiveness require a work force that is present and feeling well. A central issue that relates both to productivity and to fairness is ensuring that everyone works in an environment free of harassment.

Most research on sexual harassment has been conducted since 1979, although it seems safe to assume the problem has existed since women entered the work force. Studies on the public sector include the federal government and state governments in Florida and Illinois. In these studies over 40 percent of women and 15 percent of men workers reported being sexually harassed by supervisors and/ or co-workers.[17]

Sexual harassment is distinct from romance. It is repeated, unwanted verbal or physical sexual advances and includes, of course, those situations in which sexual favors are required as a condition of employment or career advancement. In November 1980, the Equal Employment Opportunity Commission (EEOC) issued guidelines defining sexual harassment and specifying appropriate policies and procedures.[18] Like other employers under the jurisdiction of the EEOC, state governments must comply. Some have gone beyond compliance and adopted their own rules and laws. The EEOC requires employers to inform employees and supervisors that sexual harassment is not permitted. Employers must also designate an office or individual(s)—other than one's supervisor—to whom complaints can be made. Substantial complaints must, of course, bring remedial action.

Employee Assistance Programs

Massachusetts has pioneered in going beyond providing a safe workplace to providing for the health of its employees. Massachusetts has been a leader in establishing employee assistance programs for employees with drug and alcohol abuse problems. The provision of professional counseling and help for such employees is a departure from the traditional approach of simply disciplining or firing them. In part, this new approach is motivated out of a sense of human concern and fairness. It is also prompted out of a concern for productivity.

An employee who has made valuable contributions and has the potential for more is hard to replace. If such an employee engages in drug and/or alcohol abuse and if treatment is effective, it is probable that the employer will gain more by allowing treatment than by firing the employee, perhaps having to defend that action in an appeal process, and recruiting and training a new employee. In short, although the employer takes a risk that the employee will not respond to treatment, the investment in employee assistance programs is a humane and reasonable investment in productivity.

Important features of most of these programs are that employees must participate in treatment in order to retain a job and that they might not be assigned to certain kinds of jobs while they are in treatment. The recognition that employees whose behavior might be affected by drugs could endanger themselves or others, damage valuable equipment, or disclose sensitive information is, of course, a legitimate and important concern of state governments. Some employers, including governments, have begun to test employees, systematically or randomly, for drugs. The adverse effects of drugs support efforts to identify drug users. The opposition to these efforts is based on the rights of individuals to privacy and to refuse to incriminate themselves. Some opposition is also based on doubts about the accuracy of current tests for chemicals in body fluids. This issue has occupied state governments and the federal government throughout the late 1980s.

Discipline

Sometimes employers and employees make mistakes. An agency may have hired the wrong person. A supervisor may have provided the wrong mix of encouragement and admonishment. An employee may have lost interest in his or her job and started being tardy or absent from work. A technician or professional may have failed to keep abreast of developments in his or her field. A temptation to steal or cheat may have been too much.

Discipline, which ranges from a verbal warning to firing, represents failure on the part of someone. The failure to discipline when appropriate is in itself a mistake. State governments suffer in direct ways when an employee is not doing his or her job properly and in indirect ways when other employees know that misdeeds are not being dealt with. It is, nonetheless, hard for most people to confront someone with an accusation or a negative message. Supervisors who find this part of their job distasteful can have an adverse effect on operations generally.

State governments not only are concerned about disciplining employees even when appropriate but also are committed to protecting employees from unjust or arbitrary treatment. State laws, union contracts, and federal court decisions require that state governments treat their employees fairly. The major protections for the rights of state employees are procedural. States must follow what is called "due process." This means that an employee has a right to know why he or she is being disciplined and who is making the accusation of wrongdoing. The accused employee also has a right to appeal the decision. Appeals are typically made to the immediate supervisor; then to the agency head; and then, if still not satisfied, to a third party outside the agency. Court systems provide routes of appeal beyond those in state government itself.

Public employees did not always have these due process rights. Until 1972, the U.S. Supreme Court followed what it called a "doctrine of privilege" when ruling on appeals in cases involving the discipline of public employees. According to this doctrine, individuals gave up certain rights for the privilege of working for the government. These rights included due process protections for their employment. The Court reversed itself in *Board of Regents v. Roth,* a 1972 decision.[19] Roth had been hired on a one-year contract by the University of Wisconsin— Whitewater. At the end of the year, the university told Roth he would not have a contract for the following year. The university did not explain why, and it did not allow Roth to appeal the decision. Roth persuaded the Court that public employment was a "property" (a valuable source of income) and that denial of that "property" fell within the constitutional protections guaranteeing due process. Roth also persuaded the Court that the termination of public employment threatened a "liberty interest" (the freedom to seek other employment) because one's reputation might be tarnished, making it difficult to get another job. This "liberty interest" also required due process protections.

The Court, therefore, abandoned the "doctrine of privilege" and adopted the "doctrine of substantial interest," in which it ruled that state government and other public sector employees did have property and liberty interests in their jobs that deserved due process protections when those jobs were to be taken away. Having established these principles, the Court ruled against Roth. The justices reasoned that the terms of a one-year contract were clearly different from the usual "tenure" or "permanent status" positions in government agencies. No property rights existed beyond the termination date of the contract, and the failure to renew a contract did not threaten an individual's reputation or "liberty interests."

The *Roth* principles have been applied in other cases and are incorporated in state government disciplinary procedures. Although the court case was over the issue of employment termination, due process is used for all disciplinary actions. A suspension or reprimand may be a step on the way to a dismissal, and thus the lesser penalties have to be proper and justified. Otherwise, arbitrary and unfair treatment might be used to establish an employment record that seems to support an unjust dismissal.

SUMMARY AND CONCLUSIONS

Personnel management is critical to the operation of state governments. Employees are valuable resources to a state government, and the quality of those employees and the level of their productivity have obvious implications for the formulation and implementation of public policies.

State governments are major employers. Few private businesses have 50,000 employees, most of whom are professionals and paraprofessionals. In most capital cities and in many other towns and cities, state governments, state universities, and state agencies are clearly the largest employer or among the largest employers. State governments have, for the most part, tried to be model employers. With a few exceptions, they have provided important leadership in emphasizing a mix of competence, accountability, integrity, fairness, and efficiency.

PERSONNEL EXERCISE: POSITION ANALYSIS

The purpose of this exercise is to provide experience in conducting a job analysis. As mentioned, personnel management—especially in state governments—is built on the concept of jobs or positions distinct from the people who do the jobs or hold the positions. A fundamental task of personnel management is to describe in a systematic way the duties, responsibilities, working conditions, and requirements of each job. These descriptions are then used to group similar jobs together into classifications, to develop examinations for hiring people, to construct performance evaluation instruments, and to determine compensation.

Another goal of this exercise is to increase your understanding of state government through the knowledge of what state employees do. The completion of this exercise requires an interview with someone doing the job that you intend to analyze. Wherever possible, you should also interview that employee's supervisor so that you can verify and supplement the information you receive. Written documents, such as a position description or a statutory section stating the responsibilities of the agency in which the job is located, should also be used if they are available.

It is likely that there are a number of state employees in your community. If not, work with your instructor to identify other public sector or private sector employees who do work similar to that done by some state employees.

Based on an interview with a job incumbent and, if possible, a review of relevant documents and an interview with the employee's supervisor, provide the following information:

1. Title of job
2. Title of position classification
3. Name of agency
4. Brief description of mission or responsibilities of agency
5. Summary of duties and responsibilities of position
6. Description of specific tasks, with an estimate of the time spent on each task over a daily, weekly, monthly, or annual period. (Be sure to specify which time base you are using and be sure to use the same time base for all tasks.)
7. Number of employees supervised by job incumbent
8. Description of supervisory responsibilities, if any:
   a. Hire employees?
   b. Conduct performance evaluation?
   c. Close supervision on daily basis?
   d. Loose supervision, not necessarily daily?
   e. Discipline employees?
9. Special skills required to operate machinery
10. Knowledge required to do the job—linked to tasks listed in item 6
11. Degrees, licenses, certificates required
12. Contact with people—specify if co-workers, general public, elected officials, patients, and so on. Also, specify nature of contact (give information, make arrests, negotiate agreements, provide medical treatment, etc).
13. Description of physical work environment
14. Changes, if any, planned for job

REFERENCES

1. *The Book of the States, 1986–87* (Lexington, KY: Council of State Governments, 1987), p. 298.
2. Wayne F. Cascio, *Costing Human Resources: The Financial Impact of Behavior in Organizations* (Boston: Kent Publishing Co., 1982).
3. Carl R. Fish, *The Civil Service and the Patronage* (New York: Longmans, Green and Co., 1935), p. 13.
4. Richard P. Shick, Rose Williams Boyd, and Barry Bader, "Civil Service Systems: A Short History," in Frederick S. Lane, ed., *Managing State and Local Government* (New York: St. Martin's Press, 1980), p. 75.
5. Frederick W. Taylor, *The Principles of Scientific Management* (New York: Harper and Bros., 1945).
6. Esther C. Lawton, "Job Evaluation Principles and Problems," in Harold Suskin, ed., *Job Evaluation and Pay Administration in the Public Sector* (Chicago: International Personnel Management Association, 1977).
7. Harry Kranz, *The Participatory Bureaucracy* (Lexington, MA: Lexington Books, 1976); and Nelson C. Dometrius and Lee Sigelman, "Assessing Progress Toward Affirmative Action Goals in State and Local Government: A New Benchmark," *Public Administration Review* (May/June 1984), 241–56.
8. *Griggs et al. v. Duke Power Company* (1971) and *Texas Department of Community Affairs v. Burdine* (1981). Also, see U.S. Office of Personnel Management, *Equal Employment Opportunity Court Cases* (Washington, DC: U.S. Government Printing Office, 1979).
9. David T. Stanley, *Managing Local Government Under Pressure* (Washington, DC: Brookings Institution, 1972); Joan P. Weitzman, "The Effects of Economic Restraints on Public Sector Collective Bargaining," in Hugh D. Jascourt, ed., *Government Labor Relations: Trends and Information for the Future* (Oak Park, IL: Moore, 1979); and Harry Kershen, ed., *Collective Bargaining by Government Workers* (Farmingdale, NY: Baywood, 1983).
10. Dennis L. Dresang, "Diffusion of Civil Service Reform: State and Federal Government," *Review of Public Personnel Administration,* Vol. 2, No. 2 (Spring 1982), 35–48.
11. For general texts on public personnel management, see Dennis L. Dresang, *Public Personnel Management and Public Policy* (Boston: Little, Brown, 1984); Robert D. Lee, Jr., *Public Personnel Systems* (Baltimore, MD: University Park Press, 1979); or Donald E. Klingner and John Nalbandian, *Public Personnel Management,* 2nd ed. (Englewood Cliffs, NJ: Prentice-Hall, 1985).
12. Comptroller General of the United States, *Options for Conducting a Pay Equity Study of Federal Pay and Classification Systems* (Washington, DC: U.S. Government Printing Office, 1985), p. 26.
13. Paul P. Van Riper, *History of the United States Civil Service* (Evanston, IL: Row, Peterson and Co., 1958), pp. 157–60.
14. Comptroller General, *Conducting a Pay Equity Study,* p. 3; updated by authors.
15. Helen W. Daley and Donald D. Sylvia, "A Quasi-Experimental Evaluation of Tuition Reimbursement in Municipal Government," *Review of Public Personnel Administration,* Vol. 1, No. 2 (Spring 1981), 13–23.

16. Donald L. Kirkpatrick, "Evaluation of Training," in Robert L. Craig, ed., *Training and Development Handbook,* 2nd ed. (New York: McGraw-Hill, 1976).
17. Douglas I. McIntyre and James C. Renick, "Protecting Public Employees and Employers from Sexual Harassment," *Public Personnel Management,* Vol. 11, No. 3 (Fall 1982), 282–92.
18. U.S. EEOC, "Discrimination Because of Sex Under Title VII of the 1964 Civil Rights Act, As Amended: Adoption of Final Interpretive Guidelines," *Federal Register,* Nov. 10, 1980.
19. Deborah D. Goldman, "Due Process and Public Personnel Management," *Review of Public Personnel Administration,* Vol. 2, No. 1 (Fall 1981), 19–28; and David H. Rosenbloom, "Public Personnel Administration and the Constitution: An Emergent Approach." *Public Administration Review,* Vol. 35, No. 1 (Jan.-Feb. 1975), 52–59.

SUMMARY
AND CONCLUSIONS

—————————— CHAPTER 17 ——————————
The Future of the States

We still seem to be experimenting. As we begin the third century of our existence as a country, we have still not settled on a permanent relationship between states and the federal government. Perhaps we never will. Perhaps the relationship will always be dynamic, changing with new needs, new challenges, and new opportunities.

BROAD HISTORICAL TRENDS

In the initial years, state governments were strong, if by strength we mean substantial autonomy. The colonial tradition, in which each colony was governed separately, provided each state with its own, distinct cultural, economic, and political identity. Those who struggled with framing our form of government did not fully trust a strong central government. The federal government was the product of reluctant compromise. As the country expanded westward, the concept of states, each with their own governing authority, was retained. So strong were states that some tried to secede and form their own country.

The Civil War answered fundamental questions about the limits of state sovereignty. The Great Depression and the world wars raised questions about whether the federal government was strong enough to ensure the security and the welfare of the country. Few ever questioned the responsibility of the federal government to provide for national defense. The economic crisis of the Great Depression required a quick, coordinated, and effective response. The federal government seemed to be the obvious arena for making that response.

The New Deal enhanced the scope and the power of the federal government by revolutionary proportions. The federal government assumed responsibility for

352

the welfare of individual citizens and asserted a role in virtually every dimension of the country's economy. The growth of the federal government continued through the Great Society era of President Lyndon Johnson's administration. That growth seemed all the more essential because of the visibly regressive role played by state governments in response to the civil rights movement. If individual rights were to be protected, the federal government had to do it.

Prognosticators confidently discussed the demise of state governments. The legacy of the past might preserve a legal existence for the states, but reality would be a central, national government that would determine policy for everyone. When convenient and appropriate, the federal government might use states as administrative units, but that would be the extent of a working relationship between the levels of government.

The prognosticators were wrong. By design and default, state governments have reemerged as strong, viable, and capable entities. We are back to not trusting fully a strong central government. The diversity and the distinctness of states is once again celebrated. The federal government has clearly established a position of preeminence in financial terms, through Supreme Court decisions and in the willingness of Congress and the president to address a broad range of issues. State governments, as well, have increased their capacities and their willingness to act. These are not contradictory or mutually exclusive developments.

BASES OF STATE POWER

Power can be seen both as relative influence over someone else and as a capacity to accomplish a desired end. One perspective, in other words, asks about the extent to which the federal government can determine what state governments do, or vice versa. Another perspective focuses on the states themselves to evaluate whether they have the resources and the strategies to get things done.

The power of states in the initial years after colonial rule and the power of states currently have very different bases. As mentioned in Chapter 2, the Supreme Court, in *Marbury v. Madison,* very early established the legal principle that the Constitution gave rather broad powers to the federal government. The states, nonetheless, were not heavily dominated by the federal government during this period. Washington had neither the interest nor the apparatus to dictate to the states in a wide range of policy areas. In addition, the country was not tightly knit together by an integrated economy or by an effective national transportation and telecommunications network. State governments did not have extensive resource bases or highly qualified professionals. Their capabilities were limited, but they enjoyed power in the sense that the federal government intervened minimally in their affairs.

Current state power is in part based on the quality of the people and the institutions that make up state governments. It is, of course, difficult to measure the quality of human resources. Observers do agree, however, that the elected and appointed officials of state governments are more serious and more professional than they had once been.[1] We concur with that assessment. Our confidence, and that of others, is based not only on impressions and observations but also on indicators like formal education and on the evolution of these positions into full-time or almost full-time jobs with increased, although still not always adequate, levels of compensation.

The institutional reforms included in the chapters on governors, legislatures, courts, and the bureaucracy describe some of the increased capacities of state governments. Legislators and governors now have access to staffs to help with policy analyses and with the chores of office. The terms of governors have been lengthened, generally, and chief executives now enjoy more opportunities to appoint top executives.

Legislatures not only are stronger because of staff resources, procedural changes, and longer sessions but also draw more strength through better representation. The U.S. Supreme Court mandates that legislative districts embody the principle of one person, one vote invariably links elections and legislation more effectively to the actual problems people face in the state. Power imbalances favoring rural areas meant that urban concerns were neglected. Individuals, politicians, and professionals who wanted to address major issues of current concern could now do so within state government.

Courts have also been reorganized to enhance their abilities to work effectively and efficiently. Amateur justices of the peace have, with few exceptions, become a part of history. State governments have created new courts to provide specialized services for family disputes, traffic violations, juvenile problems, and the like. Courts and processes more fully respond to the need for timely disposition of cases.

The processes for selecting state employees have, since the mid-1960s, become more sensitive to both the need for broad social representation and for job-related competence. State governments have become better employers. Compensation is fairer and more competitive than it had been. Employee rights and employee development are now meaningful principles in state personnel management systems. Budget processes provide for sophisticated analyses and informed decisions. Financial management more adequately deals with the need for accountability, flexibility, and adequate cash at those times of the year when bills must be paid. With few exceptions, state governments have developed more stable and diversified sources of revenue.

Current state power is also based on conscious decisions made by the federal government to limit its own activities and encourage more state involvement. Presidents Nixon and Reagan consolidated some categorical grant programs, with all their specific mandates and restrictions, into block grants, which have only general purposes and allow states to establish their own details. Federal agencies let it be known that they would not strictly enforce all regulations. Supreme Court justices praised rulings by state courts that elaborated on and applied general principles set by their federal counterparts.

The unprecedented growth of the federal budget deficit and national debt during the Reagan administration has also contributed to the increase in discretion available to state governments. Federal dollars have been a major force for central direction of state government activities. Dollars come with strings. The cuts in federal domestic spending have, in the same vein, led to cuts in federal mandates and restrictions.

Federal retrenchment has not been the only pattern, and changes have not always been without conflict. As noted in the discussion of transportation policy (Chapter 12), the federal government is still a major actor, despite the increased role of states. The federal government has, in fact, obstructed state planning and financing in transportation by setting obligation limits well below budget authority, delaying payments to the state, and sending inconsistent policy signals in ways that seem arbitrary. Likewise, the federal government is still very heavily involved in health and welfare programs, despite increased reliance on states for implementation. Washington still provides both requirements and restrictions on states as they design reforms and innovations in combating poverty. Most states piggyback on the federal income tax system in levying personal income taxes. When the federal government changes, so do states, unless they consciously take steps to counter federal actions.

States at times are legal adversaries of the federal government, as the latter, despite rhetoric about returning power to the states, expands its policy activities. South Dakota, with some other states cheering on the sidelines, went to court when the federal government made state laws prohibiting the drinking of alcoholic beverages before the age of twenty-one a condition of receiving federal highway monies. (South Dakota lost.) Minnesota objected to federal directives to send state National Guard troops to Central America for training exercises and road and airport construction projects.

Conflict is an inherent component of the relationships between a state and the federal government as each pursues its own goals and runs into contrary efforts of the other. Jurisdictions jealously guard their own prerogatives from encroachment by others. Interdependence among states and between states and the federal government requires cooperation, too. No doubt, the balance between conflict and cooperation will continue to be dynamic.

FUTURE DIRECTIONS

States will continue to be important actors in the governing of America, both because of their own capacities and because of the reliance of the federal government on states for the conduct of many domestic policies. This general prediction is not based on the philosophies and promises of specific presidents but on the realities of state capacities, federal limitations, and public support. Capacities and limitations have already been discussed. Public support has been evident in recent polls, which show the highest level of support and confidence in the lowest levels of government. Gallup found, in 1987, that 37 percent of the people it polled had the most trust and confidence in their local government, 22 percent in state governments, and 19 percent in the federal government. The remaining 22 percent had no opinion.[2]

How states respond to future developments depends in part, of course, on their economies. A national recession, combined with a depressed energy sector, would mean that the states would have to undergo another period of retrenchment. A recession would dampen state policy initiatives that involve increased state expenditures, such as efforts to increase teachers' pay, aid talented and gifted education programs, or establish job-training programs for welfare recipients. On the other hand, a recession would provide added impetus for the states to expand welfare reform aimed at restricting eligibility or cutting the costs of health-care services. A deep recession would probably necessitate a further round of state tax increases as well as budget cuts. It would also probably put the skids on tax concessions to business and industry because the sinking state treasuries could no longer afford the associated revenue loss. The converse scenario, that of broadened economic prosperity, would probably mean that the states would continue to pursue many of the policy initiatives that they began in the 1980s. Economic prosperity, however, would probably not affect the states equally. The South and West would still possess the advantages that have given them the competitive edge in economic development. Yet broadened prosperity would give the slower-growing states an opportunity not only to balance their budgets more easily but also to invest some of the excess revenues into improving their competitive position. Thus national economic growth might not minimize interstate competitiveness; it could just as well heighten it.

Another feature of interstate competitiveness in the near future relates to human resources more than economic or natural resources. High-technology industries, such as electronics, computers, and genetics, are not linked to the location of mineral deposits, water, fertile soil, or climate in the way that more traditional economic activities are. The major requirement for the high-technology industries is brain power. Although that might seem to give an edge to states with traditions of excellence in their school systems, in fact that is not essential as a location factor. People move, and employers transfer their employees. It is obviously easier to locate a high-technology industry where the experts are already living. University communities are, thus, major candidates. If necessary, however, the talent can be drawn from a number of places and assembled together. States competing in the future to become the home of high-technology industries will have to tout existing human resources, but in recognition of the mobility of those resources they will also have to sell quality-of-life advantages and provide financial incentives.

State policies and institutions are likely to look more similar than different as one moves across state boundaries in the future. States have the capacity and the freedom to be innovators and to experiment. The diversity that might emerge out of this orientation, however, may not occur simply because state governments are now linked by political and professional networks that make cross-fertilization of ideas and the spread of innovation more likely and more rapid. Innovations have, of course, spread throughout the states in the past.[3] The more regional patterns of diffusion are likely to be replaced by a more universal spread. Professional associations are more numerous and provide more opportunities for sharing successes and failures than had been the case in the past. Likewise, the associations linking elected officials—legislators, governors, attorneys general, and judges—have become more vibrant and effective.

Another probable trend toward homogeneity concerns electoral competition. As noted in Chapter 3, there has not been a major realignment of party loyalties in recent decades, but there has been a decline in the extent of one-party domination in states in the South, Northeast, and Midwest.[4] The increased competitiveness of the two parties has been most evident in gubernatorial elections, but minority parties have also increased their numbers in legislative chambers. Ideally, the increase in competition will lead to more participation by citizens in the political process and will enhance further the quality of people who occupy state government positions.

It is unlikely that more sharing of ideas and more similarities in electoral competition will erase differences between states and regions. The regional characteristics described in Chapter 1 are strong and vibrant. The traditions are proud ones. The establishment of common policy and administrative standards and the improvement of interstate communication take place within the context of those traditions and in the midst of the kind of economic competition described. Minimal policy standards and diverse state identities are not inconsistent. Both are likely.

SUMMARY AND CONCLUSIONS

American governance is characterized by a strong federal government and by capable state governments. Both are active, sometimes in conflict and sometimes in cooperation.

The predictions made in this chapter are safe ones. They are general and careful. More important, they are based on an understanding of the nature of state government institutions and process and of the political and economic context within which states operate.

We end as we began. We recognize the limitations of state government without joining the chorus of those who disdain the public sector. We recognize and respect the contributions and the potentials of state government, without being euphoric. But the contemporary signs, in balance, point to the rising tide of the states as policy makers and public managers.

REFERENCES

1. Larry Sabato, *Goodbye to Good-time Charlie* (Washington, DC: Congressional Quarterly Press, 1983); Alan Rosenthal, *Legislative Life* (New York: Harper & Row, 1981); and Ann O'M. Bowman and Richard C. Kearney, *The Resurgence of the States* (Englewood Cliffs, NJ: Prentice-Hall, 1986).

2. Reported in James A. Barnes, "Government as Villain. Has the Era Ended?" *Government Executive* (Jan. 1988), p. 13.
3. Jack Walker, "The Diffusion of Innovations Among the American States," *The American Political Science Review*, Vol. 63 (Sept. 1969), 880–99; and Robert L. Savage, "Policy Innovativeness as a Trait of American States," *Journal of Politics*, Vol. 40 (Feb. 1978), 212–19.
4. Malcolm E. Jewell and David M. Olson, *Political Parties and Elections in American States,* 3rd ed. (Chicago: Dorsey Press, 1988).

Index

Employment, changes in, among states, 11–12, 18–19
Employees, state government, 83, 84, 87, 91, 96, 97, 337, 338, 348. *See also* Personnel management
Energy
  changes in price of, 12
  state economics and, 11–12
Environmental Protection Agency, 290–293
Equal Employment Opportunity Commission, U.S., 294, 341, 346
Equality of Educational Opportunity, 199
Expenditures, ranking of states on, 3

Faubus, Orvil, 80
Federal Aviation Agency (FAA), 292
Federal Communications Commission (FCC), 290, 295
Federal Deposit Insurance Corporation (FDIC), 300
Federal Emergency Relief Act of 1933, 221
Federalism
  intergovernmental relations compared to, 25
  phases of, 27–28
Federal Savings and Loan Corporation, 300
Fifth Amendment, U.S. Constitution, 127
55 mph speed limit, 246, 261
Financial management, 20–21
Fiscal notes, 155
Florida, 4, 5, 6, 18, 54, 118, 175, 176, 181, 183, 185, 186, 189, 191, 205, 206–207, 260, 267, 299, 322, 342
Folsom, James, 80
Food and Drug Administration, U.S., 290
Food stamps, 226
Friedman, Milton, 232

Galbraith, John Kenneth, 30
Gallup Organization, 299, 355
Gann, Paul, 174, 181, 187

Garcia v. San Antonio Metropolitan Transit Authority, 26
Garfield, James, 339
Garreau, Joel, 4, 8, 10
General Fund, 302–303
General obligation bonds, 323
General revenue sharing, 32, 40–41
Georgia, 4, 5, 108
Gerrymandering, 100–102
Gilder, George, 227
Goodman, Robert, Agency, Inc., 53
Gormley, William, 298
Governors
  appointment powers of, 70–71
  budget and fiscal management and, 71, 78, 92–93, 160, 264, 304
  career patterns of, 79–81
  election of, 51, 54, 58, 68
  roles of, 76–79, 354
  policy initiation and, 19–21, 148–149
  staff to, 74–75
  terms of office of, 69
  transition of, 75–76
  veto power of, 68, 71, 73–74, 77, 152, 154, 167
Graham, Robert, 206
Grand jury, 133, 136
Grant and Company Manufacturing Climate Score, 19
Grants-in-aid, federal
  administration of, 95–97
  block, 31–32, 36–38
  categorical, 31, 36–38
  changes in, 30–32
  formula, 29
  matching requirements for, 30
  project, 29–30
Grant, Thornton, 284
Grasso, Ella, 79
Great Depression, 27, 69, 221, 352
Great Society, 26, 29–33, 236, 353
Greer, Frank, 53
Guiteau, Charles, 339

Hatch Acts of 1939 and 1940, 340
Hawaii, 8, 10–11, 84, 86, 132, 300, 325
Hawkins, Brett, 279
Hart, Peter D., Research Associates, 53